Sports Broadcasting

Kevin Hull, PhD
University of South Carolina

HUMAN KINETICS

Library of Congress Cataloging-in-Publication Data

Names: Hull, Kevin, 1978- author.
Title: Sports broadcasting / Kevin Hull.
Description: Champaign, IL : Human Kinetics, Inc., 2022. | Includes bibliographical references and index.
Identifiers: LCCN 2021019072 (print) | LCCN 2021019073 (ebook) | ISBN 9781492598572 (paperback) | ISBN 9781492598589 (epub) | ISBN 9781492598596 (pdf)
Subjects: LCSH: Television broadcasting of sports. | Radio broadcasting of sports.
Classification: LCC GV742.3 .H85 2022 (print) | LCC GV742.3 (ebook) | DDC 791.45/6579--dc23
LC record available at https://lccn.loc.gov/2021019072
LC ebook record available at https://lccn.loc.gov/2021019073
ISBN: 978-1-4925-9857-2 (print)

Acquisitions Editor: Andrew L. Tyler; **Developmental Editor:** Melissa J. Zavala; **Copyeditor:** Chernow Editorial Services; **Proofreader:** Leigh Keylock; **Indexer:** Beth Nauman-Montana; **Permissions Manager:** Dalene Reeder; **Graphic Designer:** Denise Lowry; **Cover Designer:** Keri Evans; **Cover Design Specialist:** Susan Rothermel Allen; **Photograph (cover):** Don Juan Moore/Getty Images; **Photographs (interior):** © Human Kinetics, unless otherwise noted; **Photo Asset Manager:** Laura Fitch; **Photo Production Manager:** Jason Allen; **Senior Art Manager:** Kelly Hendren; **Printer:** Sheridan Books

Printed in the United States of America 10 9 8 7 6 5 4 3 2 1

The paper in this book is certified under a sustainable forestry program.

Human Kinetics
1607 N. Market Street
Champaign, IL 61820
USA

United States and International
Website: **US.HumanKinetics.com**
Email: info@hkusa.com
Phone: 1-800-747-4457

Canada
Website: **Canada.HumanKinetics.com**
Email: info@hkcanada.com

E8085

CONTENTS

PREFACE

The clock is winding down, the crowd is on their feet, and the star player shoots a half-court shot to win the game. The fans are going crazy, the team is celebrating, and you could be in the middle of the action—describing the scene to the audience at home or recording highlights and interviewing players for the sportscast at night. There is one constant at the biggest sports moments in history, and that is the sports media. Broadcasters are there to shoot the video, describe the action, and talk to the key players and coaches. They essentially write the history so future generations can watch and hear what happened.

With that in mind, it should come as no surprise that sports broadcasting offers some of the most desired jobs in media, since many fans would like nothing more than to be in the stadium or arena reporting on the big game. Others might wish to talk about it as a host of a sports talk radio show or podcast. Whatever that dream job might be, the skills needed are much more than just sitting down in front of a microphone or at the anchor desk. The purpose of this book is to provide you with the information and skills needed to be a well-rounded sports broadcaster. You'll learn how to write for broadcast, shoot and edit video, and prepare for all the additional tasks needed along the way.

Simply put, this book is for anyone interested in a career in sports broadcasting. The skills taught in this book will prepare you to work in television, on the radio, or as a play-by-play or sideline reporter during a live game broadcast. In addition, you'll learn how to shoot and edit video from games and events, interview players and coaches, use social media to provide updates, and write articles for a website. There is no skill you will need as a sports broadcaster that will not be covered in this book.

In addition, this book is for all different skill levels. Readers can have some basic knowledge of broadcasting and use this book to take them to the next level. Those with years of experience might need brushing up on some of the new skills required on the job that are covered in this book. Or someone can have no experience at all when they pick up this book for the first time and be a pro by the time he or she gets to the last page.

In television broadcasting a reporter is often referred to as a "one-man band." This means that a broadcaster is shooting his or her own video, editing it, writing the story, interviewing the players and coaches, and anchoring the sportscast—essentially doing it all by themselves. When coming up with the various sections for this book, I decided I wanted this to be the "one-man band" of sports broadcasting books. This book does it all, and everything a beginning sports broadcaster needs to know will be covered in this book.

It wasn't that long ago that sports broadcasters only had to worry about the evening newscast or their radio segments. With that in mind, previous sports broadcasting books rightfully only focused on those elements of a broadcaster's daily routine. However, the job has changed. There are new types of sports broadcasting jobs popping up every year, doing remote interviews has become commonplace, writing for the web is just as crucial as writing for broadcast, and using social media has become a key part of the journalist's day. This textbook addresses all those topics while updating the skills needed for many of the traditional job duties as well. In addition, we will discuss opportunities in live sports broadcasting—both on camera and behind the scenes.

The book is divided into 13 chapters, each of which tackles a different element of sports broadcasting. We begin with some important background information on the sports broadcasting industry (chapters 1-3) before diving deep into skill-based lessons that every sportscaster needs to know (chapters 4-11). The text wraps up with helpful tips for the job search and some important ethical issues of which every broadcaster should be aware (chapters 12-13). The topics covered are as follows:

- Chapter 1—History of Sports Broadcasting: Before discussing what it takes to make it as a sports broadcaster in today's media landscape, it is important to recognize how we got to this point.
- Chapter 2—Business of Sports Broadcasting: Make no mistake about it, sports broadcasting is big business. In this chapter you'll learn about the billions of dollars spent each year broadcasting live events.
- Chapter 3—Types of Sports Broadcasting: For many years sports broadcasting jobs were limited to just a few options. However, the internet and the growth of team media have created new jobs that did not exist a decade ago.
- Chapter 4—Interviewing: One of the most important skills any broadcaster can have is the ability to conduct an interview. Since interviewing players and coaches is such a key part of the job, we start there for our skills lessons.
- Chapter 5—Writing for Broadcast: This chapter provides a look at how to write out scripts for a broadcast television sportscast or prerecorded story for either television or radio.
- Chapter 6—Writing for the Web and Mobile Devices: In addition to writing for radio and television, broadcasters need to be able to write stories that can appear on their station's website.
- Chapter 7—Shooting Games and Events: Most beginning broadcasters will be shooting their own video, so this chapter examines the skills needed to shoot games and events. It also addresses the behind-the-scenes roles in a live sports production.
- Chapter 8—Television Broadcasting: Once the scripts have been written and the highlights gathered, it is time to put it all together for the evening sportscast.
- Chapter 9—Radio Broadcasting and Podcasting: Sports talk radio remains one of the most popular outlets for fans to talk about their favorite teams, but podcasts are quickly becoming more prevalent.
- Chapter 10—Live Sports Production: Being a play-by-play announcer is the dream of many looking to enter into the field. This chapter examines the skills needed for that job and discusses other positions involved in a live broadcast.
- Chapter 11—Social Media: Many fans turn to social media when the latest sports news happens. We look at the proper way to use social media and how to create an effective social media presence.
- Chapter 12—Careers in Sports Broadcasting: Now that you've got the skills, it's time to get the job. This chapter lines up the steps needed to get the experience and materials needed to apply for that first job in the industry.
- Chapter 13—Issues and Ethics in Sports Broadcasting: Special attention needs to be paid to who is receiving coverage and what that coverage looks like.

While you might wish to dive right into the chapter that interests you the most, it is advised that the chapters be read in order. You might be ready to go shoot video at a basketball game (chapter 7), but without reading the interviewing section (chapter 4), the postgame press conference might be a struggle. Each chapter works in harmony with the others in order to create a well-rounded sports broadcaster who can be successful at any game or event.

In addition to practical information, many chapters also contain interviews with a professional. These advice sections provide additional tips from broadcasters who are working for some of the biggest media outlets in the world. Consider their advice another tool to add to your growing toolbox of skills as a broadcaster.

Many of the chapters also contain examples to demonstrate how the skills being taught might actually play out in the real world. These examples might be fictional, but they are as close to the real thing as possible, with scenarios depicting almost the exact situations you would likely face when on the job.

Student Resources in HK*Propel*

In addition to the text, HK*Propel* offers online resources to continue the lessons beyond the book itself. Within these online lessons you will see how to set up an interview for television on either a professional camera or your cellphone. In addition, you'll learn how to edit on one of the more popular editing programs, Adobe Premiere Pro. Plus, there are video clips from a college softball game on which you can practice your editing. Instead of just reading about the skills taught in this book, you will be able to practice them yourself with these hands-on examples and videos.

Instructor Resources in HK*Propel*

An instructor guide is available in the instructor pack in HK*Propel*. The instructor guide is designed to help instructors use this textbook in class. It includes an introduction, a sample syllabus, and suggestions on how to use the student activities in HK*Propel*. Chapters in the instructor guide include objectives from the book as well as writing and editing prompts that will help the instructor test students on the materials taught in the book. The instructor guide is free to adopting instructors and includes an ebook version of the text that allows instructors to add highlights, annotations, and bookmarks. Please contact your sales manager for details about how to access instructor resources in HK*Propel*.

ACKNOWLEDGMENTS

Writing this book has been an incredibly rewarding experience, but I certainly could not have done it alone. There are many people to whom I owe a great deal of gratitude.

Thank you to my friends and family for always being in my corner. I'm lucky to have such great parents and a grandfather who are always so supportive of whatever I'm doing. Thanks to my great friends Dave, John, and Justin for being just as excited about this project as I was and always asking for updates. Most importantly, thank you to Danielle for keeping me on track throughout this entire journey. It meant time away from her and Zoey, but I know I wouldn't have finished this book without either of them. Danielle read every word and provided encouragement when I most needed it, while Zoey reminded me to have some fun every now and then. I was lucky to have them both during this process.

A huge thanks to everyone at Human Kinetics for making this a reality. I am indebted to Drew Tyler for reaching out to me with this book proposal idea and then walking this novice writer through the entire process. Thank you to Melissa Zavala for her editing assistance throughout and making the final draft look better than I could have imagined. Human Kinetics published my first-ever academic journal article, so to do this book project with them is additionally meaningful.

Thank you to all the pros in each chapter who provided their expertise for this book. Early on in the writing, I made a list of people whom I wanted to feature in each chapter's Pro Advice sidebar, and every single one of them said yes. It was wonderful to reconnect with former students, reach out to old friends, and meet some of my favorite people in the business. I will forever be grateful to those who took the time to talk to me and add to the material for this book.

My dream was always to be a sports broadcaster, but once I landed that job, I realized that my favorite part of the job was working with our interns. I loved everything about being a sportscaster, but nothing could compare to seeing the excitement of the interns when they learned a new skill from me. So, a final thank you to the interns and all my current and former students who helped me realize what I really should be doing with my life. Reporting from all the games and events was something I'll never forget, but seeing my own students succeed—and hopefully the future successes of those reading this book—will always be the greatest accomplishment of my career.

Phil Cole/Getty Images

CHAPTER 1

History of Sports Broadcasting

CHAPTER OBJECTIVES

This chapter takes a trip through the history of sports broadcasting. Before understanding how to successfully do the job now, one should know the history of how the field got to where it is today. Therefore, this chapter focuses on the evolution of the broadcast sports media, including the following:

- Explaining the rise in popularity of broadcast sports on radio, television, and the internet
- Identifying key moments throughout history
- Discussing the enormous impact that cable television has had on sports broadcasting

If you ask fans to recall their favorite moment in the history of their favorite team, they can probably describe it in vivid detail. Whether it is their football team winning the championship, a basketball player nailing the buzzer beater, or their favorite soccer player scoring the goal in extra time, those plays are burned into their memories. But when it comes to those memories, how many of those fans were in attendance during that important game, and how many were watching on television or listening on the radio? The greatest moments in sports history are intertwined with sports broadcasting—whether it was watching live at the time or rewatching the highlights years later. Sports broadcasting has been there through many of the most important games and events in history. While the Super Bowl is always circled on fans' calendars, one never knows when a random Tuesday night baseball broadcast could turn into a historic no-hitter. While the athletes are there to play the games, it is the sports broadcasters who are there to capture and describe the incredible moments, often making the journalists just as much a part of the history as the games themselves.

While sports broadcasts are a key part of the world of sports now, it was not always that way. For decades, broadcasting was dominated by entertainment and news programming, with sports holding a much smaller audience. In the 1950-1951 television season, just 2 of the 30 most watched shows on television were about sports, with those primarily focused on boxing (Brooks & Marsh, 2007). However, much has changed since those early days. In 2019, 21 of the 30 most watched events on television were sports, including 13 of the top 16 (Schneider, 2019). Television and radio stations now plan entire days around sports programming, with some shelling out millions (sometimes billions) of dollars to be the exclusive home of various sports. However, sports' journey to becoming one of the biggest draws in broadcasting was not an instantaneous one. Broadcasting has evolved from a curiosity on the radio, to the biggest thing on television, to streaming on mobile devices all over the world. Figure 1.1 shows a timeline of major moments in sports broadcast history.

The Beginnings of Sports Broadcasting on Radio

While the technology behind radio had been in development for decades, it began to resemble its current form in 1906. Reginald Fessenden was the first to use radio waves to broadcast a program that had both speech and music when he transmitted a holiday concert to workers aboard a ship on Christmas Eve of that year (Fry, 1973). Within a few years, radio stations had popped up all over the United States, carrying music and news programming directly into people's homes through large home devices. Soon thereafter radio was made available commercially, and sports programming followed.

KDKA in Pittsburgh

Radio station KDKA in Pittsburgh, Pennsylvania, is recognized as one of the earliest commercial radio stations in the United States (KDKA, 2010), and sports was a big part of the programming shortly after its debut. The first-ever sporting event broadcast live on radio was a boxing match between Johnny Ray and Johnny Dundee on KDKA. On April 11, 1921, the fight's play-by-play was delivered live on the airways by the sports editor of the *Pittsburgh Post*, Florent Gibson (Romano, 2017). Less than five months later, KDKA was creating more firsts in radio. This time it was baseball: the station's broadcast of the Pittsburgh Pirates' 8–5 win over the Philadelphia Phillies was the first-ever radio play-by-play of a professional baseball game (KDKA, 2010). It should come as no surprise that KDKA was also the first to broadcast a college football game. In October 1921, the station was live for the University of Pittsburgh's win over West Virginia University (NCAA, 2020).

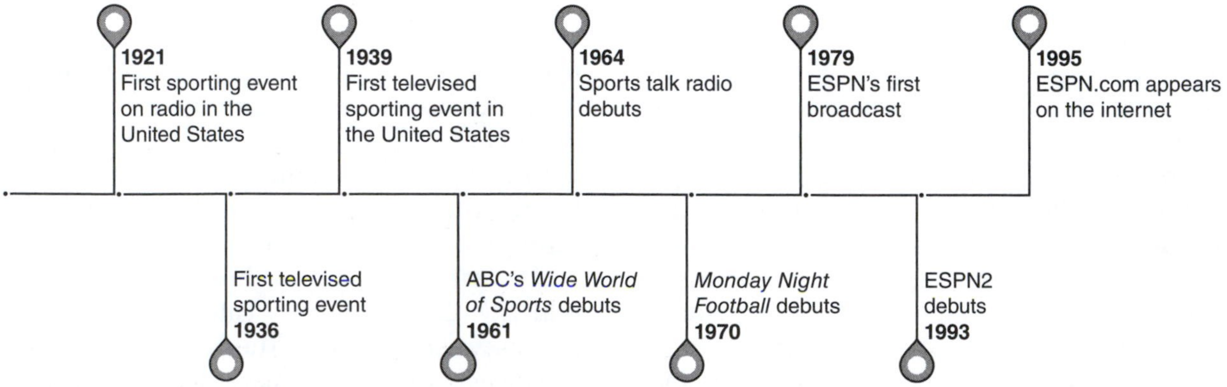

FIGURE 1.1 Major moments in sports broadcasting.

Bettmann/Getty Images

Fans in New York City crowd around a television to watch game one of the 1950 World Series.

Live . . . but Not Really

Many of the early broadcasts of sporting events were live, but they were not live at the actual game. Instead, they were doing what became known as "re-creations." During these games, someone at the stadium would send the play-by-play results as they happened back to the radio station via a telegraph wire. The announcer at the station would then read the telegraphed action and re-create what happened. While the action was traditionally described accurately, the announcers did add in their own elements to make the action more exciting, including hitting a wooden ruler against a desk to give the sound of a bat hitting a baseball (Catsis, 1996).

These re-creations were appealing to radio stations for a variety of reasons, none more prominent than the opportunity to save money. By not sending an announcer to the game, management did not have to pay for the cost of travel or telephone lines, which were expensive in the early days of radio. Instead, they subscribed to the inexpensive service from Western Union to deliver the telegraphed games or paid a newspaper reporter who was already there to call in the results to the station every couple of innings (Catsis, 1996; Nufer, 1991).

Announcer Bob Robertson would re-create Tacoma Tigers baseball road games despite often being hundreds of miles away in his home studio (Nufer, 1991). Robertson became so good at re-creating a broadcast that people would ask him how his trips to the various cities were, despite the fact that Robertson never left Tacoma. He even once fooled the Tigers' team owner (We R Tacoma, 2020). Ultimately, as technology advanced, the costs decreased, and when the audience demanded live action from the game, the use of re-creations was eventually phased out. In 1991, Robertson was credited with broadcasting the final re-created game (Catsis, 1996).

Graham McNamee

Graham McNamee was one of the first prominent play-by-play announcers in the United States. While others came before him, it was

McNamee who quickly rose to the top in the beginning years of the industry. NBC radio selected him to be its lead announcer for championship boxing fights, baseball's World Series, and top football matchups (Britannica, n.d.). However, his spot leading the way in baseball coverage came thanks to a little bit of luck. McNamee was scheduled to talk only between innings, while a newspaper reporter would provide the majority of the coverage. Instead, after just a few games, the reporter decided he did not like that the radio was interfering with his job writing for the newspaper, so he quit. McNamee slid into the top spot, and the rest is history (Catsis, 1996; Smith, 2001).

McNamee went on to have a decades-long career in broadcasting, calling some of the biggest sporting events in history, including additional World Series games, the first Rose Bowl broadcast on NBC, and the first three Major League Baseball All-Star Games (Schneider, 2019). His 1925 radio call of the World Series resulted in listeners sending 50,000 letters of appreciation to radio station WEAF. Decades after his death, McNamee was named the winner of the 2016 Ford C. Frick Award, given by the National Baseball Hall of Fame to a broadcaster who had major contributions to the sport (National Baseball Hall of Fame, n.d.).

Concerns About Radio

Live radio broadcasts meant that millions of Americans could now stay home and listen to games if they could not make it to the stadium. While that was great for fans, it created a major concern for the teams. Many feared that if fans had the option to stay home and follow along that they would never come to another game. Therefore, many teams elected not to allow live broadcasts of games, essentially banning announcers and radio stations from entering the press box. Broadcasters had to come up with ways to get around the ban, including setting up in a tree outside the stadium so they could see inside (Catsis, 1996). It was not until sponsors started advertising during these broadcasts that the stations started to relent. Owners soon realized that money they might lose on ticket sales could possibly be recovered with advertising revenues (Covil, n.d.).

Sports Talk Radio

While broadcasting live sports was an important part of the radio landscape, sports talk shows soon followed. Bill Mazer is credited with hosting the first-ever sports talk radio show when his show debuted on WNBC in March of 1964. He talked to callers about the latest sports news and even answered a variety of trivia questions from his audience (Best, 2011). Soon after, sports talk shows started sprouting up all over the country, followed by radio stations that devoted the entire day to sports programming. These all-sports stations traditionally have talk shows in the morning and afternoon, followed by live broadcasts of games at night.

Early Days of Television Sports Broadcasting

As radio was continuing to be a key part of the sports media landscape, the invention of television was about to change things dramatically. Soon, sports fans would not only be able to hear live broadcasts involving their favorite teams and athletes but would also be able to see them. Early broadcasts were very basic, using just a camera or two to get all the action, but that would eventually make way for the multiple-camera, high-definition broadcasts that are now seen on television almost every night.

Important Firsts

The first televised sporting event was the 1936 Berlin Olympics. At the time, Adolf Hitler wanted all of Germany to see the events, so he arranged for viewing stations to be set up in cities throughout the country. Ultimately, Hitler's primary goal was to drum up support for his political agenda by showing Germany, and his chosen athletes, in the best light possible. He hoped to show off the athletic successes and also technological advances of the television camera under his leadership (Given, 2016).

However, the broadcasting legacy of the 1936 Olympics is simply that they were broadcast at all. Previous to this, it was thought to be nearly impossible to broadcast an event of the magnitude of the Olympics. While coverage was limited to Germany, its success helped pave the way for other broadcasts to soon follow throughout the world.

In the United States, the first televised sporting event was a 1939 college baseball game between Columbia and Princeton. While current baseball broadcasts have multiple cameras stationed all over the stadium to capture many different angles, this first game was broadcast with just one camera stationed high above the field just to the left of home plate (Columbia Athletics, 2009). The game was broadcast on W2XBS, a television station that would eventually become WNBC, but not very many people saw it—fewer than 400 television sets were in use at the time in that viewing area (Koppett, 1999).

Even though there were not many viewers, the broadcast was a success and paved the way for sports on television as it is known today. Just a few months after that college baseball game, W2XBS televised a professional game between the Brooklyn Dodgers and the Cincinnati Reds. This time the game featured two cameras, one on the third base line and one high above home plate. An article in *The New York Times* after the game boasted that "television-set owners as far away as fifty miles viewed the action" (McGowen, 1939, para. 2). The technology was far from what it is today; the reporter wrote, "at times it was possible to catch a fleeting glimpse of the ball," certainly a long way from being able to see baseball seams during slow-motion replays on high-definition televisions (History.com Editors, 2020; McGowen, 1939, para. 2).

From these two baseball games came the rest of the sporting world on television: Just over a month later, the first football game was televised. A matchup between Fordham and Waynesburg College hit the airwaves, despite there being only about 200 television sets in New York City at the time. The game was played in the New York City area and only available locally, so fans of Waynesburg, located in Pennsylvania, could not see the game on their televisions (Caldwell, 2014). At the time, regional broadcasts were the primary means of watching live sports on television. However, in September of that year, Duke faced off against Pittsburgh in a college football matchup that was the first sporting event ever broadcast nationally, as NBC carried Duke's 19–14 win nationwide (Cramer, 2016; Halberstam, 2019). On that same day, CBS aired the first college football game in color, despite only a few cities carrying the experimental broadcast (Halberstam, 2019).

Mark Rucker/Transcendental Graphics, Getty Images

NBC transmits its first televised sporting event on May 17, 1939 in New York, showing a game between Columbia University and Princeton.

Professional Football on Television

In 1939, a matchup between the Brooklyn Dodgers and the Philadelphia Eagles on the football field did not appear to be anything worth noting. The Dodgers (not to be confused with the baseball team of the same name) were winless in their last three, while the Eagles had not won a game all season (1939 NFL League Standings, n.d.). While *The New York Times* reported on the Dodgers' win, the writer neglected to mention what ultimately made the game remarkable—it was the first professional football game ever broadcast on television. Two cameras and one microphone captured the action for NBC's broadcast to about 500 people watching at home (Fitzpatrick, 2016; Pro Football Hall of Fame, n.d.).

While the first televised game might have been played with little fanfare, it also signaled the beginning of what would ultimately become the biggest sport on television. While those initial games had a skeleton crew, games in the modern era are huge productions. NFL games routinely use between 12 and 20 cameras, while between 150 and 200 employees are working to get each game up and running every week of the regular season (NFL Ops, n.d.). These games are watched by millions. As of 2020, only 11 shows in American television history have averaged more than 100 million viewers, 10 of which were Super Bowls (Breech, 2020). The most watched television event in American history was Super Bowl 49, which had a record of an average 114.4 million viewers, peaking at 120.8 million during the final minutes of the game (Pallotta, 2015).

ABC Sports

While sports have been on television for decades, very few entities have had as great an impact on televised sports as ABC Sports. The network was long the standard-bearer for sports on television, based on their creative programming, groundbreaking football coverage, and outspoken announcers.

Wide World of Sports

ABC Sports' rise to prominence in the sports media started in 1961 with the creation of *Wide World of Sports*. The show aired most weekends on Saturdays on ABC stations throughout the United States. It was hosted by legendary

MAJOR MOMENTS

"Heidi Bowl"

As television broadcasting evolved throughout the 1950s and 1960s, a strange ending to a football game between the Oakland Raiders and the New York Jets in 1968 changed how networks would broadcast sports forever. NBC executives had allotted three hours to show the game, figuring it would be over by 7:00 p.m. EST and then they could start airing a highly publicized movie, *Heidi*. NBC had signed a contract with the movie's primary sponsor that guaranteed the movie would start on time (Haring, 2018).

As 7:00 approached, the game was far from being over. There was confusion among executives as to how to proceed, and ultimately NBC left the game in progress and started the movie with the Jets in the lead by three points (Barnhouse, 1998). However, as the movie played, the Raiders made a dramatic comeback, scoring two touchdowns in the final minute to win 43–32 (Catsis, 1996). People watching the movie had no idea this was happening until a message appeared that read "NBC SPORTS BULLETIN . . . THE OAKLAND RAIDERS HAVE DEFEATED THE NY JETS 43–32" (The Raiders Film Vault, 2019). The timing could not have been worse, as the alert scrolled across the bottom of the screen during one of the most dramatic moments in the movie. So many angry viewers called NBC to complain—both football fans complaining about missing the ending and *Heidi* fans upset about the update ruining the movie—that the network's telephone lines went down (Barnhouse, 1988).

While the game itself is ultimately just one event in the long history of football, the television ramifications of the "Heidi Bowl" continue to be felt. Professional and amateur sports leagues now have language written into their television contracts that state that games must be concluded before a network can break away from the action (Haring, 2018)—any programming that is scheduled to start after a game must be delayed until the game is over.

sportscaster Jim McKay, who started each episode with the same iconic opening lines:

> *Spanning the globe to bring you the constant variety of sport. The thrill of victory . . . the agony of defeat . . . the human drama of athletic competition. This is ABC's Wide World of Sports.*

However, in a break from most of the televised sports at the time, the games showcased on *Wide World of Sports* were not the traditional fare. Instead of baseball, football, and basketball, the show put a spotlight on lesser-known sports throughout the world. Events such as rodeo, jai-alai, cliff diving, and demolition derby made regular appearances on the show (ESPN Press Room, 2011). The show was a commercial and editorial success, winning 11 Emmy Awards, including Outstanding Achievement in Sports Programming several times (Emmys, n.d.).

Monday Night Football

Wide World of Sports might have focused on small sports, but ABC Sports' lasting contribution in the world of broadcasting is their partnership with the biggest league in the United States. In the late 1960s, NFL commissioner Pete Rozelle was looking to have one game a week air during prime-time television. The league's broadcasters at the time, CBS and NBC, had little interest in the games, so ABC was given a chance to bid. The network signed on with the NFL, and the result was 35 years of television history (Sandomir, 2005).

Monday Night Football debuted on ABC in September of 1970 with a game between the New York Giants and the Cleveland Browns. The broadcast immediately looked different from other games at the time, with ABC Sports utilizing more cameras, including some specifically designed to get more close-up shots of the action (Sandomir, 2005). Throughout the years, *Monday Night Football* covered some of the biggest games in football history, including the Miami Dolphins' upset win over the Chicago Bears in 1985. That night, 46 percent of all televisions on in the United States were tuned to witness the only loss of the season for a dominant Bears team (Florio, 2015). One of the most memorable moments in *Monday Night Football* history had nothing to do with the game at all. On a Monday night in 1980, singer John Lennon was shot and killed outside his home. As *Monday Night Football* was showing a game between the Dolphins and the New England Patriots, announcer Howard Cosell stopped describing the action and said the following:

> *An unspeakable tragedy confirmed to us by ABC News in New York City. John Lennon, outside of his apartment building on the West Side of New York City, the most famous, perhaps, of all of The Beatles—shot twice in the back. Rushed to Roosevelt Hospital—dead on arrival. Hard to go back to game after that news flash.* (TLPFAS, 2010, 0:44)

Millions of people who were watching the game for entertainment had just been told about one of the biggest news stories of the year from the football announcers (Chase, 2015).

Howard Cosell

While that was certainly a key moment in broadcast history, Howard Cosell is ultimately remembered in sports media history for much more than just his role in the John Lennon announcement. For decades, Cosell was synonymous with some of the biggest events and athletes in the world of sports, all while working at ABC Sports. Starting out as a radio host, Cosell made the transition to television in the early 1960s. His television career led him to be in the announcing booth for some of the biggest events in the sports world, but he first began to make his mark by reporting on boxing.

Cosell was one of the first broadcasters to extensively cover Cassius Clay, announcing some of his biggest fights. After Clay changed his name to Muhammad Ali, it was Cosell who became one of the boxer's most vocal supporters. Many media members refused to call Ali by his new name, but Cosell did almost from the start. Cosell also supported Ali when the boxer refused to fight in the Vietnam War, which led to Ali being stripped of his boxing championships (Sandomir, 2016). In addition to Ali's fights, Cosell became known for being on the microphone for some of the biggest boxing matches in history, including his famous

"Down goes Frazier!" call of George Foreman knocking down Joe Frazier in a 1973 fight (Slater, 2018).

Cosell's time as the commentator on *Monday Night Football* helped that show become the top-rated program on television for many years. He was also involved in ABC's Olympics coverage and World Series baseball broadcasts, and he hosted his own sports investigative show, *ABC SportsBeat* (Shapiro, 1995). However, it is Cosell's style that is likely his most enduring legacy. While most sportscasters at the time were very complimentary of athletes and sports, Cosell was one of the first to be overly critical. His distinct voice was often imitated, and the man himself was also not shy to draw attention to himself, even being labeled as arrogant. Viewers either loved him or hated him, as proven by the fact that he was once voted simultaneously the most popular and the most disliked sportscaster in America (Shapiro, 1995; Thomas, 1995).

The End of ABC Sports

Despite the decades of dominance and innovation, ABC Sports essentially came to an end in 2006. With the Walt Disney Company owning both ABC and ESPN, the decision was made to merge the two properties into one cohesive brand. Unfortunately for the continued legacy of ABC Sports, ESPN was chosen to be the dominant partner in that merger. The ABC Sports graphics, music, and name were all replaced by ESPN properties. Soon after, all sporting events shown on ABC were labeled as "ESPN on ABC" (Sandomir, 2006).

The Olympics

For decades, ABC Sports was also the home of the Olympics in the United States. While events like the Super Bowl traditionally have the biggest one-day TV viewing each year, that number is often dwarfed by the total number of people who watch the Olympics during the entire two-week run of the games. In 2008, an estimated 4.7 billion viewers worldwide—about 70 percent of the entire world's population—watched the Summer Olympics in Beijing (Nielsen, 2008).

As will be discussed more in chapter 2, the Olympics has become big business for television networks, but it did not start out that way. In the United States, the Olympics were not on television until 1960, when CBS broadcast the Winter Games from Squaw Valley, California (Billings, Angelini, & MacArthur, 2018). While the initial broadcast effort was not overly ambitious, showing barely an hour a day of events (Billings et al., 2018), a lasting technological innovation came from an incident during a ski race. During a slalom event, Olympic officials were not sure whether a skier had missed a gate when going down the mountain. To confirm the result, they asked CBS if they could review the video recording of the run. This gave CBS the idea for the innovation that is now on almost every televised sporting event: instant replay (Olympic.org, n.d.).

The Olympics began to reach higher levels of popularity during the time when ABC Sports was the broadcaster. In 1972, ABC officials made the decision to devote their entire prime-time schedule to the Olympics during the games, meaning that the Olympics were now on television every night. The result was a ratings success for ABC, and it revolutionized how networks thought about the Olympics (Billings et al., 2018).

The 1972 Olympics were also memorable for a horrific event that became one of the more famous moments in television history. Eleven members of the Israeli Olympic delegation were taken hostage by a terrorist organization that had stormed into the Olympic Village. Due to ABC's broadcasting of the Olympics, that became the channel that most Americans watched to get the latest updates (Billings et al., 2018). Broadcaster Jim McKay was on the air for 14 hours straight reporting events (Hiestand, 2008) before delivering the news that all the hostages had been killed:

> *When I was a kid, my father used to say, "Our greatest hopes and our worst fears are seldom realized." Our worst fears have been realized tonight. They've now said that there were eleven hostages. Two were killed in their rooms yesterday morning, nine were killed at the airport tonight. They're all gone. (McKay, 2002, para. 11)*

While ABC was synonymous with the Olympics for decades, that would soon change as NBC took over coverage in 1998 and refused to relinquish that control well into the 2000s. Coverage under NBC changed, because the network focused more on storytelling and less on the actual events themselves (Billings et al., 2018). One of the main reasons for this was that NBC executives wanted to attract female viewers, and they believed that women were more interested in the storylines and less interested in the results. While this decision has led to some criticism of that coverage, the decision has led to their desired result. In 2016, more women than men watched the first six nights of NBC's Olympic coverage (Best, 2016). This makes the Olympics unique because there are very few sporting events that have more female than male viewers.

Impact of Cable Television

While cable television might currently be seen as a way to watch a variety of channels about almost anything, that was not the goal of the technology when it first debuted in the United States. Many Americans were receiving their television signal through antennas located on the television. While millions of people watched their favorite shows through this method, there were large parts of the country that were still without a workable signal. Those living in areas with tall mountains had difficulties getting a clear signal through their antennas, so cable was created as a way in which everyone could get a television signal. In 1948, cable systems were created in Arkansas, Oregon, and Pennsylvania through which people could connect from their homes to the community antenna tower (CCTA, n.d.).

By the late 1950s, cable companies began recognizing that cable could be used for more than just transmitting local channels. Instead, the focus quickly turned to offering a variety of programming options beyond just a few stations. However, the Federal Communications Commission (FCC) continued to debate how to regulate this new technology before finally loosening regulations in 1972 (CCTA, n.d.). Perhaps not surprisingly, it was a sporting event on cable a few years later that is often credited with the rapid growth of the satellite and cable industry.

"Thrilla in Manilla"

In 1972, cable's first pay TV network debuted with the name Home Box Office (HBO) (Kissel, 1992). While HBO might be primarily known for movies and TV series today, the channel had a strong sports presence when it premiered. In fact, the first-ever program on HBO was not a movie but a hockey game between the NHL's New York Rangers and Vancouver Canucks (Leverete, Ott, & Buckley, 2008). These early days of HBO were fairly limited, because only those within a few hundred miles of New York City were able to get the channel (Koplovitz, 2015). However, emerging satellite technology would soon allow for nationwide broadcasts. A year later, during a demonstration of these satellites, HBO arranged to show a live boxing match in New York City to an audience watching in Los Angeles. While the fight's broadcast went off without a hitch, there were still some concerns about cost and reliability (Leddy, 2015). Those concerns would quickly vanish a few years later following one of the most famous sporting events of all time.

In 1975, Muhammad Ali and Joe Frazier were set to face off in the third and final bout between the two. Frazier had won the first fight, while Ali had won the rematch. The third matchup was scheduled to take place in the Philippines (Anderson, 1975). HBO had arranged for a live satellite feed to broadcast the video back to the United States. The head of programming for HBO was gambling that a successful fight broadcast would prove the value of cable television (Koplovitz, 2015). When the fight started that night, it was clear that that gamble would pay off.

Bob Rosencrans, the president of a cable company, said, "The fighters looked like they were in the next room, the picture quality was that extraordinary. We knew we had a winner. We knew this was a big day" (Leddy, 2015, para. 18). While Ali was the winner in the ring that night (Anderson, 1975), the real winner

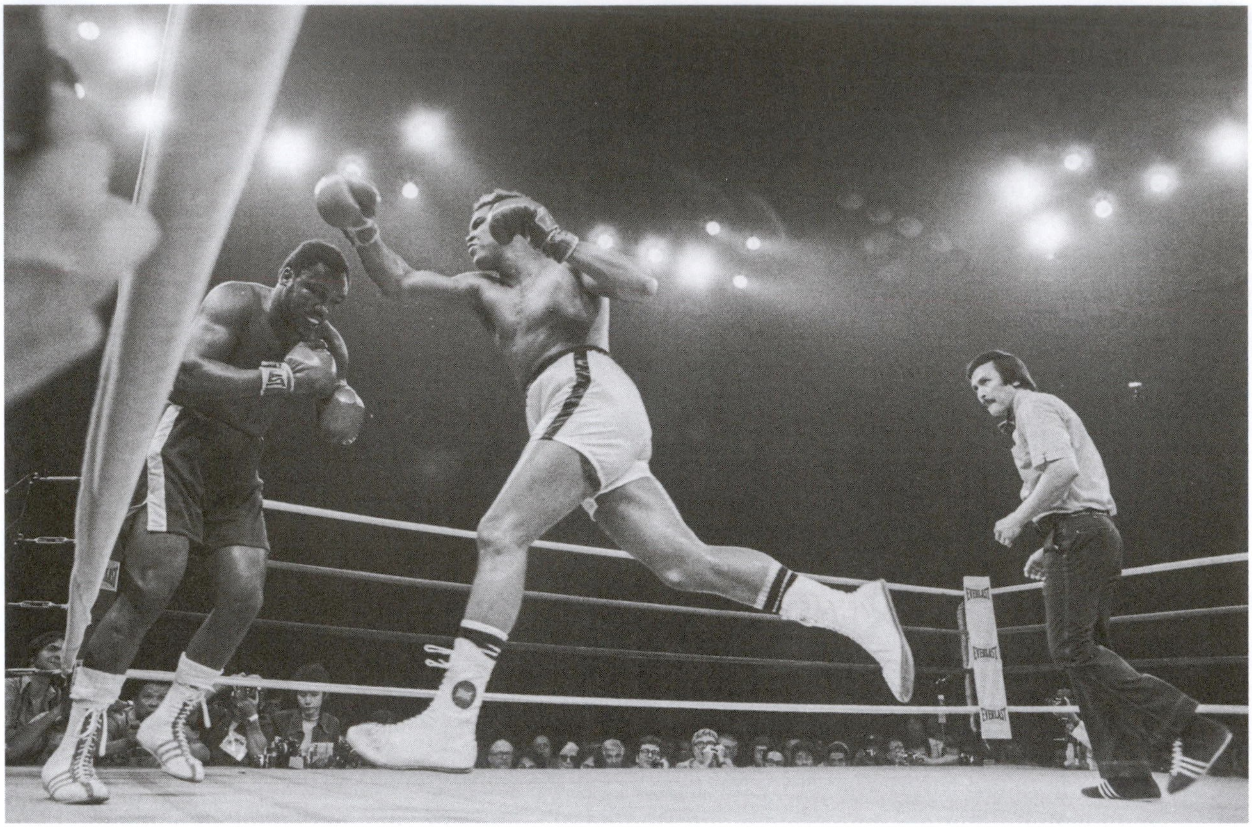

Bettmann/Getty Images

The "Thrilla in Manilla" between Joe Frazier and Muhammad Ali was one of the first broadcasts to demonstrate the possibilities with satellite television.

might have been cable television. Following the successful broadcast, cable companies all across the United States raced to install their own satellite dishes in order to show events from around the world (Koplovitz, 2015).

ESPN

When it comes to sports broadcasting, perhaps no media outlet has had more of an impact on the landscape than ESPN. For decades, sports television was dominated by regional broadcasts in which the audience primarily saw games and highlights of only the teams in their area. ESPN changed everything by bringing sports throughout the world to cable audiences in the United States. If a sports fan lived in New York, they previously would only have had news about New York teams from the local media. However, on ESPN, that New York–based fan could get highlights of the Miami Dolphins, Houston Astros, or Los Angeles Lakers.

The Early Days of ESPN

While ESPN is the home for national sports, that was not the goal when the initial owners came up with the idea for a sports television network in 1978. Connecticut residents Bill and Scott Rasmussen wanted to create a cable television channel that was devoted entirely to Connecticut-area sports and shown exclusively in that part of the country. The ESP Network, or Entertainment and Sports Programming Network, would focus on the University of Connecticut, the NHL's Hartford Whalers, and other teams in that area. However, after some initial research, and examining the financial bottom line, the owners determined that buying a 24-satellite feed that could reach the entire United States was actually cheaper than sending the channel to just Connecticut through nonsatellite means. With that in mind, the father and son duo elected to go with the nationwide option, and the concept of what ESPN would become soon began to change (Miller & Shales, 2011; Vogan, 2015).

After securing a location in Bristol, Connecticut, to build the headquarters, the owners quickly moved to secure the rights to show various sports. A deal with the NCAA allowed ESPN to show 18 different college sports, including championship games, giving the network some programming to build their evenings around. Anheuser-Busch became one of their first sponsors, inking a deal that was, at the time, the largest advertising contract in cable television history. While giving over a million dollars to a network that had not yet been on the air might have seemed like a gamble at the time, Anheuser-Busch guessed that sports fans were beer drinkers, so they determined that it was a good place to advertise (Miller & Shales, 2011).

With major college sports and a tentpole sponsor on board, ESPN debuted on September 7, 1979. As the network hit the air, anchor Lee Leonard told the audience: "If you're a fan, *if you're a fan*, what you'll see in the next minutes, hours, and days to follow may convince you that you've gone to sports heaven" (ESPN Front Row, 2018, 0:03). After a brief explanation of how the satellite technology worked, and the first edition of *SportsCenter*, the network was off and running.

While college sports were part of the network's early programming, those were just about the only recognizable, mainstream sports on ESPN at the time. The first-ever sporting event broadcast on ESPN was men's professional slow-pitch softball. Other early sports included Australian rules football, tractor pulls, skeet shooting, and karate (Rosenthal, 2019). With that lack of traditionally popular sports, the network did not exactly become the runaway success that one might expect. In fact, while it might seem crazy now, ESPN almost did not survive their first few years in business. With few viewers and a lack of sponsors, ESPN was losing over a million dollars a month (Vogan, 2015), but Anheuser-Busch re-upped its sponsorship, giving the network an additional $5 million that may have saved it from going out of business (Kohler, 2013).

The arrival of professional sports helped increase ESPN's demand among customers. With the NBA, USFL, and NHL all on ESPN, the days of relying on fringe sports to make up the vast majority of the network's programming was quickly coming to an end. Fans of these sports were calling their cable company to demand that ESPN be part of the channel lineup. Additionally, in 1984, the original owner of ESPN, Getty Oil, had been purchased and the new owner wanted to get rid of any holdings that were not part of the oil business. The network was bought by broadcast company ABC, and by 1985, with new owners and an increased demand, ESPN had turned a profit for the first time (Vogan, 2015).

SportsCenter

While ESPN has undergone numerous changes throughout the years, one constant has been *SportsCenter*. The show debuted on the network's very first day on the air in 1979 and has been a staple ever since. It traditionally airs multiple times a day, seven days a week, with a rotating cast of anchors and reporters. However, during some specific time slots, there is a chosen, dedicated host. For example, in 2015, ESPN announced that Scott Van Pelt would be solo anchor for *SportsCenter* every weeknight at midnight EST (Coelho, 2015).

SportsCenter primarily focuses on news and highlights from the world of sports. While other programming on ESPN might feature just one sport, *SportsCenter* consists of stories from all the major events and tends to deliver the news with some additional analysis. The show is often very polished, unlike the debate shows that tend to consist of two personalities arguing back and forth.

One of the lasting legacies of *SportsCenter* is that it brought national sports to a local audience. The impact this had trickled down to sports broadcasts throughout the country. While local sports broadcasters would talk about the local teams during their segments on the news, they would also report much of the national news and scores from that night. However, with *SportsCenter* reporting on all the national news, fans no longer needed the local sportscasters to deliver that information. Therefore, those working in local news had to readjust their focus, spending less time on national highlights and more time with the local teams.

While perhaps not a key part of the broadcasting legacy of ESPN, the commercials for *SportsCenter* have provided some of the most memorable moments. In 1995, the network debuted its "This is *SportsCenter*" advertising campaign. These tongue-in-cheek commercials gave a humorous take on how the show was put together behind the scenes. In the ads, mascots, sports stars, and various celebrities played a key role in how the show is created. Over 400 of the commercials were produced, and they proved to be incredibly successful for the network (Fleming, 2020), winning both Best in Show for advertising contests and being credited with creating a positive impression of the network among viewers (Sunset, 2008).

1987: The Turning Point

While ESPN was quickly becoming a major player in the world of sports broadcasting, it officially announced its arrival in 1987. The NFL was one of the biggest U.S. sports organizations at the time and had some of the highest viewership numbers each week during the season. However, since the beginning of televised games, NFL contests were only on local over-the-air channels such as ABC, CBS, and NBC. In 1987, that changed forever. ESPN agreed to pay the NFL $153 million to show eight Sunday night regular season games, four preseason exhibition games, and the Pro Bowl all-star game for the upcoming three seasons (Fabrikant, 1987). ESPN's president at the time called it "the most significant sports agreement in cable television history" (Pierson, 1987, para. 20). The preseason games a few months later earned the biggest sports ratings in cable history (Chad, 1987), and demand for the network was at all-time high. The acquisition of NFL coverage was cited as the reason for 700,000 new ESPN subscribers, making it the first cable network to be in 50 percent of homes (Shales & Miller, 2011). Additionally, the television ratings for the network in 1987 showed a 33 percent increase over 1986 (Nagle, 1988).

ESPN Expansion

ESPN was successfully bidding on sports to show, and millions of fans were willing to watch, so network officials moved forward with expansion. The company debuted ESPN2 in 1993, with a goal of attracting younger viewers. They focused on sports popular with a different audience from that of traditional ESPN, such as hockey, arena football, and BMX racing (Frager, 1993). However, when it came to creating demand for the network, ESPN went to a more traditional sport, college basketball. Duke versus North Carolina was one of the biggest rivalries in the sport at the time, and ESPN put the 1994 game on ESPN2. If fans wanted to see the next chapter in this matchup, they needed to call their cable company and demand that ESPN2 be added to the channel lineup (Chansky, 2005). Eventually, executives moved the network away from the focus on younger sports, and instead it simply became an extension of ESPN, even dropping the ESPN2 name (Leitch, 2007).

This was hardly the end of ESPN's expansion: ESPNews debuted in 1996 as a 24-hour sports news channel, ESPN Classic (bought in 1997) showed games from years earlier, and 2005's creation of ESPNU focused on college sports (Cotey, 2005; Hofmeister, 1997; Sandomir, 1996). Thanks to the increasing popularity of college football in the 2010s, ESPN's next expansions all happened with that focus in mind. As the University of Texas was debating leaving the Big 12 and joining a different football conference in 2011, ESPN offered the university a 20-year, $295 million contract to create the Longhorn Network (Fang, 2015). UT took the deal and stayed in the same conference. The Longhorn Network focused almost exclusively on University of Texas sports by showing studio shows, live sports, and analysis of Longhorn athletics. Announced in 2013, ESPN's next new channel covered an entire conference instead of just one team. The SEC Network was a joint partnership between the Southeastern Conference (SEC) and ESPN, in which the network carried hundreds of sporting events, including over 40 football games from the league (Sandomir, 2013). The network proved to be a success for both the SEC and ESPN (Morton, 2019), so a new partnership formed soon after. With a similar format, the Atlantic Coast Conference (ACC) worked with ESPN to debut the ACC Network in 2019 (Hale, 2018).

ESPN's Competition

While ESPN has long been the dominant force in sports on cable, they have not been without competition along the way. CNN/SI debuted in 1996 as a joint venture between cable news giant CNN and the popular sports magazine *Sports Illustrated*. While the network had the journalistic backing to succeed, it was not profitable because it was not in nearly enough homes to attract sponsors. By 2002, CNN/SI was out of business (Associated Press, 2002).

Other sports networks have done little to slow the momentum of ESPN. NBC Sports Network (NBCSN) went through two different iterations, Outdoor Life Network and Versus, before settling on the NBC branding after a 2011 sale. While ESPN shows games from professional football and basketball, NBCSN has the rights for less popular sports such as auto racing and hockey (Badenhausen, 2013). The network has also embraced European soccer leagues, with the hope of attracting fans of that sport (Sandomir, 2015). However, in early 2021, NBC Sports announced they were stopping operations of the network (Pallotta, 2021). CBS Sports Network originally debuted as the National College Sports Network, a cable station devoted to showing just college sports (Umstead, 2002). After being purchased by CBS in 2006, the emphasis on college sports remained, while also adding programming involving other sports such as mixed martial arts (Martin, 2020).

While NBC Sports Network and CBS Sports Network appeared to not be actively trying to challenge ESPN for cable sports supremacy, Fox Sports took direct aim when it debuted Fox Sports 1 (later shortened to FS1) in 2013. The network created an aggressive marketing plan to become an alternative to ESPN and hired former ESPN employees, created studio shows, and developed *Fox Sports Live* as a direct competitor to *SportsCenter* (Baysinger, 2013). In 2015, the network used an ultimately unsuccessful "embrace debate" strategy in which afternoon debate-style shows took center stage instead of news and highlights. While it has not made the ratings dent it may have hoped, FS1 has become an alternative to ESPN (Reedy, 2019).

League and Team Networks

In addition to traditionally owned media networks, teams and leagues are also utilizing cable television as a way to reach their audience. On January 1, 2009, Major League Baseball debuted the MLB Network, a channel owned and operated by the league with the sole purpose of reporting on the sport. While it might have seemed revolutionary, MLB was hardly the first. In fact, the NFL Network for football, the NBA Network for basketball, and the NHL Network for hockey were already on the air by the time the baseball-only channel debuted (Sandomir, 2008).

Additionally, team-owned networks have allowed teams to essentially focus on themselves. In 2002, the New York Yankees created the YES (Yankee Entertainment and Sports) Network. The network airs Yankees games and documentaries about the Yankees, and it simulcasts a daily radio show from the Yankees play-by-play announcer (Reynolds, 2014; Sandomir, 2001). The channel is everything a New York Yankees fan could ever want, which is exactly what the team is aiming for. Following the success of YES in both viewers and advertising dollars, other professional sports teams have created their own cable networks.

The Internet

While sports broadcasting has undergone years of evolution from radio, to broadcast television, to cable television, the future might be focused more on the internet. Fans no longer need to be in front of their televisions to watch live games, while fans of sports talk radio can listen to almost any show throughout the country on each station's respective website. Additionally, the internet has opened up more opportunities for smaller broadcast outlets to be heard by a bigger audience.

Livestreaming

Many high school sports programs use the internet to livestream audio or video from their games. Depending on how elaborate a production the school wishes to create, a few cameras and additional technology can be purchased, and with a few clicks on the computer, games can be streamed live across the world. In fall 2020, as several state guidelines limited the number of fans in the crowd due to the COVID-19 virus, schools turned to these livestreaming methods as a way to allow more people to watch the games (Sidelinger, 2020).

Watch All the Games

For fans, perhaps the biggest advantage that the internet has provided is the opportunity to see every game in a professional season, no matter where the viewer lives. In 2001, Major League Baseball announced they were planning to stream every game on the internet to fans for a fee (Hu, 2001). This was the beginning of MLB.TV, an internet service run by the league itself in which fans can stream games directly to their computer, phone, tablet, or television through a streaming device. The service is ideal for the displaced fan. For example, Boston Red Sox fans living in South Carolina would not be able to get the local Boston coverage of their favorite team. However, through MLB.TV, fans can stream every Red Sox game, even though they live over 900 miles away from the stadium. Other leagues soon followed suit, with NBA League Pass and NHL.tv each providing similar options.

While it is only one game a week, the NFL's partnership with Amazon also signaled that league's entry into streaming. In 2017, the NFL announced that their new Thursday night regular season games would be shown live on Amazon's streaming platform Amazon Prime. Fans would not need a cable subscription, or a television, to watch this Thursday night game

MAJOR MOMENTS

ESPN+

While the internet has allowed for smaller broadcast outlets, including high schools, to broadcast live online, bigger networks are embracing online streaming as well. Perhaps no commitment to this streaming technology was bigger than ESPN's decision to create ESPN+ in 2018. However, at the start, many wondered whether ESPN had misread what the audience was really looking for.

The network initially announced that ESPN+ would be a place to watch sporting events from around the world, including some not traditionally shown on the television network. One estimate was that there would be more than 10,000 games available to stream on ESPN+. Additionally, ESPN's wildly popular *30 for 30* sports documentaries would be available on the service, along with some new programming designed specifically for ESPN+ (Draper, 2018). However, what would *not* be on it drew much of the early attention. Network officials were careful to point out that ESPN+ would be the home for sports "not available" on television (Statt, 2018). That means that for $4.99 a month, sports fans were paying for sports on their phone or streaming device, but those sports would not include the NFL, the biggest college football games, and network programming such as *SportsCenter*. One popular website labeled the initial offering "underwhelming" and "a missed opportunity" (McAtee, 2018).

However, sports fans loudly disagreed. ESPN+ had over one million paid subscribers within five months of launching (Melvin, 2018) and had 8.5 million subscribers less than two years later (Sengwe, 2020). For additional content, ESPN reached an agreement with the mixed martial arts organization UFC to have ESPN+ be the exclusive home for all the fight company's pay-per-view bouts starting in April 2019. At the announcement of the partnership, UFC president Dana White said, "Streaming is the future" (Mullin, 2019).

as long as they were a subscriber to Amazon Prime (Wingfield, 2017). The partnership was such a success that the league expanded the partnership to allow for Amazon to stream a playoff game starting in 2021 (Flint, 2020).

Social Media

The NFL first attempted a Thursday night streaming package with Twitter (Selyukh, 2016), demonstrating the emergence of social media in broadcast sports. While that experiment lasted just one year before the NFL moved to Amazon Prime, other leagues have since taken their games to Twitter (Voepel, 2020). Facebook reached a deal with Major League Baseball to be the exclusive home for 25 games during the 2018 season, meaning fans wanting to watch had to log into Facebook first before watching (Valinsky, 2018).

In 2017, ESPN launched *SportsCenter* on Snapchat. New episodes were made exclusively for the service and were available twice a day during the week and once a day on weekends. Each episode topped out at around five minutes long (Ota, 2017), and the format was geared to the younger audience that was already using Snapchat (Esposito, 2018). After about two months in existence, *SportsCenter* on Snapchat was getting more than 2 million unique viewers a day, with 75% of those viewers being between the ages of 13 and 24 (Brady, 2018).

CHAPTER WRAP-UP

SUMMARY

Sports broadcasting's evolution from radio experiment to one of the biggest entities in the media is remarkable. Early radio stations quickly recognized the demand for sports programming and put baseball and boxing events on the schedule. When television debuted, sports followed shortly behind. ABC Sports led the way to a revolutionary boom for televised sports, with fans being the biggest beneficiary. Viewers could now see their favorite athletes in action, while national programming allowed for athletes from all over the country to suddenly not feel so far away. Additionally, programs such as *Wide World of Sports* brought nontraditional sports to the mainstream.

However, televised sports really hit it big after the creation of cable's ESPN. A channel devoted entirely to sports 24 hours a day, seven days a week, and 365 days a year meant that, no matter what the time, there was always going to be sports on television. Partnerships with the major sports leagues soon followed, and a brand extension brought new networks to the ESPN family.

As sports broadcasting continues to evolve, the internet promises to become an important part of the future. Small high school games and professional championship games can both be streamed directly to computers or other mobile devices. This is great news for teams and leagues that previously could not afford to be on television, but ultimately it benefits the fans most. The more places one can get broadcast sports—whether on radio, television, or the internet—the better it is for fans who want to keep up with the latest sports news, games, and highlights.

Phil Cole/Getty Images

CHAPTER 2

Business of Sports Broadcasting

CHAPTER OBJECTIVES

While radio and television stations bring the fun and excitement of sports into the homes of millions of people throughout the world, sports broadcasting is also big business. Networks such as ESPN pay billions of dollars to show live sports, while local television and radio stations invest much of their budget in covering the sports in their area. With all that money involved, this chapter focuses on the business of sports broadcasting, including the following:

- Understanding how ratings work and why they are important
- Explaining why investing in live sports broadcasting is desirable for radio and television stations
- Discussing some of the key moments in history that turned sports broadcasting into a billion-dollar industry
- Recognizing what role market size plays in local radio and television
- Understanding the impact "cord cutting" might have on the future of broadcast sports

This chapter will discuss many different business aspects of sports broadcasting, the most important of which is the "rating." The rating of a television or radio program is the approximate number of people who are watching. For television, the Nielsen Media Research company gathers ratings throughout the United States. For decades, Nielsen sent written diaries to consumers, and those television viewers would report in writing what they watched during a certain time period. Over the years, the process became automated, and now Nielsen is able to get that information electronically.

Ratings

Ratings are often reported in numbers and shares. For example, the 2021 Super Bowl between the Kansas City Chiefs and the Tampa Bay Buccaneers drew a 38.2 rating and a 68 share (Porter, 2021). That means that of all the television households in the United States, 38.2 percent of them were estimated to have tuned into the game. Additionally, of all the television households that had a television on during that time, 68 percent were estimated to have been watching the game. Viewership is also reported in average and peak viewers. For example, the previous season's Super Bowl averaged 99.9 million viewers but peaked at 103.5 million late in the fourth quarter (Breech, 2020).

While those numbers were reported, the truth is that Nielsen does not know *exactly* how many people were watching the game. Not every television set in the United States is monitored, so instead, the company uses a small sample of viewers and extrapolates those number to the entire population. In 2016, the company used just over 0.03 percent of all the homes in the United States to determine what everyone was watching (King, 2017). It is entirely possible that all the Nielsen homes are watching something completely different from the rest of the country, causing results that are wildly inaccurate. However, that is unlikely because Nielsen takes special care to ensure that they have a diverse audience and not one that could sway the results (Nielsen, n.d.). What ratings can do more than anything is show trends. For example, in 2014, a Houston Astros game received a 0.0 rating in the city of Houston, meaning that none of the 574 metered televisions watched the game (Tayler, 2014). While technically that means no one watched the game according to the ratings, that is probably not the case. One can safely assume that at least one of the 500,000 households in Houston tuned in, but one can also confidently say that the actual number of viewers was not very high.

Ratings can also be impacted by streaming services. As mentioned earlier, the 2021 Super Bowl had a rating of 38.2. While the television audience accounted for 91.63 million viewers, another 5.7 million watched on streaming platforms. That was an all-time high for the Super Bowl, up 65 percent from the previous year (Porter, 2021). So while the television ratings were lower, those numbers did not account for the millions watching via streaming.

While networks want to have the highest ratings possible, those numbers provide more than bragging rights. Ratings are used by the television networks to determine how much to charge companies to advertise during the program. If ESPN can demonstrate through previous ratings that millions of people will be watching *Monday Night Football*, then they can go to advertisers and essentially promise them that millions of people will be watching their commercials. The more viewers who are expected to watch, the more money a network can charge.

Why Live Sports?

The sports media, and specifically the broadcasting of live sports, has become one of the most valuable entities in media. In a landscape full of prime-time programming and blockbuster movies, what is it about sports that has media outlets willing to spend billions of dollars to broadcast the games? The simple answer is that sports are "DVR-proof."

For example, in 1976, millions of people tuned in on Tuesday nights to watch the latest episode of the popular show *M*A*S*H*. However, as technology advanced, the need to watch shows "live" decreased, and viewers are now just as willing to watch these shows at their own convenience. People can record episodes through a digital video recorder (DVR) or stream them through a variety of different online options and then watch them when they are ready. In 2019, the finale of the show *The Big Bang Theory* attracted 23.4 million viewers, but over 5 million of them watched the episode not on that Thursday when it aired live, but in the three days afterward through either a recording or streaming (de Moraes, 2019). In addition to the ability to watch when convenient, recording these shows also means that viewers have the opportunity to fast-forward through the commercials.

While there may not be a need to watch a sitcom live, that is not usually the case for sporting events. It is highly unlikely that a football fan would record the Super Bowl and wait several days to watch it. By the time that fan sat down to enjoy the game, he or she would already know the final score and all the key plays—that is why sports is considered DVR-proof. Sports fans want to watch games live so they can talk about it with friends, follow along on social media, and know the biggest plays as they are happening. Since those fans are watching live, that means they are also watching commercials. This makes live sports especially appealing to advertisers because they know their product pitches will not be fast-forwarded through.

With a captivated live audience who cannot fast-forward through promotions for the channel itself or commercials for products, it should be no surprise that these networks want to spend billions on live sports through expensive television rights deals.

Rights Deals

Radio and television stations pay billions of dollars to be the exclusive home for various sporting events so that fans only have one option when it comes to watching those games. In 2020, American television companies spent a combined $21 billion to show live sporting events (Draper, 2020). While networks will pay billions to show the biggest and most popular sports, there is even money out there for sports that might not be on the front page of the local newspaper. For example, in 2020, Fox Sports agreed to a four-year deal worth six figures annually to show the professional fishing league Bassmaster (Ourand, 2020).

The NFL

The NFL is the biggest of all the traditional sports leagues when it comes to television rights fees in the United States. The sport consistently has the highest ratings, meaning that all the major networks want to be a part of the action. In addition, NFL executives have successfully recruited new and unexpected bidders to spend millions of dollars to show the games both on television and online. As the league expands to new viewing nights and times, the money should continue to roll in from broadcasters.

Early Years of NFL Broadcasts

While weekly NFL games are a major television event in today's media landscape, it started out a much humbler affair. In 1964, CBS paid the NFL just over $28 million dollars to broadcast games for the next two seasons, a price that surprised even the league commissioner (Adams, 1964). That era was different, not only when it comes to the money spent, but also the broadcasts themselves. While networks now spend billions of dollars to be the exclusive home of each Super Bowl, the first-ever AFL–NFL Championship Game (Super Bowl I) was broadcast on CBS and NBC at the same time, each broadcast with its own announcers. The two networks paid a total of $9.5 million to show the game to an audience of approximately 50 million viewers. That might not sound like a lot compared to today's numbers, but it was about 25 percent of the entire United States population in 1967 (Fang, 2015; Flood, 2020).

That first Super Bowl demonstrated the demand for football on television. By 1978, the Super Bowl was garnering over 100 million viewers, and in 1982, television networks signed a combined $2.1 billion contract with the NFL to continue showing the games for the next five seasons (Fang, 2015). The rights fees would continue to rise gradually, traditionally rotating between the same few networks. At the time, the leagues and channels were content with that partnership, because the relationship was not really about making the biggest profit. A CBS executive said that NFL owners "were in it less for the money and more for the thrill of being an owner," while the television networks simply did not want to lose money on the deals (Curtis, 2018, para. 38). However, that would soon change, as the business of broadcasting live sports, especially football, was never the same after 1993.

Fox Sports Changes Everything

For decades, American television had three main commercial stations—ABC, CBS, and NBC. In 1986, a fourth broadcast station was created, with Fox entering the competition, attempting to turn the "Big Three" into a "Big Four." However, the early days of Fox did not exactly do much to get the country's viewers excited. *The Late Show Starring Joan Rivers*, a direct competitor to NBC's *The Tonight Show*, flopped in the ratings, and seldom-watched prime-time programming consisted of sitcoms labeled "crude" such as *Married . . . With Children* and a cartoon titled *The Simpsons*, of which even the then-president of the United States was critical (Bennetts, 2016; Petski, 2017; Weinstein, 1989). It was clear that Fox was attempting to be something completely different from the three legacy networks, but that had not resulted in commercial success. Additionally, while Fox was supposed to be a national network, it was not available nationally—only 91 percent of the country had a local Fox station (Lippman, 1990). In order to survive, network executives would need to find something that could get viewers to tune in and get affiliates to want to be part of the network. In 1993, Fox found that mystery draw that suddenly made it a major player in sports broadcasting.

Starting in 1956, the NFL was part of the programming at CBS. However, when the rights to the games traditionally on the network were up for grabs in 1993, CBS offered the NFL $250 million a year to renew (Curtis, 2018). Fox swooped in and outbid CBS's proposal by more than $100 million a year, securing the rights for four years for a total of $1.6 billion (Curtis, 2018; Sandomir, 1993). The head of Fox, Rupert Murdoch, said at the time, "We're a network now. Like no other sport will do, the NFL will make us into a real network" (Wulf, 1993, para. 4). Fox was using sports as a way to increase its own profile and was willing to spend billions to do it.

Ultimately, the Fox deal ended up costing CBS more money in the long run. After losing out on half the games in 1993 by refusing to pay more than Fox's $400 million a year, CBS executives found themselves having to bid $500 million a year in 1998 to win the other half of the games from NBC (Sandomir, 1998). Suddenly, broadcasting NFL games was a billion-dollar business. Owners recognized that these television deals could make them a remarkable amount of money, while networks were resigned to the fact that showing games was going to cost them a small fortune.

More Packages Equals More Money

While those Sunday packages are where the majority of the bidding takes place, it is far from the only media money the NFL makes from selling rights. The NFL has successfully divided up their games into a variety of different television packages that networks can bid on.

For decades, the most prominent of those additional deals was *Monday Night Football*. In 1970, the NFL offered this new Monday night package to ABC, CBS, and NBC. Only ABC was interested, and they paid just $8.5 million for that first season (Sandomir, 2005). That turned out to be a bargain price because the rights fees quickly jumped up. By 2004, ABC was paying $550 million a year to show the Monday night games (James, 2004). In 2005, *Monday Night Football* moved from broadcast television to cable, when ESPN agreed to pay $1.1 billion for the next seven seasons (Shapiro & Maske, 2005). In 2011, ESPN upped that to $1.9 billion a year when they renewed through 2021 (Sandomir, 2011). One ESPN writer compared ESPN's investment with creating a blockbuster movie: "ESPN pays the NFL nearly $2 billion a year to air *Monday Night Football*, which is like staging a $120 million Harry Potter every week" (Fainaru-Wade & Fairaru, 2013, para. 28).

Streeter Lecka/Getty Images

When Fox Sports acquired the rights for NFL games, the business of sports broadcasting was changed forever.

At the same time that ESPN was reupping their deal, the NFL also announced a partnership with NBC to be the exclusive home for *Sunday Night Football* (Shapiro & Maske, 2005). Previous to that, in 1987, the NFL made the then-controversial decision to create a Sunday night package that would air on cable. Some NFL executives were nervous about taking the games off of broadcast television (Reedy, 2019), but the deal ultimately proved to be a success. In 1987, ESPN won the rights to show eight games a season (Chad, 1987), while by 1990, TNT and ESPN split the package with each airing half of the season (Reedy, 2019). In 1998, ESPN successfully bid $600 million to be the sole home of the Sunday night package (Shapiro & Farhi, 1998). When ESPN swapped to *Monday Night Football*, NBC paid $600 million a year to take over the games on Sunday evening (Hiestand, 2005). That turned out to be a good decision for NBC, as *Sunday Night Football* was the most watched show in prime-time for nine years in a row starting in 2011 (NBC Sports Group, 2019).

By the mid-2010s, it was clear that football fans could not get enough of the NFL, and ratings demonstrated that many were watching all day on Sunday and again on Monday night. With that in mind, and with the possibility of yet another television deal on which networks could bid, the NFL announced a new Thursday night football game in 2006. However, those early games had more of a selfish purpose. The NFL had recently created the NFL Network, but due to disagreements with some cable companies, the channel was not available everywhere (Gagnon, 2013). For the NFL, this meant fewer viewers and, in turn, less money they could charge for advertising. In order to increase demand for the network, the league put these Thursday night games on the NFL Network, resulting in fans calling their cable company and demanding it be added to the lineup. By 2013, the plan had worked, and the

NFL Network was in 70 million cable homes (Gagnon, 2013).

The NFL now had less motivation to keep the games on the NFL Network, so the league quickly worked out financial partnerships with other networks, including CBS in 2016, NBC in 2017, and Fox from 2018 to 2022 (Garcia, 2018). However, two surprising broadcasters also paid millions to show the games online. The social media network Twitter paid $10 million to stream the games in 2016, while online retail giant Amazon paid $50 million to stream the games on its Amazon Prime service the following season (Breech, 2017). The NFL had found new ways to increase the broadcasting money it could make by including nontraditional broadcasters in the bidding. For the legacy television networks, these moves by streaming services signaled a new competitor in the world of rights fees.

In 2007, the NFL played a game in London, England, hoping to expand the global popularity of the sport. This overseas game quickly became a yearly staple on the schedule, and as the NFL started experimenting with games in London, the media implications were hard to ignore. Due to the time zone differences, those regular season games in London traditionally start in the morning in the United States. An early kickoff is outside the traditional Sunday afternoon viewing window, but these select games still aired on either CBS or Fox as part of their already purchased agreement. However, as the NFL contemplated adding a weekly game to London, instead of just one or two a year, that could mean yet another television package that could be up for bid. Certainly some media outlet, maybe even an online-only option, would pay millions to be the exclusive home of the 9:30 a.m. Eastern time kickoffs (Koo, 2019).

ESPN's Investment in Live Sports

When it comes to live sports, no network has made more of a commitment than ESPN. This interest in showing live games started before the network even debuted, when ESPN reached an agreement with the NCAA to show a variety of sports. From there, the network slowly built up a portfolio of other live sports, including showing the NBA from 1982 to 1984. The deal allowed ESPN to broadcast 40 regular season games and 10 playoff games each season (Cozart, 2014). In 1985, ESPN signed a three-year deal to become the home for the NHL (Nagle, 1986). While both deals were modest and only lasted a few years, each ultimately had bigger implications. By having a successful partnership with major sports leagues, ESPN proved that they could be trusted to broadcast games professionally. Therefore, when the NFL was looking to expand into cable in 1987, it was ESPN that was at the front of the line ready to bid. As discussed in chapter 1, this $153 million partnership was considered the biggest deal in cable television history and confirmed the network's commitment to showing live sporting events (Pierson, 1987).

From there, ESPN was off and running to acquire live sports. Starting with the 1990 season, ESPN agreed to a 4-year, $400 million deal to show Major League Baseball (Gerard, 1989). By 2002, the NBA was back on ESPN after a multi billion-dollar partnership was announced (Stewart, 2002). From 2002 to 2004, the NBA, NHL, MLB, and NFL were all on ESPN. However, these were mostly regular season games. The Super Bowl or World Series games were still being shown on the traditional broadcasting powers such as ABC, CBS, Fox, and NBC. While ESPN was getting games, it was missing out on the games that would get the highest viewership and, in turn, allow them to charge the most for advertising. With many of these sports leagues locked up in long-term deals with networks, there was little opportunity for ESPN to break into major professional sports. However, when a college sport had one of its big events up for grabs, ESPN put in a startling bid.

As with most major sporting events, the college football national championship game, known previously as the Bowl Championship Series (BCS), aired on over-the-air television, meaning a viewer would not need to subscribe to cable to watch the game. From 1998 to 2006, the BCS aired on ABC before moving to Fox in 2006 (Stewart, 2004). However, with that partnership set to expire after the 2010 season, Fox announced it would not pay more than $100 million a year to renew the deal. ESPN's executives, however, had no problem going much higher and submitted a bid of $125 million for the television, radio, and digital rights to the games from 2011 to 2014 (Zinser, 2008).

ESPN had previously spent millions to acquire numerous sporting events to show on its channel, but this deal was different. Now, for one of the first times ever, a major sporting event that was previously available to everyone was going to be shown only on cable. After losing the bid, Fox Sports officials immediately pointed out this fact by releasing a statement that read, "Unfortunately, the university presidents and B.C.S. commissioners . . . decided to take their jewel events to pay television" (Zinser, 2008, para. 9). The deal was immediately recognized as a potential sports broadcasting game changer, that "could pave the way for other championship events to leave broadcast" (Lewis, 2008, para. 4). That's exactly what happened, as the NCAA men's basketball championship moved to cable's TBS for every even-numbered year between 2016 and 2024 (Sandomir, 2016). In the years following, ESPN doubled down on that commitment, agreeing to pay $5.64 billion in a 12-year deal to continue being the home of the college football championship game (Bachman, 2012).

That deal with college football is just the tip of the iceberg for ESPN when it comes to live sports rights. In 2020, the network has deals with the NFL, MLB, and NBA. Plus, smaller deals with various college conferences and major golf and tennis tournaments add up. That means that each year, ESPN pays about $7.5 billion in rights fees just to show sporting events (Crupi, 2020).

Soccer

While sports that have long been popular in the United States routinely bring in television deals worth millions—and sometimes billions—there are only so many of those sports to go around. Therefore, networks have had to go outside traditional sports to find new programming to fill the demand for live games. Soccer has long been the most popular sport in the rest of the world, and in the mid-2010s, American networks took a shot that international soccer leagues could be just as popular on television in the United States.

NBC Sports, through both the main NBC channel and the cable channel NBC Sports Network, was the home of the popular European soccer league Premier League starting in 2013, and reupped with the league in a six-year, one-billion-dollar deal in 2015 (Gaughan, 2015). NBC was hardly alone, as ESPN and CBS each paid tens of millions of dollars to broadcast other top soccer leagues in the world (Bassam, 2019; Lucia, 2019). In 2011, Fox paid $425 million to be the English-language home of the World Cup in the United States for both 2018 and 2022. When that deal was extended to 2026 without allowing for other bids, ESPN was surprised they were not allowed to make an offer (Parker, 2015). That demonstrated the demand for soccer, as ESPN was disappointed that they were unable to spend hundreds of millions of dollars.

The growth of soccer on American television showcases how networks are always looking for "the next big thing." Leagues such as the NFL and NBA are already popular, but if a network can find a sport and get in on the ground floor, then the network can grow with it. If NBC can be known to fans as "the soccer channel," that gives them a huge advantage when talking to advertisers and other leagues when negotiating deals.

The Olympics

While there are a variety of sports to broadcast, and any number of television networks ready to pay the big bucks to show them, one of the most impressive sports media deals has involved an event that only happens for just a few weeks every other year. For two weeks, the Olympic Games—either Winter or Summer—capture the attention of fans throughout the world. While the Games don't last very long, the financial impact they have on the business of sports media is enormous.

In 1960, CBS paid just $50,000 to be the first television station to broadcast the Olympics in the United States (Spence, 1988). After that,

Pro Advice

© John Ourand

John Ourand

Media reporter for *Sports Business Journal*

The business of sports media has become so big that there are now journalists whose job it is to report on the networks doing the sports reporting. John Ourand is one of those media reporters, having worked at *Sports Business Journal* since 2006. He is widely regarded as one of the industry leaders on the subject, appearing on a variety of media outlets to give the latest business updates on sports media. Ourand has seen many changes in his time on the beat—from the rapid growth of ESPN to the growing influence of streaming networks.

Why is sports broadcasting such big business?

Live programming, even before streaming services became available, was the only thing that people were able to watch or had to watch *at that time*. The whole idea of the live telecast is that you can watch it as a community. For television, it also generally attracts a younger, male demographic, which is what advertisers are interested in reaching. They're able to sell advertising around it, and because they bring in so many audiences, they're able to convince cable and satellite operators to pay for their channels too, so they end up with a dual revenue stream—all predicated on sports.

Is there one moment that signified sports broadcasting was big business, or was this a gradual evolution?

I do think that you can point to a couple of different moments that really showed the power of sports to drive the business of television. One of those is in the late 1980s when the NFL sold a package to Turner and to ESPN, which really helped the cable industry grow. It certainly helped propel ESPN to the sort of model that it became. Then, in 1993 Fox, a relatively new network, outbid CBS for the NFL rights. Fox had only been around for a couple of years, and it bought the NFL rights, and, based on the NFL, it was able to expand the broadcast network. And then in 2008 ESPN outbid Fox for the BCS by about a billion dollars. At the time ESPN was a little cable channel. That was really one of the first times that broadcast networks looked and thought "Wow, ESPN is bigger than we are right now, and we have to do something to arrest that."

Sports broadcasting is obviously big business now, but what do media outlets need to do to still be big business 20 years from now?

I think the smartest company out there is Disney, who have really started leaning into streaming. What they've done with ESPN+ is a vision for the future, turning the focus onto streaming. NBC is trying to get more sports onto Peacock. CBS and CBS All-Access, Warner Media and HBO Max, are also looking into streaming more sports. Fox is really the only one without a streaming network. I've been writing this for about a decade, you know: "watch out here comes Amazon, watch out here comes Facebook." Those big tech companies are so much bigger than these TV networks, and we've all been waiting for them to come in and pluck out some of these rights. And what Disney, NBC, and CBS have done is set up their own streaming services in order to get those rights and try to keep them away from the big tech companies.

the Olympics rotated between ABC, CBS, and NBC for decades, with each bidding slightly more than the other to be the exclusive channel of the Games. A variety of technological innovations happened along the way, such as when ABC broadcast the majority of the 1968 events in color, a revolutionary move at the time (Noriega, 2018).

The Olympics have become synonymous with NBC as the network has paid billions of dollars to be the exclusive television broadcast home of the Games in the United States.

While technology was constantly evolving, one of the first big financial initiatives regarding the Olympics took place in 1992 when NBC debuted the Triplecast. The network worked with cable companies to create a pay-per-view system in which customers could order a specific channel (Red, White, or Blue) that would show events live from Barcelona, Spain, the site of the 1992 Olympics. NBC believed that this channel option would be appealing to fans who did not want to wait until the tape-delayed showing of the events on NBC that night. Fans had the option of paying between $95 and $170 for various packages (Sandomir, 1992). Unfortunately for NBC, they misread the market and very few signed up. Media experts estimated that NBC lost somewhere around $100 million on the Triplecast (Mulligan, 1992), but that only tells part of the story. NBC's decision to put the events on multiple channels at the same time, as opposed to everything being on just NBC, was lauded as an excellent innovation that allowed more choices for the fans (Stewart, 1992). In the end, that proved to be the lasting legacy of the Triplecast.

While networks were willing to spend millions of dollars to show the Olympics, they were also looking for a way to recoup some of that money. For the 1992, 1994, and 1998 Winter Olympics, CBS took an unconventional route of reselling some of the rights they had already acquired. Cable channel TNT agreed to pay CBS tens of millions of dollars to be the American cable television home for the Olympics, traditionally showing less popular sports that CBS would likely not air (Dempsey, 1996). Once again, fans were able to benefit from this business decision as the Olympics could now be seen on more than one channel.

Olympics coverage, at least in the area of the business of sports broadcasting, can be divided into two different eras: before and after

NBC made the decision to invest heavily in the Games. For years, television stations paid a relatively modest amount to be the home of the Olympics. That included the bid NBC made to be home of the 1988 Summer Games in Seoul, South Korea. However, it was a decision later in 1988 that changed the financial conversation around the Olympics forever.

While ABC and CBS each bid around $350 million that year to broadcast the 1992 Olympics, NBC swooped in with a bid of $401 million (Sharbutt, 1998). That was the first step toward NBC making the Olympics one of the biggest, and most expensive, media events in sports broadcasting. Soon after, despite losing a reported $100 million on those 1992 Olympics, NBC paid another $456 million to broadcast the 1996 Summer Games (UPI, 1993). From there, the network was off and running with its Olympic partnership, and thanks to their big pocketbook, it made sure that no one else would get in on the action.

In 1995, NBC paid $1.27 billion for the television rights to the 2000 Summer Olympics and the 2002 Winter Olympics (Sandomir, 1995a). Less than six months later, the network and the International Olympic Committee agreed to another deal without even letting other networks bid. This time, NBC paid $2.3 billion for the rights to the 2004 Summer, 2006 Winter, and 2008 Summer Olympics (Sandomir, 1995b). Suddenly, bidding on the Olympics was no longer a multimillion-dollar proposition. NBC had made it a multibillion-dollar business, and it was not done there. After spending another $2.2 billion to show the 2010 and 2012 Olympics (Abrahamson, 2003) and $4.38 billion for the 2014, 2016, 2018, and 2020 Olympics (Riley, 2011), NBC made sure no one else would be able to show an Olympics for a very long time. In 2014, they paid $7.7 billion to be the home of the next seven Games, meaning that NBC would remain the broadcast home until at least 2032 (Isidore, 2014).

While NBC's Triplecast might have been a financial dud in 1992, the concept of airing events on multiple channels at the same time is still part of NBC's schedule. In 2016, the network showed events not only on NBC, but also on Bravo, CNBC, Golf Channel, MSNBC, NBC Sports Network, USA Network, and two temporary channels that showed only soccer and basketball. In addition, the NBC Sports app and website allowed for livestreaming of various events (Associated Press, 2016). Additionally, in 2017, NBC created The Olympic Channel, a 365-day-per-year channel devoted to Olympic sports (Stanhope, 2017).

Cable Fees

One of the biggest revenue streams for cable stations comes directly from the cable companies themselves. For example, cable companies pay ESPN for the right to carry that network on their system. Of course, that cost is pushed directly to the consumer, as customers pay about $9 each month on their bill to have ESPN as part of their channel selection, whether they watch it or not. Viewers pay similar monthly fees for the Fox Sports channels, NFL Network, and other sports-specific channels (Gaines, 2017).

While some non–sports fans have pushed back at having to pay for these channels, the cable companies have kept them on the bill, focusing on what might happen if those channels were not available. *Sports Business Journal* media writer John Ourand (see earlier) summed up why these companies may have no choice but to carry these networks: "If the University of South Carolina is playing on ESPN and the cable operator in South Carolina doesn't carry ESPN, imagine how many people are going to dump that cable operator for another just in that one state" (personal communication). With that demand, ESPN has a dual-revenue model. The cable companies pay them a rights fee just to be able to show the network and then ESPN is also able to charge for advertising. When a game is shown on ESPN, the network is essentially getting paid twice—once by the network and once by the advertisers.

Cord Cutting

While sports broadcasting remains a major part of television viewership, the question now has shifted to whether television itself will remain a major part of sports fans' lives. Millions of

MAJOR MOMENTS

Michael Phelps Equals Ratings

It might sound crazy that a network would force the Super Bowl to start at 10 a.m., but that is essentially what NBC did in 2008. At the time, swimmer Michael Phelps was attempting to become the first person ever to win eight gold medals in the same Olympics. His races were set to be the biggest story and were sure to bring in a record number of viewers. However, while Phelps was preparing for his races, the business going on behind the scenes was a competition of a different sort.

NBC had paid hundreds of millions of dollars to show the Olympics in 2008 and quickly made Phelps the biggest star of the Games before the events had even started. Because of that, it was no surprise that Phelps' races were lined up to be the biggest viewership draw for NBC. The only problem for the network was that the 2008 Olympics were taking place in Beijing, China. A traditional 8:00 p.m. race start in Beijing would be a 7:00 a.m. start in New York, which would likely not result in the most viewers possible. While NBC had tape-delayed events in the past, doing this for the biggest races of the biggest star would likely open them up to a great deal of criticism.

However, in the end, it ultimately came down to the business of sports broadcasting. NBC pays more to broadcast the Olympics than all the world's other broadcasters combined. With that in mind, NBC went to the International Olympic Committee (IOC) to suggest the swimming events start in the mornings in Beijing so that they would be on in the evenings in the United States. With all the money NBC had invested, the IOC had little choice but to allow the change (Carter, 2008). So, for the first time ever, Olympic finals in swimming were held between 10 a.m. and noon local time, meaning the races would air live in prime time in the United States (Crouse, 2008). Of course, it helped NBC's cause that Phelps himself had endorsed the unorthodox start time (Carter, 2008).

As expected, Phelps' races turned out to be a ratings bonanza. The 2008 Olympics were, at the time, the most watched U.S. television event of all time, while the live broadcast of one of Phelps' races was the most watched Saturday night on NBC in 18 years (Gorman, 2008; Hibberd & Landreth, 2008). Perhaps just as important to NBC, starting the races in the morning did not affect Phelps—he won all his races on his way to capturing those record-setting eight gold medals (Newberry, 2008).

---

consumers are ditching cable television and relying only on streaming services to get their entertainment. While losing customers is obviously bad news for cable companies, it also directly impacts the networks that are on cable as well. Each network gets a set amount of money from each subscriber, so if people are canceling their subscriptions, networks are losing out on that revenue stream.

Cord cutting is impacting the entire television industry; networks such as the Disney Channel, USA Network, and CNN all have reported a drop in viewership as people leave their cable subscriptions behind. Sports networks are facing similar drops, with all of them facing a decline in viewers from 2018 to 2019 (Andreeva & Johnson, 2019). However, while this is an industry-wide issue, it is ESPN that may have the most to worry about. In 2011, ESPN was in over 100 million households in the United States (Gaines, 2015), but that number had dropped to about 83 million in 2020 (Strauss, 2020). The main concern for ESPN is that each one of those customers was paying more than $7 a month, so that is about $84 a year they have lost from each of their millions of customers. While that loss of revenue is concerning for ESPN, it may also face wider-ranging problems. John Ourand said that the drop in cable customers may have sports leagues wondering how many ESPN viewers will ultimately be left: "Nobody believes it is going to go down to zero, at least no time soon, but if it goes down to 50 million, will leagues want to go to cable?" Ourand is essentially saying that if games that used to be seen in 100 million homes are now only being seen by 50 million homes, that maybe those leagues should rethink where they broadcast the events.

ESPN has already taken steps to try to solve the cord-cutting problem. As discussed in chapter 1, ESPN+ was the network's way to enter into the streaming battle. If people are not watching as much cable television, ESPN still needs a way to recoup the money that was lost. By charging almost the same amount as they were getting from cable subscriptions, ESPN is still able to keep customers and, hopefully, keep the teams and leagues from looking elsewhere when it comes to broadcasting games.

CHAPTER WRAP-UP

SUMMARY

While fans watching and listening to sports broadcasts are focused on the game on the field, the network executives are playing an entirely different game behind the scenes. The business of sports broadcasting is a billion-dollar industry, with networks looking to be the home of the events that bring in the biggest audience, no matter what the cost. Fox's investment in the NFL turned broadcast television from a "Big Three" into a "Big Four." A 30-second commercial during the 2020 Super Bowl cost $5.6 million, simply because advertisers can be nearly certain that almost 100 million people will see it thanks to the draw of live sports and the inability to fast-forward through commercials (McClintock, 2020). Meanwhile, NBC has spent billions of dollars to make sure that no other network can get in on the ratings bonanza that is the Olympics. Ultimately, sports broadcasting exists because, for many networks, it is a money-making experience. As long as live sports continue to bring in millions of viewers, expect networks to continue making investments in showing the latest games and events.

Phil Cole/Getty Images

CHAPTER 3

Types of Sports Broadcasting

CHAPTER OBJECTIVES

From television to radio to the internet, there are any number of job possibilities for those looking to enter the field of sports broadcasting. However, while the goals of all of those broadcasters is to talk about sports, the job descriptions are anything but the same based on where they work. Therefore, this chapter focuses on the different types of sports broadcasting, including the following:

- Distinguishing between the different types of sports broadcasting
- Recognizing the impact that internet streaming has had on sports broadcasting
- Understanding how team media has become a key player in the world of sports broadcasting

The term "sports broadcasting" is ultimately very broad. Saying "I want to be a sports broadcaster" could mean a variety of different things. There are television broadcasters who work for national stations reporting at major events or local stations focusing on high school sports. Those broadcasters interested in audio journalism can host a sports talk show on the radio or possibly create a podcast that can be distributed globally. For those wanting to be live at the big games, the options of internet streaming or live sports production and announcing may be appealing. While the majority of jobs in this field will have broadcasters working for traditional media outlets such as commercial television stations or radio stations, some journalists are now employed by the teams and leagues themselves. With all these different options available, it is important to distinguish between the various types of sports broadcasting.

National Television

When people first think of sports broadcasting, they may immediately think of the national sports media outlets that are on television throughout the United States. This is not surprising. Sports fans can turn on their televisions at any hour of any day and find a channel that has someone talking about sports. Additionally, weekends are traditionally full of live sporting events that are broadcast throughout the country. It is perhaps no surprise that the majority of the most watched television events in the history of the United States are sports (Breech, 2020). ESPN is certainly the most prominent national sports television broadcaster, but league-specific networks such as NFL Network have created more options for those looking for sports coverage.

While live games will be discussed later in this chapter, this section will focus on what are known as **studio shows**. These are programs that traditionally have anchors or commentators reporting on or discussing the latest sports news. Perhaps the most famous of these studio shows is ESPN's *SportsCenter.* As the network's longest running show, *SportsCenter* is the show in which ESPN airs daily highlights, interviews players and coaches, and tells additional stories about sports throughout the world. Highlight shows such as this one are shown throughout the country, so the audience is a national one. Therefore, these shows tend to focus on the sports that are the most popular and will attract the most attention. For example, *SportsCenter* would likely spend a great deal of time talking about and showing highlights of a matchup between two highly ranked college football teams but ignore a game between two unranked teams because of the lack of national appeal.

Some studio shows focus more on journalism and less on highlights. On ESPN, the programs *Outside the Lines* and *E:60* have been the longtime standard-bearer for investigative journalism. *Outside the Lines* has won multiple Sports Emmy Awards, Edward R. Murrow Awards, and Peabody Awards for their work covering controversial topics in the world of sports (Hall, 2019).

For many years, national sports networks such as ESPN and FS1 were filled almost entirely with studio shows when they were not showing live games. Some specialized in one sport, such as *Baseball Tonight* and *NFL Primetime*, both airing on ESPN. However, many national sports broadcasts have included more **debate shows** in their programming. These shows consist of several media members debating various topics live on the air. This format became increasingly popular following the debut of *Pardon the Interruption* (*PTI*) on ESPN in 2001. *PTI* featured two writers from *The Washington Post*, Tony Kornheiser and Michael Wilbon, debating the day's topics. They did not show highlights or report on the day's news. Instead, they simply argued about the day's topics, often yelling over one another to make their point. The program turned into a massive success for ESPN (Hofheimer, 2016; Miller & Shales, 2011) and eventually became the blueprint for several other shows on the network. The era of "embrace debate" became a key part of ESPN's programming as shows such as *First Take* and *Around the Horn* followed the lead first set by *Pardon the Interruption* (Ravanos, 2020). Very little (if any) actual reporting happens on these shows. The hosts, who are almost always sports reporters or former athletes, are provided a list of topics and argue different sides of those topics. For example, a May 2020 episode of *First Take* featured the two hosts debating which player had the best chance at being the NBA's best in the future (ESPN, 2020). In addition to showing a variety of these shows, the network has invested financially in them. Stephen A. Smith, one of the hosts of *First Take*, became the highest paid on-air employee at ESPN in 2019 when he signed a deal worth $8 million a year (Marchand, 2019). While these shows are increasingly popular among sports fans (TV News Desk, 2020), they are often criticized for their lack of journalistic values (Gaines, 2013).

Local Television

While national television sports broadcasters may get the majority of the attention when it comes to major sporting events, hundreds

Christopher Capozziello/Contributor

SportsCenter on ESPN is the longest running show on the network having debuted on the very first day back in 1979 and is still going strong today.

of local sports broadcasters throughout the United States are covering events that are likely only of interest to those living in that specific area. For example, while a professional football game might get the attention of people all over the country, a high school football game in Alexandria, Louisiana, may only be of interest to those who are residents of that city. These local sports broadcasters are the ones covering high school events, interviewing the coaches of college teams beyond just the popular sports, and highlighting the accomplishments of local athletes doing remarkable things.

Before explaining the daily routine of a local sports broadcaster, it is important to summarize how local television works. The United States is divided up into 210 **television markets**, ranging from the biggest (New York City is Market #1 because it is the most populated) to the smallest (Glendive, Montana, is Market #210 because it has the least number of viewers). Instead of being seen throughout the country like ESPN, the newscasts in each market are limited to the people living in that specific viewing area. For example, a sportscaster in Denver, Colorado, will be on television in the Denver area but nowhere else in the country. Therefore, local sports broadcasters are encouraged to emphasize the "local" in their job title. A sportscaster in Columbia, South Carolina, will talk about high school sporting events that take place in that area but probably not show highlights of the New York Yankees. Fans of the Yankees who live in that city have a variety of places in which they can get highlights of the team, so the Columbia sportscaster should focus on what fans can only get from him or her: in-depth coverage of local teams and athletes. However, a local sportscaster in New York City would show Yankees highlights because even though they are a national brand, they are still local to the fans who live in that area.

Local sports broadcasters will often work for the ABC, CBS, Fox, or NBC affiliates in a city, although some may work for an independent station or one of the less prominent national networks. In some cases, local sports broadcasters may work for two of these networks at the same time. Several stations throughout the country have entered into **shared services agreements** with what used to be their competition within the same market. In these arrangements, two stations agree to share news operations while still legally acting as two different entities (Yanich, 2011). For example, the NBC affiliate in Wilmington, North Carolina, has a shared services agreement with the Fox affiliate in which the two share a building, engineering personnel, and news resources (Finlay, 2011). For the television stations, combining resources can be a financially beneficial decision as they can save costs (Malone, 2012; Stelter, 2012; TVNewsCheck, 2013). For the sports broadcasters, this combination means they are often appearing on multiple stations on the same night. For example, a sports broadcaster in the Wilmington market can give the highlights of a high school volleyball match at 10 p.m. on the Fox station and then show them again on the 11 p.m. newscast on the NBC station.

ESPN is home to more than 6,500 employees worldwide (ESPN Press Room, n.d.), with most employees specializing in one job such as anchoring, reporting, shooting video, recording audio, social media, and producing shows. However, in local television, a sports broadcaster often has all those responsibilities because the entire sports department is usually quite small. In a 2019 survey of local sports broadcasters, more than two-thirds of the respondents (67.1 percent) said their sports department contained just two employees (Hull & Romney, 2020). That means that local sports broadcasters are not just showing highlights on the late local news, but they are often the ones shooting the video for those highlights as well. All of the sportscasters who had been on the job less than five years in that 2019 survey said they shoot their own video at least half of the time, with 60 percent reporting they shoot their own video "always," and an additional 18.9 percent saying they shoot "most of the time" (Hull & Romney, 2020). That can change as the markets get bigger. For example, sportscasters in New York City and Boston do not shoot their own video, as they have videographers (some solely devoted to doing sports) who will gather the video for them.

Therefore, in smaller markets where local sports broadcasters often get their first jobs, a day at work can prove to be very busy. For example, in a typical day, the local college basketball team might have practice at 1 p.m. The sportscaster would have to get to the office before then to get his or her camera equipment and then drive to the practice. After shooting an interview with the coach and the star player, the sportscaster would get some video of practice before heading back to the television station. While there, he or she would decide the order of the 6 p.m. show, go through the interview with the coach and player to pick out appropriate sound bites, and then write and edit the entire show together. During this time, the sportscaster would also update the website and send out some social media posts. After anchoring the 6 p.m. sportscast, the local sports broadcaster would drive to two different area high schools to get video from the basketball games going on that night. After returning to the television station, he or she would edit together the various games, update earlier stories with new video and scripts, and include any new stories that have developed. Then it would be time to send out final scores on social media, anchor the 11 p.m. news, and update the website again before calling it a day. With that in mind, it is no surprise that local sports broadcasters in their first job often report working long hours throughout the week. Of the 76 beginning broadcasters surveyed in 2019, only 4 said they worked 40 hours a week or less, while 44 of the 76 (57.9 percent) said they worked 50 or more hours a week (Hull & Romney, 2020).

While working in small, beginner markets can lead to some long days, the goal of most in the profession is to move on to bigger cities. Local sports broadcasters, especially in smaller cities, rarely stay in one place for very long. In local television, the most common way to get promoted is not to get a better job within the current station but to move to a bigger city doing the same job at a different television station. Therefore, local sports broadcasters, especially early in their career, lead very nomadic lives. For example, in 2020, Emily Gagnon was a sports anchor and reporter in Atlanta, Georgia (Market #10). However, in her first six years in the industry, her career took her all over the country. Gagnon started in Meridian, Mississippi (Market #190), for a year and three months before moving to Tyler, Texas (Market #114), for a year and one month. She left Tyler to work as a sideline reporter for Comcast in Atlanta for less than a year and a half, before anchoring in Wichita, Kansas (Market #72), for a little over two years before ending up in her current job in Atlanta (Gagnon, n.d.). (For more information about being a television sports broadcaster, see chapter 8.)

Sports Talk Radio

Sports talk radio consists of hosts discussing that day's big sports news. These types of shows have become so popular among fans that stations have devoted their entire day's lineup to sports talk shows. New York City's WFAN was the first station to go to a 24/7 all-sports format (Sullivan, 2013), but they were certainly not the last. Reporters in 2012 estimated that there were nearly 700 all-sports stations throughout the United States (French & Kahn, 2012).

Traditionally, the hosts will talk about the day's events, take calls from listeners, and conduct interviews live on the air. These shows are usually several hours long, with numerous commercial breaks throughout. The hosts are often broadcasters or former athletes who have transitioned to a career behind the microphone.

National or **syndicated** shows are played throughout the United States and have more of a national focus. For example, ESPN Radio hosts will focus their attention on the major sports news of the day of interest in the country. While these shows are national, they are picked up by local radio stations and played in cities in the United States. Therefore, they often do not have the local appeal of a host in that city. Local radio sports talk shows help to fill that void. These shows are specific to one area and are usually the most popular among fans interested in the local teams.

Podcasting

While there are still many opportunities on radio for those looking to get into audio journalism, the rapid growth of the popularity of

Cindy Ord/Getty Images for SiriusXM

Sports talk radio is a popular way for fans to hear the latest sports news. Many stations have devoted their entire daily schedule to sports.

podcasts has created a new outlet for sports broadcasters. **Podcasts** are digital audio files that can be downloaded and played at the listener's convenience. Originally developed due to the creation of Apple's iPod (the word is a combination of iPod and broadcast), podcasts rose in popularity thanks to the variety of options and the ease of listening. People can listen to podcasts on demand while doing other things (such as traveling to work, exercising, or doing housework). A 2020 report from Edison Research found that more than one-third of Americans ages 12 and up listen to podcasts regularly, reaching over 100 million people in the United States each month (Edison Research, 2020). By June 2020, there were more than one million different podcasts available for download (Lewis, 2020).

Podcasts can be about any number of topics, but shows about sports are some of the most popular among listeners. Sports fans can listen to podcasts about sports as a whole, individual sports, specific teams, and even fantasy teams. ESPN was one of the early adopters of the podcast, launching its first in 2005 (Keller, 2018). By late 2019, the sports media giant offered more than 35 original podcast options for listeners, plus podcast versions of shows from ESPN Radio. As a whole, ESPN had 40 million downloads in just the month of December in 2019 (McCarthy, 2020).

For sports broadcasters, podcasts are an appealing option because they are relatively easy to produce and provide opportunities for content that may not be available on traditional broadcasts. For example, many podcasts are simply broadcasters having in-depth conversations with sports celebrities. An evening sportscast on the local news is normally less than four minutes long, so only one quick segment of that interview can be used from that talk. On a podcast, the entire conversation can be played in its entirety. Scott Van Pelt, an anchor at ESPN, said, "A podcast allows as much leeway as we'd like. To take the deeper dives with guests, and flush out topics that matter will be fun" (McCarthy, 2020).

At ESPN, it was Bill Simmons that was one of the first to embrace this format. His show, *B.S. Report*, became one of the early sports podcast hits and is credited with helping "launch a sports podcast revolution" (Spanberg, 2018). In the years since his show debuted in 2007, sports podcasts have popped up about any number of topics and have proven to be profitable as well. ESPN is estimated to earn well over $10 million a year just from podcasts (McCarthy, 2020), and Bill Simmons, who left ESPN to start the new venture *The Ringer* in 2016, elected to focus much of the attention of that new entity on podcasts. *The Ringer*'s podcast ad sales were more than $15 million in 2018 (Mullin & Flint, 2019), and Simmons sold the company to streaming company Spotify for $250 million in early 2020 (Shaw, 2020). (For more information on sports talk radio and podcasting, see chapter 9.)

Internet Streaming

The ability to easily **stream** video and audio over the internet has created another way in which sports broadcasters can reach their audience. For decades, ESPN was only available with a cable subscription, but the creation of ESPN+ allowed for some of the network's programming to be watched without having cable. Additionally, sports streaming-only options such as DAZN have been created. These streaming options have live games and studio shows, creating a host of new jobs for sports broadcasters.

Internet streaming has also allowed for smaller organizations to put their sports online. Once the camera equipment is purchased, livestreamed games are relatively inexpensive to produce. This can allow for high schools, colleges, and other independent teams/leagues to broadcast games to an online audience. While television is still the main format in which people watch sports, these streaming options have given opportunities for less publicized sports to have a worldwide audience.

Sports broadcasters can also use internet streaming to reach their audience in more ways than before. Streaming options such as Facebook Live give broadcasters a chance to report live from almost any location with just their cellphones. With the push of a few buttons, broadcasters are instantly streaming live video to their audience without needing an entire

SANJAY KANOJIA/AFP via Getty Images

Fans are now able to stream games directly to their phones, meaning the action is with them wherever they go.

camera crew or a production satellite vehicle. Through these livestreams straight from their phone, broadcasters can give an update on what is happening at the event while also interacting with followers who have the ability to type in questions that show up on the screen.

Team Media

For decades, if a team or player wanted to get information out to the public, they would have to rely on the news media to help deliver that message. Teams have public relations officials or **sports information directors** (SIDs), whose job it is to provide information to the media while also helping to facilitate interviews. For college sports, SIDs are members of the university, and their job is to protect and publicize the university (Gisondi, 2011; Schultz, 2005). A **press release** with information about the team would be sent to the media, and then ultimately it would be up to the newspaper, television, or radio station to decide if they want to report on that story. In some cases, such as a team transaction or update, the news will almost certainly be reported. However, that was not always the case. For example, if a team was having a charity event and invited the local television station to attend and cover it, there was no guarantee that the media would show up. Additionally, even if the media did show up, it is possible that the media might report the story differently (ignoring the charity angle, for example) than how the team would have liked. In order to avoid this happening, teams began reporting on themselves.

In the late 1990s, the NFL's Cincinnati Bengals hired Geoff Hobson, a sportswriter at the *Cincinnati Enquirer*, to write for the team's website, Bengals.com (Jenkins, 2000; Pérez-Peña, 2009). Bengals officials said that, despite being their employee, Hobson was still an independent reporter who could report on the team as if he were still working for the newspaper (Trumpbour, 2007). However, several controversial topics were not covered

MAJOR MOMENTS

And the Winner Is . . . Periscope

While there are legitimate options available for fans looking to use video streaming, some fans have found ways to watch without paying for them. Instead, people have used illegal streams to watch sporting events from around the world. This was happening in the shadows for years but hit the mainstream in 2015, when Twitter's livestreaming app Periscope made headlines during one of the biggest boxing fights of the decade.

After years of hype around a possible matchup, Floyd Mayweather Jr. and Manny Pacquiao finally agreed to meet up in the boxing ring. The fight would take place in Las Vegas, and those who could not be in attendance could order the fight on high definition pay-per-view (PPV) for approximately $100, making it the most expensive PPV program in boxing history (Pedersen, 2015). However, that's not how thousands of people ended up watching it.

Shortly after the fight began, people who had ordered the fight began pointing the cameras on their phones to the television and broadcast livestreams of the fight through Periscope. One fan even created a livestream from directly inside the arena by aiming his phone at the ring (Busbee, 2015). A reporter wrote about how she watched the match via Periscope, "hopping from stream to stream," before ultimately settling on one: "The stream I ended up watching for half the night was in Spanish. It had more than 10,000 people in it at its peak" (Warren, 2015). It is unclear exactly how many people watched the fight illegally through Periscope, but one report estimated that it was possibly millions (Warren, 2015).

While some of the feeds were taken down during the fight after complaints from the rights holders, new ones popped up almost immediately (Sandomir, 2015). Officials with Top Rank, which represented Pacquiao, said shortly after the fight that they planned to pursue legal action against Twitter (Pfeifer, 2015), but it is unclear if they followed through on that threat. This demonstrates the battle that sports broadcasting companies have with technology. While many will utilize livestreaming apps for their own benefit, they can do little to stop people from broadcasting within their own homes. Ultimately, Twitter (which owns Periscope) decided to work with boxing officials to avoid a repeat of the illegal streams during Mayweather's next fight later that year (Mannix, 2015). However, on the night of the Pacquiao fight, while it was Mayweather who was declared the winner by unanimous decision, Twitter CEO Dick Costolo had a different champion. He proclaimed on Twitter, "And the winner is . . . @periscopeco" (Costolo, 2015).

---

on Bengals.com, with the most prominent omission from his reporting being a lack of stories about the team's proposed new stadium (Jenkins, 2000). While writing for the *Cincinnati Enquirer*, Hobson was one of the main critics of the stadium, but his mentions of the proposed deal with the city nearly disappeared with his Bengals.com job (Jenkins, 2000; Trumpbour, 2007). Additionally, and perhaps the biggest departure from working from a traditional media source, the team's public relations director admitted that some of the phrasing was changed in Hobson's stories to make the Bengals look better (Jenkins, 2000).

The Bengals may have been the first to hire a team reporter, but the flood gates were now open. Each team in Major League Baseball, the National Football League, and the National Basketball Association now has its own sportswriter (Pells & Newberry, 2009), and college athletic departments have hired journalists for their websites (Yanity, 2013). In some cases, teams cited budget cuts at local newspapers, leading to less coverage for the team, as the reason they needed to hire their own reporters (Pérez-Peña, 2009). These writers report on the team but admittedly cover them differently than traditional journalists would because they are a part of the team themselves (Affleck, 2016).

These team media members are doing almost everything that traditional media members are doing but are simply doing it while being employed by the team. This has led some to wonder if these team writers are practicing journalism or public relations. One longtime sportswriter leaned clearly on the side of public relations, saying, "It's the difference between reading propaganda and information" (Affleck, 2016, p. 353). However, some team media members see it differently. When addressing why he did not cover an off-field controversial topic on Rams.com, the Los Angeles Rams in-house beat writer said, "My job is to be a football reporter" (Mirer, 2018, p. 256). Ultimately, an examination of a University of Washington team media member may have found the best answer to the question whether he was a journalist or a public relations practitioner: It depended on the day. After writing an article for the team's website (GoHuskies.com) in which he mentioned how frustrated some of the players were after a loss, the coach told him, "You don't want the kids wondering whose side you are on" (Yanity, 2013, p. 485). This implied that the writer is a member of the team (public relations) and not an independent observer (journalism).

While there may be a debate about whether these team reporters are traditional journalists or not, one thing is not up for debate: Team media is one of the fastest growing areas of sports journalism. J. A. Adande, a longtime sportswriter for multiple newspapers and ESPN, said, "For a while now, the biggest growth in sports media jobs has been for teams and their websites" (Strauss, 2020). It is easy to see why. For example, if someone wanted to cover the University of Florida, years ago they could work for the television stations or newspaper in Gainesville, Florida. However, now they can work for FloridaGators.com (the website of the athletics department), create content for the coach's weekly television and/or radio shows, work for the SEC Network, or write for SECsports.com. The team's website alone has articles, videos, photo galleries, social media accounts, radio shows, and podcasts that are all created by Florida Gators athletics employees. Chris Harry is a senior writer for the website who covered the team for a Florida newspaper for over 13 years before being hired by the athletics department (Harry, n.d.). On his FloridaGators.com bio, he wrote that his job was "To tell the story of University of Florida athletics from the inside by hopefully giving readers (and Gator fans) some insight not available through traditional media outlets; a peek behind the curtain, if you will" (FloridaGators.com, n.d.).

Team media jobs can be very appealing for those looking to work in sports journalism, often because of access. Just like traditional media reporters, team journalists go to games and interview the players, but they can (usually) avoid reporting on any controversial topics while also having additional access to the team that others may not have. On FloridaGators.com, Harry wrote that the best part about working for the school was "a chance to see things from the other side. I spent nearly 30 years as newspaper reporter writing about teams, coaches and players. Since coming to work at UF, my context of how athletics operate . . . has changed, thanks to the new lens from which I now watch it all unfold" (FloridaGators.com, n.d.). Additionally, they are still using many of the same skills needed to be a broadcaster at a professional television station, such as interviewing athletes, shooting video of games, and putting together stories. Finally, the grind of working in a small television market as a local sports broadcaster, trying to get to bigger cities and higher paying jobs, may not be appealing to everyone. Instead, working for team media may be an excellent alternative.

Live Sports Production

Live sports production is the broadcasting of live games either on television, radio, or the internet. As stated in the previous chapter, live game broadcasts are big business. Stations spend millions (and sometimes billions) of dollars to broadcast live games on their station. While this provides a huge financial windfall for teams and leagues, it also gives the networks programming that can allow them to charge high advertising rates.

There are traditionally two different types of broadcast outlets that show live games: national outlets and local or regional outlets. While they both have the same goal of showing the game, how they go about doing it can be very different.

Pro Advice

© Caroline Frazier

Caroline Frazier

Team Media reporter

Caroline Frazier has worked for both the NFL's Indianapolis Colts and Carolina Panthers as a team reporter. In both cases, she was employed by the team, not by what might be considered a "traditional" media outlet such as a newspaper or television station. Frazier's job had her doing sideline reports during games on the teams' radio broadcasts, creating content for the social media pages, and conducting on-camera interviews with players on the teams' websites.

Frazier, a University of South Carolina graduate, did not have dreams of becoming a team reporter. The reason, she said, is that she did not know that such a job was even a possibility. "When I was in college, my job did not exist," Frazier said. "There were only three team reporters when I was in school." However, once she found out that she could work in sports through this avenue, she knew exactly where her future would lie.

How would you summarize what team media is?

It's more like a marketing agency than a newsroom. We are the Carolina Panthers agency and that's how we operate. We have a full video team, graphics team, photo team, social and web, radio, podcasts, and writers. We all collectively come together to put out content for the team. Everyone is involved. We are not your traditional local newsroom.

What is one of the big differences between working for team media as opposed to the traditional media?

With internal (team) media, we are more proactive than reactive. Everything you're seeing from traditional media is very reactive. Something has happened, so they must go cover it. For internal media, we know what's coming. We need to be proactive in how this news gets out, how we want it to represent the brand that we work for, and how it's going to ultimately reflect on those who are the big players in our brand. So anything that we do in team media reflects on our owner, our head coach, and our general manager.

What are some of the different expectations for team reporters?

A great example is when the Panthers hired Matt Rhule as the head coach (in 2020). Everyone in traditional media is out trying to get feelers on who (the Panthers) are interviewing, when are they interviewing them, and how can they be the first one to break it. For about a week, I had a piece of paper that said who they're interviewing and when they're interviewing. We knew. I could have tweeted it, but I would have gotten fired. I'm not a breaking news reporter, unless we think it's a good public relations move. I'm not breaking it as soon as I'm hearing it. I'm going to know about it for days. This is very different from what breaking news reporters are doing.

Where are you trying to reach the team's fans?

Everywhere. You are not just going for one platform. You're not just creating a video that's going to go on one platform. You need to come up with content that can be easily shared across all platforms. But you have to prioritize. What we're at is usually a one-time thing. For Rhule's hire, we decided that we were going to prioritize video, then photo, then written. Where do we release this? You have social media, and then within social media, you have TikTok, Twitter, Instagram, Facebook, YouTube, and the website. We decided to put social media first. That's always kind of our priority.

The national media stations show games involving teams from all over the United States. For example, when Fox broadcasts an NFL game between the Cowboys and the Packers, these games are often shown throughout the country, no matter where the audience lives. Due to the fact that it is on nationally, it is not necessarily die-hard fans of the two teams playing watching the game. If the Cowboys and Packers have the two best records in football, then fans of all of the teams may tune in to Fox because it has the potential to be a good game, even though their favorite team is not playing. However, in addition to showing that game, Fox is also showing numerous other games throughout the day and sometimes at the same time as the big game of the week. Therefore, instead of specializing in one team, they focus on the league as a whole. The announcers for national games are traditionally impartial and simply give an account of what is happening while also providing analysis during the action.

The local/regional broadcasts are ones in which the station specializes in showing games from local teams. These games are only available locally on the radio or television (unless a special national package is purchased). Due to the fact that the games are only shown locally, the stations assume that the majority of people watching are already fans of the team. These games are traditionally not impartial, as the announcers are not necessarily employees of the media outlet but instead sometimes work for the team. For example, nearly every Boston Red Sox game is shown on the New England Sports Network (NESN). This channel is available on cable systems throughout the New England area where the Red Sox are the most popular baseball team. On a game night on NESN, there is a Red Sox–centric preview show before the game starts, the in-game announcers are the same for nearly every game (usually including a former popular Red Sox player), and there is a postgame show that analyzes the game from nearly every angle. Later that night, NESN will rerun the game as part of their late-night programming. Due to the narrow focus of this channel on the Red Sox, NESN would likely never show a game between the Royals and the Twins because that is not the focus of their coverage. These national and local/regional splits also exist in radio, with both national and local announcers covering games for their respective audiences.

During a live sports production, the most visible people to the audience are the play-by-play broadcaster and the color commentator. These are the two people who are describing the action during the game and whose voices can be heard throughout. Occasionally, depending on the size of the broadcast, there will also be a sideline reporter who gives updates from the field level. However, those three broadcasters are far from the only ones present at a live sports broadcast. There are numerous behind-the-scenes people who run cameras for television broadcasts and help with the production for audio broadcasts, to make sure everything runs smoothly. (For more information on live sports broadcasts, see chapter 10.)

CHAPTER WRAP-UP

SUMMARY

The world of sports broadcasting is a vast one. For decades, broadcasters had the option of working for either television or radio stations to cover the sporting news of the day. The internet opened up an entirely new avenue of broadcasting sporting events and reaching fans throughout the world. The creation of team media has given broadcasters who might have worked for a traditional media outlet a way to work for a college or professional team. Therefore, those who wish to enter the profession have a variety of paths to take in order to try to reach that goal. As this book moves forward, more detailed information will be given on the various jobs available and how aspiring journalists can be successful in those professions.

Phil Cole/Getty Images

CHAPTER 4

Interviewing

CHAPTER OBJECTIVES

This chapter spotlights one of the most important elements of the job for a sports broadcaster: interviewing. The audience wants to hear directly from those involved in the story. Therefore, this chapter focuses on getting interviews, including the following:

- Understanding the different question types when conducting an interview
- Differentiating between four main interviewing methods
- Knowing what to do before, during, and after an interview
- Knowing how to properly set up a camera to record an interview

While sports broadcasters and journalists can describe the action happening during games, there is no one better to talk about what happened than the people actually participating in the games. Why did the coach make that substitution? Why did the catcher call that pitch sequence that led to the game-winning strikeout? Why did the team's leading scorer not start today's game when she has started every other game? In many cases, the journalist can make an educated guess, but it is the participants themselves who can give the exact reasoning through an **interview**.

There are many aspects of games that fans can already understand by watching. A loyal fan knows what the big hit in a baseball game was or who scored the most goals in a soccer match. In fact, in many cases, the fans at home know just as much, or perhaps more, than the media members. Therefore, the ability to interview athletes and coaches is one of the job responsibilities that separates journalists from fans. Without the media asking questions, fans would not know why things happened and the "behind-the-scenes" details of the teams and players. The journalists get the "why" to add context to the "what." For example, the golfer used a five wood on the 14th hole: We know *what* happened, but *why* did she choose that club? The journalist is there to find out, and he or she does that through interviews.

Types of Interviews

Not all interviews are the same. Often, everything that an interviewee says during a conversation can be used in a broadcast. However, in some cases, the information provided by the interviewee cannot be used by the reporter. It is very important for the broadcaster and the person being interviewed to be in agreement regarding what type of interview is taking place. The Associated Press (n.d.) has defined four different types of interviews: on the record, off the record, on background, and on deep background.

On the Record

This is the most common type of interview that a broadcaster will do. If a recording device is present (and the interview subject is aware that the conversation is being recorded), then it is assumed that the interview will be "on the record." This means that everything within the interview can be used, including the information, the source, and direct quotes of what is said, for example, "Wildcats assistant coach Jenny Johnson told Action News that Kristina Smith will be the team's new first baseman for the rest of the season, replacing Pamela Bell." That statement may then be followed by a sound bite from coach Johnson explaining why that change was made.

Off the Record

These interviews take place when a recording device is not present and the person being interviewed has made it explicitly clear that the information they are giving to the reporter is not to be used during the broadcast. Therefore, the information, the source, and any direct quote could not be used. The reporter may use the off-the-record information to call other people relating to the story to try to have it confirmed. In the Wildcats softball example, the reporter would not be able to broadcast any of the information that coach Johnson provided until getting it confirmed by another source.

On Background

Much like off-the-record interviews, this type of interview takes place when a recording device is not present. In this case, the source has agreed to allow the broadcaster to report the information but not where the information came from. In these situations, the person being interviewed may feel comfortable providing the story details but not comfortable revealing that he or she was the one who told the news media. For our softball example, a broadcaster could say, "A source within the Wildcats softball team told Action News that Kristina Smith will be the team's new first baseman for the rest of the season, replacing Pamela Bell." While the information is still there, it is no longer attributed to a specific person.

On Deep Background

These will take place without a recording device present in order to protect the identity of the person providing the information. In these cases, the source does not want to be identified at all—even with a vague identifier. For the Wildcats softball team, the broadcaster could only say "Action News has learned that Kristina Smith will be the Wildcats' new first baseman for the rest of the season, replacing Pamela Bell." There is no identifying information about where the story came from.

For broadcasters, "on the record" sessions should be the most common form of interviewing. This allows the broadcasters to use the interviewee's own voice for a story instead of quoting them indirectly. In the on-the-record example about the softball team, the broadcaster was able to provide the information, followed immediately by a sound bite from the coach to give her perspective.

Conducting the Interview

Interviewing is not as simple as showing up to a practice or game and starting to ask questions. Sports broadcasters have to be prepared before the interview, follow several important steps during the interview, and be sure to reflect afterward about how the interview went.

Before the Interview

Before the sports broadcaster can even start the interview, he or she needs to be as prepared as possible. This primarily involves doing research beforehand. If a reporter shows up unprepared for an interview with a coach or player, that could damage the reputation of that journalist. What research should be completed ultimately depends on the type of story being reported.

- *A story previewing a game:* The reporter should know how each team has played lately, what happened the last time these two teams played each other, who the key players on each team are, and what additional story elements may be present. For example, are these two teams rivals? Is there a player that used to be on one team that is now on the other? Much of this information can be gathered online.
- *A feature story about an athlete:* The reporter should know the personal history of this athlete, what makes him or her worthy of a story like this, and what questions will get to the real story about the athlete. To get this information, a broadcaster may need to read older news stories, look at online resources, and talk to others who know the athlete well.
- *A game recap:* After the conclusion of the game, the reporter should look at the game statistics to determine what might be key moments during the contest, what players had either a good game or a bad one, what this game means in the "big picture" of both teams, and what is next on the schedule.

Once reporters have done research before the interview, they should prepare ahead of time a few questions to ask during the interview. While some veteran reporters may be able to "wing it" and come up with questions on the spot, it is better to have a few questions ready to ask for when the interview session begins. That may involve writing them down on a notepad or simply having a few mentally ready. For journalists, interviewing is similar to how an athlete prepares for a big game. A football player would not play an opponent without doing some scouting first, so a journalist should not show up to an interview without doing some research ahead of time.

Types of Interview Questions

Before asking questions, it is important to know the difference between the two main types: **open-ended** and **closed-ended**. Open-ended questions allow the interview subject some flexibility in his or her answers. They are often opinions and not facts. For example, an open-ended question to a women's tennis player might be, "Why do you think you can win this tournament?" She could take her response in a variety of different ways, talking about her game ("I've been practicing my forehand a lot and I think that it gives me a new weapon that should help put me over the top"), the environment ("I feel really comfortable on this court because we practice here all the time, so it feels like home to me"), or how confident she is ("I think I'm the best player here and if I play up to my potential then no one here can stop me").

A closed-ended question is designed to get a specific response out of someone. They often can be answered in just a word or very short sentence. An example of a closed-ended question might be, "What racket are you playing with this weekend?" There is only one quick answer the player can give—the name of the racket ("the new RocketTech 800")—and that usually ends that line of questions. Instead of getting a well-thought-out opinion-based answer from the athlete, the journalist instead gets a four-word response that is simply a fact.

For broadcast interviews, open-ended questions are almost always more effective because they usually lead to longer answers that are ideal for a radio or television broadcast. Open-ended questions can also be used to ensure that the player/coach can give their true answers. "How do you feel after that win?" is a much better question than "How happy are you right now?" That player might not be happy for whatever reason, but the wording of the second question forces him or her to talk about the happiness they may not be necessarily feeling. For example, a football wide receiver may be upset following a 35–0 win because he believes he was not thrown the ball enough.

Starting the Interview

How the broadcaster starts the interview will depend on who is being questioned and what type of interview is taking place. However, one of the main goals during the start of any broadcast interview is to make sure that everything is recording properly and check the **audio levels** so that they are not too loud or too soft.

For a large press conference or an interview with multiple reporters present, reporters can speak into their own microphone briefly before the interview starts to ensure that everything is working properly. The reporter simply holds the microphone up to his or her own mouth and says a few words to check that the **VU meter** is moving and that the sound is not overmodulated.

For a one-on-one interview, there are more options for those first questions depending on who is being interviewed. If the subject is not a well-known person (a fan, for example), then the goal of the first question should be to identify that person. The broadcaster should ask: "Please say your name and spell it for me." This allows the broadcaster to get the proper pronunciation (in case he or she needs to say it in the story) and the correct spelling for any on-screen graphics or web stories that will accompany the piece. When the person is saying his or her name, it is also a good time to check the equipment and the audio levels.

If the subject is a coach or player who is familiar to the audience and the reporter, then they do not need to be identified on the recording. For example, asking multiple Super Bowl–winning quarterback Tom Brady to identify himself and spell his name seems somewhat silly. Without that opportunity to ask this simple question, the broadcaster needs to recognize quickly if everything is set up properly with the camera and microphone during the first answer. Therefore, in order to avoid missing a key answer due to faulty equipment, the first question should be something broad that will likely not be used during the broadcast. During the response, the broadcaster can check to make sure that all the equipment is working properly and that the audio is recording at an acceptable volume.

During the Interview

Once the interview begins, it is up to the journalist to do his or her best to make sure that the exchange is pleasant for both the journalist and the person being interviewed. Interviews are essentially a partnership, so both the reporter and the interview subject should be happy with the final result. The interview subject wants to make sure that their message is getting across, and the reporter is looking for sound bites and information that can be used within his or her story.

Ask Simple Questions to Get Simple Answers

Broadcasters need their subjects to keep the answers simple. This is unlike a written story because if something is confusing, the reader can simply go back and reread the piece. However, broadcast viewers and listeners only get one chance to hear the story. Therefore, to get simple answers, the broadcasters should ask simple questions. That means avoiding two-part questions and overly complex tactical questions. While broadcasters may wish to show off their football knowledge ("Coach, what happened on that zone read play in which the safety cheated up and caused the interception on the fly route?"), that will likely get a very complex answer from the coach. For the average viewer or listener at home, this answer will not mean much to them because many football fans do not know the intricate details of the game. Broadcasters must remember that the majority of the audience are likely casual fans, so a detailed Xs and Os breakdown of a football play may be confusing.

Additionally, if something is confusing to the broadcaster, then it will almost certainly be confusing to the viewer. If the interviewer does not understand something that the subject says, he or she should ask for clarification in a follow-up question ("Coach, you said that the zone defense was dropping too low. What do you mean by that?").

Pay Attention

While asking questions is obviously an important part of a reporter's job during an interview, the reporter should also be listening closely to what the subject is saying during the answers. While interviewers may have a list of questions they plan to ask, they should be prepared to deviate from that list. They should not be simply writing down the responses, or simply waiting to ask the next question on their list. While the interview may be about a specific topic, the answers could lead to a situation in which an entirely different story emerges or a key piece of information is revealed. For example, say a hockey player is asked about that night's game and the response is, "It was great to get a goal tonight. It is especially great because I found out right before the game that my wife is pregnant. So, to get a win today is really special." If the broadcaster is not entirely paying attention while thinking about the next question to ask, checking audio levels on the recorder, or distracted by others in the room, then he or she may have only heard the beginning and the end of the answer—"It was great to get a goal tonight . . . a win today is really special." Now, a key event in this player's life—and an excellent addition to the story—is missed.

The Power of Why Questions

While there may be some value in occasionally asking wordy and complex questions, the most effective question is often "why?" This is not a good question to a basketball coach: "In the first half your team seemed to struggle with the full-court press. Do you think that led to the 15–0 run by the other team?" The wording of that question gives the coach a possible answer with which he may or may not agree. In that same scenario, this would be a much better question: "Why do you think the other team went on a 15–0 run in the first half?" The simple "why" question allows the coach to come up with his own reason why his team was outscored 15–0 at one point.

Ultimately, the purpose of the interview is to get the subjects to give their opinions or explanations. The reporter's job is to give the information and have the participants talk about why it happened. For example, the coach does not need to say, "That 15–0 run put us down by 10 points." That's a fact that the reporter can say. A better use of the interview is to tell us *why* that run happened, what the team did to respond, and what impact that scoring drought had on his team. A good way to remember this is that *reporters give facts, interview subjects give opinions and emotion.*

In order to get that opinion and emotion, reporters should ask questions that can get the subject to give details beyond just the facts. This is another reason why the "why" question can be so effective. The reporter can talk about how the team has a new starting quarterback (facts), but the coach can give the emotion and opinion that go beyond the simple facts. Questions could include:

- How hard was it to make this change at quarterback?
- Why was now the time to make the change?
- How do you feel the former starter will handle this change?

None of those questions should provide simple straightforward factual answers. Instead, the audience will get to know the opinions and emotion behind the decision.

You're in Charge

Whether interviewing a high school swimmer or a multi-time Olympic gold medalist, the reporter must remain in control of the interview. Many upper-level athletes and coaches receive media training that can help them either avoid questions they wish not to answer or give answers that do not provide any substance for the interviewer. Reporters must remember that they cannot let the subject decide what questions are being answered. If someone does not provide an acceptable answer, the reporter

Pro Advice

Courtesy of Walter Cronkite School of Journalism and Mass Communication.

Brett Kurland

Director of sports programs at Arizona State University's Walter Cronkite School of Journalism and Mass Communication

One would be hard-pressed to find someone more passionate about interviewing than Brett Kurland. "It's my favorite topic" said the former television producer and current director of sports programs at Arizona State University's Walter Cronkite School of Journalism and Mass Communication. "It's the most important tool in journalism," Kurland said. "As far as I'm concerned, it is impossible to be a good journalist if you're not good at interviewing."

Kurland worked in television for more than 15 years, producing multiple sports documentaries for a variety of television networks including ESPN, NFL Network, and the NHL Network. A key part of his job on those productions was interviewing some of the biggest sports stars in the world. He said, "If I walked out of an interview and I didn't learn anything new, I probably didn't do a great interview. It's the one real true tool that journalists have."

What makes a good interview question?

Questions should be open, lean, and neutral. Open: use open-ended questions. Lean: short and to the point. Neutral: you don't want to introduce any bias or anything like that. Also, you don't want to give people in an interview "off-ramps." Imagine you're driving down the freeway and there are the off-ramps. You want to keep them going. So, when someone is looking for an off-ramp, trying to change the subject or avoid your question, you bring them back on.

Not every interview is an easy one. How should a reporter handle an interview when he or she has to ask tough questions?

You don't want the tough question to be the first question. You have to build up that relationship and build up that rapport. But at the same time, you can't be afraid to ask the tough questions.

After Tiger Woods crashed the car on Thanksgiving and all the information comes out about his affairs, (ESPN's) Tom Rinaldi gets the first interview with him. And it is a beautifully perfect interview because he gets Tiger to talk. He doesn't accuse Tiger, he asks him neutral questions, he's listening to what Tiger is saying, asking follow-ups, and doesn't give him off-ramps. Imagine how different that interview would have been if Rinaldi opens with "So, how could you cheat on your wife? How could you do that?"

I know you don't like it when reporters use "talk about" instead of asking a question. Why is that a bad way to conduct an interview?

To be frank, it's lazy. You're giving up complete control of the interview. You need to engage someone when you're interviewing. These athletes get interviewed all the time. So, if you don't show any effort, they're not going to show any effort. So, if you say, "talk about," they're going to say, "this person isn't really invested so I'm just going to give them some generic answer."

Many young journalists find it intimidating to do interviews with athletes, because these players are legends in many of their eyes. How can beginners get past that awe factor?

It is rare to meet someone who went into sports journalism who didn't grow up a sports fan. They grew up idolizing these athletes, or just the concept of athletes. You want to show that we're on the same level here, not the eight-year-old looking for an autograph. When interviewing (baseball player) Paul Goldschmidt, you don't go up to him and say, "Excuse me, Mr. Goldschmidt, would you mind talking to me?" Instead it's, "Hey Paul, I'm Brett from Arizona PBS . . ." and then your question. You want to show that we're on the same level here. An athlete is somebody who is particularly good at one thing, and it happens to be that sport. You're particularly skilled at being a journalist. So, you're on the same level.

Can it be intimidating? Absolutely, initially. But you have to cut through that. There's a sense of "oh my gosh, that's such and such. I've watched him on TV." They're just regular people who happen to be really good at sports and make a lot of money. Otherwise, they're regular people. The more you remind yourself of that, the better off you are.

should ask the question again, worded slightly differently, to let the athlete know that he or she did not answer the question. If necessary, a reporter can politely interrupt the subject if they are talking at length about a topic that is not relevant to the interview topic.

The Last Question

For news reporters, the last question in the interview should almost always be "Is there something I didn't ask you that you think our viewers/listeners should know about?" Often interview subjects have one specific piece of information that they want to talk about, but if that never comes up in the interview, they are left without being able to discuss it. This open-ended final question allows the interview subject to talk about that item. In many cases, the answer to that question could lead to an entirely different angle to the story and result in several follow-up questions.

For sports reporters, that may not always be the best final question. For example, a head coach or player probably is not going to reveal any information about the team that was not specifically asked about. Instead, the reporter may ask a variation of the question, such as "anything else new?" or "any other changes I didn't ask about?" These are generic enough that the coach might be willing to provide information about a topic that was not brought up during the interview.

Working With a Difficult Interview Subject

While one would hope that every interview will go smoothly, that is not always the case. In some situations, the purpose of the interview alone can cause challenges. When a new head coach is hired, the interview is usually light-hearted and non confrontational. The coach is happy, excited to be interviewed, and likely wants to make a good impression with both the fan base and the media. However, the interview can be difficult if that coach is later fired. The coach may be angry, the fans upset, and the tone much more serious. In some cases, athletes simply do not want to speak to the media. Seattle Seahawks running back Marshawn Lynch had no interest in talking to reporters before the 2014 Super Bowl; however, NFL rules stated that he had to attend the week's large media event. Instead of answering questions, Lynch either provided short, unusable answers or said, "I'm here so I won't get fined" (Branch, 2015, para. 6). The phrase become so synonymous with Lynch that he personally trademarked it less than a year later (Payne, 2015).

Broadcasters can usually tell how an interview is going to go even before the first question is asked. If the interview is likely going to be a difficult one, the reporter, if possible, should attempt to deescalate the tension. He or she can let the subject know that the interview will only take a short amount of time ("just a couple of quick questions, coach"), focus on topics that might make the subject happier ("That was a tough loss, but what was a bright spot tonight?"), or change the topic slightly ("What will be the focus of the next game?"). Finally, in some cases, no matter what the interviewer does, the subject will not be happy. In these cases, it is sometimes best to end the conversation early once there has been at least one usable sound bite.

MAJOR MOMENTS

Kevin Durant Strikes Back

In February 2019, professional basketball player Kevin Durant was playing out the final year of his contract with the Golden State Warriors. The speculation was that the All-Star would leave the team at the end of the season, and many media members had reported that. Durant, who previously had been very cordial and accommodating with the media, staged a brief boycott of the press. After nine days of not talking with writers and broadcasters, Durant sat down for a contentious press conference with several members of the local media.

Durant was not happy that the focus of several stories was the belief that he might leave: "Y'all come in here every day, ask me about free agency, ask my teammates, my coaches. You rile fans up about it. Let us play basketball" (Boren, 2019, para 2). When asked why he had enacted his silence from the media, Durant responded, "I didn't feel like talking the last couple of days. I just ain't feel like it" (Boren, 2019, para 6). Ultimately, it appeared the questions about his future made Durant feel as if the media was out to get him. He said, "I just don't trust none of y'all" (KNBR, 2019, 2:20).

Finally, in an effort to shift the topic to basketball, something Durant had asked the media to do, reporter Tim Kawakami asked Durant, "How are you playing and how is the team playing?" Durant responded by saying "I'm done. You know you don't care about that" and walked off of the press conference podium (KNBR, 2019, 2:50).

The press conference showcased the difficulties that athletes and reporters can have during a contentious time. In this case, Durant could not understand why the media was so focused on him possibly leaving the Warriors after the season. Meanwhile, the media could not understand why he would not want to talk about his free agency. In this case, there likely would not have been anything that could have been done during the press conference to appease Durant. However, he had an opportunity to talk about how he felt directly to the media. The two sides had a cordial working relationship for the rest of season before Durant eventually did leave as a free agent in July 2019 (Cacciola & Stein, 2019).

After the Interview

After the final question has been asked, the first thing a reporter should do is thank the person with whom they just finished the interview. If someone set up the interview (such as a public relations person for the team or school), then the reporter should be sure to thank that person as well. Interview subjects are taking their own time to work with the media, and if the reporter shows appreciation it could make it easier to get a follow-up interview at another time. This does not mean the reporter should be "sucking up" to the athlete or coach, but a simple "thank you" afterward is encouraged.

Following the interview, especially early in a broadcaster's career, it is important to review the interview to recognize what worked well and what did not. Like an athlete studying game tape to improve, broadcasters should listen back to the interview in order to improve for the next one. What questions led to great answers? What questions led to a subpar answer from the interviewee? Did the interview subject appear uncomfortable at any point? By analyzing what went right and what went wrong, a reporter can have a better idea of how to move forward with future interviews.

Finally, in order to know exactly what the person in the interview said, the reporter should transcribe the interview, a process also known as **logging**. When logging an interview, every word a person has said is written down by the reporter after listening to the recording. It is important to write down every word and not just summarize what is said by the interview subject. For example, if a softball team picks up a big win over a rival opponent, the head coach would likely be interviewed. That brief interview would be transcribed by the reporter as follows:

Reporter (:00): This was obviously a big win against your rival. What did you like about your team tonight?

Coach (:05): I liked the win, that's for sure. But I thought our pitching really stood out. Janet on the mound was outstanding. She threw a complete game shutout and I liked that she was challenging hitters. In previous games, if she threw a couple of pitches outside the strike zone, she would have a hard time coming back. Today, everything was right where it needed to be, and that makes it really hard for whoever is facing her. She's really good when she's got command of her pitches.

Reporter (:27): In addition to that great pitching, your team got some timely hits. This is the third game in a row that you've scored more than five runs. What's been different lately?

Coach (:35): I think our players are more relaxed. I felt like they were really pressing at the beginning of the season—trying to hit a home run on every swing. We've told them that there is nothing wrong with a single. Not everything has to go over the fence. So I think they're starting to embrace that mindset more, and we've been able to string together a couple of hits. That's how you score runs.

Reporter (:55): Unfortunately, you don't have much time to celebrate this one. You've got tomorrow off, but then right back in action on Friday. How do you keep this momentum going?

Coach (1:02): Yeah—the schedule isn't doing us any favors, that's for sure. This is a big win, but we've got a lot of the season still to play. But we'll go into Friday's game feeling really good about ourselves after this one. We're getting people out on the mound, scoring runs, and in a good spot mentally. I think we all know that if we keep playing like this, we're a tough team to play.

The transcription reports who said the quote, at what time the quote happened in the recording, and a word-for-word account of what was said. For the purposes of clarity, the reporter does not need to transcribe each "um" and "ah" that is said. However, by getting the exact wording, the script will be easier to write because one will know the proper wording instead of just a vague idea of what was said. Also, by writing down the time that it occurred on the recording, the editing process will be easier because the reporter will not have to search for the selected sound bite. If the reporter wants the quote where the coach is talking about the offense, the reporter knows it starts at :35 thanks to the transcription. How all of this helps the reporter when writing for broadcast will be discussed further in chapter 5.

Shooting the Interview for Television

Asking good questions is an important part of any interview situation. However, for television broadcasters, properly recording the video is perhaps just as crucial to the process. If the interview is out of focus, the incorrect color, or **overmodulated**, then the content of the answers will not make much difference because it likely will not be able to be shown on television.

There is not one answer to "How does someone get video of an interview?" because sports broadcasters usually participate in three very different ways of talking to players or coaches: **press conferences, group interviews,** and **solo interviews**. There are advantages and disadvantages to each, and the video setup and organization is quite different as well. Figure 4.1 lists items needed for each of these settings.

Press Conference

A press conference is an interview in which many members of the press are invited at once to hear from someone in a formal setting. In the world of sports, a press conference normally takes place before or after a major event. For example, a basketball team may have a press conference before the season, a day or two before each game, immediately following a game, or there may be a final press conference after the season. Press conferences may also take place if a major event has occurred, such as

INTERVIEW CHECKLIST

Press Conference

- ❑ Video camera
- ❑ Tripod
- ❑ Handheld microphone with stand
- ❑ Cables to connect from camera to microphone or to mult box
- ❑ Headphones to monitor audio during recording
- ❑ Camera card to record interview onto

Group Interview

- ❑ Video camera
- ❑ Tripod (but you likely won't have time or space to use it)
- ❑ Handheld microphone
- ❑ Cables to connect from camera to microphone
- ❑ Light for camera
- ❑ Headphones to monitor audio during recording
- ❑ Camera card to record interview onto

Solo Interview

- ❑ Video camera
- ❑ Tripod
- ❑ Lavalier and handheld microphone (preferable to use lavalier)
- ❑ Cables to connect from camera to microphone
- ❑ Light for camera
- ❑ Headphones to monitor audio during recording
- ❑ Camera card to record interview onto

FIGURE 4.1 List of items needed to conduct an interview.

the hiring or firing of a head coach. In the world of sports, the press conference often begins with the player or coach making an opening statement, followed by a question-and-answer session from the assembled media. On rare occasions, only one of those will take place, such as a statement with no questions permitted or an athlete simply asking for questions.

Advantages and Disadvantages

The advantage of a press conference is that the person doing it is often required to be there for a certain amount of time with the explicit purpose of answering questions from the media. This can help journalists because the subject is mentally prepared to answer questions, so they might be in a better mood to answer them. This is not always the case, however, so journalists should be ready for anything when entering the press conference room.

In a press conference, questions will come from all of the journalists in the room, which can be both an advantage and a disadvantage for an individual reporter. It is an advantage because someone may ask a question that others had not thought of. However, it can also be a disadvantage because there is not an opportunity to have exclusive answers. All the answers that the person gives can be used by everyone in the room. That means no **"scoops"** or individual stories can come from this scenario.

Another disadvantage of a press conference is that they are impersonal. It is hard to develop a relationship with the person in front of the room when the reporter is one of many in attendance. This distance creates a scenario in which questions and answers are game-centric and do not allow for the journalists to ask questions that might allow the audience to get to know the player or coach outside of the action.

Setup

Press conferences will take place in a designated location decided upon by the team. Most major sports teams have a specific room dedicated to hosting these events. The player or coach will sit or stand in front of the room behind a table or a podium, while the media is facing them. The media section will have rows of chairs for the reporters to sit in and a section for the video cameras to set up to record the press conference.

Television broadcasters should set up in the back area of the room in order to get the best video angles of the press conference and to not block other journalists. A **tripod** should always be used for a press conference and should be raised to a height at which the camera will stand higher than the media members sitting in the chairs in front.

Lighting is usually not a concern during these press conferences, as they often take place in rooms that have ample lighting. Using the light provided, the photographer should **white balance** the camera so that the camera can determine the various colors. This is usually a button on the side of the camera. Once the athlete or coach enters the room to begin the press conference, the photographer should **zoom** in as close as possible on that person's nose and then focus. This will ensure that the subject is in focus during the interview. Once the person is in focus and the white balance

Alex Grimm/Getty Images

In a press conference, the athlete or coach is in front of the room, while the gathered media asks questions from the audience.

has been acquired, the photographer should zoom back out to a shot in which the top of the person's head is at the top of the frame and the bottom of the frame is at about the middle of the person's chest.

There are normally two different options for collecting sound during a press conference. The first option is to simply run a microphone cord from the camera to a microphone placed on the desk or the podium in front of the person giving the press conference. In smaller settings, this is often the most common way in which to hear what the person is saying for the recording. In bigger press conferences, there may be a **mult box**. This is a device with multiple outputs so that many different media organizations can all get sound from the same microphone. It splits one audio signal (the sound coming from the microphone at the table or podium) into several signals (MacAdam, 2015). The photographer would simply plug one end of the microphone cord into the camera and the other end into the mult box. No matter which audio-gathering method is used, it is a good practice to wear headphones when recording interviews. That will allow the photographer to be sure that the audio is recording correctly into the camera.

Group Interview

A press conference is usually a somewhat formal event featuring the key participants in the game, such as the head coach or the person that scored the game-winning goal. However, the media will often want to speak with other players involved in the game as well. If that is the case, a less formal group interview will take place, in which multiple media members will crowd around a single player to ask him or her questions. These interviews usually take place after a practice or game.

Advantages and Disadvantages

The advantage of the group interview is that it allows for the broadcaster to get an additional interview with a player on which they may want to focus. For example, the player who scored the game-winning goal is an obvious interview at the podium during the press conference, but the broadcaster may also want to talk to the player who had the assist on that goal. By having the opportunity to interview additional people, there are more sound bites to pick from when putting together the story.

One disadvantage of the group interview is the same as the press conference, in that everyone who participates in that session has the same answers. Once again, this means that there is no chance for an answer to appear on only one media outlet. Additionally, the group interview can, at times, be slightly chaotic, with media members all rushing to get to the same player in a very small area. With all of the journalists and their equipment in one space, it can be a cramped situation.

Setup

Much like the press conference, the location of a group interview is usually predetermined by the team. These often take place in the locker room, in a hallway, or on the field after the game or practice is over. Additionally, these interviews often come together quickly, with a team official bringing over the player or coach to the set location and the media members all rushing toward the subject. Due to the urgent nature of group interviews, sports broadcasters should not use tripods because there is not time or space to set up properly. Instead, photographers should hold the cameras themselves, either balancing them on their shoulders if it is a larger camera or holding them in front of them for a smaller camera. The camera should be at eye level with the person that is being interviewed.

To pick up the audio from the interview, a **handheld microphone** should be used. These microphones will pick up the audio from what is directly in front of it, so they are perfect for an interview that will be quick and in a loud environment (like a locker room). The journalist should hold the microphone, not the person being interviewed. As always, the photographer should be wearing headphones to be sure that the audio is recording correctly.

The lighting needed may depend on where the interview is taking place. Locker rooms are often well lit, so no additional steps will need to be taken. However, a hallway could be darker.

Kevin C. Cox/Getty Images

In a group interview, the athlete or coach will often stand in the locker room and be surrounded by several media members asking questions.

If that is the case, the photographer should turn on an additional light on the camera. White balancing should not take place until after the lighting situation has been settled.

When the interview is set to begin, the photographer should zoom into the subject's nose, focus on his or her nose, and then zoom back out. The resulting shot should have the top of the person's head at the top of the frame and the middle of the person's chest at the bottom of the frame.

Solo Interview

Occasionally, a sports broadcaster will be granted a one-on-one interview with an athlete or coach. Depending on the level of the sport being covered, this could be a rare occurrence. For example, it may be challenging to get a solo interview with a member of the United States soccer team, but getting a one-on-one interview with a high school soccer player should be relatively easier.

Advantages and Disadvantages

The advantage of a solo interview is that it can provide an opportunity to ask questions beyond the traditional game-centric topics. Solo interviews are ideal for feature stories in which aspects of the subject can be focused on stories off the field of play. In press conferences, questions usually focus on very specific aspects of the game. In a one-on-one situation, reporters can ask questions that might only be relevant to their story and not waste the time of the others in the room. There are few disadvantages to a solo interview. However, in this situation a broadcaster must be even more prepared than for other types of interviews because he or she is the only one asking questions, and there is no possibility for another journalist to ask a question the reporter may not have thought of.

Setup

With a solo interview, there is a possibility for the reporter to have more control over the location of the interview. While an interview with a basketball player may still need to take place at the arena, the journalist might be able to decide where in the arena it will take place. For example, the interview setup could take place in the stands, under the basket, or on the bench. If a photographer has the option of choosing the location, it is important to remember that the background of the interview is a key part of the framing. The goal is to pick a spot that is relevant to what the story is about. For example, a soccer player could be interviewed on the soccer field with the goal behind him or her. It is also important to pick a background that is not overly distracting or overly boring. A background with a lot of activity would not be an ideal location because the viewer may be more interested in what is happening behind the interview than what the person is saying. Putting the interview subject in front of a white wall is going to create a situation that is not interesting visually.

Once a location for the interview has been chosen, the interview should be framed up in the **viewfinder**. The camera should be at eye level with the subject. If the camera is higher than the subject, it will make him or her appear smaller; if it is lower, it will be a shot of the bottom of his or her chin. Putting the camera at eye level produces the most visually appealing shot. As with the previous interview styles, the photographer should zoom all the way in on the person's nose, focus, and then zoom out to begin the framing process.

Every solo interview should be framed to have the top of the person's head at the top of the frame and the top of their chest at the bottom of the frame. The subject should be slightly off-center, leaving "looking room" to one side. The subject should look at the person conducting the interview, leaving more "looking room" in front of the person, as opposed to behind them. Viewers should be able to see both eyes of the person being interviewed, so it should not be a profile shot of the person. Finally, no part of the reporter should be shown in these shots.

While setting up the interview, the placement of the reporter is an important part of the process. After setting up the camera on the tripod, the reporter should be as close to the camera as possible, either immediately to the left or right of the lens. This helps to ensure that a profile is not seen in the shot. The reporter should be on the side of the camera from which there is more look space.

In addition to the camera being eye level with the subject, the interviewer should be eye level as well. The person being interviewed should never be looking down or up during the interview, so the reporter's face should be even with the camera lens. When the interview is about to begin, the reporter should tell the subject, "You can look at me, don't look directly into the camera."

If possible, a **lavalier microphone** should be used for a solo interview. These small microphones clip onto a person's shirt, allowing the reporter to have both hands free. The framing of the shot should be zoomed in enough so that the wire for the microphone cannot be seen during the interview. The photographer could ask the subject to run the wire under his or her shirt, but zooming in close enough can also solve the issues of the exposed wire. The microphone should be clipped on the side the subject is facing (the side with more "looking room") and be about 8 to 12 inches from the person's mouth. The top of someone's shirt is a good location to clip a lavalier microphone.

In some cases, the reporter may wish to use a handheld microphone instead of a lavalier microphone during an interview. The handheld microphone picks up the audio from what is directly in front of it. In the case of a loud location, the photographer should use the handheld microphone because it will be better at picking up the sound from the interview without all the surrounding noise. When using a handheld microphone, the person being interviewed should never be the one holding it. Instead, the reporter should hold the microphone about 5 to 10 inches away from the subject's mouth.

Since the solo interview can take place in a variety of locations, different lighting situations must be considered by the photographer. The dominant light should fall evenly on the subject's face. Light behind the person will create a silhouette effect in which the subject's face will be completely dark.

JUDY GRIESEDIECK/Star Tribune via Getty Images

In a solo interview, the reporter has a one-on-one opportunity to ask the athlete or coach questions with just the two of them—and perhaps a photographer—present.

If interviewing outside during the day, the most important thing to be aware of is the sun. The light given off from the sun can cause many headaches for a television broadcast. If the sun is directly behind the person, his or her face will be dark. If it is to the side, then only half of that person's face will be well lit, while the other half will remain dark. Therefore, the best spot for the sun to be during an interview is directly in front of the subject so they are looking directly at it. If interviewing outside, the photographer should avoid putting a subject in front of a window because it will cause the same silhouette effect as placing someone with their back in front of the sun.

Multiple Solo Interviews

In some cases, a reporter may need to conduct multiple solo interviews for a story. For example, if there is a story about a player overcoming an injury, the reporter may wish to interview that player, the coach, and the team's medical person. If all the interviews are going to appear in the same story, it is a good policy to change the location and angles for each interview. Instead of shooting each interview in the gym in the exact same seat in the bleachers, one interview could be in that spot, one could be facing a different direction, and the other could be in the locker room. Mixing up the locations helps provide a more pleasing visual story for the viewer. If the location cannot be moved between interviews, the photographer can simply have the subjects face different directions. While not perfect, it will still give a slight impression that the shots are different.

If a story involves two people on the opposite side of an issue, such as the two quarterbacks of rival high schools, the interviews should be framed with the people facing in different directions. For example, the quarterback of East High School would face left, while the quarterback of West High School would face right. This gives the impression that the two interview subjects have differing opinions on a topic.

Distance Interview

In 2020, the COVID-19 global pandemic forced sports journalists to add a new type of interview to their options. With social distancing dictating that people stay at least six feet apart from each other, media members were banned from the locker room and all in-person press conferences were canceled. Instead, interviews were taking place over video-conferencing software. The players and coaches would sit in one room while the media members would sit in various locations away from the players. This took away from the face-to-face interaction but still allowed for the media to speak to the athletes.

Mitch Brown, a sports broadcaster in Lexington, Kentucky, found himself doing distance interviews with athletes and coaches throughout the summer of 2020. He said the setup certainly was not as intimate as a face-to-face interview because more people were there and, at times, questions can be interpreted differently through a screen. However, Brown also said that there are some positives to this format: "Honestly, people on the other side getting interviewed are a lot more comfortable. They're usually at home or in a room by themselves, so they don't have all these eyes watching them physically. On Zoom, they have time to process the question and gather their thoughts as opposed to feeling like they need to answer it instantly." He also cited an advantage for the broadcasters themselves: "It's not bad being on your couch and doing an interview."

While the sessions are taking place in different locations, the skills needed to have successful distance interviews are not much different from those used for an in-person interview. When multiple media members are present, broadcasters should treat these distance interviews similarly to group interviews or press conferences. If it is a one-on-one interview, completing the interview as if it is a solo interview is advisable.

Interview Access

Professional and college sports teams and leagues make great efforts to make the players and coaches available for interviews with the media. In the professional ranks, leagues have rules that allow the media access to the players before and after each game. Major League Baseball allows accredited media members access to the clubhouse from 3 hours and 30 minutes before the game until one hour prior to the game. The media is also required to have access to the clubhouse no later than 10 minutes after the final out of the game (MLB, n.d.). In the NFL, the media is given access to the locker room during the season for interviews for a minimum of 45 minutes on Monday, Wednesday, Thursday, and Friday, and the head coach must be available at least 4 days during the week for interviews. Similar to the MLB policy, locker rooms must be open no later than 10 to 12 minutes after the completion of the game (NFL, n.d.).

In the NCAA, the rules vary from school to school and sport to sport. While the professional leagues have set standards that each team must enforce, it is a challenge in college due to the variety of schools and sport sizes that exist throughout the country. It would be difficult to put the same restrictions on a small school's volleyball team and a large school's football team. The best policy is to call ahead to the Sports Information Director (SID) for the individual school and sport to see what the policy is for the team you would like to cover. Due to the NCAA's hands-off approach regarding the media during the regular season, each team can make its own media policy. This can create some difficulties for the local media members.

For example, several U.S. college football programs do not allow freshmen to talk to the media. The coaches of these programs often say that this policy is for the benefit of the player. University of Alabama head coach Nick Saban is one of those with this policy, saying, "I'm for protecting our players and helping them develop. We eventually want that guy to be able to talk to the media and do a good job with it" (Gribble, 2012, para. 20). At the University of South Carolina, former head coach Will Muschamp did not allow his freshmen to talk to the media: "Some of our guys don't always know how to handle questions the right way. We have some things in place to help them handle the media" (Whittle, 2016, para. 5).

This policy can prove to be a major deterrent for the media if one of the best players on the team is a freshman. In 2012, Texas A&M University freshman Johnny Manziel was not just the star of the Aggies football team, he was also considered the best player in college football. While his play on the field dazzled the media, no one had heard from him off the field because of head coach Kevin Sumlin's policy on freshmen not speaking to the media. However, when it became apparent that Manziel might have a chance to win the Heisman Trophy, annually awarded to the best player in college football, Sumlin changed his policy for just Manziel to allow the quarterback to get some additional national media attention (Huston, 2012; Pendergast, 2012).

If a college team reaches the NCAA Tournament, then the governing body of college athletics has more control over what coverage teams must provide for the media. The NCAA designated a 10-minute "cooling-off period" after the conclusion of a game for a coach to be with the athletes. The coach and athletes must report to the designated interview room after that time. The coach is required to talk to the entire media during the NCAA tournament and not just a specific media member or organization (NCAA, n.d.).

High school policies are similar to that of the NCAA in that each school has its own policy. It is a good practice to call ahead to the individual school in order to speak directly to the coach or the school's athletic director. That person can let the journalists know when the best time is to get interviews from the coaches or the players. Many states do have a media policy when schools reach the pinnacle of the sport and make it to the state championships. For example, in Louisiana, a formal press conference in a designated interview room follows the championship games in volleyball, football, and basketball. State officials determined that the losing coach will enter the interview room first and all one-on-one interviews will take place after the conclusion of the press conference (LHSAA, n.d.).

CHAPTER WRAP-UP

HK*PROPEL* ACTIVITIES

There are two videos in HK*Propel* for how to set up an interview. Video #1 shows a reporter using a professional video camera to interview a subject. Video #2 shows a reporter using a phone to interview a subject. Each video features narration from the author of this book describing the proper way to set up an interview. Using these videos and the information provided in this chapter as a guide, students should conduct an interview of a classmate while using proper video framing.

SUMMARY

Interviewing is one of the most important and difficult parts of a sports broadcaster's job. While the reporter should give the facts and statistics surrounding a sporting event, it is the participants themselves who provide the "why" for what happened at the game. Broadcasters must also be aware of the differences between interviewing situations, whether it is a press conference, group interview, or solo interview. With proper interviewing techniques, the reporter can give the audience a better sense of what happened. Many steps must be followed before, during, and after an interview to ensure that it is completed properly.

While asking questions is the most obvious part of any interview, television broadcasters must also be aware of the technical aspects of an interview that can make or break the question-and-answer session. Proper framing is key to having a video that is visually pleasing for the viewer. That means the video should be in focus, have the correct color, and show the subject from the top of the head to the middle of the chest. Additionally, the reporter should be sure to use the best microphone depending on the type of interview being conducted.

Finally, reporters should remember that interviewing is essentially a team activity. Both the reporter and the interview subject should be pleased with the final result. Therefore, reporters should make every effort to make interviewees as comfortable as possible through questions that allow both coaches and players to give their opinions about events surrounding the team.

Phil Cole/Getty Images

CHAPTER 5

Writing for Broadcast

CHAPTER OBJECTIVES

Writing for broadcast can be one of the most difficult aspects of the job for new journalists to understand. It is very different from all previous styles of writing that most people have been taught throughout school. Therefore, this chapter focuses on writing for broadcast, including the following:

- Recognizing the difference between the various types of broadcast news stories
- Utilizing proper broadcast writing style
- Formatting a script for television and radio
- Writing a complete script suitable for broadcast

The game is over, the statistics have been analyzed, and the interviews have been collected. It's now time to write the broadcast story. For games and events, journalists have to write a story that makes the audience feel like they were part of the action and in the front row at the game. However, for broadcast, journalists are writing scripts for the ear and not the eye. Therefore, the stories have to be easy to understand for the listener.

Types of Stories

Not all broadcast stories are the same. For television, some contain video, are prerecorded, or have part of an interview included at the end. For radio, the inclusion of a sound bite from a subject covered in the story can change the entire formatting of a piece. Each situation will lead to a different style of writing from the broadcaster. Therefore, it is important to recognize the difference between the types of stories based on the content included in them.

Television Stories

Several types of stories can appear on an evening television sportscast. Each has a specific purpose, and the sports broadcaster must decide what works best depending on the story (Filak, 2019; Halbrooks, 2018; Harrower, 2013).

- *Reader:* The anchor reading a script while being shown on television. These stories should only be used if there is no video available or if the story is exceptionally short. These can run anywhere from 15 to 20 seconds.
- *Voice-over (VO):* The anchor reading a script while video is played on the screen. The video should be relevant to what the story is about. For a sports broadcaster, a VO could be the anchor talking about a basketball team, with practice video playing on the screen. A VO usually lasts between 20 and 30 seconds.
- *Sound on tape (SOT):* An edited piece of an interview showing the interview subject talking on camera. A SOT should not be much longer than 15 seconds.
- *Voice-over to sound on tape (VO/SOT):* A combination of the VO and SOT. The anchor reads a script with video playing on the screen. After the anchor is done reading the story, a sound bite from an interview will play. For example, when sports broadcasters are previewing a game, the VO could contain video of practice, followed by a SOT that was a short soundbite from a coach talking about the opponent. The combined VO/SOT should be about 45 seconds.
- *Package (PKG):* A package is a self-contained story that includes multiple recorded reporter tracks, about three different sound bites, and relevant video to match what is being described by the reporter and the interview subjects. A package should be about a minute and 30 seconds.
- *Highlights:* Television sports broadcasters also have to write a script to go along with game highlights. Highlights show the best or most important plays in a particular game. While these are technically considered a VO, the writing and style that goes along with them is different from a traditional news-style voice-over. More information on highlights will be given in chapter 8.

Radio Stories

For radio broadcasters, there are also different types of stories that they must decide among when writing about sports. Obviously, they do not have to worry about video during these, so there are no voice-overs in radio. While some of the types of stories are the same, there are some differences between television and radio stories (Kern, 2008).

- *Reader:* anchor reading a script with no other audio elements included in the story
- *Actuality:* sound bite from a prerecorded interview
- *Wrap:* similar to the television package (PKG) in which a reporter records his or her voice track and includes sound bites from relevant people

Broadcast Writing Style

Writing for broadcast is different from how people are taught to write their entire lives. Writing a 30-second VO is almost the complete opposite of writing an 11th-grade history paper. With that in mind, there are multiple differences between broadcast writing and traditional writing.

Write for the Ear, Not the Eye

Broadcasters must remember that when writing for radio or television, the script is being written for the ear, not the eye. If there is something unclear in a print or online story, the reader can go back and reread the confusing part in order to get some additional clarification. However, in the world of broadcast, there is only one chance to hear the story. Unless someone is recording a sportscast, the first time hearing the story will be the only time to hear the story.

Therefore, the best advice for a journalist when writing a story for broadcast is to picture each script as a conversation with the audience and both keep it simple and "write like you talk" (Butera, 2015). If two friends were chatting over breakfast and one asked, "What happened at the Tigers game last night?", the friend's response would not be a complicated play-by-play description of the contest. Instead, a quick, easy-to-comprehend conversational recap would make more sense (Butera, 2015). That same idea is true for broadcast writing (see Script Formatting section later in this chapter for guidelines for punctuation and capitalization).

Option A: THE TIGERS LOOKED GREAT. THEY SCORED 21 POINTS IN A ROW AND WON 35–7. CHAD SMITH SCORED THREE TOUCHDOWNS.

Option B: THE TIGERS BEAT THE SHARKS 35–7 AFTER CHAD SMITH SCORED ON TOUCHDOWN RUNS OF 14 YARDS—25 YARDS—AND 8 YARDS. THE GAME WAS TIED AT SEVEN APIECE BEFORE THE TIGERS SCORED THREE STRAIGHT TOUCHDOWNS IN ORDER TO GET A LEAD THEY WOULD NOT GIVE UP.

While both are technically correct, Option A sounds much more like something that two friends would say to each other. Option B is much less conversational, and therefore is less pleasing and perhaps confusing to listen to. Therefore, Option A would be the correct broadcast style because it is more conversational and, therefore, would be much easier for the audience to understand when listening at home.

Option C: TICKETS FOR FRIDAY NIGHT'S FOOTBALL GAME ARE SELLING FOR 20 DOLLARS EACH. THAT'S MORE THAN THE USUAL 10 DOLLAR PRICE BECAUSE THIS IS A PLAYOFF GAME AND THE PRICES ARE DECIDED BY THE STATE INSTEAD OF THE SCHOOL.

Option D: IF YOU'RE PLANNING ON GOING TO THE FOOTBALL PLAYOFF GAME THIS FRIDAY—GET READY TO PAY A LITTLE MORE. TICKETS ARE 20 DOLLARS INSTEAD OF THE USUAL TEN. THAT HIGHER PRICE IS DECIDED BY THE STATE BECAUSE THEY ARE IN CHARGE OF PLAYOFF TICKETS.

Again, both are technically correct, but Option D is much more conversational. Additionally, Option D personalizes the story for the viewer. If possible, broadcasters should visualize that they are talking to just one person, instead of an entire audience. If there is an opportunity to personalize a story (IF **YOU'RE** PLANNING ON . . .), the broadcaster should take advantage of that. One television broadcaster wrote, "You should treat every news story as if it were a one-on-one conversation at the dinner table with your viewer" (Butera, 2015, p. 11).

Short, Simple Sentences

While a high school English teacher might encourage students to write long and flowing sentences, full of descriptive language and multiple details, that is not proper broadcast writing style. Instead, broadcast sentences should be short and contain only one idea in each sentence. One suggestion is that sentences should be between 8 and 12 words (Butera, 2015).

Option A: THE HEAD TENNIS COACH AT EAST HIGH SCHOOL IS HEADING TO SOUTH HIGH. ZOEY SMITH WILL BE THE NEW HEAD COACH AT SOUTH STARTING NEXT SEASON.

Option B: ZOEY SMITH—THE HEAD TENNIS COACH OF EAST HIGH SCHOOL—WILL LEAVE THAT JOB AT THE END OF THE SEASON TO BECOME THE NEW HEAD TENNIS COACH AT SOUTH HIGH SCHOOL.

Option A has one thought in each sentence, while Option B has all of the information contained within one longer sentence. For broadcast writing, Option A would be the better choice because it has short, quick sentences that are easier for the broadcaster to read and easier for the audience to understand when listening to the story.

Option C: THERE WILL BE NEW SECURITY MEASURES AT THE STADIUM THIS WEEKEND AND EACH PERSON ATTENDING WILL HAVE TO EMPTY THEIR POCKETS AND GO THROUGH A METAL DETECTOR.

Option D: THERE WILL BE NEW SECURITY MEASURES AT THE STADIUM THIS WEEKEND. EACH PERSON ATTENDING WILL HAVE TO EMPTY THEIR POCKETS AND GO THROUGH A METAL DETECTOR.

These two examples are practically the same. However, turning Option C into two sentences makes Option D the better choice for broadcast writers. Short, simple sentences allow for easier understanding by the audience and also give the reporter a chance for a natural pause in between the two ideas when reading for broadcast.

What Is Happening Now?

Broadcasting is a medium in which the audience is expecting to know what is happening right now. The newspaper contains yesterday's news, while broadcasts focus on what is happening in real time. When starting a script, it is important to talk about the aspect of the story that is still current. That does not mean that a reporter should make up a "false present" in which broadcast writers make news that is not actually happening now seem current (Butera, 2015). This is not a natural way to talk and can make the broadcaster seem foolish. For example, if an athlete broke the world record in the long jump in the afternoon, someone would never describe it hours later as "Michael Jones jumps for a new record." Instead, the broadcaster should talk about what is currently happening: "There is a new world record holder in the long jump."

Option A: THE MARLINS LOST THEIR THIRD STRAIGHT GAME LAST NIGHT.

Option B: THE MARLINS LOOK TO SNAP THEIR THREE-GAME LOSING STREAK TONIGHT.

Option B is today's news. Instead of focusing on what happened last night, the broadcaster is updating the information to talk about what is going on today.

Talking about what is happening now is especially important for the first sentence (also known as the lead sentence) of a broadcast script. The opening line of a story is never about something that already happened; instead, the first sentence should talk about what is happening right now.

Option C: ALL THE TICKETS FOR SATURDAY'S GAME WERE SOLD EARLIER THIS WEEK.

Option D: SATURDAY'S GAME IS SOLD OUT.

Option D tells the audience what is happening right now—the game is sold out. While Option C is correct, it gives the impression that the news happened hours ago and there is nothing new to report.

Option E: THE EAGLES WERE CONSIDERING MAKING A CHANGE AT QUARTERBACK.

Option F: BRYCE SIMPSON WILL REMAIN THE STARTING QUARTERBACK FOR THE EAGLES.

Option F tells the audience what is happening right now—Simpson will be the quarterback. Option E is in the past tense.

Don't Overuse Numbers and Statistics

It is nearly impossible to talk about sports without using numbers and statistics. For many, the statistics are what make the games interesting. However, broadcasters must be careful not to overuse numbers when writing the script because those numbers can lead to confusion for the audience. For example:

IN SUPER BOWL 49, NEW ENGLAND PATRIOTS QUARTERBACK TOM BRADY WAS 37-OF-50 FOR A 74% COMPLETION PERCENTAGE. HE THREW FOUR TOUCHDOWNS AND TWO INTERCEPTIONS. HIS TOUCHDOWN PASSES WERE FOR 11 YARDS—22 YARDS—4 YARDS—AND 3 YARDS.

This script contains a great deal of information that would likely be of interest to the listener. Despite that, there are simply too many numbers for the audience to process and understand completely. Since broadcasters are writing for the ear, they need to keep the script as simple as possible, and that can be done without relying too heavily on numbers.

TOM BRADY THREW FOUR TOUCHDOWN PASSES IN THE PATRIOTS SUPER BOWL WIN.

Fans are more likely to remember that one important fact than they are all the information provided in the first example.

Use Active Voice

When writing for broadcast, journalists should use **active voice** instead of **passive voice**. In active voice, the subject acts upon the verb (I drove the car). In passive voice, the subject is the recipient of the verb's action (The car was driven by me). By flipping the order and adding the preposition *by* to the sentence, the sentence goes from active to passive (Traffis, n.d.). Broadcast writing stresses what is happening now, and active voice helps to achieve that style of writing. Active verb sentences can be created using the following format: Subject—Verb—Object (Butera, 2015).

Option A: JIMMY HENDERSON RAN THE FOOTBALL FOR 135 YARDS.

Option B: THE FOOTBALL WAS RUN FOR 135 YARDS BY JIMMY HENDERSON.

Option A would be the better choice for sports broadcasters because it is written in active voice.

Write to Video

For television broadcasters, the video is a key part of a written story. One good rule of thumb is: "If I see it, I should hear it. If I hear it, I should see it." If a reporter is talking about a big play in a baseball game, the video should be showing that play. In a package, if a reporter is specifically talking about a certain person, the video should be of that person as the reporter is talking. For example, if a reporter in a package says, "Scooter Johnson is leading the team in scoring this season," then the video should be video of Johnson as that line is being said. If a key piece of video needs to be pointed out, the reporter can write specifically to that video. If counterfeit tickets are being sold for a football game, the reporter could hold up the fake tickets and say, "These tickets are the fake ones that students need to be on the lookout for. You can tell they are fake because they don't have a hologram on them." By saying "*these* tickets," the reporter is referencing the tickets in the video. The reporter can then show a close-up of the tickets to demonstrate that they do not have a hologram on them.

Using Sound Bites

As stated in chapter 4, interviews are a key part of how a broadcaster tells the story of the day. A pregame interview with a coach can preview the big rivalry matchup, while a postgame interview with the player that scored the game-winning goal can let the fans know what the player was thinking when he lined up the shot. In a broadcast story, the reporter should not use the entire press conference or an entire interview on the air. Therefore, the reporter has to pick a good sound bite, or brief portion of the interview, that can be a part of the sportscast.

What Makes a Good Sound Bite?

Reporters give facts, while interviews should provide emotion and opinion. Broadcasters are supposed to be impartial and unbiased, and they should be the audience's trusted source to deliver information. Reporters should not be giving opinions but should instead focus on giving the facts in the story.

For example, a hockey coach says the following: "Tommy Simpson will miss the next six weeks with a knee injury. It hurts so much to lose him, but we feel good about the guys that we do have. I think we'll be able to play well and still win. Hopefully Tommy will be back soon." In this scenario, the broadcaster should say that Simpson is hurt with a knee injury. The sound bite from the coach would start with "It hurts so much . . ." and include the rest of the

Kai Schwoerer-ICC/ICC via Getty Images

Including sound bites is an important part of writing for broadcast. A SOT with the coach following a big win should be included in the script.

quote because that is the coach's opinion. While the broadcaster may feel the same as the coach, it is more effective to hear that statement from the coach than from the reporter.

Similarly, having the interview subject state facts is essentially a waste of time during the newscast because the audience wants to hear the "why" from the players and coaches and not the "what." For example, no one would want to have a sound bite from a coach in which he says, "We won 6–2 tonight. It is our third win in a row, and we are still alive for a playoff spot." That is all information that the broadcaster can (and should) be saying. Instead, the audience is ready to hear from the coach about how important this is for the team: "This is huge for us. We needed this win badly and the guys came through big time. Three wins in a row is huge. Let's hope we can keep it going."

Option A: "We have sold 15,000 tickets for tonight's game."

Option B: "It's incredible that a high school basketball game can sell this many tickets."

Option B would be the better sound bite to use during a sportscast because it gives someone's opinion instead of simply stating a fact. The reporter can give the information about the number of tickets that have been sold during the script.

The length should also be considered when selecting a sound bite for the sportscast. Ultimately, a sound bite should be between 12 and 18 seconds. Anything shorter than 12 seconds is so short that the audience would have a hard time comprehending what the story is about. By the time they recognized the person and established what they are talking about, the sound bite would be over. Anything longer than 20 seconds has the potential to drag on and become boring to the audience.

In order to pick the best sound bite, broadcasters must know everything the person in the interview said. That can be done through the logging of interviews. (See chapter 4 for more information on logging.) Once everything the interviewee has said has been recorded, the reporter has a better idea of what part of the interview he or she wants to use. For example, in October 2019, the NFL's Carolina Panthers were playing the Tampa Bay Buccaneers in London. Two days before the game, then–Panthers head coach Ron Rivera held a press conference that tackled a wide range of topics. The following is one question and answer from the press conference (Panthers.com, 2019):

Reporter: Does playing over here act as a disadvantage?

Ron Rivera: We've talked about it. I've tried to get them to understand that both teams have to come over here. So, there's no reason not to feel like you have a great experience in front of you. I told them to focus and I use a friend of mine's saying: "Be where your feet are." So, wherever you are, focus in on wherever you are 100 percent. When you're on the practice fields, when you're in the meeting room, when you're on the game field, be where you are. When you're not, be with your family, your friends and around town, enjoy that. It's a great experience, and for some of these guys, it might be a once-in-a-lifetime experience. It's been terrific, it really has. I got an opportunity to go out about town last night and just be with other folks. What a great experience. The people here in the UK, the people here in London have been very warm.

Rivera's answer took 47 seconds, which is much too long for a sound bite that would be broadcast. Therefore, the reporter will have to divide it up into various quotes and decide which parts to include. By logging the press conference answers, the reporter now knows exactly what was said by Rivera, making it much easier to select the quotes to use. Which sound bite is chosen will depend on the angle that the reporter is taking.

For Rivera's answer, if the reporter wanted to discuss the disadvantages of playing in London, he or she might use this sound bite:

I've tried to get them to understand that both teams have to come over here. So, there's no reason not to feel like you have a great experience in front of you. I told them to focus and I use a friend of mine's saying: "Be where your feet are." So, wherever you are, focus in on wherever you are 100 percent.

However, if the focus of the story was the reception the team has been getting in London, then this sound bite would be more appropriate:

It's a great experience, and for some of these guys, it might be a once-in-a-lifetime experience. It's been terrific, it really has. I got an opportunity to go out about town last night and just be with other folks. What a great experience. The people here in the UK, the people here in London have been very warm.

Even though both sound bites come from the same answer that Ron Rivera gave to a question, each is relevant only for a specific type of question. By using the interview log, the reporter is able to specifically look for sound bites that fit with the topic of the story. Without logging the interview first, the reporter may not realize that this one question provided sound bites that could be used for two different topics.

Writing Around a Sound Bite

Including a sound bite in the script allows for the audience to hear directly from someone involved in the story. As stated in chapter 4, interviews can provide additional context to what is going on at an event or game. Once the broadcasters have picked out a sound bite they want to use in the script, they need to figure out how to include it in the story. This should not be done by simply putting the sound bite anywhere. Instead, the broadcaster must write around the sound bite to make it flow naturally with the rest of the story.

The lead-in to the sound bite is the reporter's way of introducing what is about to be talked about by the interview subject. It should prepare the audience for who is about to speak and what they are about to be talking about. For example:

Reporter: HEAD COACH BILLY SIMPSON SAID THIS COULD BE A BIG WEEK FOR THE FRESHMEN ON THE TEAM.

Sound bite from Simpson: Our guys are banged up and we're going to be looking deep onto the depth chart to see who can step up with all these injuries. Some of our young guys are going to get an opportunity that they haven't had in previous weeks.

In this example, the reporter lets the audience know that Billy Simpson is about to speak and that he is specifically going to talk about the freshmen. Simpson's sound bite then discusses injuries and how they will give the younger players a chance to play. The audience was prepared to hear about this because of the lead-in.

Several lead-in techniques must also be avoided by the reporter because they are inefficient or do not add anything to the story. Perhaps most importantly, the reporter should be sure not to repeat exactly what the person is about to say in the lead-in. In broadcast, the time allotted is usually short, and every word matters tremendously. Therefore, it is a waste for both the broadcaster and the audience to simply repeat what is about to be said. What ***not*** to do:

Reporter: RUNNING BACK ANDRE JACKSON WILL MISS THE REST OF THE SEASON AFTER SUFFERING WHAT HEAD COACH BILLY SIMPSON SAID IS ONE OF THE WORST INJURIES HE'S EVER SEEN.

Sound bite from Simpson: This is one of the worst injuries I've ever seen. It looks like Andre will miss the rest of the season.

The lead-in to coach Simpson's sound bite adds nothing new to the story because Simpson is about to say the exact same thing and therefore wastes the time of the audience. This lead-in would work better:

Reporter: RUNNING BACK ANDRE JACKSON LEFT THE GAME IN THE THIRD QUARTER AND HEAD COACH BILLY SIMPSON SAID IT DOESN'T LOOK GOOD.

Sound bite from Simpson: This is one of the worst injuries I've ever seen. It looks like Andre will miss the rest of the season.

The new lead-in gives some additional information (when the injury happened) and lets the audience know that Simpson is about to talk about how bad the injury is.

Reporters should also avoid very generic lead-ins that do not provide any substance for what is about to be said. For example, the following lead-ins should ***not*** be used:

- "We caught up with head coach Billy Simpson who said this about the game . . ."
- "Head coach Billy Simpson shared his thoughts on the game . . ."
- *SOUND BITE* ". . . says head coach Billy Simpson"
- "Head coach Billy Simpson expresses his views on the game . . ."
- "Head coach Billy Simpson told us his thoughts on the game . . ."
- "We asked head coach Billy Simpson what he thought about the game . . ."

None of those lead-ins provides any information beyond "we talked to Billy Simpson." The news angle for the story is not that the reporter talked to Simpson, it is what Simpson said. Therefore, reporters should create a lead that has some substance and key information in it.

Reporter: HEAD COACH BILLY SIMPSON SAID AFTER THE GAME THAT THE FRESHMEN CAME THROUGH THIS AFTERNOON—LIFTING THE TEAM BOTH ON AND OFF THE FIELD.

Sound bite from Simpson: The whole team was down because of Andre's injury, but I knew the young guys were going to be able to come in and play well. It's a big win for us.

Writing Different Types of Scripts

While broadcast writing is the same no matter what type of story is being used, the formatting will be different based on the story type. A 20-second reader will be written much differently than a 90-second package script. The goals of both are different, but the broadcaster should still be aiming to make the story easy to understand for the audience.

Reader

A reader should be short and to the point. In television, because it is a visual medium, stories with video accompanying them can go a little longer because the journalist has the opportunity to reference the video that is being shown on the screen. Without that video, television viewers are left only looking at the anchor reading the script. Therefore, the story should be about 20 seconds and only contain the most important information.

Highlights

There is not one correct way to do highlights during a television sportscast. Watching 20 different sportscasters would likely provide 20 different styles. Since there are different ways of doing highlights, there are instead some general tips that should be followed no matter the style of the sportscaster.

The first highlight should be an **establishing shot** that shows something happening at the game that is not a play. This can be video of the coach, fans, cheerleaders, or anything that is not game action. During this time, the broadcaster can give some information about the game, the teams participating, or key players. Once the establishing shot has been finished (about five seconds), the broadcaster then begins the highlights of the game. No matter what the style of the broadcaster is, he or she must make sure that the audience can follow along easily and understand what is happening during the highlights. If the broadcaster prefers to use a bunch of pop culture references, movie lines, or funny remarks during the action, the audience must still be able to understand who is scoring, what happened during the clip being shown, and the final score. A good piece of advice for highlights is the "grandma rule": even with all the modern references to current music, actors, or jokes, broadcasters should ask themselves "would a grandma understand this and be able to follow along?"

While many broadcasters do try to use song lyrics, movie quotes, and catchphrases throughout their highlights (with varying levels of success), perhaps most importantly, sportscasters should be themselves. Broadcasters often get caught up in mimicking the style of a famous sportscaster or trying to be something they are not. If telling jokes and being silly

Jim Rogash/Getty Images

ESPN's Stuart Scott was known for his distinct and unique writing style and on-air delivery while working at ESPN.

Pro Advice

© Jeff Butera

Jeff Butera

Author of *Write Like You Talk* and news anchor in Fort Myers, Florida

Jeff Butera has literally written the book on broadcast writing. The television news anchor in Fort Myers, Florida, is the author of *Write Like You Talk: A Guide to Broadcast News Writing*, one of the most highly regarded books on the subject of broadcast writing. His book (available at http://WriteLikeYouTalk.com) is used in hundreds of newsrooms and classrooms in the United States.

While the book is aimed more at news writing, Butera admits the crossover between news and sports is more apparent than ever before. "When I was a teenager, all I wanted was to be on ESPN. I idolized the guys on *SportsCenter*." He took the advice of ESPN anchors Dan Patrick and Keith Olbermann, who suggested that if you wanted to be a sportscaster, there was just as much value interning in the news department as there was interning in the sports department. Butera said, "A huge portion of the things you cover in sports are really just 'news' stories about athletes. I just logged onto the ESPN website. They have six stories posted at the top of the page. Know how many of them are about an actual game? Zero!"

What are the key steps a broadcaster should follow when writing a broadcast script?

I have four tenets of effective broadcast script writing:

The first is "One Sentence, One Thought." Say one thing in a sentence; don't cram four things in there.

Second is "8 to 12 Words per Sentence." Your writing should be tight and succinct. Anything longer than 8 to 12 words will sound like a run-on sentence and force you to breathe at an inopportune time.

The third is "#WriteLikeYouTalk." Treat each story like you're having a conversation with the viewer. They can't respond to you, but you should imagine them listening to you. Talk to them like a normal person. Truthfully, sports folks tend to be better at this than news people.

Finally is "No Clichés." Unlike the previous tip, sports folks tend to have a much bigger problem with this than news people. Phrases like "He's on fire," "On paper, they're the team to beat," and "It all comes down to this"—clichés are bad writing. Instead of writing something someone has written a million times before, be the first person to write a phrase. Challenge yourself. Your writing will improve, and your viewers will respond.

How important is it to make the stories understandable to the audience?

Clarity is key. It doesn't matter how creative, clever, or cool you think your writing is. If I can't understand what the heck you're talking about, then what's the point? Your first priority should always be effectively, efficiently, and accurately communicating the story to your viewers. If you look at a story like a cake, consider clarity the basic ingredient. Anything you can add to that by way of creative storytelling is just icing.

How can sportscasters make the stories understandable to non–sports fans?

You always have to take into account who your audience is and make reasonable guesses about how much they know. If you work for ESPN, you know someone most likely voluntarily tuned into a sports channel, so they probably have a basic working knowledge of sports. Don't patronize them by explaining what pass interference is. But if you're doing sports on local news, yes, you should assume a big chunk of your audience probably isn't well versed in the sports world. Always just make your best estimation of how much you need to explain so they understand your story.

is that broadcaster's personality, then they can embrace that during the highlights. However, if they are more reserved, those pop culture references will feel forced and will not be as authentic to the audience.

The time given to a highlight depends on the game being reported on. If it is an important game involving local teams on a local sportscast, then the highlights could go longer than 30 seconds. However, if it is an out-of-town game, or one that does not have as much importance, then the highlights should be 30 seconds or less. Most sportscasters only have a certain amount of time to get in all their different games, so some highlights will have to be shorter than others. On a busy day, some games may get only one highlight in the sportscast.

Straight News VO

For television sports broadcasters, reading and writing for highlights will be a major part of the time on the anchor desk. However, there are also many instances in which the sportscaster will be reading a news VO. For example, a game preview, a coach being hired or fired, and a player injury update would all be stories that could be a part of a local sports broadcaster's show.

In these instances, three to four sentences should be able to clearly summarize the story. Start with the most important information first and then provide the accompanying details afterwards. As broadcaster Jeff Butera writes in his book *Write Like You Talk*, VOs should be "story sandwiches" that grab the audience's attention at the beginning with a compelling lead (the top piece of bread), provide the important details (the meat), and then wrap the story up with an important fact or detail (the bottom piece of bread) (Butera, 2015).

In television, the video should match up with what the story is about. If the piece is updating the status of an injured player, the video should show that player in a game or sitting on the bench while out with the injury. The lead sentence will let the audience know what is coming (IT LOOKS LIKE THE WILDCATS WILL BE WITHOUT THEIR STAR CENTER FOR A LITTLE BIT LONGER . . .). When the video begins to play, the important details will be conveyed by the anchor (HEAD COACH TIMMY SMITH SAYING TODAY THAT GREG JONES WILL MISS THE NEXT THREE GAMES. . . . JONES HAS BEEN BATTLING A SORE ANKLE FOR THE LAST TWO WEEKS AND HASN'T PLAYED SINCE NOVEMBER . . .). The script should then wrap up with an important detail (THE WILDCATS CERTAINLY MISS HIM—THE TEAM HAS LOST FOUR IN A ROW WITHOUT JONES IN THE LINEUP . . .).

VO/SOT

A VO/SOT is similar to the news VO described previously. However, instead of simply wrapping up the story with a fact or statistic, the broadcaster must remember to write in the sound bite properly. Including the sound bite, VO/SOTs are usually about 45 seconds. In the example above, the script can remain unchanged, except for a line at the end introducing what the sound bite is going to be about (COACH SMITH IS STILL LOOKING FOR THAT ONE GUY TO STEP UP TO FILL THE VOID . . .). Then the SOT would play on the screen.

Packages

A package is a self-contained story including both sound bites and reporter tracks. Most news packages should be about one minute and 30 seconds long. There are many different ways to get to that time recommendation, but an easy way for beginners is as follows:

Reporter track (12 seconds)
Sound bite (15 seconds)
Reporter track (12 seconds)
Sound bite (15 seconds)
Reporter track (12 seconds)
Sound bite (15 seconds)
Reporter track (12 seconds)
Total: 1:32

Those times do not have to be exact, but if they are close, then it should be a good way to get to approximately a minute and 30 seconds.

A good rule is that no reporter track or sound bite should be longer than 17 seconds.

When formatting a package, the reporter should divide up the story into three parts: a beginning, middle, and end.

1. *Beginning:*

   Why should the audience care?

   Grab the viewers' attention, so put the best video first.

2. *Middle:*

   What does the audience need to know?

   Reporters give us facts, while sound bites and interviews give us emotion and opinion.

   Include key facts and statistics to support the information in the sound bites.

3. *End:*

   Provide a summary and conclusion.

   Include any final relevant facts and statistics.

   Bring it back full circle to how the story started.

One possible way to write a broadcast package script is by using the **diamond structure.** In this style, the storytelling order is similar to the shape of a diamond (figure 5.1). The story starts with a very narrow focus. The beginning would introduce the main character and the topic of the story. After establishing the focus of the story (the top of the diamond), the content of the piece widens out to give more information, facts, and statistics that will help discuss the topic in greater detail (the middle of the diamond). After providing the context and details needed to explain *why* the story is important, the reporter can return to the narrow focus that was the start of the piece (the bottom of the diamond). This further showcases the main character and reminds the audience about why they should care about this story.

For example, if using the diamond structure when doing a story about a player scoring her 100th career goal, the reporter would start the story by talking about the player. The reporter could talk about her start in the game, how she ended up on the team, and perhaps a personal anecdote (top of the diamond). The middle of the story would give more of a statistical angle to the piece, providing facts and numbers that would help to further emphasize how important a milestone this was. The middle would also be an ideal time to place a sound bite from another person involved in the story, such as the head coach, that can provide some additional context to how impressive this accomplishment was (middle of the diamond). The story would then circle back to the athlete with a sound bite from her that gives her opinion about how important this record is to her or how she plans to celebrate the accomplishment (bottom of the diamond).

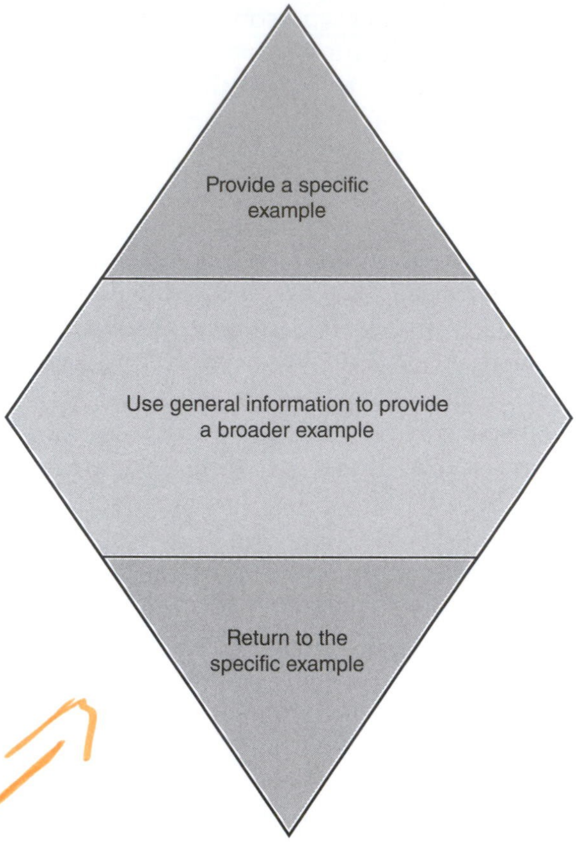

FIGURE 5.1 The diamond structure of storytelling.

After the Writing is Done

Whether it is a 15-second reader or a 90-second package, the reporter should always read the script out loud when finished. A broadcast story will eventually have to be read out loud, so it is a good idea to practice it before having to do it "for real." Reading it out loud will help the reporter recognize if some sentences are too wordy, too long, or do not make sense when being read aloud.

Script Formatting

Each broadcaster will have his or her own style of writing and may approach stories completely differently. However, for uniformity, each broadcaster at a newsroom should stay consistent with formatting of the script. This will make it easier for other members of the newsroom (such as the producer and the director) to know what is happening during a script.

It should be noted that each newsroom may have its own respective rules, so some of these suggestions may change based on where the broadcaster works. However, for the most part, these formatting tips are universal.

- Anchor and reporter scripts are written in ALL CAPITAL LETTERS, while sound bites should be in sentence case. For example:

Reporter: HEAD COACH TIM JOHNSON IS EXCITED ABOUT THE OPPORTUNITY.

Johnson: This is a school that I have been following for a long time. I think it is the best job in North Carolina and I'm ready to get started.

- Commas should not be used in broadcast script writing. Instead, reporters should use ellipses (. . .) or dashes (—) to indicate a pause.

JOHNSON—THE NEW HEAD COACH—IS ORIGINALLY FROM NEW YORK CITY...

- Spell out print symbols. Since the reporter is saying the word out loud in broadcast, the word should be written so. Instead of $25, the broadcaster would write 25 DOLLARS. Instead of 88%, the broadcaster would write 88 PERCENT.
- Write out the words for numbers one through ten, and hundred, thousand, and million. Instead of 3,000,000, the broadcaster would write THREE MILLION. A broadcaster does not want to try to be counting zeros and commas when quickly saying a number out loud.
- Complex numbers should be rounded off when possible. Instead of saying that Walter Payton rushed for 16,726 career yards, a broadcaster would say WALTER PAYTON RUSHED FOR OVER 16 THOUSAND YARDS IN HIS CAREER.
- Write out the date instead of using numbers. Instead of July 4th, a broadcaster would write JULY FOURTH. For years before 1999, a hyphen should be used to break up the year in the natural spot. THE LAKE PLACID OLYMPICS TOOK PLACE IN 19-80.
- For acronyms, the reporter should use hyphens, not periods, to separate the letters (U-C-L-A and N-B-A, for example). In some cases, there are two options: N-C-A-A or N-C- double-A would both be acceptable. However, do not use hyphens if the anchor is supposed to read the abbreviation as a word. For example, NASCAR stands for the National Association for Stock Car Auto Racing, but no one calls it N-A-S-C-A-R. Instead, it is simply read like it is spelled.
- Difficult-to-pronounce names should be spelled out phonetically. Former NFL quarterback Jake Delhomme's name is not pronounced the way it looks. The broadcaster would enter it into the script as DA-LOAM. Spelling out names phonetically can also help with names that are spelled the same but have a variety of pronunciations. For example, Stephen Jackson and Stephen Curry both played in the NBA, but their first names are not pronounced the same. Therefore, when entering each's name into the script, the reporter would likely use the phonetic spelling: STEVEN JACKSON or STEFFEN CURRY.
- The director of the show needs to know when the broadcaster wants the video and sound bites to start. The reporter can signify this by typing <TAKE VO> into the script when the video should start

and <TAKE SOT> when the sound bite should begin.

- The director also must know when to put identifiers into the broadcast. Commonly known as **lower thirds**, these graphics take up a small portion of the bottom of the screen and list the name of the person and their occupation. In sports, these lower thirds can also have a final score in them. While every newsroom may be different, a common command would be to enter <L3>Name/Occupation into the script.

Examples of Scripts

In order to demonstrate how one story can be told in a variety of different broadcast types, the following fictional event will be used: A local college basketball team has hired a new head basketball coach. This is the type of story that local sports broadcasters would cover quite frequently. High schools and colleges often hire new coaches for sports on campus, while professional teams may make announcements regarding the hiring of both head coaches and new assistants. Therefore, this is a good example of a story that could be told in a variety of different ways. As is usually the case, the university has sent out a press release with many of the details of the hire, while the sound bites from the press conference can be used during the broadcast.

The following quotes are from the press conference:

> **Head coach Scott Jackson:** This job is a dream come true. As a New Yorker, I'm very familiar with the Vikings program and I think it is a real sleeping giant. I think we've got a good foundation here and I am excited about what the future holds. I can't wait to get started. It's funny, when this job came open, I told my wife "pack your bags, honey, because I'm applying for that job and I'm going to get it." I just knew it was the right fit for me and that I was the right fit for here. I think we're going to win a lot of games. I know that it's been a few years since this team went to the postseason, but that doesn't matter to me. I told the players when I met with them this morning that everyone here has a clean slate. I don't care what has happened before, I only care about what will

PRESS RELEASE

FOR IMMEDIATE RELEASE

March 15, 2019

Scott Jackson is Vikings New Head Basketball Coach

Albany, NY—Scott Jackson was introduced as the 15th head coach in New York State University men's basketball history on Tuesday. Jackson will look to rebuild a Vikings program that hasn't made the postseason in the last six seasons. After spending the last eight seasons as an assistant coach at Wilmington (NC) College, this will be Jackson's first head coaching opportunity.

During Jackson's time at Wilmington, the Waves went a combined 167–85 and made a national postseason tournament in all but his first season there. Last season, Jackson was a finalist for the "Assistant Coach of the Year" award.

An Albany, NY, native, Jackson returns to his home state to lead the Vikings program. As a collegiate player, he was a star guard at Northern New York College for four seasons, playing in 121 career games. He finished with 1,104 points, and at the time of his graduation, he was the school's all-time three-point leader with 196.

Jackson replaced Bob Quarterman, who stepped down as the NYSU head coach after three seasons.

###

happen starting now. Play hard and make good decisions. That's all I ask. Do that and we'll win a lot.

Athletic director Thomas Zip: It was clear immediately that Scott was our guy. He has had a lot of success as an assistant coach and everyone we talked to about him just couldn't say enough great things. We know he's ready to be a head coach, and his attitude is going to get a lot of people excited. We're already excited, and we're showing that by the financial commitment to Scott, too. It is a five-year deal, and he's now the highest paid head coach in the history of the program. But, and I feel very strongly about this, I think it's going to be money well spent.

Basketball player D'Andre Vick: The whole team met with him this morning, and all the guys walked out of that meeting fired up and ready to play. He seems like an awesome dude, and you could totally tell how excited he was to be there and meet with us. You know, it's been a rough couple of years, so I think we need that energy in the locker room. It's great he's here. Can't wait to get started.

A video from the press conference shows Zip introducing Jackson, Jackson putting on a NYSU hat, Jackson's family, the crowd, and various additional shots of Jackson interacting with people in the crowd and with some of his players. The television station in Wilmington has also sent video of Jackson coaching Wilmington College from last season.

Reader

<Anchor on camera>

NEW YORK STATE UNIVERSITY HAS A NEW HEAD MEN'S BASKETBALL COACH TONIGHT . . .

SCOTT JACKSON REPLACES BOB QUARTERMAN WHO STEPPED DOWN AT THE END OF LAST SEASON . . .

JACKSON WAS MOST RECENTLY AN ASSISTANT COACH AT WILMINGTON COLLEGE IN NORTH CAROLINA . . .

Script Explanation: In this reader, the broadcaster only gives the main details of the story—that a new coach was hired, who it is, and where he is from. For both television and radio, readers should not be overly long. For television, because the anchor has chosen not to use video, the script is shorter than usual because it is not visually interesting to have the anchor talking on camera for a long period of time.

VO

<Anchor on camera>

NEW YORK STATE UNIVERSITY HAS A NEW HEAD MEN'S BASKETBALL COACH TONIGHT . . .

<Take VO>

SCOTT JACKSON WAS INTRODUCED TO THE MEDIA AND FANS THIS AFTERNOON AT A PRESS CONFERENCE ON CAMPUS . . .

JACKSON COMES TO THE VIKINGS FROM WILMINGTON COLLEGE IN NORTH CAROLINA . . .

LAST SEASON JACKSON WAS A FINALIST FOR THE ASSISTANT COACH OF THE YEAR AWARD . . .

IT IS A FIVE YEAR DEAL FOR JACKSON—AND IT MAKES HIM THE HIGHEST PAID COACH IN SCHOOL HISTORY . . .

JACKSON REPLACES BOB QUARTERMAN WHO RESIGNED AT THE END OF LAST SEASON . . .

Script Explanation: The first sentence from the reader remains the same, but the addition of video allows for a more detailed script in which the reporter can write directly to the video. Since the video is showing the press conference, the reporter should specifically reference the press conference in the first sentence after the video starts. The VO also allows for some additional information to be in the story that was not in the reader, i.e., both the Assistant Coach of the Year nomination and the contract details (which were in a sound bite from the athletic director and not in the press release).

VO/SOT or Radio Actuality

<Anchor>

NEW YORK STATE UNIVERSITY HAS A NEW HEAD MEN'S BASKETBALL COACH TONIGHT . . .

<Take VO>

SCOTT JACKSON WAS INTRODUCED TO THE MEDIA AND FANS THIS AFTERNOON AT A PRESS CONFERENCE ON CAMPUS . . .

JACKSON COMES TO THE VIKINGS FROM WILMINGTON COLLEGE IN NORTH CAROLINA . . .

LAST SEASON JACKSON WAS A FINALIST FOR THE ASSISTANT COACH OF THE YEAR AWARD . . .

JACKSON WILL HAVE A TOUGH JOB AHEAD OF HIM—THIS TEAM HASN'T MADE THE POSTSEASON IN SIX SEASONS . . .

BUT ACCORDING TO THE COACH—IT'S A NEW DAY AND FRESH START FOR EVERYONE INVOLVED . . .

<Take SOT>

<L3: Scott Jackson / New NYSU head basketball coach>

I know that it's been a few years since this team went to the postseason, but that doesn't matter to me. I told the players when I met with them this morning that everyone here has a clean slate. I don't care what has happened before, I only care about what will happen starting now. Play hard and make good decisions. That's all I ask. Do that and we'll win a lot.

Script Explanation: The script for the VO/SOT is very similar to the script for the VO. However, now the broadcaster has to consider the SOT that is going to be chosen. Due to this new addition to the story, some of the information written about will change, and there now needs to be a proper lead-in to the sound bite. Even though the reporter interviewed three different people, the big story of the day is the new coach, so the best decision is to pick a sound bite from him and not the others. The fans at home are (hopefully) excited about the new coach and likely do not know much about him, so the broadcaster should put the coach front and center with the sound bite. The information about the contract is important but does not necessarily fit in this new version. Therefore, the broadcaster may wish to write a separate VO for after this story to include details about the contract.

For the radio actuality, the script can be the same. The differences would be that there would not be any direct references to video because the radio story would not have the video to accompany it.

Package (television) or Wrap (radio)

<Anchor>

THE SEARCH FOR A NEW MEN'S HEAD BASKETBALL COACH AT NEW YORK STATE UNIVERSITY IS OVER . . .

SCOTT JACKSON TAKES OVER A PROGRAM THAT HAS SEEN SOME TOUGH YEARS LATELY . . .

REPORTER CAROLINE DINESH HAS THE STORY . . .

<Take Package/Wrap>

Nat sound pop from Zip: It's my pleasure to introduce Scott Jackson (applause)

IT IS ALL SMILES AT THE PRESS CONFERENCE FOR NEW VIKINGS HEAD MENS BASKETBALL COACH SCOTT JACKSON . . .

BUT BEHIND THOSE SMILES IS THE REALITY THAT THIS TEAM HASN'T MADE THE POSTSEASON IN SIX SEASONS . . .

<L3: Scott Jackson / NYSU men's head basketball coach>

Scott Jackson: That doesn't matter to me. I told the players when I met with them this morning that everyone here has a clean slate. I don't care what has happened before, I only care about what will happen starting now. Play hard and make good decisions. That's all I ask. Do that and we'll win a lot.

JACKSON COMES FROM WILMINGTON COLLEGE IN NORTH CAROLINA—WHERE HE WAS A FINALIST FOR THE NATIONAL ASSISTANT COACH OF THE YEAR AWARD . . .

JACKSON'S NEW SCHOOL CERTAINLY BELIEVES IN HIM . . .

THEY HAVE GIVEN HIM A FIVE YEAR DEAL—AND IT IS THE HIGHEST SALARY FOR A BASKETBALL COACH IN SCHOOL HISTORY . . .

HIS NEW PLAYERS ARE ALREADY ON BOARD . . .

<L3: D'Andre Vick / NYSU senior guard>

D'Andre Vick: The whole team met with him this morning, and all the guys walked out of that meeting fired up and ready to play. He seems like an awesome dude, and you could totally tell how excited he was to be there and meet with us. You know, it's been a rough couple of years, so I think we need that energy in the locker room.

JACKSON SAYS THIS OPPORTUNITY IS ABOUT MORE THAN JUST THE MONEY—IT'S HOME.

THE NEW YORK NATIVE SAID HE KNEW INSTANTLY THAT THIS WAS THE JOB FOR HIM . . .

Scott Jackson: It's funny, when this job came open, I told my wife "pack your bags, honey, because I'm applying for that job and I'm going to get it." I just knew it was the right fit for me and that I was the right fit for here. I think we're going to win a lot of games.

JACKSON'S TEAMS IN WILMINGTON MADE THE POSTSEASON THE LAST SEVEN YEARS—A TREND HE'S HOPING TO CONTINUE WITH THE VIKINGS . . .

REPORTING FROM N-Y-S-U—I'M CAROLINE DINESH . . .

Script Explanation: For a package, it is important to pick one particular angle that can go throughout the entire story. For this piece, the reporter has decided that the team's struggles in the past is that common theme. It is mentioned in the first reporter track, Jackson's first sound bite, Vick's sound bite, Jackson's second sound bite, and the final reporter track.

Using the diamond structure discussed previously in this chapter, the story started with introducing Coach Jackson (the top of the diamond). This allows the audience to "meet" the new coach immediately, which is the correct angle to take since he is the big story of the day. The reporter should not make the audience wait to get their first look at the coach. The middle of the story (and diamond) contains the background information and supporting details on the hire. These details include his coaching past, more information about the contract, his current players' reactions, and the fact that Jackson is a New York native. Finally, the story circles back to Jackson at the end (the bottom of the diamond) by using another sound bite from him that talks a bit about his family and excitement about the job. Remembering that not all of the audience are die-hard sports fans, the reporter chose to include the anecdote about telling his wife he was going to get the job. This allows the audience to get to know the coach outside of his basketball ability. Finally, the story wraps up with a statistic about Jackson's postseason success at his previous job before the reporter sign-off (see figure 5.2).

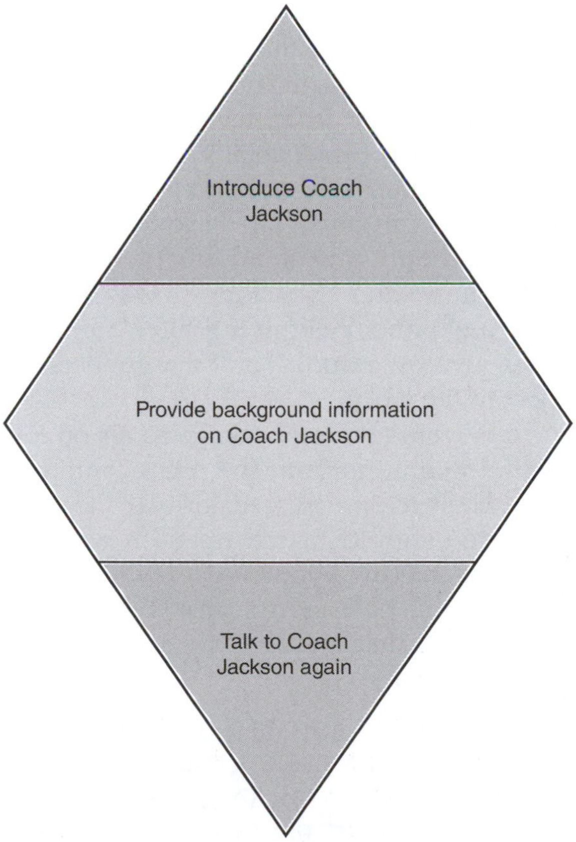

FIGURE 5.2 The diamond structure in action during this story on Coach Jackson.

Even with the extended script time compared to a VO or VO/SOT, there are still elements to the press release and interviews that did not make the final script. There is no mention of the previous coach, Jackson's college playing career, or that everyone the school talked to about Jackson really liked him. The reporter will often have to make difficult decisions about what to include and what not to include. This is also true for interviews. Just because a reporter interviews someone does not mean that the person has to be in the story. In this case, the athletics director was one of the options for the sound bites, but the reporter preferred the sound bite from the player. In order to decide what to include, the reporter should focus on the main angle of the story and then decide what information and interviews will further that chosen direction. The interview with the athletics director was not a complete waste of time, however, as it was in that interview that it was revealed that Jackson would be the highest paid coach in school history and that it was a five-year deal. Both of those facts were mentioned by the reporter.

The reporter giving the contract information also worked well with the idea that "reporters give facts and interviews give emotion/opinion." The contract details and the fact that Jackson is a native New Yorker are facts that the reporter can say, while Jackson giving his opinion ("I only care about what will happen starting now" and "I just knew it was the right fit for me") and Vick giving his ("He seems like an awesome dude") add a more personal aspect to the story.

If this were a video package to air on television, the images from the press conference would likely make up the majority of the video. The video should match up with what the reporter is talking about. Next is the reporter track from the package, followed by a possible piece of video that could be edited into the story during those lines.

IT IS ALL SMILES AT THE PRESS CONFERENCE FOR NEW VIKINGS HEAD MENS BASKETBALL COACH SCOTT JACKSON . . . (VIDEO: Jackson at the press conference smiling and people in the audience smiling. Everyone should look happy in this video since that is what the reporter is referencing.)

BUT BEHIND THOSE SMILES IS THE REALITY THAT THIS TEAM HASN'T MADE THE POSTSEASON IN SIX SEASONS . . . (VIDEO: Players in attendance, wide shot of room that press conference is in, other assorted items in the room that represent NYSU. There is not an exact way to show what the reporter is talking about here, so keeping the video as generic as possible, while still giving the audience a sense of being at the press conference, is important.)

JACKSON COMES FROM WILMINGTON COLLEGE IN NORTH CAROLINA—WHERE HE WAS A FINALIST FOR THE NATIONAL ASSISTANT COACH OF THE YEAR AWARD . . . (VIDEO: Jackson coaching at Wilmington College, provided by the Wilmington television station.)

JACKSON'S NEW SCHOOL CERTAINLY BELIEVES IN HIM . . . (VIDEO: NYSU administration at the press conference. The reporter is talking about the people who hired him, so the video should be of those people.)

THEY HAVE GIVEN HIM A FIVE-YEAR DEAL—AND IT IS THE HIGHEST SALARY FOR A BASKETBALL COACH IN SCHOOL HISTORY . . . (VIDEO: Jackson at the press conference and some additional shots of the administration.)

HIS NEW PLAYERS ARE ALREADY ON BOARD . . . (VIDEO: Players at the press conference talking to each other and talking to Jackson. This is appropriate here because the reporter is discussing the impact of the new coach on the players.)

JACKSON SAYS THIS OPPORTUNITY IS ABOUT MORE THAN JUST THE MONEY—IT'S HOME.

THE NEW YORK NATIVE SAID HE KNEW INSTANTLY THAT THIS WAS THE JOB FOR HIM . . . (VIDEO: Jackson's wife and family in the audience, with close-up shots of Jackson looking happy at the press conference. The sound bite is about to discuss how Jackson told his wife he was going to get the job, so showing video of her here will help to establish that she is about to become an element in the story. Using video of Jackson looking happy will demonstrate how this is an exciting career move for him.)

JACKSON'S TEAMS IN WILMINGTON MADE THE POSTSEASON THE LAST SEVEN YEARS (VIDEO: Jackson coaching in Wilmington)

—A TREND HE'S HOPING TO CONTINUE WITH THE VIKINGS . . . (VIDEO: Jackson at press conference)

REPORTING FROM N-Y-S-U—I'M CAROLINE DINESH . . . (VIDEO: medium shot of press conference room. This generic video is a good way to close out the story because it matches up with a simple sign off from the reporter.)

CHAPTER WRAP-UP

HK*PROPEL* ACTIVITIES

HK*Propel* includes ten fact sheets from various games and events. Using that information, students will write broadcast scripts.

SUMMARY

When writing a story that will be broadcast, reporters first must decide what type of story should be used to deliver the information. Will the story have a sound bite? How much information needs to be included to help determine the length of the piece? Once those decisions are made, the broadcast style of writing should be used to help tell the story on television or on the radio. Using short, easy-to-understand sentences that are written to be heard and not read, the broadcaster gives the latest information (What is happening now?) so that the audience knows what is current. Sound bites play a key role in a broadcast story, allowing the audience to hear directly from the affected party. Therefore, journalists should find the bites that can best add the person's opinion or emotion to the story in approximately 15 to 20 seconds. The goal of a good broadcast story is to tell the latest information in a clear and succinct manner that is suitable for listening.

Phil Cole/Getty Images

CHAPTER 6

Writing for the Web and Mobile Devices

CHAPTER OBJECTIVES

The job duties of a sports broadcaster have evolved in recent years, with increased importance placed on writing stories that would appear on websites and mobile devices. While the content is similar to what would appear on the radio or television, the writing style is completely different from the traditional broadcast format. With that in mind, this chapter focuses on writing for the web and mobile devices, including the following:

- Formatting and writing a story for a website
- Recognizing the increased importance of websites in broadcast media
- Understanding the differences between writing for a newspaper, writing for computers, and writing for content on mobile devices
- Utilizing the inverted pyramid style of writing

For decades, broadcasters only had to worry about their television or radio broadcasts. However, the growing importance of webpages to a media outlet's coverage (and the financial bottom line) has forced broadcasters to make web writing a part of their reporting. Instead of simply writing a broadcast story, reporters now have to also create content that can appear on the media outlet's website.

Everything that was discussed in the "Writing for Broadcast" lessons in chapter 5 should essentially be forgotten when it comes to writing for the web. The rules of broadcast do not apply to the website story (Butera, 2015), so a simple "copy and paste" from the broadcast script to the website story will not do. Instead, broadcasters have to rewrite the story, often from scratch, in order to make it acceptable for those reading on the web.

Increased Importance of the Web

The early days of television and radio websites demonstrated that broadcast stations did not place much emphasis on the online product. WECT, the NBC affiliate in Wilmington, North Carolina, used to simply copy and paste their broadcast scripts onto the website (WECT, 2000). Stories were not rewritten into a newspaper-style story format, so the website read more as a copy of the newscast and less as a complement to the broadcast coverage.

While the vast majority of Americans who get news from local television stations do still get it from television sets (76 percent), the number also getting it from the stations' websites or social media is slowly increasing (22 percent) (Pew Research Center, 2019). Almost 90 percent of Americans (89 percent) get at least some local news digitally, with 41 percent saying they do so often (Pew Research Center, 2019). Additionally, popular social media websites such as Facebook drive a large amount of traffic to television news websites (Knight Foundation, 2019), making them a destination for people looking to get the latest news updates. With increased readership online, and a new potential for revenue, broadcast media outlets have put added emphasis on their websites.

Writing the Story

When writing a sports story for a website, it is difficult to know the exact direction to take because not everyone has the same game experience. Some of the audience are die-hard fans who watch every play and know all the statistics, while others are casual fans who perhaps, at best, know the names of a handful of players. Journalists need to keep both of those fan types in mind when writing because focusing on just one will likely alienate the other. If it is too technical, the casual fan will be uninterested; if there is no more detail beyond just the basic stats, die-hard fans will be wanting more. Therefore, it is important to stick to the facts of the game for the casual fan while providing quotes from interviews with the players to please the die-hard fan looking for more information.

The Inverted Pyramid

Whether writing for the web or for a newspaper, the traditional **inverted pyramid** has been a staple of media writing for decades. The inverted pyramid style states that the most important information in the story should be placed in the first paragraph, with supporting details and additional information following it. In simple terms, a story using the inverted pyramid style should go from "most important" to "least important." With some people spending just a few seconds on an article, the inverted pyramid style might be more important than ever. If one assumes that a reader skims the first paragraph (or just the first sentence) of a story, then that beginning becomes the best chance to deliver the most important information. There is no reason to "bury the lead" and save the important part of the story for the middle paragraphs. The audience should be able to stop reading a story at any point and still be able to understand what it is about.

In the world of sports, games obviously happen in chronological order: Team A scores first, and then Team B scores three times in a row to win 3–1. However, that's not necessarily how the story should be formatted. In this case, if the story were written in the order things happened, a reader would learn about Team A scoring in the first sentence and perhaps stop reading the story, not realizing that Team B actually won the game.

> *Chronological order:* In Saturday's game against the Bombers, Greg McGuire scored the first goal of the game for the Cardinals to give them a 1–0 lead. After McGuire's

goal, Josh Butler, Oliver Slater, and Cameron Forsyth each scored to put the Bombers in the lead 3–1. The final score was 3–1.

Inverted pyramid: The Bombers scored three unanswered goals on Saturday to beat the Cardinals 3–1.

Figure 6.1 shows the general format that all written journalism pieces should follow on the web. The story should start with the most important information (the lead), then provide supporting details (additional information), and then wrap the story up (background information).

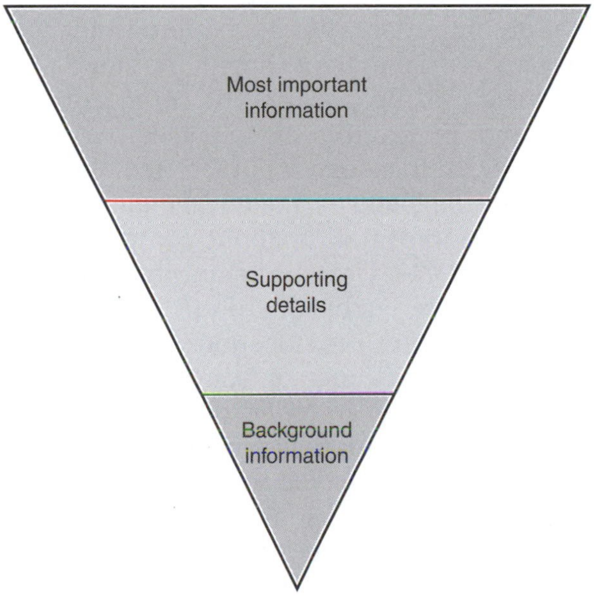

FIGURE 6.1 The inverted pyramid.

The Lead

The first part of the inverted pyramid is the **lead**. This should be the most important information in a story. If a reporter were asked to summarize his or her story in one or two sentences, those two sentences should be the lead paragraph. A website visitor should be able to read just the lead paragraph and be able to know what the story is about.

The lead should contain answers to the basic questions: who, what, where, when, and, frequently, why and how (Wiggins, Smith, & Sisk, 2017). If a reader has the answers to all of those questions, he or she will be able to fully understand what is happening in the story. The author should not start writing the web story until he or she can answer all of these questions.

To determine what should be included in the lead, one should decide what is the most important part of the story. A Major League Baseball team plays 162 regular season games each season, so the fact that the Boston Red Sox won a Tuesday night regular season game in the middle of July is not the only fact that should be included in the lead. Therefore, using the inverted pyramid, the author must determine what else is newsworthy enough to be in the lead. Did a particular player have a noteworthy game? Does the final score impact a winning or losing streak? Is the team now in first place? The author should use the "so what?" question when writing a lead. A simple lead of "The Red Sox beat the Orioles 8–5 Tuesday night" is not overly impressive in a full 162-game season. Yes, the Red Sox won, but so what? What makes this win noteworthy? However, a lead that contains "J.D. Martinez hit his 200th career home run, Xander Bogaerts added a solo shot, and Mitch Moreland capped the power surge with a three-run drive that carried the Red Sox past the Baltimore Orioles 8–5 Tuesday night" (Associated Press, 2019, para. 1) adds to the information beyond just the final score. It describes the fact that the Red Sox hit three home runs, including a career highlight home run for J.D. Martinez. While the final score remains just another in the season-long list for the Red Sox, this lead demonstrates what about this game is particularly newsworthy.

Perhaps the best way to determine the answer to the "so what?" question is to use the who, what, where, when, why, and how questions. When taken all together, the answers to those questions should tell the audience why the story is important. In the 2019 baseball off-season, the New York Yankees signed free agent pitcher Gerrit Cole. After gathering the important information, the author of the article is able to answer the six questions needed to determine the "so what?"

Who? The New York Yankees.

What? Signed free agent pitcher Gerrit Cole.

Where? New York.

When? Tuesday night.

Why? Cole was considered the best free agent available in the off-season.

How? The Yankees gave Cole a nine-year, $324 million contract. It is the largest contract for a pitcher in baseball history.

While players sign with new teams in the off-season each year, Cole's signing is different for a variety of reasons. Therefore, answering the "so what?" question can be done by addressing the fact that this is a record contract and that Cole was the top free agent available. With those facts listed, the Associated Press lead was written as follows:

The New York Yankees landed the biggest prize of the free agent market, adding Gerrit Cole to their rotation with a record $324 million, nine-year contract Tuesday night, a person familiar with the deal told The Associated Press (Blum, 2019, para. 1).

The lead contains the important information that readers need to know: The Yankees signed the best player available for a large amount of money. Therefore, if all readers want to know are the important details, they are getting that information in just the lead paragraph.

Throughout this chapter, an example of an injured football running back will be used to demonstrate how to write a web story. In this type of story, the journalist must let the reader know all the important details of the injury in the lead by answering the basic questions listed above. While die-hard fans may want to know all the details of the injury, a casual fan might only read the lead and get all the information that he or she needs. With that in mind, this would be an acceptable lead:

Stingrays running back John Sucich is unlikely to play against the Anteaters on Thursday in Miami because of a broken left hand. Sucich injured the hand during practice on Monday.

The major elements are all there: Stingrays running back John Sucich (WHO) is unlikely to play against the Anteaters (WHAT) on Thursday (WHEN) because of a broken left hand (WHY). Sucich injured the hand during practice (WHERE and HOW) on Monday (WHEN). This lead paragraph is just two sentences and a total of 30 words. All the important information is there and the reader can leave the story after just reading the lead and know the major news aspects of the story.

Supporting Details

Following the lead paragraph, the next part of the story should provide supporting details for the piece. The middle paragraphs will add additional details in the order of their importance, keeping in mind that the reader will rarely make it through an entire story online. Therefore, this section offers additional details that are important, but not so important that they are crucial to the telling of the story.

These middle paragraphs often contain facts and quotes from the impacted parties in the story. In the story about Gerrit Cole signing with the Yankees, the middle paragraphs contained information about comparatively large contracts, Cole's pitching history, and the Yankees recent history (Blum, 2019). While this information provides more information about the significance of Cole's signing, it is not vital to know in order to understand the story. Keeping with the theme of the inverted pyramid, the information contained in the middle paragraphs should still go from most important to least important.

In the example of the injured running back, the subsequent paragraphs can contain information about the Stingrays, the impact of Sucich's injury, and how the injury was suffered. Therefore, the next paragraphs may be as follows:

Sucich, the Stingrays leading rusher with 1,423 yards, was injured during a drill at Monday's practice. Sucich was tackled by linebacker Dave Shaw and fell awkwardly on his hand. He immediately walked to the sideline and did not return to practice.

The Stingrays are hoping to have Sucich ready for the playoffs and are leaning towards having him miss multiple games to rest. Miami (10-3) can clinch a playoff berth with a victory over the Anteaters on Thursday.

The paragraphs after the lead provide additional information about the story. Readers now know how good Sucich is (the team's leading rusher), how he was injured (fell awkwardly after being tackled), what the team is going to do (possibly rest him), and how the team is doing (can clinch a playoff berth with a win). None of that information was important enough to include in the lead paragraph, so adding it into the story later is a good way to provide the additional details.

Using Quotes

As with broadcast writing, quotes provide firsthand accounts of the action straight from the people involved in the story. These quotes should provide a sense of why the story is important and what the people impacted by the story are feeling (Wiggins et al., 2017). When reading a story online, the audience will often already know the result of the game being written about, so it is the quotations that provide information that the reader may not know. For example, it is likely that most visitors to ESPN's website the day after the Super Bowl already know the result. Instead, they are looking for more information, often provided in quotes from players and coaches, beyond just the final score. Therefore, quotes should offer new information or an expert opinion or be entertaining (Gisondi, 2018).

There are three ways to use quotes within a web story: indirect quotes, partial quotes, and direct quotes. **Indirect quotes**, also known as **paraphrasing**, are when an author does not use the exact words from the interview subject and instead summarizes a general idea stated by the subject. For example, suppose a baseball coach said, "We're going to start Burrow at third base this week." That direct quote is not something a reporter would want to use in his or her story because it is a simple fact he or she has reported. As stated in previous chapters, reporters give facts while others provide emotion or opinion. Therefore, an indirect or paraphrased quote might appear in the story as follows: Coach Stephens says they will start Burrow at third base this week. A paraphrased quote does not need any special punctuation or formatting to appear in the story.

Direct quotes are used when a reporter wants to include in his or her story exactly what a subject has said. Such quotes are used to allow the person in the story to tell his or her own version of the events and provide additional context to the basic facts written about by the reporter. When using direct quotes, authors should be sure to use the exact quote, word for word, of what the person being interviewed said. Additionally, using direct quotes helps reduce the risk of misreporting someone's ideas.

To format a direct quote, quotation marks should be placed around the words said by the subject. Periods and commas should go within those quotation marks, with the attribution part of the same sentence. Therefore, formatting of a quote should be: "The quote from the person is here," the person said.

Direct quote examples:

"Oklahoma is the best team we've played all year," Smith said.

"I think I'm going to be good to go for the Alabama game," Thurmond said. "It's the biggest game of the year and I wouldn't miss it."

Partial quotes are when just a small portion of what someone says is used in a web story. It is essentially a combination of an indirect quote and a direct quote. The words used by the subject are put in quotation marks, while the rest of the quote is paraphrased by the writer. These are used to put added importance or emphasis on a key word or phrase. For example, if a head coach said, "Michael Jordan was unstoppable tonight," a reporter may use a partial quote and write, Coach Dogg described Jordan as "unstoppable." By using only the word "unstoppable" from the quote, it demonstrates that the coach felt a specific way about Jordan.

When quotes are used, the author must also attribute who is saying the information. **Attribution** is when a journalist states who said the quote or who provided the information to the reporter. It is important for a reporter to attribute information because it informs the reader who provided the information in the story.

When formatting a quote using attribution, the correct sequence is as follows: direct quote, then the speaker, and then the verb. A good way to remember this is by using the inverted pyramid again. What is said is the most important, followed by who said it, and then that it was said (Stovall, 2012). For example: "We think Burrow starting gives us the best chance to win," Stephens said. For quotes that are multiple sentences, put the attribution at the end of the first sentence. For example: "We think Burrow starting gives us the best chance to win," Stephens said. "He's a good hitter and he matches up nicely against their starting pitcher."

Continuing the injured running back example, since Sucich is a key member of the team, one can safely assume that the head coach will have a comment on this injury. A quote from the coach will add additional substance to the story because he can provide details beyond the facts. Once again, reporters give facts and interview; subjects provide opinion and emotion. Therefore, a quote from the coach should provide his opinion on the injury, how he will handle it, and what he says will be the impact on the team.

> *Stingrays head coach Justin Schrager said Tuesday that he won't pressure Sucich to return from injury before he's fully ready. "Until he's 100 percent, until he's ready to go, we're not going to get him out there before he's ready to play," Schrager said. "We've been able to show we can win in a lot of ways. We're not finished just because our top guy is hurt."*

The paragraph starts with a paraphrased quote from Schrager about how he will handle Sucich's injury. It then transitions to the direct quote from Schrager. Including both the indirect and direct quote allowed the writer to get additional information directly from the coach into the story.

Wrapping Up the Story

To finish the story, the author can present some general background information or the least important information that has not yet been relayed. When writing the final parts of the story, reporters should ask themselves, "If this wasn't in the story, would my audience still know all the important details?" If the answer to that question is "no," then the author should move some of those facts to an earlier portion of the story. However, if the answer is "yes," then that information is acceptable for the conclusion to the story.

A final paragraph to wrap up the story of the injured running back might discuss who will play in Sucich's absence. While this is important information, Sucich is one of the best players on the team, so the majority of the article will focus on him. However, who will have the bulk of the carries with him injured is worth mentioning. Therefore, the story can conclude with the following:

> *Schrager said the Stingrays will likely feature Xavier Zezima at running back on Thursday. Zezima has rushed for 304 yards and two touchdowns this season as Sucich's primary backup.*

Since Zezima is the primary backup, one could have probably assumed that he would get most of the carries with the injured starter out. Had the Stingrays made a trade or signed a well-known veteran to play in Sucich's place, that information likely would have been moved to

G Fiume/Getty Images

Peter Gammons' move from *The Boston Globe* to ESPN was one of the first major moments in broadcast stations embracing the possibilities within websites.

the lead or immediately after the lead because it was a surprising development. Instead, since Zezima is the projected player to benefit most from Sucich's injury, and that would have been the expected news for the reader, this news can be relegated to the final paragraph.

The completed story now has a lead, supporting details in the middle paragraphs, an indirect and direct quote from the head coach, and information on who will play in the injured player's place. The finished story reads as follows:

Stingrays running back John Sucich is unlikely to play against the Anteaters on Thursday in Miami because of a broken left hand. Sucich injured the hand during practice on Monday.

Sucich, the Stingrays leading rusher with 1,423 yards, was injured during a drill at Monday's practice. Sucich was tackled by linebacker Dave Shaw and fell awkwardly on his hand. He immediately walked to the sideline and did not return to practice.

The Stingrays are hoping to have Sucich ready for the playoffs and are leaning towards having him miss multiple games to rest. Miami (10-3) can clinch a playoff berth with a victory over the Anteaters on Thursday.

Stingrays head coach Justin Schrager said Tuesday that he won't pressure Sucich to return from injury before he's fully ready. "Until he's 100 percent, until he's ready to

MAJOR MOMENTS

Peter Gammons to ESPN

In 1969, Peter Gammons joined the staff of *The Boston Globe* as a reporter covering the Boston Red Sox. While at *The Globe*, Gammons created a weekly Sunday baseball notes column in which he gathered news from teams all over the country and reported them in a one-page story. Gammons' column is considered a "staple of baseball news coverage." One baseball reporter wrote, "Gammons' column each week was a revelation, a fountain of information and entertainment, and something I immediately would try to emulate in the nascent days of my own checkered career" (Pascarelli, 2009, para. 17). Another remembered how, as a college student in Nashville, TN, he would spend two dollars a week on the Sunday *Globe* just to read the column (Olney, 2009).

Known as a newspaper reporting legend, it was perhaps surprising when, in 1989, Gammons announced he was leaving *The Boston Globe* for a job at broadcasting giant ESPN. Gammons said he was "purely a print guy" when ESPN hired him (Miller & Shales, 2011, p. 154), but the network wanted someone who could contribute both on-air and online. While his appearances on *Baseball Tonight* and *SportsCenter* opened him up to an entirely new audience from those who read him in the newspaper, it was the online content that helped usher in the increased importance of online written content for broadcast stations. Gammons wrote an Insider column for ESPN.com that was similar to his Sunday Notes column that had previously appeared in the newspaper. The website was just a few years old when Gammons began writing for it (ESPN Press Room, n.d.), and he helped add to the credibility of the site. Former ESPN.com columnist Bill Simmons said that ESPN hiring Gammons was "the biggest moment in the history of sports coverage on the Internet" because it made it "ok to read sports on the web" (Demers, 2017, para. 109; Testa, 2009, para. 12). "That was the all-time game changer because, once they got him, and once people like my dad had to figure out how to get to ESPN.com, that changed everything," Simmons said (Demers, 2017, para. 110).

In 2004, Gammons was named the J.G. Taylor Spink Award winner during the 2005 Baseball Hall of Fame induction ceremony (ESPN.com, 2009). The award is given to a journalist "for meritorious contributions to baseball writing" (Baseballhall.org, n.d., para. 2), and Gammons was given the award for his time at both *The Boston Globe* and at ESPN. Citing a desire for a less demanding schedule, Gammons announced he was leaving ESPN in 2009. Following his departure, ESPN's executive vice president said that Gammons' "contributions to ESPN will never be forgotten" (ESPN.com, 2009, para. 6).

go, we're not going to get him out there before he's ready to play," Schrager said. "We've been able to show we can win in a lot of ways. We're not finished just because our top guy is hurt."

Schrager said the Stingrays will likely feature Xavier Zezima at running back on Thursday. Zezima has rushed for 304 yards and two touchdowns this season as Sucich's primary backup.

Writing for Online

Please note that this chapter is not titled "writing for print media." Broadcasters will likely not have to write stories for the newspaper, but instead will focus on writing stories that will appear on their media product's website or mobile app. While several of the principles of writing are the same for newspaper and online, research has demonstrated that people reading online approach articles differently than they do reading articles in a newspaper.

Newspaper readers spend about 15 minutes a day reading the newspaper (The Missouri Group, 2020). However, when it comes to online reading, most people say they only scan articles that appear on websites, while a minority say they are reading word for word (Moran, 2020). Perhaps even more surprising, 17 percent of page views last for less than four seconds (BoardStudios.com, 2017). That means that readers are more likely to spend less than four seconds on an online article than they are to read the entire story. Therefore, reporters should write their online stories as if they only have 30 seconds of their readers' attention for each story. They should ask themselves the following: What important information must a reporter share before the audience clicks away to the next story (The Missouri Group, 2020)?

In addition to websites on desktop and laptop computers, news consumers are getting their information increasingly from mobile devices. More than half (51 percent) of Americans who get news online do so primarily through a mobile device instead of through a computer (27 percent) (Pew Research Center, 2019). For sports fans, the ESPN app had almost 24 million unique users in just one month alone in 2019, an increase of 16 percent from the previous year (Adler, 2019).

Writing Style for the Web and Mobile Devices

With this increased emphasis on reading articles on websites and mobile applications, reporters need to adjust how they write some online content. With readers likely to spend just a few seconds on an article, a reporter has to make those seconds count. Therefore, specific to web writing, journalists need to format stories slightly differently than if the article were appearing in a newspaper.

- *Write concisely:* Since the majority of readers will never make it to the end of a web story, the text should be as concise as possible. Readers are always a click away from leaving a website or story, so reporters should avoid unnecessary words and get directly to the point of the article.
- *Have a strong introduction:* Keeping the inverted pyramid style in mind, the reporter should have a very strong introduction. This gets to the important part of the story quickly and gives the reporter the opportunity to interest the reader immediately. Also, if the reader does decide to click or swipe away from the story before the conclusion, it allows the reporter to still have gotten the point of the piece across in the beginning paragraph.
- *Use short paragraphs:* No one wants to read large blocks of text on their phone or on a computer screen. Breaking up the story into smaller, easier-to-read paragraphs may motivate the reader to move along farther in the story.
- *Add multimedia elements:* To complement the content in the story, add photos to help break up the piece and make it easier to scan on a phone. Visuals also help break up any large blocks of text that appear.
- *Use links:* **Links** to previous stories related to the current news will allow the reader to feel as if they are in control of where the story goes next. If they want previous information, they can click on one of the selected links that will take them to stories that will provide supplemental details. For example, on the story with the injured running back, a link to Sucich's bio page on the Stingrays website could be included (Brooks et al., 2020; Gisondi, 2018; Hu, 2011; The Missouri Group, 2020).

Pro Advice

Courtesy of Michaela Baker Taylor.

Manie Robinson

Sports media instructor at the University of South Carolina

By the time Manie Robinson started his career at *The Greenville News*, the organization's website was already an important part of the newsroom operation. However, that emphasis increased even more just a few years later. "It was well known that we were now a digital organization that happens to print a newspaper," Robinson recalled. "Now you had to think about timing, immediacy, breaking news, and it had to be on the web first."

Robinson became one of the newspaper's primary reporters dedicated to Clemson University football, including covering two of the team's national championship seasons. His reporting earned him two South Carolina Sportswriter of the Year awards from the National Sports Media Association and more than a dozen South Carolina Press Association awards. In 2020, Robinson joined the faculty at the University of South Carolina as the journalism school's first dedicated sports media instructor. Some of his early lessons for his new students involved something with which he was very familiar: teaching them how to write stories for websites.

How is writing for the web different than writing for a newspaper or broadcast?

You want to think about "what can pull the reader in." When you're already into this medium, there are so many things that can pull things away. Even on your own website, there are ads that you want people to pay attention to. What are the elements of the story? What are the characters of the story that can keep them in the story? Characters became more important than the blow-by-blow.

Are there other elements beyond just the article's body that are different on the web?

We had to think about what other elements can you add beyond just the written word to keep people in that story. You have to be more cautious about how you write headlines. Don't give away too much in the headline, but don't make it a clickbait headline. There's a balance there, so we put a lot of time into that. Also, SEO (***Search Engine Optimization***) became part of the strategy not just in the headline for searchability but also how often are you using key words in the body of the story and how high they are. It's a lot more strategy to writing online, as opposed to method.

Ultimately, no matter if it is online or not, isn't writing still writing?

Oh, absolutely. The craft of it doesn't change. What makes it effective and what makes it clear doesn't change. Just because you are on that platform doesn't mean you do away with AP style, because I think those things matter. You still want to be professional. You assume it is more laid back, but when you're still writing for a publication, you still need to adhere to those guidelines. Character, flow, clarity, pace—all those principles apply.

Associated Press Style

The Associated Press Stylebook is a must-have for all journalists writing articles for the web. The **Associated Press** (AP) is a United States news agency that provides news articles and information to media outlets throughout the world. In 2018, the Associated Press estimated that more than half of the world's population saw news from the AP every day (Associated Press, n.d.a). More than 15,000 news outlets and businesses worldwide use the Associated Press to provide news updates to their audience (Associated Press, n.d.b).

In order to have writing uniformity for their journalists throughout the world, the AP created a style guide for journalists to follow. Initially designed just for their own writers, AP style has been adopted at newsrooms and businesses throughout the world and millions of copies of the rules have been sold worldwide (Stokes, 2005). *The Associated Press Stylebook* has more than 5,000 entries that provide a consistent style on capitalization, spelling, numerals, and word usage. It is updated each year with a new edition, so writers should consult the most recent edition of the book for the latest style developments or visit the Associated Press website.

In addition to providing information that is useful for all types of stories, a specific section of the book is dedicated to sports. In this section, common sporting events, terms, and grammar usage are discussed. Following are a few highlights from the sports section of *The Associated Press Stylebook* (Froke, Bratton, Garcia, McMillan, & Schawrtz, 2019):

- *Abbreviations*—It is not necessary to spell out commonly known leagues on first reference. For example, MLB can be used instead of Major League Baseball.
- *Numerals*—Use figures when preceding a unit of measure or points, as well as for team records or game numbers. For example, first place; 10th inning; Game 6; the team's record is 6-5-1; Johnson was 6 for 20 for 215 yards and two touchdowns.
- *Pregame, preseason, postseason, postgame*—One word, no hyphen.
- *School names*—Use abbreviations on first reference only for well-known schools with unique acronyms (such as UCLA). Abbreviations are acceptable on second reference when the shorthand is commonly used and clear.
- *Scores*—Use figures exclusively, placing a hyphen between the totals of the winning and losing teams. For example, The Gamecocks beat the Tigers 42-3.
- *Titles*—Job descriptions and informal titles are lowercase. For example, coach Bill Love; running back Carl Sanderson.

The guide also provides proper spelling and formatting for sport-specific terms. For example, in boxing, *knockout* is a noun and adjective, while *knock out* is a verb.

Rewriting a Story from Broadcast to Print

In chapter 5, a fictitious press release and press conference interviews were used as a guide to demonstrate how to write various broadcast stories. In that scenario, Scott Jackson was hired as the head men's basketball coach at New York State University. Jackson's hiring was covered by the media with a broadcast reader, a VO, a VO/SOT, and a package.

This chapter examines how to write a web story. In order to demonstrate the differences between a broadcast script and a web story script, a new press release will be used. For this scenario, it is three years into the future and, unfortunately for Jackson, his time with the Vikings was not successful. The school has removed him as head coach following another disappointing season. What follows is the press release announcing that move.

The only information available with which to write the story is what is contained within the press release and additional research done by the reporter. That research can contain information from the press release when Jackson was hired (see chapter 5). Additionally, an online search would reveal that star player D'Andre Vick broke his leg before Jackson's first season and never suited up for his new coach due to the injury.

The school did not make the athletic director or any players available for an interview, and repeated phone calls to Jackson went unanswered. For a broadcaster, that means that there is no interview to use as a SOT or an actuality, so a reader or VO must be used. Therefore, for the broadcast script, there is limited information beyond just the details.

Broadcast Script

<Anchor>

AFTER MUCH SPECULATION—N-Y-S-U MADE IT OFFICIAL TODAY . . .

THEY HAVE FIRED HEAD MEN'S BASKETBALL COACH SCOTT JACKSON . . .

<Take VO>

PRESS RELEASE

FOR IMMEDIATE RELEASE

April 8, 2022

Athletics Announces Change in Leadership of Men's Basketball Program

Albany, NY New York State University athletics director Thomas Zip today informed Scott Jackson of his decision to relieve the third-year coach of his duties and begin immediately a national search for a new leader for the Vikings' men's basketball program.

"I would like to thank Coach Jackson for his hard work and contributions to our program," Zip said. "I have tremendous respect for Coach Jackson. He has represented NYSU with dignity and class and we wish him the very best."

"I met with our student-athletes and staff today to inform them of my decision and to make clear New York State University's commitment to a championship-caliber men's basketball program."

Jackson was named the fifteenth head coach in NYSU history. In three seasons, he posted a 29-63 overall record. Jackson's first two NYSU teams finished with matching 10-20 records. His third season saw a drop to a 9-23 record.

The NYSU men's basketball program has participated in 10 national postseason tournaments in school history, including a trip to the semifinals in 2012.

"We have a passionate fan base and remain committed to achieving excellence at the highest level," said Zip. "We are now engaged in a national search to identify the next head coach of NYSU men's basketball."

Jackson's record at New York State University:

Year 1: 10-20 overall, 5-13 in Empire Conference

Year 2: 10-20 overall, 5-13 in Empire Conference

Year 3: 9-23 overall, 3-13 in Empire Conference

Total: 29-63 overall, 13-39 in Empire Conference

###

DESPITE ARRIVING WITH A LOT OF PROMISE—JACKSON HAD THREE LOSING SEASONS FOR THE VIKINGS . . .

HE FINISHED WITH 29 WINS AND 63 LOSSES . . .

THIS PAST SEASON THE TEAM WON JUST THREE GAMES IN THE EMPIRE CONFERENCE . . .

ATHLETIC DIRECTOR THOMAS ZIP SAID THE SEARCH FOR A NEW HEAD COACH WILL BEGIN IMMEDIATELY . . .

Script Explanation: There is little room for additional information in the 30-second VO that a broadcaster would write. The record is included, and the information that the search for a new coach is already beginning. With no on-camera quotes from any of the impacted parties, the story cannot be expanded to a VO/SOT. However, the web story would have room for additional information beyond just the story and can use some of the quotes from the press release.

Web Story

New York State University fired men's basketball coach Scott Jackson on Sunday after three seasons in which the Vikings failed to win more than 10 games in each season.

NYSU made the move two days after finishing a 9-23 season with a blowout loss in the Empire Conference tournament. That left Jackson 29-63 overall and 13-39 in the Empire Conference.

"I would like to thank Coach Jackson for his hard work and contributions to our program," NYSU athletic director Thomas Zip said in a statement. "I have tremendous respect for Coach Jackson. He has represented NYSU with dignity and class and we wish him the very best."

The former Wilmington (NC) College assistant was hired by NYSU to replace Bob Quarterman. Jackson's time with the Vikings got off to a difficult start when the team's leading scorer, D'Andre Vick, broke his leg before Jackson's first season. Vick left the team shortly after the injury.

Jackson, a New York native, was a finalist for the Assistant Coach of the Year award while at Wilmington College. A search for his replacement at NYSU has already begun, according to Zip.

The NYSU men's basketball program has participated in 10 national postseason tournaments in school history, including a trip to the semifinals in 2012.

Story Explanation: The story follows the traditional inverted pyramid format. The lead sentence contains the important information a reader would need to know if that were the only part that was read: New York State University fired men's basketball coach Scott Jackson on Sunday after 3 seasons in which the Vikings failed to win more than 10 games in each season.

Who? Scott Jackson

What? Was fired as men's basketball coach

Where? New York State University

When? Sunday

Why? The team failed to win more than 10 games in each of his three seasons.

The how was not answered in the lead, but the reader can safely assume that the firing was done in a traditional and noncontroversial way. If the firing had occurred in a way that was rare or unique, that would have been placed in the lead. For example, the University of Southern California fired football coach Lane Kiffin in 2013. Instead of informing him of the decision on campus in his office, the athletic director called Kiffin off the team bus and fired him at the airport at 3 a.m. following a loss. The unusual story of circumstances surrounding that firing made the lead portion of the story when reported (Witz, 2013).

The middle paragraphs of the story provide supporting details that give the reader more information about the decision to fire Jackson, answering questions that the reader might have.

Why was Jackson fired? NYSU made the move two days after finishing a 9-23 season with a blowout loss in the Empire Conference tournament. That left Jackson 29-63 overall and 13-39 in the Empire Conference.

What does the administration have to say about this? "I would like to thank Coach Jackson for his hard work and contributions to our program," NYSU athletic director Thomas Zip said in a statement. "I have tremendous respect for Coach Jackson. He has represented NYSU with dignity and class and we wish him the very best."

Are there reasons why Jackson wasn't successful? Jackson's time with the Vikings got off to a difficult start when the team's leading scorer, D'Andre Vick, broke his leg before Jackson's first season. Vick left the team shortly after the injury.

What's Jackson's history? The former Wilmington (NC) College assistant was hired by NYSU to replace Bob Quarterman. Jackson, a New York native, was a finalist for the Assistant Coach of the Year award while at Wilmington College.

When will a new coach be hired? A search for his replacement at NYSU has already begun, according to Zip.

The story then concludes with some basic information about the NYSU program that is not necessary to the story but provides some background details about the program: The NYSU men's basketball program has participated in 10 national postseason tournaments in school history, including a trip to the semifinals in 2012.

CHAPTER WRAP-UP

HK*PROPEL* ACTIVITIES

HK*Propel* includes examples of broadcast scripts. Using the lessons in this chapter, students can create their own web stories based on the scripts provided in HK*Propel*.

SUMMARY

The focus of broadcasters' jobs used to be just the time they were on television or on the radio. The importance of websites has added a new responsibility to their workday. Now a website story will almost always have to accompany any story that makes it to the broadcast airways. However, these website stories should not be just a simple "copy and paste" from the broadcast script. The skills used in web writing are very different from those used in broadcast writing. Using the inverted pyramid as a guide, reporters should put the most important information in the very beginning of the story, followed by additional details that will add to the story. When appropriate, quotes from the impacted parties should be added to the story in order to add their emotion and opinions to the facts presented by the reporter. A successful web story will present information in a way that enables the reader to leave the story at any point and still understand what it is about.

Phil Cole/Getty Images

CHAPTER 7

Shooting Games and Events

CHAPTER OBJECTIVES

When it comes to television broadcasting, a sportscaster is sometimes only as good as the video that accompanies his or her stories. While the broadcaster can describe the game, it is the highlights from the games or events that makes viewers feel like they were there. Therefore, this chapter focuses on shooting video of games and events, including the following:

- Knowing what to shoot and where to stand during a variety of games
- Knowing what to shoot during an event
- Identifying the different types of shots needed when using a video camera
- Understanding the shooting locations during a live sports production

One of the job perks of being a sports broadcaster is the opportunity to spend a large portion of the working day at sporting events. However, for many local television sports broadcasters, especially in their first jobs, going to the games involves a lot more than just sitting in the press box and casually watching the action. In fact, it is quite the opposite. Local television sports broadcasters will often have to shoot the video that will air on the evening newscast. That means carrying around heavy cameras, making sure they are in the right spot to catch the best angles, and thinking about what shots are necessary for that evening's highlights. Additionally, television sports broadcasters may have to attend press conferences, practices, and other sports-related events that will require them to shoot video for that evening's sportscast.

Types of Shooting

A television sports broadcaster will likely shoot two different types of stories: games and events. If he or she is shooting games, those will likely be turned into **highlights** on the evening sportscast. Highlights are essentially a VO that contains some of the most important plays from a game back-to-back with the sportscaster describing the action. For example, if a hockey team wins 2–0, the three highlights would likely be the two goals and a save from the goalkeeper who had the shutout. An event would be something that would be eventually turned into a VO, VO/SOT, or package during the sportscast. Events could include practices, press conferences, or appearances by athletes at a location in which they are not playing (such as a charity event). Highlights and events are not only two distinctly different types of stories, they also require two different mindsets when shooting video.

Shooting Highlights

When most people think of television sports broadcasters, they probably think of highlights. If there is a big game, it is the local sports broadcaster who is there, shooting the action and showcasing the best plays during that evening's sportscast. The purpose of highlights is to give a brief recap of game, showcasing the key plays that led to the final result.

Format of Highlights

How to edit highlights will be covered in chapter 8, but it is important to understand the format of broadcaster-shot highlights before heading out to a game. When broadcasters show highlights of televised games, they are limited to what networks such as ESPN show during the game. For example, if a broadcaster wants to show an assistant coach, he or she has to hope that ESPN will put that coach on camera during the broadcast. When shooting their own highlights, broadcasters can choose exactly what will be shot to get on television.

Despite that freedom, most highlights will follow a very specific format. For the average game, a set of highlights will last about 30 seconds. That time will include a brief cutaway at the beginning, followed by approximately three plays from the game, with some additional cutaways in between each play. More important contests, such as a rivalry, championship, or a game with a historic storyline, can go longer than 30 seconds and would include several additional highlights beyond the traditional three. No matter how long the broadcaster plans to go with the highlights, he or she knows exactly what they must shoot when they are at each game: several cutaways and successful plays from both teams. Knowing what to be looking for in advance makes the process of shooting sports much easier.

Cutaways

A key part of shooting sports is getting multiple cutaways. Therefore, it is important to understand what this entails. A **cutaway** is a shot of something that is not part of the main action. For example, at a high school football game, the primary action is the actual game. However, many things are happening at the game that a broadcaster can get a cutaway of beyond just the play on the field. At most games there are cheerleaders, mascots, fans, coaches, and the band. When one really considers what makes high school football special, it is often the combination of those things that creates the atmosphere, not just the game itself. Therefore, broadcasters should shoot all of those things to make the audience feel like they are at the game and work to include some elements throughout the highlights. When a player scores a touchdown, a shot of the cheerleaders celebrating will add to the moment on video. When the quarterback throws an interception, a cutaway of an angry coach immediately afterward will help set the tone. Often the right cutaways can help increase the effectiveness of a highlight video.

Individual Sports

There is not a universal answer to the question, "How do you shoot a game?" Instead, the answer varies, sometimes dramatically, based

Scott Varley/MediaNews Group/Torrance Daily Breeze via Getty Images

Sports broadcasters want to make sure they are standing in the right spot to get the best angles of the biggest plays.

on the sport being shot; for example, shooting football is very different from shooting a tennis match. This section will break down how to shoot various types of sports.

Football

In many cities throughout the United States, the most popular sport is not in the professional ranks or in college—instead, it is high school football. Local sports broadcasters, especially those working in **markets** that have small towns, will shoot many high school football games throughout their careers. Some cities have entire Friday night football shows that air after the late newscast that show only high school football. Regardless, the skills for broadcasting high school games are the same as for professional and college games.

Most sportscasters will stand just a few steps outside the sidelines when shooting football for highlights. This gives a good vantage point and allows the sportscaster to get close to the action. Once a videographer gets to a game, he or she should pick one sideline and stay there for the entire time he or she is there. Otherwise, the **180-degree rule** would be violated. The videographer should pretend there is an imaginary line that runs down the middle of the field from goalpost to goalpost, and once he or she arrives at a game, all the shots should be on the same side of that line. Violating that rule can disorient the viewer because if a running back is running left to right in one shot and the photographer goes to the other side of the field for the next play, the same player would be running right to left in the next shot. That's why televised college and professional games always have the cameras set up on just one side of the field.

Once the game has started, a sportscaster should stand so that the action is coming at him or her. That means standing about 15 yards ahead of the line of scrimmage. This is ideal because it allows for good shots of running backs going up the field or following a pass through the air. The only exception for standing on the sidelines would be if a team is getting close to the end zone. For any plays inside the five-yard line, videographers should stand just outside the back of the end zone to get the players running right at them for the touchdown. While some sports involve picking a spot and standing in one place the entire time, football is the complete opposite. In fact, if done properly, shooting football games can be a strenuous cardio workout. Every time the team moves up or down the field, the videographer needs to move with them after the play. Twenty-yard run? As soon as the play is whistled dead, the videographer is also running 20 yards down the field, while carrying the camera, so that he or she can be in the right spot ahead of the new line of scrimmage before the next play begins. This happens after every play throughout the game. Due to this constant movement, both during and after plays, the camera should not be on a **tripod** while shooting football.

While having the action come at the broadcaster should work the vast majority of the time, there will be the occasional play in which the action is going the other way and there is nothing that can be done. For example, a football player is running down the sidelines toward the broadcaster and fumbles. The other team picks it up and runs 70 yards the other way—away from the photographer—for a touchdown. In that case, the audience will be looking at players' backs as they run in the other direction. While these are usually big plays, they also happen fairly rarely, so having the action go the other way is a chance the videographer has to take.

When framing up a shot in football, zoom in on the line of scrimmage before the ball is snapped, so that just the quarterback and a few offensive linemen are in the frame. After the ball is snapped, there should be a very minor zoom to show the quarterback from head to toe, and that framing should be kept for the majority of the play if the action is in the middle of the field. If the action is coming directly at the videographer, he or she should zoom out so that more of the player can be seen as he gets closer. If the action is going toward the other sideline, then zooming in would be effective because it will make the player appear less far away. If the ball is passed, follow the ball in the air into the receiver's arms, although that can be difficult for beginning videographers.

Basketball

Unlike football, shooting basketball involves finding one spot and staying there for the entire game (figure 7.1). When shooting for highlights, the ideal spot to be is on one of the end lines (also called the baseline), relatively close to one of the corners. This allows for a clear view of the basket and the players on the court. For a high school game there are bleachers on both sides of the gym but likely not any seats along the end line, so the videographer can stand in his or her spot while shooting a game. However, for a college or professional game, the arenas are usually much bigger than a high school gym, so there will likely be people sitting in seats along the end line. Therefore, the videographer must sit down while shooting so that he or she is not blocking the fans in the seats. In both cases, the camera should be either on the videographer's shoulder or held in front of him or her, depending on the size of the camera.

The simple rule for basketball is "follow the ball." When the ball is passed from player to player, the videographer should keep the camera trained on whomever has the ball. When a shot is taken, the videographer should follow the ball through the air and, hopefully, through the net. After the point is scored, the camera should pan back to the player who made the basket for a few seconds. When reading highlights, bringing the camera focus back to the player who scored the basket allows the broadcaster to give some more information about that player. If LeBron James scores, the broadcaster can give James' statistics while running back on defense. After shooting the player running back on defense, the broadcaster can get a very quick shot of the scoreboard. This shot will not make the air in all likelihood, but it will help the broadcaster when editing the highlights. Having that scoreboard shot will

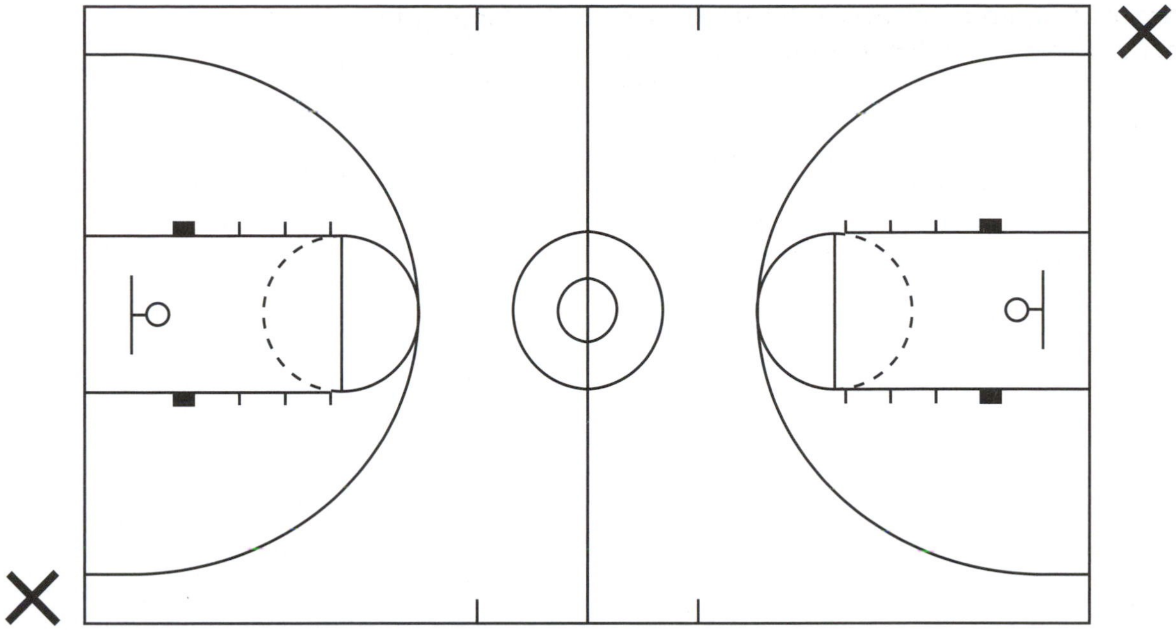

FIGURE 7.1 The camera location for shooting basketball could be in the corner of the court.

allow the broadcaster to say what the score was after that point. For example, WNBA player A'ja Wilson has the ball close to the basket. The videographer follows Wilson as she shoots and follows the ball in the air as it goes in. After seeing the ball go in, the videographer pans back to Wilson to show her running back on defense. After a few seconds, the camera should be pointed up at the scoreboard just to get a quick shot of the score. Then it is back to shooting the action and waiting for the next basket to repeat the process.

For basketball, the framing should depend on where the player is standing in relation to where the videographer is stationed. If a player is standing at the top of the key, then a full body shot, from head to toe, would be appropriate. As the player gets closer to the camera, such as standing right underneath the hoop, the videographer can zoom in to show the player from the waist up. Basketball can be difficult because the ball moves quickly, so the journalist working the camera needs to be ready to zoom in and out quickly while also paying close attention to the focus.

Baseball or Softball

Where to stand during a baseball or softball game often depends on the configuration of the stadium. For larger stadiums, standing behind home plate in an elevated location (such as the concourse area right behind the seating) is probably the "easiest" place to shoot a game. Easiest is in quotes because baseball and softball are very difficult sports to shoot. Unlike basketball, where the ball ultimately has to go through the hoop for a point, the small, fast-moving baseball or softball can go to a variety of locations on the field with a successful result. Therefore, the videographer has to wait to see where the ball is heading before following it. From the spot behind home plate, with the camera on the tripod, the videographer should start the shot with the pitcher in the top of the frame and the batter in the bottom of the frame. As the ball is put into play, the videographer can slowly zoom in on the ball as it moves throughout the field. If the game situation calls for it, once the ball has settled, the camera should be panned back toward home plate to get video of the runners scoring.

However, for high school games without a lot of seating, there is not usually a variety of options for where to stand. Often, the best location is standing on the field next to the dugout. In some cases a high school head coach will let the videographer stand right in the dugout to shoot, but it is wise to ask before setting up there. From this angle, the videographer should hold the camera (no tripod) and zoom in on the batter. As the batter hits the ball, the camera should follow the ball until the play is over, only moving away to get a runner touching home plate. It should be stated that it is incredibly difficult to shoot baseball from this angle because the ball moves so quickly. Figure 7.2 is a diagram of potential camera positions.

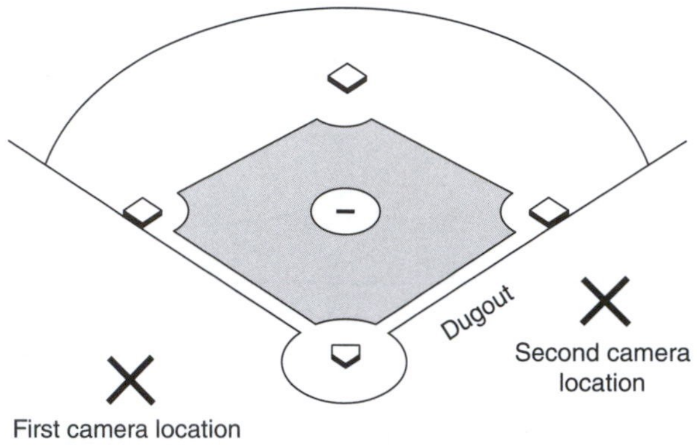

FIGURE 7.2 Baseball shooting camera positions.

Volleyball

Volleyball is a unique sport in that there are two different locations from which to shoot it and either one can be successful. Videographers can stand either in the bleachers to get footage from a high angle or shoot at court level on one end line on one side to get the action in front of them. While each can result in quality highlights, they require very different methods of shooting.

For the videographer who decides to stand in the bleachers, he or she should find a spot that is slightly off to one side of the net. There is often a referee that is perched up high for volleyball, and that referee can be in the way of shots if the videographer stands directly behind him or her. Standing to one side can help eliminate that potential problem. The videographer should be high enough in the bleachers, with the camera on the tripod, so that about six players can be seen on the screen at one time and the ball can be followed smoothly back and forth without needing to use jarringly fast movements from the camera (figure 7.3).

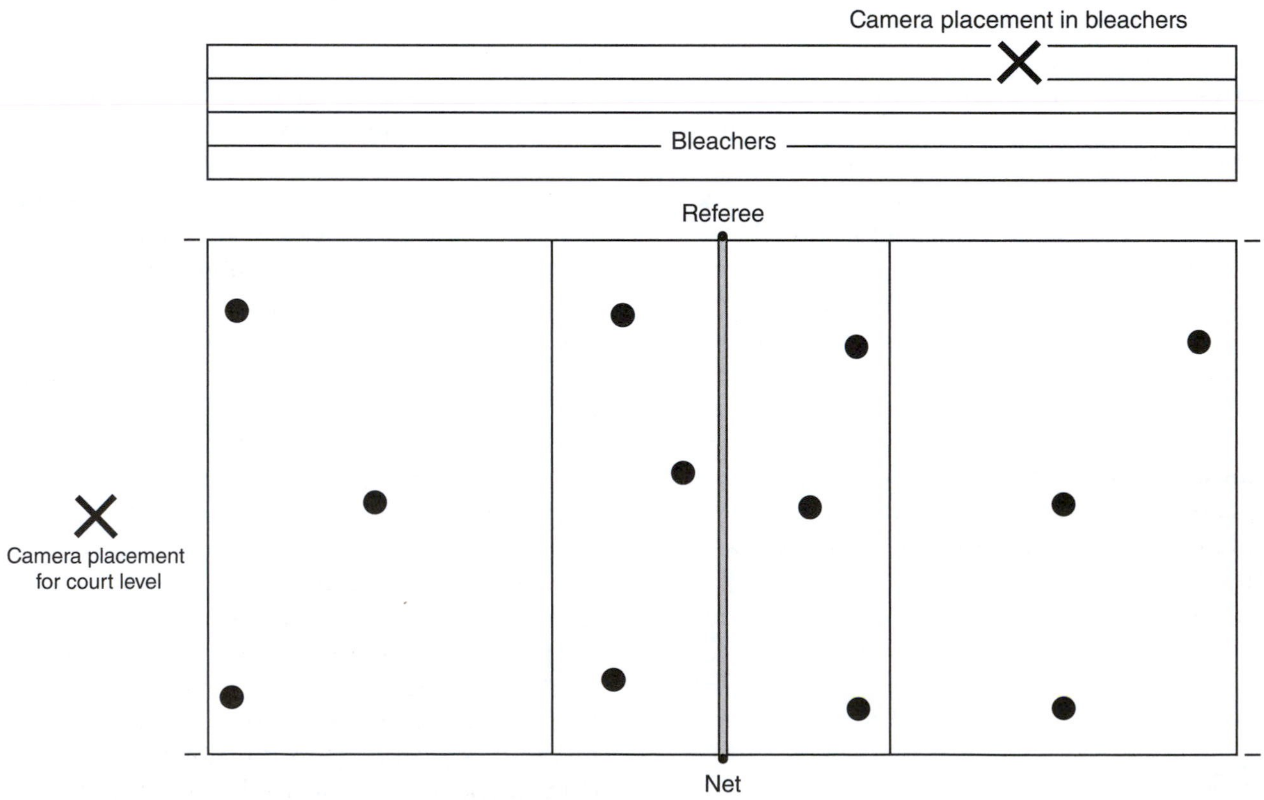

FIGURE 7.3 Videographer positions for shooting volleyball.

Reprinted by permission from I. Kleinman, *Complete Physical Education Plans for Grades 5 to 12*, 2nd ed. (Champaign, IL: Human Kinetics, 2009), 572.

The videographer who stands on the floor should set up behind one end line with the action immediately in front of him or her. The camera will be held by the videographer, and he or she will follow the ball through the air as it is being hit. The ball moves very fast in volleyball when it is being hit over the net, so the camera should not be zoomed in so closely that the ball might get lost during the shot.

Soccer and Hockey

While it may not seem like soccer and hockey would have much in common based on the climate and game location, shooting the two sports for highlights is actually quite similar. If possible, one of the best ways to shoot these sports is to stand high in the bleachers as close to midfield or midice as possible. Shooting from field or ice level is an option, but because of the size of the field or rink, getting action at the other end from where the videographer is standing can be difficult. The players will look very small, even when zoomed in all the way, and that will not make for good video. Instead, standing in the bleachers and putting the camera on a tripod provides a good view of the action and allows the videographer an easier shot to follow the ball or puck. Like basketball, the rule for either sport is to follow where the ball or puck is going. The players cannot score without it, so there is no sense shooting anything else while the action is happening.

For both sports, the framing should be not as tight as in previously discussed sports. Instead, the camera should be wide enough for about six players to be seen on the screen at all times. The videographer should be tight enough that the audience can recognize who is controlling the ball or puck, but not so tight that only one player can be seen. If the action is too tight, the camera will be quickly jolting back and forth after every pass and shot, and that can be unenjoyable for the viewer to watch. When the ball or puck is passed or shot, the videographer simply pans to keep it in the center of the frame while the players battle for it.

Golf

Golf is one of the more difficult sports to shoot simply because following a very small and very fast-moving white ball through the air can be a challenge. In some cases it is hard enough to follow a golf ball with the naked eye, let alone through the lens of a camera. Therefore, for beginner sports broadcasters, it is wise to stick with short chips and putts for highlights.

Using a tripod, the videographer should set up far enough away from the green in order not to be in the way of the golfers but still be close enough to be able to see the ball going into the hole. Some tournaments may have very explicit rules about where videographers can stand, while other, smaller events (such as a high school or college tournament) may leave it up to the individual journalist. In those cases it is important for the journalist to remember that the golfer should have the final say in where the videographer can stand. If a golfer asks a videographer to move to a different location, he or she should do so without complaint. When the player begins to set up to take the putt, the videographer should stand perfectly still and not make any noise. Only after the ball has been struck should any camera movements, such as a zoom or pan, take place.

Multiple Events at the Same Time

Some of the more difficult sports to shoot are those in which there are multiple events happening at the same time. For example, showing winners of every race, throwing event, and jumping competition at a track meet would take much more time than a sportscaster will have allotted for his or her sportscast. The same can be said for a swim meet with multiple swimming and diving heats, wrestling competitions with various weight classes, and team tennis events in which there are five or six matches going on at the same time. There are two different ways in which to shoot such events.

Option one is to focus on one or two specific athletes or events at the competition. This could mean showing highlights of only the tennis match between the two top players on each team, a really important race at a track meet, or the wrestling match that involves the defending state champion. While this does allow for more detailed highlights of that one aspect, it does not allow for the broadcaster to tell the entire story of the event. In some cases, that can lead to misleading video. For example, showing just the matchup of top players in the team tennis match between the Eagles and Buccaneers might result in highlights that show the Eagles player winning that match. However, if the Buccaneers won every other match and therefore the entire team event, showing a highlight of a celebrating Eagles player while the broadcaster is talking about how the other team won will look awkward.

Option two allows for broadcasters to take a wider look at the event without giving specifics. In this case the broadcaster would essentially shoot a number of cutaways and not actual highlights. At a swim meet, for example, he or she could shoot video of a few different races in which the swimmers go in and out of frame from different angles, someone doing a high dive, a coach on the side of the pool, fans cheering, swimmers diving into the water at the beginning of a race, and other swimmers on the side of the pool talking to each other. None of those shots give a very specific example of what happened during the event, but putting them all together gives the viewer a sense of what it was like to be there. With those generic shots from the swim meet playing, the broadcaster could read a script like the one here:

> THE HOGGARD HIGH SWIM TEAM IS THE MIDEASTERN CONFERENCE CHAMPION YET AGAIN . . .
>
> THE VIKINGS TOOK THE TITLE EARLIER TODAY AT THE U-N-C-W POOL—THEIR 18TH COMBINED TEAM CHAMPIONSHIP IN THE LAST 20 YEARS . . .
>
> THE BOYS AND GIRLS TEAMS AT HOGGARD BOTH FINISHED IN FIRST PLACE . . .
>
> NEW HANOVER HIGH SCHOOL FINISHED SECOND ON THE GIRLS SIDE—WHILE ASHLEY HIGH FINISHED SECOND ON THE BOYS SIDE . . .

The issue with this format is that individual swimmers do not get the credit they likely deserve. For example, according to a newspaper recap of the event above, four Hoggard swimmers won multiple solo races (Fuller, 2019), but the broadcaster is not able to list them individually because he or she did not get specific video of each. Therefore, broadcasters must decide, based on the event, which is the better way to shoot a large sporting event based on the goal of the recap during that night's sportscast.

There are obvious exceptions when shooting events with multiple aspects going on at the same time, such as if a local player is in a state championship event or if a specific athlete is about to do something historic or remarkable. In those cases, it is best to shoot the one athlete performing while still shooting it as a VO full of cutaways. If a high school wrestler is in a match that could make him undefeated for the year, the broadcaster could get shots of him warming up, talking to his coach, stepping onto the mat, wrestling during the actual match, and celebrating afterward (or acting dejected if he lost). A similar format could be used for a swimmer in a race, a tennis player in a match, and a track star in his or her respective event.

Always Check Ahead

The tips for the sports discussed here are based on general conditions at various stadiums and arenas. However, sports broadcasters should always check with event officials when arriving at a game to see if there are specific rules for that location. For example, a baseball stadium may have seating behind home plate that is reserved for fans and not the media. A golf tournament may have a policy in which there are certain places the media cannot stand. Some football teams may strongly enforce rules that state the media has to stand behind a certain line, while that same policy is a little more relaxed elsewhere. Every time sports broadcasters go to a new location, they should check to see what the policies are for shooting locations. This can be a simple conversation with a sports information director or an athletic director, for example: "I normally shoot basketball games from the corner on the baseline. Am I fine to do that here?"

Framing for Shooting Sports

Sports broadcasters should make sure proper **framing** is being used. The camera should not be zoomed out so wide that the audience at home cannot make out which player is which. At the same time, if the camera is zoomed in too tight, it can lead to very fast and confusing camera movements trying to follow the ball. Those quick **pans** and **zooms** can lead to a disorienting experience for the viewer. Instead, the broadcaster should have a few players in the frame at all times—close enough to be able to identify the players but wide enough to allow for camera movement following the ball that will not be overly jarring.

Look Out!

Standing on the sidelines at a game or at a practice can be a dangerous event. For football, large players in full pads can be running toward the sidelines and tackled directly into a photographer. A foul ball could be hit right to where a sportscaster is standing. A basketball player diving to save a ball that has gone out of bounds could end up in a broadcaster's lap. In many cases, a collision between the player and broadcaster, or the ball and a sportscaster, cannot be avoided. This can be pretty painful for the broadcaster and can also lead to some expensive repairs for a broken camera. In many cases these collisions happen so fast that little can be done to get out of the way. However, simply paying close attention to the action and anticipating where the action might be heading can occasionally help. Most importantly, there is no need for photographers to be "heroes" or a "tough guy" when a player or ball is barreling at them. They should move as fast as they can to get out of the way.

The Shot Is Ruined

There is one second left on the clock and the home team is down two points. They need to go the length of the court to win, so only a full court prayer of a shot will win the game. The ball is inbounded, the player heaves the ball, baseball-style, with one arm. It is flying through the air, it has the distance and is aimed right at the basket, and just as it is about to go through the hoop . . . the referee stands right in front of the camera. The crowd goes crazy as the ball flies through the net for the game-winner, while the videographer is stuck looking at the referee's backside through his viewfinder. Instead of video of the winning shot, there is instead video of a referee blocking the action.

A version of this exact scenario has happened to nearly everyone who has shot video at a sporting event. Unfortunately, there is nothing that can be done to prevent this. The best philosophy is simply to keep shooting, get the reaction of the players celebrating, and hope it does not happen again.

Shooting Events

While games are obviously a large portion of the shooting responsibilities of a sports broadcaster, they are hardly the only event worth shooting. In fact, many other sports-related events can be important parts of a broadcaster's sportscast. For example, a press conference for a major team announcement, a high school athlete signing her letter of intent to play sports at a specific college, or a dinner honoring a local coaching legend would all be events that a local sportscaster would surely cover. Even a practice would be a different way to show video of a team beyond what is shown at a game. Therefore, it is important to recognize that these events are shot much differently than a game highlight would be.

For events, the key is to think about the shooting in the style of repeated cutaways. There is not a "play" that would be shot in the form of a game recap. If a basketball player makes 10 three-pointers in row in practice, the videographer would likely not show all 10 of them during the story. Instead, there should be a variety of shots that tell the entire story of the practice, and not just the one player in a long shot. Ultimately, the video from an event should capture what it is like to be there so the audience can feel like they were there also.

Practices

Video from a practice is one of the best ways to get highlights of a team in a more intimate and staged setting. Not all coaches, especially at the professional and college levels, will allow the media to attend an entire practice, but there may be opportunities to get some footage for a brief period of time. Using cutaways, the videographer can tell the story of what is happening at these practice sessions. The videographer can get several shots of the coaches, the players warming up, a drill the team is doing, a wide shot that helps set the scene of what is going on, and several close-up shots of players' faces.

Press Conferences

While press conferences are usually designed to provide sound bites for the media, in some situations the press conference itself can be news. In those cases, what is available to shoot will depend almost entirely on the tone of what is happening at that event. If it is an announcement of a head coach getting hired, it will likely be a packed room, perhaps even with some fans, the coach's family, the leadership of the team or school, and usually a presentation of some sort where the coach is given a jersey or hat with which to pose. Those press conferences are usually pretty easy to shoot because there is a lot happening and everyone is in a good mood. The press conference after the coach has been fired is certainly much less festive. There will not be much to shoot at this event, so the videographer will have to get a few different shots of the leadership person speaking about the firing, some shots of the entire room, people mingling before the press conference starts, and perhaps some additional video of other media members who are also there for the event. Unfortunately for videographers, most press conferences are similar to the coach-firing ones in that there is not much going on beyond the coach at the podium. Even mid-week game preview press conferences are usually not very visual events.

Signing Day

There is rarely a more jovial event for a sportscaster to cover than **signing day**. At these events, high school athletes will announce where they are going to college to continue playing their sport. These will often take place in the high school's library or gym, with other

MAJOR MOMENTS

Super Bowl Media Day

For decades, Super Bowl Media Day was simply an event in which media members could interview the players participating in that year's big game. The event would take place in a hotel, conference room, or the stadium at which the game was going to be played (Wilder, 2019). Newspaper and television reporters would surround the various players and ask them questions about the upcoming game (Moore, 2020). There was not much for a sports broadcaster to shoot at these events beyond the interviews with the players. However, in the 1990s Super Bowl Media Day became about more than just the game. The NFL started allowing media members who were not sports reporters to attend the event, and that opened the door for some unconventional "reporters" with very unconventional questions. Late night talk show comics, actors in wedding dresses, puppets, and hosts dressed up as superheroes became part of the show (Bieler, 2016; Moore, 2020).

For sports broadcasters hoping to get video of Super Bowl Media Day, the event is now much more involved than just the players at podiums. Instead, Media Day has become more about the spectacle than the actual event. Therefore, stories about Media Day instead often focus on everything else happening and not nearly as much on the players themselves (Bieler, 2016; Wilder, 2019). For sports broadcasters, a story recapping the event will likely include video of the players at the podiums, but also video of all the other offbeat "media members" in attendance.

To further prove that the event has become more than just a way for journalists to interview players, the NFL eventually opened Media Day up to the public. The fans can sit in the stands of the stadium (for the cost of a $25 ticket in 2020) and watch all the action unfold live in front of them.

Ray Chavez/Media News Group/The Mercury News via Getty Images

When it comes to covering high school sports, one of the biggest days of the year is signing day.

students, coaches, and the player's family in attendance. While many of these occur on the same day throughout the United States, they almost all follow the same format. Traditionally, the athletic director or principal will welcome everyone to the event and say a few words, the player will be sitting at a table at the front of the room, the player will sign his or her name on the document, a family member will cry tears of happiness, everyone in the audience will clap, and a small celebration usually happens afterward.

However, while most signing days are the same, in recent years these events have fallen into one of two categories: known and unknown. A known signing day occurs when the athlete has made it very clear where he or she plans to attend. This athlete has made the announcement weeks or even months earlier that School X was going to be the choice. For these signing days, there is little drama to the event because the athlete and his or her family will usually show up wearing a shirt from that college or university, and there will be signs or logos of that school all over the podium. For these known signings, getting shots of the shirts and the logos helps to reinforce the script that will say where the athlete is signing.

Many athletes, especially high-profile ones, are now making their signing day an unknown event. An athlete may narrow down his or her college choice to a top three and then reveal which one he or she will be playing at on that day. In a simple ceremony, the athlete will have hats of the finalists on the table and then put on the chosen school's hat to announce the winner. Sometimes the reveals have become more elaborate. Athletes are now trying to trick the audience by implying they were going one place but then announcing they are going elsewhere. In 2019, recruit Donell Harris wore a University of Florida sweatshirt to his signing day, only to take it off during the ceremony and put on a Texas A&M University hat (Rill, 2019). In 2018, Quay Walker picked up a University of Tennessee hat and started to put it on his head before tossing it to the side and revealing that he was wearing a University of Georgia shirt (Lambert, 2018). It has become more and more apparent that sports broadcasters must keep shooting during signing day until pen is put to paper. That first reveal might not be the final reveal, so if a videographer moves away from the player to shoot video of the crowd, the actual team selection might be missed. As recent history has shown, just because a player puts on a specific school's hat does not mean he or she is done with the theatrics.

Charitable Event

Athletes and teams will often participate in charitable events as part of their commitment to the community. In many cases, the media will be invited to these events in order to showcase the team's charitable side. Videographers should get a variety of different shots from the location in order to tell the story of what is happening. These shots could include a variety of videos of the players, different angles of what they are doing, the people attending the event, and anything else that makes the viewer feel like they are part of the action. In most cases, the videographer can use the tripod and move around the location to get different angles and shot types.

Shooting Strategies

While shooting games is pretty straightforward, the strategies involved in shooting a VO or a package are almost entirely different. These shooting strategies are used on a daily basis by news videographers, but with so much of the sports world more than just games, it is important for sports broadcasters to be well versed in how to shoot like a news reporter.

Recognize What the Story Is About

Preparation to shoot an event should start before the videographer even arrives at the location. Having a plan is key to making sure that no important video is missed or there are not any wasted shots. This comes to down to understanding what the story is going to be about. For example, if a broadcaster is going to do a story about a new head coach's first practice in charge, he or she should consider what might be talked about during the story. The script will likely mention the coach in a variety of ways, such as teaching the players, working with his or her new assistants, being in the gym for the first time, and facing the pressures of being on the job. Therefore, at practice, the videographer should be getting as many shots of the coach in action as possible. These shots should include the coach talking to players, giving instructions, and working with assistant coaches. By planning ahead, the videographer will be able to get a large number of shots that will match up with what he or she will likely be talking about during the evening news.

Shoot Everything . . . And Then Get More

There is no such thing as having too much video after leaving an event. If the reporter thinks he or she is going to need 10 shots of the coach during the practice, then the reporter should leave with at least 15 shots. While everything might be going well at the event, a reporter could return to the newsroom to find out that a couple of the video clips did not turn out as well as expected. Perhaps the reporter talked more about a specific, unexpected aspect of the story but not enough video was taken of that aspect. The key to any event video is to get as much video as possible . . . and then get more. A good rule of thumb is that when a reporter thinks he or she has enough video, they should get five more shots before leaving.

Move Around

When shooting a basketball, baseball, or soccer game, a videographer often stands in one spot for the entire contest. However, when shooting a VO or a package, the videographer should move around in order to show the action from a variety of different angles. Having an entire 40-second VO or a 2-minute package with video all from the same location is not going to be visually pleasing to the viewer. Therefore, the videographer should be moving around during the event to get shots from a variety of different spots. For example, if a videographer is shooting a high school football practice, he or she should move up and down the sidelines and get different groups that are participating.

Pro Advice

© Mitch Brown

Mitch Brown

Sports director—WDKY

While many local sportscasters get an on-air job and then have to learn how to get better at shooting video, Mitch Brown went the other way. The sports director at WDKY in Lexington, Kentucky, started his career as a videographer before transitioning into a sports reporter. Even as he has added to his work responsibilities, Brown's love of shooting has continued, with him saying "it has always been my favorite thing to do."

Even though he enjoys it, there is no debating that shooting video is not for the faint of heart for beginners. However, Brown says that while it might be overwhelming at first, it does get easier: "Every time you go out and shoot, you remember that basic photog checklist: white balance, iris, volume is on, and all of that. It becomes a checklist that in the beginning is physical, then becomes mental, and then becomes second nature."

How does shooting your own video help you put your stories together?

I know how I want a story to be shot. If I want to do a minute and a half package, I know I'm going to have to overshoot. That might not sound like a lot of time, but, for me, I like to do a lot of quick cuts, so that's why it helps me. I don't want to usually rely on someone else to get all the little nuances that I see that they might not. Everyone's eye is different.

What is the most important thing to remember when shooting events such as press conferences or practices?

I'm looking for ways to make something out of nothing. If you go to practice, you get a couple of clips of them running plays and stretching. But I'm thinking of it in a 30-second video. How many clips can I fit into 30 seconds? At a practice, or a charity event, you're looking to show faces that people will recognize.

How about shooting games? What's the most important thing to remember there?

Work on shooting a little bit wider and just following the ball. As long as you follow the ball, everything will be fine when it comes to shooting sports events. Football, basketball, and soccer are all the same—you just want to follow the ball. Baseball, you want to shoot a little wider.

Of course, I'm shooting the plays, but I'm big on getting the fan reactions. There is so much going on around you that you zone in on the game and forget about all the fan reactions. They are the gold money shots at a game. Get the atmosphere.

Why are those fan cutaways so important?

You'll see so many highlights on air that just go from play to play. And I don't get any feel for the game because I don't get any atmosphere. I love to start with the entrance of the home team or a wide shot of the crowd. I don't care if you show me just one fan, or two fans; it is going to help you break up the video because some of those cuts aren't going to look as good if you don't have those shots.

Once you've shot the video at the game, what's a tip for when you're editing it all together?

Make sure you let the play breathe. Don't just cut the clip off right afterwards. Let the play breathe. Show me some celebration. Then you can move onto the next play.

These different angles and locations will also give the audience a sense of being right in the action instead of standing far away and having the photographer zooming in.

Be Smooth and Steady

Sports action can be difficult to shoot because it often happens very quickly. For example, a baseball will rocket off a metal bat in the college game so fast that a videographer cannot help but to jolt the camera quickly to follow it. While these quick-moving shots are often necessary during game highlights, they can be distracting if they are simply happening during a VO of an event. If a story is about a charitable event involving a team, a VO full of quick zooms and wild pans will distract the viewer watching the video and prevent him or her from paying close attention to what the reporter is saying. Therefore, any camera movements, whether a zoom, pan, or **tilt**, should be slow and smooth in order to not be distracting to the viewer.

Video can also be distracting if it is very shaky. Therefore, when possible, videographers should use a **tripod** in order to ensure it is steady. A tripod is a three-legged stand used to keep the camera stable. When a videographer holds the camera or puts it on his or her shoulder when shooting, the resulting video may not be steady because there is not a solid base. If the videographer has to zoom in, or if it is very windy outside, then the video will almost certainly be shaky. A tripod will keep the camera steady and allow for video to be shot that will not be distracting. In most cases, the camera simply slides onto the top of the stand and locks into place. The tripod can then be manipulated for smooth camera movements such as a pan or tilt.

180-Degree Rule

The 180-degree rule is a video guideline that states the camera should stay on one side of the action at all times. In order to achieve this, the videographer should draw an imaginary straight line down the middle of the field and stay on one side of that 180-degree line for the entire time they are at the game. This keeps the subjects consistent when they are looking or moving in a specific direction. For example, if a camera is on one sideline for a play, the team with the ball will look as if they are running in one direction. However, if that camera moves to the other side of the field for the very next play, the team will suddenly be going in the opposite direction. This can be very disorienting for the audience watching at home. This is why when professional sports are televised, the camera angle is always from the same side of the field or court throughout the game.

Types of Shots

Not every shot in a story will be eye-level with the subject and at the same framing size in the camera. In fact, a videographer should make an effort to get a variety of different angles and framing sizes in order to make sure that not every piece of video looks the same. A mixture of shots will create something that can be visually pleasing to the viewer and show the story from more than just the usual perspective.

Wide, Medium, and Tight Shots

When shooting sports, the easiest method to get a variety of types of shots can involve using different framing sizes. At a practice, it may be difficult to get different angles because the videographer may be constricted to a very small portion of the field. However, using the zooming technology on the camera will allow the videographer to get shots of the subject with different framing sizes. The three most common framing sizes are wide, medium, and tight (figure 7.4).

A **wide shot** is used to establish a full picture of what is happening at a scene. If a person is in the frame, his or her entire body is shown. Additionally, the video is wide enough so that what is in the background can be clearly identified as well. This allows the viewer to know where the action is taking place. In a VO, the wide shot can often be the first shot in the edited piece because it can be used as an establishing shot for what is happening and where it is taking place. For example, a wide shot of a football player at practice would

FIGURE 7.4 Some type of stadium background should be seen easily in the wide shot, less easily in the medium shot, and barely at all in the tight shot.

show their entire body throwing the ball while also showing enough of the practice field for the viewer to easily identify what the player is doing. However, while location context is important, the video is often so wide that it may be difficult to identify the emotion on the person's face because the shot is so wide.

For a **medium shot**, the videographer can zoom in slightly to show less of the person's body but see a better angle of their face. A football player would be shot from the waist up, with just some of the background easily identifiable for the audience. When shooting a VO or video for a package, a medium shot is often the most common type of shot that will be used. Every shot should not be a medium one, but it is a wise decision to make most of them from that size because it is a nice mix between wide and tight.

A **tight shot** will focus on just the main aspect of the video and will be as close as possible to the action. The shot should be close enough so that the subject can be identified but not so close that they cannot be identified. A tight shot of a football player at practice would have just his face in the photo. The audience may not be able to tell that the player is throwing the ball or where he or she is located. A tight shot is sometimes referred to as a close-up shot.

High- and Low-Angle Shots

While many shots are at eye level with the subject, a shot taken from a different angle can provide a different vantage point for the viewer. A high-angle shot would occur when the camera is up high and looking down upon the subject. These shots make the subject seem small and weak because the camera placement has the viewer at home essentially looking down on the person in the video. This type of shot is not used very often in sports video because there is little reason to make an athlete appear weak. However, the opposite low-angle shot is used quite frequently in sports. In a low-angle shot, the camera is placed below the subject and is looking up at him or her. This shot, sometimes referred to as the "hero shot," makes the subject appear strong and powerful. Often in televised sporting events, these shots are used as the athletes are warming up before the game starts.

Sequence Shooting

One of the methods to help show what is happening at an event is the use of **sequence shooting**. This is a process in which a videographer will get a variety of shots from one location with the goal of telling the story of what is happening there. Two of the main goals of sequence shooting are to promote continuity and compress time (Frechette, 2012). It might take someone 5 minutes to complete a task, but through sequence shooting, a videographer and editor can decrease that time to about 30 seconds and make it easier to use for television. Having continuity helps make sure that all the shots go together and have a progression that makes sense. Otherwise, the viewer can be disoriented (Frechette, 2012). For example, if a person is putting together a puzzle, a properly assembled sequence shooting session will show the puzzle going from start to finish. If a sequence is not used, the puzzle might be half completed in the first shot, just started in the second shot, done in the third shot, and then half completed in the fourth. This process can leave the viewer confused and distracted by what is happening in the video.

One of the more popular methods to complete a sequence shot is the use of the **five-shot rule**. In this strategy, the videographer should get five very distinct shots that can be edited together in order to create a sequence: a close-up of the subject's hands, a close-up of the subject's face, a medium shot of the subject, an "over-the-shoulder" shot to provide a point of view of the person, and finally an unusual or creative shot (Frechette, 2012). For most sequences, those are the basic five shots that should be included, but the videographer should not stop there. Getting additional shots from a sequence will help fill additional time that might be needed for a VO or a package.

For sports broadcasters, a great time to use sequence shooting is during signing day. This event is not the most visually appealing, and the entire process from the principal's introduction to the celebration afterward can take well over 30 minutes. Therefore, using sequence shooting can help speed up this process and turn it into a 30-second event for broadcast. Getting a variety of shots from signing day can create a VO that utilizes the five-shot rule and condenses the amount of time it takes to tell the story. Following is an example of the order in which a 35-second edited VO could showcase several shots from the five-shot rule with some additional shots for more coverage of a planned signing day.

- Shot 1: Medium shot of athlete at podium (five seconds)
- Shot 2: Medium shot of athlete's coach in attendance (three seconds)
- Shot 3: Tight shot of athlete's face (five seconds)
- Shot 4: Tight shot of athlete's hands signing the commitment paper (three seconds)
- Shot 5: Wide shot of audience clapping after the athlete signs (five seconds)
- Shot 6: Medium shot from behind the players, over their shoulder, as they talk to teammates afterward or hug their parents (five seconds)
- Shot 7: Medium shot of a logo of the school the athlete signed with (four seconds)
- Shot 8: Tight shot of athlete's face as he or she interacts with audience after signing (five seconds)

It's Time to Shoot!

Much of a videographer's shooting technique is practiced and planned before shooting even a second of video at an event. For example, if he or she is going to a practice to do a story on Abigail May, a high jumper who just broke the high school state record, the videographer is going to know before getting to the practice that video of the athlete warming up, running down the track, jumping over the bar, landing on the mat, talking to her coach, and interacting with teammates will be needed. Additionally, the videographer should plan to get a variety of shot sizes, not violate the 180-degree rule, and, if possible, get some high- and low-angle shots of May as she is warming up and jumping. Having a plan ahead of time is key to making sure that all the necessary shots are collected at the event.

Getting the Shot

When shooting an event, the process before getting each shot should follow a basic order. In the following example, a videographer is at a practice and wants to shoot video of a soccer player for a feature story. First, if possible, the camera should be put on a tripod to keep the shot steady. Second, he or she should pick out what the first shot will be. In this case, the soccer player is sitting on the field stretching, so that will be a good time to get a shot during which the player will not be moving too much.

Once the first shot has been decided, the videographer should zoom in as close as possible, all the way in, to the player and use that opportunity to **focus** the camera. If the shot is focused from this close vantage point, it will be in focus from every other depth. If possible, the camera should also be **white balanced** during this time. White balancing is when the videographer, through the push of a button, tells the camera what is white. The camera should be zoomed in on something white, the button pushed, and then the camera will adjust to these new settings. Once the camera knows what is white, it will be able to determine other colors. Once one white balance has been acquired in a location, it does not need to be repeated before every shot. However, if the camera moves to a location with different lighting (outside to inside or if clouds appear, making it darker), then a new white balance should be taken.

After focusing and white balancing, the videographer should then zoom back out to the proper framing that he or she wishes to have for that shot. Using either a wide, medium, or tight shot, the **viewfinder** will show what will be recorded in the video. Once that shot has been established, the videographer should hit record. A good tip for beginning videographers at this point is to simply take a step back from the camera. Many beginners want to immediately zoom in, pan, tilt, or stop a shot almost immediately after starting it. Instead, the shot should be held steady for about 12 seconds, allowing for the best five consecutive seconds of video to be used when editing. Therefore, taking a step back and away from the camera will reduce the temptation for the videographer to start touching the camera. If a camera zoom, pan, or tilt is part of the shot, the videographer should record for a few seconds before starting that movement, have the movement go no more than five seconds, and then have a few seconds at the end before stopping the recording.

After getting that first shot, the process is repeated all over again for the next one. In order to get a variety of angles, the videographer should move to a new location and repeat order of picking out a shot, putting the camera on the tripod, zooming in, focusing, white balancing (if necessary), zooming out to the desired shot size, hitting record, holding the shot for 12 seconds, and then stopping the recording. This happens over and over again until enough video has been acquired from the event.

Lighting and the Sun

Perhaps nothing can ruin a good outdoor shot more than the sun. The ball is flying through the air, the videographer tilts up to follow the ball through the sky, and suddenly the camera is aimed directly into the bright sun. That makes it almost impossible to continue following the ball and also will not be very appealing for the viewer watching at home. In game situations, there is not much that can be done about this, but during an event or an interview, the videographer should always be aware of the dominant light's location and plan accordingly.

Having a dominant light source can actually help light up a shot. When in a location, the videographer should identify the brightest light and make sure that it is falling on the subject. Additionally, that light should be behind the videographer and not behind the subject. If the light is behind them (often when they are sitting in front of a window or directly in front of the sun), the light will be too bright and will make the subject appear **backlit**. In this framing, the subject will appear very dark because the strong light will be the focus and will dominate the frame. Therefore, the subject should essentially be looking directly into the sun when getting video of him or her.

Additionally, paying close attention to the amount of light in the area can impact how the shots turn out. If there is too much light, the video will be overexposed—sometimes referred to as "hot" in the broadcast industry—making it difficult to see what is happening. If there is not enough light, the video will be too dark. On a professional video camera, there are features, such as the **iris**, **gain**, and **ND filter**, that can help in these scenarios. The iris helps to control the amount of light coming through the lens and can be both opened and closed. The gain button can be used only to increase the brightness of a video, while the ND filter—sometimes referred to as "sunglasses for the camera"—can help darken video shot outside if the sun is overly bright.

Think About Sound

In chapter 8, the process of video editing will be discussed. However, as strange as it may sound, editing really starts when the videographer is still out shooting video. He or she needs to be thinking ahead about what video will be needed when assembling the piece on the editing timeline. Perhaps one of the most important aspects of editing is the inclusion of sound. Very few live events that a news station will cover will have the distinct sounds involved in sports. A baseball practice has a coach yelling, players huddling, the crack of the bat hitting the ball, a player stepping on a base, and the snap of the ball landing in a glove. While watching these clips from practice will tell the story, it is often the *sounds* from an event that resonate more with the viewer at home. Therefore, when a videographer arrives at an event, he or she should not just be looking for things to include in a story, but also listening and asking, "What are the sounds that are occurring that I will need to include in my story?"

Broadcasting Full Games

While sports reports on the evening news are a popular way to catch up with the latest sports news, little can compare to watching the game live. Games from all over the world, from a variety of different sports, are broadcast on a daily basis on a multitude of television networks. Whether it is the NBA finals or a college soccer match, live television sports production has become big business, and the various networks have invested millions of dollars in making sure the broadcasts are visually appealing and easy to watch. (More information on live sports production can be found in chapter 10.)

Shooting a Full Game

When shooting complete games to be broadcast live, some minor changes apply to how a local sports broadcaster should shoot highlights. Perhaps most obviously, many more videographers will be present. For example, while a local sports broadcaster would be on his or her own shooting a college basketball game, there may be five videographers shooting a game for a television broadcast. There are usually three positioned up high, with one at center court and the other two on the opposite sides of the team benches. Those three cameras can all follow the ball during the action but can also get close-up cutaways of the benches to get the coach's reactions. Two more videographers would be stationed on the end lines, with one under each basket. They are there to get the action from a different vantage point and also get close-up shots of the players. For an important game, such as a national championship or a big rivalry, there may be twice as many cameras to get all the extra excitement surrounding the event (Clapp, 2015).

When shooting games for broadcast television, the videographer must remember that he or she is always "on." When shooting basketball, getting shots of the scoreboard and zipping the camera around to find the ball are acceptable because those shots will not make the broadcast. However, for live television, the videographer must assume that the camera is always live. With one push of a button from the director, any shot can make the air. If the videographer is not focused on the action, is out of focus, or is missing key plays, that shot could unfortunately make the broadcast.

Sports that are usually shot by a solo videographer are captured slightly differently during a television broadcast. A basketball game would be shot similarly to a soccer game, in that the primary camera should be at a higher angle and framed wide enough so that a little less than half the court is in the frame when the game is going on. These cameras that are located high up should be on a tripod so they can be steady throughout the shot. Shots from this angle should use what is known as a **zone focus** to ensure that the players are in focus the entire time. For this kind of shot, the videographer prefocuses on the field of play knowing that everything that comes into that area will be in focus, eliminating the need to constantly refocus while shooting the game (Owens, 2016). Cameras that are underneath the basket will be located on the videographer's shoulder so he or she can follow the action quickly. These shots will be similar to those of a solo videographer shooting the game for highlights. He or she will follow the ball and then pan back to the shooter who made the basket afterward—the only difference is that the videographer will not get a shot of the scoreboard.

Other sports will be similar to the basketball setup, with cameras both up high and at field level. The low-level shots are used primarily for **instant replays**, while cameras placed higher are used for the live game action.

CHAPTER WRAP-UP

SUMMARY

Shooting games and events is hardly the most glamorous part of a sports broadcaster's job. It often involves lugging around heavy equipment at press conferences and sporting events, running around to get the best shots possible, and then hustling back to the television station to edit the footage before that evening's sportscast. Despite the stress and difficulty involved, shooting video is crucial to the success of a sportscast. Highlights and video from events allow the audience to get a firsthand visual account of what happened. Therefore, it is important for broadcasters to learn the proper way to use a video camera and tell a story visually. Being aware of the various shooting strategies, the different types of shots, and what to do when out at an event will help when gathering video. Additionally, knowing where to stand when getting highlights of various sporting events can ensure that the audience will be able to follow along with what the broadcaster is showing during the evening sportscast.

Phil Cole/Getty Images

CHAPTER 8

Television Broadcasting

CHAPTER OBJECTIVES

Being a television sports broadcaster is much more than just sitting at an anchor desk and reading a script. Therefore, this chapter focuses on television broadcasting, including the following:

- Distinguishing between local sports broadcasters and national sports broadcasters
- Creating a rundown for an evening sportscast
- Editing highlights from a game or an event
- Understanding the skills needed to anchor a sportscast
- Recapping the daily routine of a local sports broadcaster

When the red light on the video camera lights up, it is time for television sports broadcasters to shine. Whether they are in the studio or live out at a game, they are often the eyes and ears for the audience at home, delivering highlights and recaps from the biggest games and events in the sports world. However, while the most visible moments of a television sports broadcaster's job are the few minutes in which he or she is actually on television, there is much more involved with the job than simply reading highlights.

Local or National?

As first discussed in chapter 3, there are two different types of television sports broadcasters: ones that work for a national television outlet and ones that work for a local television station. National sports broadcasters traditionally have many years of experience and work in large departments in which there are multiple people who split up the daily tasks. At ESPN, there are producers, editors, videographers, social media experts, and anchors who all have very specialized jobs. Local sports broadcasters work at the various major television network affiliates located throughout the United States. In the city of Savannah, Georgia, for example, there is an ABC affiliate (WJCL), a CBS affiliate (WTOC), a Fox affiliate (WTGS), and an NBC affiliate (WSAV). All four stations have local newscasts that cover the news, weather, and sports for that city. This setup is similar to how many people in cities throughout the United States get their local television news. Since this book is an introduction to sports broadcasting aimed at those looking to start or just beginning in the field, this chapter will instead focus on the job duties involved with being a local sports broadcaster because those are traditionally entry-level jobs in smaller cities.

Unlike ESPN, these local television stations often have sports departments of just one or two people who have to do all the various jobs needed to get a sportscast on the air. Several of the skills needed to be successful have been discussed in previous chapters in this book, including interviewing athletes and coaches (see chapter 4), writing broadcast scripts (see chapter 5), writing website stories (see chapter 6), and shooting video of games and events (see chapter 7). (How sports broadcasters use social media will be reviewed in chapter 11.) Therefore, this chapter will be devoted to three additional duties for local sports broadcasters: producing the sportscast, editing video, and anchoring.

Producing a Sportscast

Deciding what stories are told in the evening newscast is traditionally determined by the **producer**. This person decides the order in which stories will be told, often writes many of the stories, and makes sure that the show is timed out accordingly. In local television, especially in beginning markets, the anchor will often serve as the producer for his or her own show. Therefore, not only are the anchors the ones reading the stories, they are also the ones deciding which ones will be discussed and in what order. However, some strategic planning must take place when a sports broadcaster is making those decisions.

Think About the Audience

Sports broadcasters should remember that the sportscast is not for their benefit but is instead designed for the audience. While a story might be of interest to the individual broadcaster, he or she must first think about what the audience as a whole will be most interested in. When it comes to local sports broadcasters, the most important part of the title is "local." Fans can get highlights of national sporting events almost anywhere. A supporter of the NFL's Pittsburgh Steelers can get highlights of a Sunday game on ESPN, Fox Sports, NBC, The NFL Network, and a variety of online sources including social media networks such as Facebook and Twitter. Therefore, unless that local sports broadcaster works in Pittsburgh or the surrounding area, there is little need to spend much time covering Steelers because fans can get that in a variety of places.

Instead, the local sports broadcaster should focus on what only he or she can provide, and that is the best (and sometimes only) coverage of the local teams within that city. That includes colleges, high schools, and other sports teams and athletes that would not get national attention. This is often why many television stations devote entire segments to high school football on Friday nights in the fall. An exception to this "only-local" highlights policy might be if a local athlete is playing in the professional ranks. For example, if an NFL kicker played high school football in the sports broadcaster's city, then highlights of that kicker's NFL game, showing only his kicks, would be acceptable to show during a sports broadcast. Perhaps the best motto for a local sports broadcaster is "local, local, local."

Different Shows Have Different Goals

There are traditionally two main sportscasts in a local sports broadcaster's day—the early newscast (6:00 p.m. on the East Coast) and the late newscast (11:00 p.m. on the East Coast). There may be additional broadcasts based on the individual station, but those are the two primary focuses. During the weekdays, when traditionally sports are not played in the afternoon, these shows have two different goals. The early newscast is used to provide information on stories from that day, preview games happening that night, and perhaps give a quick recap of a big story from the night before. The late newscast is almost all highlights, showcasing games that happened that evening. A big story from earlier in the day might be repeated again on the late news. Weekend sportscasts are almost always very heavy on highlights for both the early and late shows because games will start as early as noon EST, which is often plenty of time to get full game highlights into the early sportscast.

Assembling the Rundown

Once the stories have been selected, it is time to start putting them into the **rundown**. The rundown is the order in which the stories will appear in the newscast. The local television newscast is traditionally divided up into several different sections (known as "blocks") separated by commercial breaks. A typical newscast rundown format is as follows:

A-block: This the beginning of the newscast and is where the biggest news stories of the day will be located. There may also be a quick update on the weather in this segment.

Commercial break

B-block: This second section of the newscast is often dedicated to feature stories that do not have as serious a tone.

Commercial break

Weather: This entire section will have the weather segment.

Commercial break

Sports: The sportscast traditionally is toward the end of the show.

Commercial break

Wrap-up: Newscasts will end with an upbeat and happy story (often referred to as the **kicker**), followed by a final look at the weather. If there was breaking news earlier in the show, an update may be included here before the show ends.

The news producer's only role with the sports section is to determine how much time the sportscast will have during that show. Once that information is provided (and it is traditionally the same every night) sports broadcasters then have to create their own rundown within the main news rundown. Most television newsrooms use specialized software for putting together a newscast; two of the most popular rundown news production software programs are ENPS and iNews. These programs are used for producing, timing, and organizing television news broadcasts. Additionally, ENPS was developed by the Associated Press, so the latest news wires from that organization are integrated directly into the interface of the program.

Figure 8.1 is an example of a sports segment rundown in ENPS. The sportscast is during the "D-block," so the pages are labeled D1 through D6. Chapter 5 discussed the different types of stories, and both a VO and a SOT are used in this rundown. The show starts with a VO about the Pro Day for the football players at the University of South Carolina. The anchor then transitions to a VO and SOT about the

D0	PSA9				CLIP X	2:00	0:00	04:54:01 PM	04:52:0
D1	GAMECOCK PRO DAY	VO	PETER	CAM 3	CLIP X	0:35	0:00	04:54:47 PM	04:54:0
D2	MENS BASEBALL	VO	PETER	CAM 3	CLIP X	0:30	0:25	04:54:50 PM	04:54:3
D3		SOT TAG	PETER			0:10	0:10	04:55:20 PM	04:55:0
D4	CLT HORNETS	VO		CAM 3	CLIP X	0:25	0:25	04:55:58 PM	04:55:1
D5	OLYMPICS	VO		CAM 3	CLIP X	0:20	0:23	04:56:27 PM	04:55:4
D6	WWE MAYOR	VO	PETER	CAM 3		0:30	0:23	04:57:29 PM	04:56:0
D7	TEASE FOUR	VO	ANCHOR	CAM 2:2		0:10	0:07	04:57:31 PM	04:56:3
E0	PSA10				CLIP X	2:00	0:00	04:58:29 PM	04:56:4

FIGURE 8.1 A rundown of a sportscast in ENPS software.

Courtesy of University of South Carolina, Kevin Hull.

baseball team. The TAG after the SOT means that the sports anchor will say some additional things about that story before moving onto the next story, a VO about the NBA's Charlotte Hornets. That is followed by back-to-back VOs for the Olympics and a lighthearted story about a professional wrestler who is the mayor. The rest of the rundown displays the anchor's name (Peter), which camera the anchor should look into when talking (primarily camera 3), and how long is allotted to each story (35 seconds for the Gamecock Pro Day, for example).

Figure 8.2 shows the Gamecock Pro Day script from that rundown in ENPS. The information at the top shows which camera the director should take (camera 3, with just one person being shown), that the monitor should be behind the sportscaster, and the name of the anchor (Peter). Peter's script is in all capital letters, with his on-camera anchor lead at the beginning before the TAKE VO, which signifies when the show's director should start playing the VO highlights.

The Flow

While deciding what to put into an evening sports broadcast can be challenging, sports broadcasters also have to consider the order in which those stories should go. Each individual story should flow naturally from one to the next so the audience can easily follow along. For example, if the 11:00 p.m. newscast has highlights from four different high school football games, it would make the most sense to group those together instead of showing two football games, highlights of a high school soccer match, and then going back to the other two football games. Therefore, common sports should be grouped together when possible.

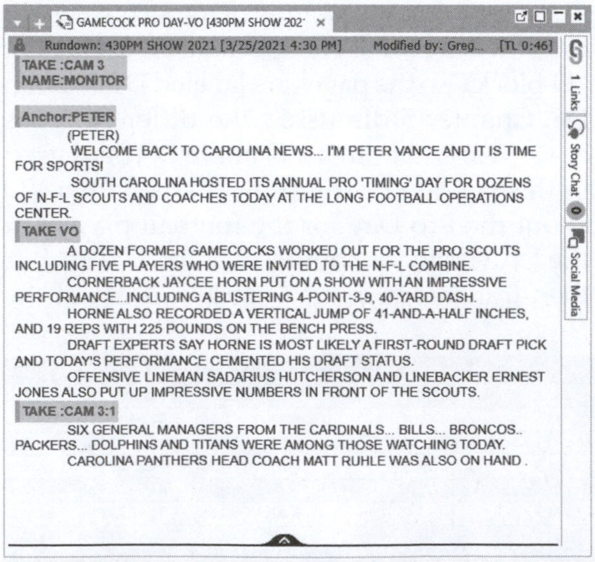

FIGURE 8.2 An example of a script format for a story in ENPS.

Courtesy of University of South Carolina, Kevin Hull.

How often the audience sees the sports anchor can also contribute to the flow of the show. Traditionally at the start of the sportscast, the broadcaster is "on camera," so the viewers can see the anchor as he or she welcomes them to the sportscast and begins the first story. These **on-camera leads** provide a sentence or two of information before the highlights start so that the viewers will know about the importance of this game. An on-camera lead for a high school volleyball match might be:

> IT HAS BEEN A HOT START TO THE SEASON FOR THE MICHAELS HIGH SCHOOL VOLLEYBALL TEAM . . .
>
> THE HURRICANES HAVE WON FIVE IN A ROW AND ARE CURRENTLY
>
> RANKED NUMBER THREE IN THE STATE RANKINGS . . .
>
> TONIGHT THEY LOOK TO KEEP IT GOING AGAINST COUNTY RIVAL WALLACE HIGH . . .
>
> << take VO >>

The audience should see the sportscaster at the beginning of each show, but it is not necessary to see him or her at the beginning of each *story*. While grouping together similar stories, sportscasters should consider wiping from one to the next. In television, a **wipe** occurs when the video from a story ends and the video in the next story begins to play immediately, with the anchor not appearing on camera again. If the sportscaster has four high school football games to show, there might be an on-camera lead for the first one before wiping from the first to the second, then the second to the third, and then the third to the fourth. While this can be effective for show flow, it also means that

Pro Advice

© Lina Washington

Lina Washington

Sports anchor and reporter, KPNX in Phoenix, Arizona

With a father who was a National Championship–winning football player, Lina Washington had little choice but to become a sports fan herself. However, while her dad might have gotten her love of sports started, it was Washington herself who took that passion and turned it into a career. She started working as a local sports broadcaster in Bakersfield, California, after graduating from college and then jumped up to one of the top markets in the country to work in Sacramento, California. In Sacramento, the Emmy Award winner covered everything from the NBA to high school sports to the local weekend warriors. Now reporting for the NBC affiliate in Phoenix, Arizona, she said she would not change it for anything: "I have friends who work in retail and engineering, and software, and all these things, and I can't imagine myself doing any of those things. I'm thankful to be able to do this."

When most people think "sports broadcaster," they probably immediately think of ESPN. But you're one of the hundreds of* local *sports broadcasters throughout the United States. Why are local sportscasters important?

It's so important to focus on local sports because those athletes wouldn't have the exposure otherwise. That's my favorite part, just being able to travel and build these relationships with these athletes, coaches, and families. While they're validating what you're doing as a storyteller, you're also validating all the work that this family and this athlete put in for this moment. You know the stats of who makes it to the pros is very small, so for a lot of these people, this is their goal to remember these special moments with these people they grew up with doing something they love. At the end of the day, some reporter in some small town was sitting down with this athlete and laying the foundation for future interviews to come. It all starts at the high school local level, and that's why it's so important.

What is it like when you see these local athletes reaching lofty heights?

I've only been working in sports broadcasting for seven years or so, but I've gotten to the point where kids that I gave Athlete of the Week to in high school football are now having their names called on *ABC College Football Saturday* and *Sunday Night Football*. It really makes me catch feelings in a way because I saw these kids with their parents after they lost a game, and I know what that moment meant for them. Now they're onto some bigger and better things playing for the Patriots or playing for a college football championship contender. You hear the little nuggets that they get in on sideline reporting or whatnot, like yes, I knew that kid had experiences five years ago because we were telling that story at his local high school banquet.

What is the biggest misconception about local sports broadcasters?

People think you're getting your nose powdered in commercial breaks and you have someone carrying your camera. No, that's not what it is. It's me putting on all my makeup, buying all of this expensive stuff to look good for four seconds on camera. I'm driving in sleet to this town for this game and then going to another game and going back and writing all the names and knowing how to pronounce them, and getting the scores right.

What skills do you think are really important to be a good sports broadcaster?

Well, you have to be flexible. You have to be kind of addicted to the adrenaline. It's a rip-and-run kind of field. You have to be willing to work. You have to be willing to adapt. I went to Arizona State University from 2008 to 2012. I started learning editing on tape, but we were the last class to work on tape at school before we transitioned to SD cards. Between that, and the use of Twitter, and the use of phones, I've had to adapt and change how I go about storytelling and content gathering, presentation, all of that. I can only imagine what it's like for people 10 or 20 years older than me in this industry. So, you definitely have to be flexible and able to adapt.

there cannot be as much background information provided by the anchor. Sometimes, there might be time for just one sentence that can be said during the cutaway at the beginning:

<< take VO >>

IN VOLLEYBALL ACTION . . .

THIRD RANKED MICHAELS HIGH
HOSTING WALLACE HIGH . . .

Using wipes effectively can also help during nights when there are several different games to show and the broadcaster is concerned about time. By avoiding on-camera leads, the broadcaster is able to save 10-15 seconds per highlight.

Editing Video

Local sports broadcasters will often shoot their own video during their first jobs in the industry, but getting video is just the first step when it comes to getting the stories on the air. (How to shoot the various games and events is reviewed in chapter 7 of this book.) These video clips need to be edited together in order to tell a succinct story about what happened.

The process of video editing has become increasingly easier over the years. For decades, highlights were shot on videotapes. Those tapes were then searched for the best plays, with those plays then copied onto a different tape in some sort of sequential order. This process, known as **linear video editing**, was the main way in which video was edited for television broadcasts for decades. The integration of computers and digital materials into the video-gathering process has led to the rise in **nonlinear video editing**. In this method, video is ingested into a computer from either a tape or a camera card containing different clips. These clips are then edited together on the computer using specialized software before the finished product is exported for viewing. Most video editing is now done through nonlinear methods.

Editing Software

Not every news station uses the same editing software, so while journalists may learn on one system, they might suddenly need to learn another at a new job. Popular editing programs at television stations include the newsroom-specific programs Edius and Avid, while some rely on the more commercially available Final Cut Pro and Adobe Premiere Pro. However, it is not the editing program that makes the difference in the edit; it is the editors themselves who can make or break the story by choosing the right video clips and assembling them in a way that successfully tells the story of the event. (Visit HK*Propel* for a tutorial for editing in Adobe Premiere Pro.)

Editing Highlights

The goal of an edited highlight is to tell the story of the entire game through just a few plays. It may seem challenging to reduce a 3+-hour game into about 30 seconds, but a good highlight package can make the audience feel like they have watched that entire game by just following the broadcaster's short recap. Much of the work for editing highlights happens before sitting down in front of the computer.

Traditionally, editing highlights should not start until the game is over; however, an exception can be made if the score is very lopsided and the outcome is not in doubt. Editing too early can result in possibly having to recut the story due to an unexpected comeback or remarkable play. For example, a baseball team might have a two-run lead in the ninth inning, but finishing editing the highlights just seconds before the dramatic game-winning walk-off three-run home run would lead to a very frustrated broadcaster having to start all over. By waiting until after the game ends, the broadcaster will know the result, key plays, and eye-catching statistics.

As discussed in chapter 7, sports highlights are often very similar no matter what the sport. A traditional 30-second highlight will start with a cutaway and then show approximately three plays from the game, with a cutaway following each play. These postplay cutaways should match up with what happened in the highlight. For example, if a team scores, their cheerleaders or fans could be shown celebrating. If a team has a turnover, a shot of the coach being upset could be shown. Game highlights should always end with the team that won doing something good. If South Carolina beat North Carolina 35–7 in football, it would be confusing to the viewer to see a North Carolina player scoring a touchdown while hearing that they lost the game.

There is no set length for each individual play in a highlight; they should be long enough for the viewer to establish what is happening, but not so long that the viewer loses interest before the play is over. For sports where there is a stoppage in action, the individual highlight should be an entire play, so the broadcaster would set an "In" point right before the ball is snapped in football or right before the pitch is thrown in baseball or softball. For sports with more continuous action, such as baseball, hockey, or soccer, the full highlight should be slightly less than 10 seconds. In the case of these sports, perhaps set the "In" two passes before the point or goal is scored.

Most sports will have highlights in which the content is edited in a similar fashion: a cutaway—video of one team scoring, the other team scoring (or a big play), and then an additional score of whichever team won the game to end. If the game is a blowout, then all the highlights may be from the same team. To demonstrate a typical game recap highlight, a high school football game between the Nash High Lions and the Hall High Frogs will be used as an example. The broadcaster was told that Hall High won the game 21–7. Table 8.1 would be an appropriate script to go along with the accompanying highlights.

The highlights have a cutaway to start, which allows the broadcaster to talk about the game and give an additional piece of information ("first place on the line . . ."). The first highlight has the touchdown, while the script gives the name of the player, what happened, and the resulting score. After the touchdown, a cutaway of the cheerleaders breaks up the action on the field and shows that Hall High is happy after scoring. The Nash High touchdown is next, once again giving the name of the player, what happened, and the updated score. The cutaway after that score shows the Hall High coach upset with the result. Finally, because Hall High is the winner of the game, the highlights will end with a score from them. The script provides additional game-wide

TABLE 8.1 Example Script With Highlights

Script	Highlight
A BIG GAME IN THE EASTERN CONFERENCE TONIGHT—HALL HIGH HOSTING NASH HIGH . . . FIRST PLACE IS ON THE LINE . . .	Hall High football players running onto the field before the game (cutaway)
HALL HIGH GETS ON THE BOARD FIRST . . . CARL KERR RUNS IT IN FROM TEN YARDS OUT . . . 7–0 FROGS . . .	Carl Kerr 10-yard TD run Hall High cheerleaders celebrating
BUT THE LIONS ANSWER RIGHT BACK . . . MATT WILSON FINDS EVAN SHARP FOR THE 22-YARD TOUCHDOWN . . . WE ARE TIED AT SEVEN . . .	Matt Wilson to Evan Sharp TD pass Hall High coach upset
HALL TAKES THE LEAD FOR GOOD IN THE SECOND QUARTER . . . IT'S KERR AGAIN—HIS SECOND T-D OF THE GAME . . . HE FINISHES WITH 121 YARDS RUSHING AND TWO SCORES . . .	Carl Kerr 3-yard TD run Players celebrating after the score
HALL HIGH IS THE WINNER, 21–7 . . . THEY'RE NOW ALONE IN FIRST PLACE IN THE EASTERN CONFERENCE . . .	

information, including the total yards and touchdowns, before ending with the final score.

Editing Events

As discussed in chapter 7, not everything on a television sports broadcaster's agenda is a game. Instead, press conferences and practices can often be daily stops in which they have to get video for the evening's sportscast. While highlights can be fairly straightforward to edit (simply show the big plays), sometimes creative editing has to take place to ensure that video of an event is exciting for the television viewer to watch.

It is recommended to first quickly look through the shots to see what the editor has to work with. With that in mind, the broadcaster should then write the script before editing video from an event. This way the broadcaster can use the script to match up the video to his or her own words. A good rule to follow when editing is "If I see it, I should hear it." If the reporter is talking about something at the 10-second mark of the script, the editing should be done so that the specific thing that is being talked about will be on the screen during that time. Otherwise, the video may not match up with what the broadcaster is talking about, which could prove to be confusing to the viewer. If a broadcaster says, "Wilson will miss the next two weeks with a leg injury," but video of Smith is playing, the viewer might be left wondering if it is Wilson or Smith that is injured because the script and the video are telling two different stories.

When it comes time to edit an event, the **assembly edit** should be done first. This is the process of putting down the clips in the order in which they will ultimately be seen on the broadcast. A popular way to edit events is by using the shots gathered during sequence shooting in order to visually inform the viewer about what happened there. (See chapter 7 for more information on sequence shooting.) Each shot should be no more than about five seconds but can be significantly shorter if it matches up with the script. A final event VO should be about 45 seconds, with the understanding that only about the first 30 seconds or so will actually make the broadcast. After the assembly edit, the **sound edit** is the next step to make sure that all the volume is at the appropriate levels. A person should be able to hit "play" and not have to turn the volume up and down repeatedly during the video, so the key is to keep the audio levels consistent throughout.

Editing a Package

Editing a package is essentially a two-step process. The first step is to edit together the primary audio of a story, also known as the **A-roll.** This normally consists of the reporter's voice track and the interviews. This is primarily an edit for audio purposes, with the goal making sure that everything sounds correct when done. However, the A-roll does not leave a very visually appealing video when finished because the reporter's voice track either contains no video or video that is not very interesting.

Therefore, the next step is the **B-roll** in which the reporter track is covered with video that was shot out in the field. It is the supplemental video that helps tell the story visually to help support what the reporter and the interview subjects are discussing. When B-rolling, the broadcaster should pay close attention to the script to ensure that the video matches up with what is being talked about during the story ("If I see it, I should hear it"). For example, if a package about a high school volleyball team has the line "NICOLE DUNCAN LEADS THE TEAM IN KILLS," then the video that editing positions with that should be of Nicole Duncan. This is why it is important to have the script close by when editing a story.

In addition to the video, attention should be paid to the audio when B-rolling. When the reporter is talking in the voice track, the audio from the video should also be heard. This is known as **natural sound**, or the sound that occurs naturally in the field. For example, the story about the high school volleyball team from the previous paragraph should have the sounds from the volleyball practice or game that goes along with the video. Using the motto of "If I see it, I should hear it" as a guide, if there is video of a volleyball being spiked during a package, then the viewer should also hear the sound of a volleyball being spiked while the reporter is talking. When editing a package, the audio from the interviews and the reporter track will go on one audio channel (A1), while the natural sound from the video will go on a different audio channel on the timeline (A2). (Due to the additional importance of natural sound in audio-only pieces, the topic will be discussed in much greater detail in chapter 9.)

Editing a package can be intimidating at first, but it is essentially just combining many of the basic skills that are learned when first editing. If a broadcaster can edit video onto a timeline and also cut sound bites from interviews, then a package is simply putting them all together into one self-contained piece.

Anchoring the Sportscast

While anchoring is perhaps the most public part of a sports broadcaster's job, it is also often the last part of his or her day. It is not until after the research is done, the day is planned, the games or events are shot, the sportscast is produced, the scripts are written, and the video is edited that it is time to anchor the show. Despite being last on the agenda, it is hardly the least important.

A sample of 100 different sportscasters throughout the United States might result in 100 different styles and techniques when the show starts. Therefore, there is no one piece of advice that will work for everyone. Perhaps the best tip that can be provided is that sportscasters should simply be themselves when at the anchor desk. While other sportscasters can be watched for tips, simply trying to be a carbon-copy of someone on ESPN will likely not result in a successful career. Instead, broadcasters should be themselves.

The Teleprompter

When on the anchor desk, the scripts that have been written into the newsroom software will show up on the **teleprompter**. This device displays the scripts electronically on a piece of glass directly in front of the camera for the anchor to read during the sportscast. The difficult aspect of using a teleprompter is to make it sound like the anchor is talking, not reading. One of the best ways to help avoid the impression of reading is for broadcasters to familiarize themselves with the script before going on the set. While the broadcaster will likely have written the words, he or she may have done that hours before the show begins. Therefore, all scripts should be reread in the minutes before the sportscast.

Stick to the Script . . . Except With Highlights

For straight VOs, the broadcaster should write the script out beforehand and stick to that script when on the set. There is no need to ad-lib a story that has specific facts and statistics. By going off-script in those moments, the broadcaster becomes more likely to make a mistake such as saying the wrong name or giving an incorrect detail. These mistakes will hurt a broadcaster's credibility, so sticking to the already-written script will help to avoid any mistakes when on the air.

However, highlights do allow for a little more freedom for the sportscaster. While some anchors do write out the highlights word for word, others instead rely on a **shot sheet** (sometimes called a cut sheet) (see table 8.2). These documents take the place of a script and instead simply have a description of the highlight, along with perhaps an important fact.

The shot sheet contains just the basic information of what happened in very simple, bullet-point–style sentences. This allows the anchor to ad-lib during the highlights, perhaps adding in some of their own descriptive words and reactions to help tell the story. Beginning broadcasters may wish to write out their highlights completely, while eventually working their way up to a shot sheet when they feel more comfortable.

Speak Clearly and Have Fun

Obviously, a key aspect of anchoring a sportscast is talking directly into the camera. The anchor should speak at a speed that is not so

TABLE 8.2 Example Football Shot Sheet

Situation	Action	Result
2nd quarter . . . Game is tied 7–7 Hall High has the ball 1st and 10 from the 3-yard line	CARL KERR runs untouched to the left for the TOUCHDOWN	HALL HIGH takes a 14–7 lead . . . CARL KERR: 121 yards rushing Two touchdowns

fast that it becomes hard to understand, but not so slow that it is monotone and boring. The middle ground between the two will also allow for the sports broadcaster to enunciate words properly so that they can be better understood. Not enunciating words is a mistake that many beginning broadcasters make, as they often start speaking so fast that parts of words are accidentally dropped when reading out loud. Ultimately, the key to anchoring is to sound conversational and relaxed while not sounding like a script is being read.

Anchoring a sportscast should be a fun experience for the anchor and the audience watching. Sports traditionally have a lighter tone and often give the viewers a break from the serious aspects of the rest of the newscast. Therefore, sports broadcasters should do their best to have lots of energy, smile often, and remember that sports are, most often, not life or death. Sportscasts should be entertaining, and the viewers, even if their teams came out on the losing end, should enjoy watching the show. A sportscaster's tone should lie somewhere between the straightforward and plain delivery of the news anchor and someone who is over-the-top showmanship anchoring. It should be entertaining, but not distracting. However, it is also important to remember to be serious when necessary. When former NBA star Kobe Bryant was killed in a helicopter crash in January 2020, sports broadcasters should have refrained from smiling and having a good time when reporting the news to instead match the tone of the story.

Practice, Practice, Practice

No one is a good television sports anchor overnight. Instead, the key to becoming a successful anchor is practice. It ultimately takes many, many shows before someone finally gets comfortable on the desk giving highlights and reading scripts. The repetitions are especially helpful when using the teleprompter: the more time spent using that device will help make the reading seem more second nature. Practicing reading out loud can help, too. When reading a website or newspaper, one can practice reading it out loud for extra repetitions.

Additionally, in order to improve, a broadcaster should record his or her sportscasts and watch them afterward. What was successful? What looked good? What caused an issue? Watching the show twice, the second time with the sound off, will help draw attention to the body language and facial expressions to determine if those need any adjusting in future shows.

A Day in the Life of a Local Sports Broadcaster

It should be noted that while this section will discuss the "typical" day for a local sports broadcaster, in reality there is no such thing. Every day is different, which is one of the aspects of the job that makes it so exciting. Friday nights during high school football season are filled with driving all across the viewing area getting highlights at various games. However, the summer months are often relatively quiet with high school and college sports taking a break. Weekend games sometimes start at 1:00 p.m., so those can prove to be long days for a broadcaster, who will end up working almost a 12-hour day. Therefore, for the purposes of this section, the local sports broadcaster (the fictional Sophie Scott) is working a Tuesday in February, which is right in the heart of high school and college basketball season.

MAJOR MOMENTS

The Big Show

While *SportsCenter* has been ESPN's flagship news and highlights show since the network's inception in 1979, the show took on a different persona from 1992 to 1997. In that time period, the evening edition of *SportsCenter* was primarily hosted by Keith Olbermann and Dan Patrick. With those two at the helm, the show became must-see television for sports fans, and their own version became known as "The Big Show."

Their show was different from almost anything that had been on the network previously. Their show was humorous, featured a great deal of ad-libbing, and had smart, well-written scripts (Curtis, 2019). The shows became incredibly popular for sports fans everywhere, including famous celebrities from Jerry Seinfeld to Bill Murray (Miller & Shales, 2011). They even had fans among others in the business—one writer observed that "every wannabe sportscaster" was essentially doing a poor impression of the two on their own evening sportscast (Curtis, 2019, para. 6).

The label "The Big Show" was actually not given to the show by ESPN executives, but was coined by the hosts (Miller & Shales, 2011). They were quick to refer to their show by that title whenever possible, even cowriting a book called "The Big Show," which gave readers a behind-the-scenes look at the show (Olbermann & Patrick, 1997). No matter where the description came from, it ultimately was a fit. Olbermann and Patrick's version of *SportsCenter* is still considered the gold standard of the program, even though Olbermann's contentious departure from ESPN for Fox left many of the network's executives with an unfavorable opinion of the former host (Miller & Shales, 2011). However, when ESPN was set to celebrate the 40th anniversary of the network in 2019, they invited the two back to anchor *SportsCenter* that night. And so, for one night only, Olbermann and Patrick were back on ESPN's airwaves giving "The Big Show" to homes across the United States (Scott, 2019).

Morning

A local sports broadcaster's shift is traditionally at night because he or she has to be a part of the late newscasts. Therefore, the mornings and early afternoons are spent reading stories online, calling sources for story ideas, and updating social media if there is a breaking news situation. This is also time to look at the schedule of games that day to decide which ones might be worth covering at night. In this city, Tuesday night is a popular one for high school basketball, so the sport broadcaster will likely have to shoot a game or two after the 6:00 news.

As of mid-morning, no urgent stories need added attention, so Sophie calls the local college's sports information director (SID) to find out when the men's basketball team is practicing today and if it would be possible to interview the coach and a player beforehand. Tomorrow night the team has a big conference game, so these interviews would be used to preview the game during today and tomorrow's shows. The SID reports that practice starts at 2:00 p.m. and that, if she could be there by 1:30, there should be time for a quick interview with the coach and a player. Sophie has the advantage of covering a smaller school, so arranging these interviews is easier. Big programs often make players and coaches available once a week at a time designated by the school, so the media has to work around the school's schedule. In this case, because the school is smaller, they work closely with the local media to get as much coverage as possible.

The Early Afternoon Interview

A local sports broadcaster's shift would normally start around 2:30 p.m., but with the interview opportunity, today is an early arrival. Sophie arrives at the station around 1:00 and quickly gathers the camera equipment to take to practice. The camera bag includes the video camera, a wireless microphone, a handheld microphone, headphones, and assorted cables and batteries. After grabbing a tripod to complete the kit, she hops into a station vehicle and is off to the arena.

Sophie arrives at the arena by 1:20, which gives her time to get everything set up. By getting there early, she will not be rushed and should allow for a more pleasant interview since she will not be scrambling to get ready while the coach has to wait. She finds a spot to conduct the interviews in front of the school's modest trophy case and sets up the tripod with the camera on it. She elects to use the handheld microphone because this will be a quick interview, so there will not be time to attach the wireless microphone to the coach and player. As promised, the coach emerges from the locker room with the SID shortly after 1:30, and Sophie is told she has about five minutes to talk to the coach. Approximately seven questions later, the coach is heading into the gym and the star player takes his place in front of the camera. After another quick interview, Sophie thanks the SID for helping to set up the interviews and gets back in her car to return to the television station.

6:00 Show Prep

Sophie's sportscast airs during the 6:00 p.m. news, so she has some time to prepare after getting back to the station a little after 2:00. She checks her email to make sure that nothing important has happened since she was at practice and then starts to formulate the rundown of her show. Today she has three minutes for her sportscast. As of now, her rundown is:

High school basketball preview—VO (:45)

Tonight's games—Graphic (:15)

Tomorrow's college basketball game—VO/SOT (1:00)

Last night's women's college game—VO/SOT (:45)

NBA player scores 55 points last night—VO (:15)

There are several high school games tonight, including the top team in the state playing, so she decides to show video of them. The graphic will list the other games on the schedule. The interviews she just got at practice will be part of the VO/SOT preview, while she will use highlights and interviews from last night when recapping the women's game. Finally, since she works for a local station, Sophie does not traditionally show NBA highlights, but she believes the 55 points was a big story when it happened last night, so she adds it.

Most broadcasters will write their scripts before editing the video. This allows them to pick video that matches up with what they chose to write about. Sophie's high school basketball preview will focus on Hart High School, the local team that is also the top-ranked team in the state. Tonight, they are playing Lynch High School, a team that has just three wins on the season. Since this will likely be a mismatch, Sophie focuses her script on Hart High while mentioning that Lynch High is having a tough season. After that story ends, a graphic will appear on the screen along with the other games in town. Assuming the timing works out, Sophie is also hoping to get highlights of Windham High against Smith High, so she is sure to include that in her script.

She will then come back on camera to introduce the college basketball preview for tomorrow. The coach mentioned in his interview that he has been pleased with the play of the seniors lately, so Sophie will focus her script on that before the SOT from the coach about that topic airs. After the SOT, the video from last night's women's game will run. The team forced a season-high 22 turnovers in their win, and the team captain talked about that in the postgame press conference. Therefore, Sophie will focus on the defense in her script before playing the sound bite. Finally, the script about the 55-point game will be relatively quick and just give the main details.

The early sportscasts during the week often consist primarily of **file video**, or video that has been used previously. Sophie selects video from Hart's previous game to serve as her video for the high school basketball story and video from the local college's last game for that story. Since her story about the women's game focuses on their defense from last night, she goes through the entire game footage and recuts a new highlight package consisting of great defensive plays. Finally, she cuts highlights of the NBA player's 55-point game that aired last night on ESPN.

Just before 5:00, an email arrives in her inbox from the local college saying that guard Adam Mathis will play tomorrow after missing the last three games with an ankle injury. It certainly would have been better to have found this out earlier so Sophie could have asked the coach about it during their interview, but it is still worth putting in the show. She quickly writes a social media post about the news and then creates a new rundown in which the NBA player's 55-point night is out:

High school basketball preview—VO (:45)

Tonight's games—Graphic (:15)

Tomorrow's college basketball game—VO/SOT (1:00)

Mathis returns tomorrow—VO (:15)

Last night's women's college game—VO/SOT (:45)

Sophie writes up a brief script about Mathis' return and finds file video of when he scored 15 points in a game from earlier in the season. In addition, she writes a story for the website about the news and posts another update on social media with a link to her newly written web story. At 6:20 p.m., she is at the anchor desk reading her sportscast.

Shooting High School Basketball

The early show is over, but Sophie's day is still just beginning. During the week, games typically take place at night, and she has high school basketball on her agenda. In her city, the girls' games take place immediately before the boys' games, so she's hoping to get highlights from three different contests. She grabs the camera gear again, loads into a station vehicle, and is off to Hart High School.

Sophie walks into the Hart High gym just as the fourth quarter is starting. She finds a spot in the corner of the gym (see chapter 7 for tips on shooting basketball highlights) and gets a cutaway and video of several baskets from both teams before Lynch High pulls away late to win 50–41. After the final buzzer sounds, she makes her way to the scorer's table to get copies of both rosters and also find out the leading scorers for the game. There are no rosters available to take with her, so she simply takes video of the scorebook with her camera so she will have the names and numbers recorded.

There is a short break in between games, so Sophie again shoots video of the scorebook to get the boys' roster and then goes back to her spot on the corner to shoot the game. As expected, Hart High, the top team in the state, takes a commanding lead early, and it is 22–8 after the first quarter. That will be more than enough highlights for Sophie, so she leaves and heads to Smith High School for her second game.

It is halftime of the boys' game when she arrives at Smith High, so Sophie quickly gets the rosters for each team and finds a spot to shoot. In back-and-forth action, each team scores eight baskets in the third quarter. Sophie decides she has enough highlights, so she leaves to head back to the station and begin preparing her 11:00 p.m. show.

11:00 Show Prep

Traditionally, local sports broadcasters are given more time in the late local news because most games happen at night. Sophie is no exception, and she has been given 3 minutes and 45 seconds for her segment during the 11:00 p.m. show. Before creating a rundown, she once again checks her email and social media to make sure that there was not a major story that occurred when she was out shooting the basketball games. It appears to be a quiet night so far, so she tentatively creates a rundown:

Lynch High at Hart High boys—VO (:45)

Windham High at Smith High boys—VO (:30)

Boys scoreboard—GFX (:15)

Lynch High at Hart High girls—VO (:30)

Girls scoreboard—GFX (:15)

Feb 21–25 – youtube Sav Knights

Tomorrow's college basketball game—VO/SOT (1:00)

Mathis returns tomorrow—VO (:15)

NHL game—VO (:15)

Since the Hart High boys are the top team in the state, she makes the easy decision to start her show with that game. She will then wipe directly to the other boys' game she has highlights of before showing a boys' scoreboard. Sportscasters typically keep boys' games and girls' games clumped together to help with the flow of the show but should not automatically default to starting with the boys. The best game with the biggest storyline should always be the lead, regardless of the gender of the athletes. In this case, the Hart High boys are the clear lead due to their state-wide prominence.

Sophie will wipe from the boys' scoreboard to the Lynch and Hart High girls' game and then show the girls' scoreboard. It is back on camera after that to do another VO/SOT about the men's basketball team, but this time choosing a different angle to the story from what she did earlier. The story about Mathis returning will be next, before wrapping it up with a quick highlight from the state's NHL team that played tonight.

She can safely edit the Lynch/Hart girls' and boys' games because she knows the result of the girls' game and can safely assume that the Hart boys will win. She will wait until there is a final score reported in for the Windham/Smith boys' game because she wants to end the highlight with the winning team, and it was too close to call when she left. For the two games she can edit, she picks a cutaway and three baskets, writing down the numbers of the players who scored so she can identify them by name using the rosters she got video of while at the gyms.

The hockey game is also over, and she edits a video from the television broadcast that is a cutaway of the coach and the game-winning goal. Since she's a local sports broadcaster, she wants to focus her attention on the most local part of her show, and that is the high school games and the college basketball team tomorrow. While the hockey team is in her state, they are not located in the same city, so just one quick highlight will be enough. Finally, Sophie rewrites the basketball preview story and picks a new sound bite that is different from what she ran earlier. Additionally, the Mathis story will be slightly rewritten, but the same video will air, so she does not need to reedit anything.

As the night proceeds, Sophie gathers final scores from the area basketball games, adds them to her two scoreboards, and posts them to social media and the television station's website. These results are either called into the station, emailed to her, or posted on social media. The Hart High boys won by 30 points, so her gamble to edit those highlights before getting the final score was a good decision. However, as the minutes tick by and it gets closer to showtime, she still does not have a final score for the Windham at Smith boys' game. She leaves voicemails with the coaches and athletic directors and continues to search social media for any indication of who won. Finally, at 10:45, the Windham head coach returns her call to let her know that his team won 66–52. She quickly edits together three baskets from the game, ending her highlights with a Windham basket so that they are celebrating when she talks about them winning the game. Tonight ended up coming right down to the wire thanks to that late score, but Sophie is ready to go when her sportscast begins at 11:25 p.m.

Wrapping Up

The show is over, but there are still some final items on a local sports broadcaster's to-do list before it is time to call it a day. As discussed in chapter 6, the website has become a key part of news delivery, so Sophie will update the sports section with some video from tonight's games and the story from today's college basketball practice. Finally, in order to know what to expect tomorrow, she takes a quick look at the schedule so she has an idea of the stories she is going to be talking out and if anything needs to be set up in the morning. Then it is time to head home and get ready to do it all again tomorrow.

CHAPTER WRAP-UP

HK*PROPEL* ACTIVITIES

HK*Propel* includes both a written walkthrough on video editing and a video narrated by the author demonstrating how to edit softball highlights. For student practice, clips from that softball game have also been included at HK*Propel* with six practice scripts to edit from. Additionally, examples of rundowns from all over the United States on the same night are provided online to demonstrate the variety of sportscasts based on the location and market size of the various sportscasters.

SUMMARY

This chapter focused on the job duties involved with being a local sports broadcaster. While many may assume that anchoring the sportscast is the most important part of the day, it is but a small part of the daily routine. Television sports broadcasters are conducting interviews, writing scripts and website stories, shooting and editing highlights from games, and producing the sportscast.

Ultimately, the job of the local sports broadcaster comes down to thinking about what story will be most interesting to the audience watching. This helps to determine story selection, highlight order, and whom to interview when previewing and recapping games. Local sports broadcasters in smaller cities simply cannot compete with ESPN when it comes to covering national sporting events, so instead they should focus on the advantages they do have. In most cases, those advantages include the opportunity to focus on the sports in that community. That means greater attention on high school sports and local college action and showcasing individual local athletes doing amazing things. The audience can get national highlights any number of places, but highlighting local high school games is how these sports broadcasters can make their mark.

Phil Cole/Getty Images

CHAPTER 9

Radio Broadcasting and Podcasting

CHAPTER OBJECTIVES

Many of the skills needed to be a successful audio sports broadcaster are different from those used in television. Additionally, the rise of audio broadcasting has created a variety of new job possibilities. This chapter focuses on radio broadcasting and podcasting, including the following:

- Understanding the differences between television and radio broadcasting
- Recognizing the importance of writing for the ear and natural sound
- Describing the various roles in a radio sports talk show
- Evaluating the reasons for the increase in the popularity of podcasting
- Identifying the various steps needed to start a podcast

Sports broadcasting on television has been proven to be a multi billion-dollar business, but even as television continues to be a major power, it is audio broadcasting that is having a renaissance. The increased popularity of podcasting has opened the door for new voices to be heard with few barriers to reaching a mass audience. Additionally, internet streaming has allowed sports talk radio and radio play-by-play announcers to have global audiences as the broadcasts can be listened to anywhere.

It is fairly obvious that the biggest difference between radio and television broadcasting is the inclusion of video on television. In many cases, the pictures tell the story in television, as the viewers can simply watch what is happening on their own. However, with radio, the role of the broadcaster becomes more important to the story because he or she has to act as the eyes for the listener.

Radio Stories

Just as television news has video news packages that are self-contained stories, radio broadcasts have **wraps** with a similar format. The reporter will interview people ahead of time, write the script, and then edit the story into a piece that will run about two minutes. However, when writing a radio piece, writing for the ear and using natural sound has become increasingly important.

Writing and Reading for the Ear

In chapter 5, the importance of writing short, simple sentences was emphasized. This skill is even more important in radio because there is no visual element to reinforce what the reporter is discussing. In television, a viewer can often determine what a story is about by simply watching the video, but there is no way to fall back on that option in radio. Radio scripts should sound conversational so that the listener feels as if the story is being told directly to them. Therefore, not only do such scripts need to be written clearly, they also need to be spoken clearly. Radio broadcasters should be sure to speak at a pace at which listeners can understand them and also emphasize key words that are important to the story. (Tips on how to format the script to help with this skill are found in chapter 5.)

Using Natural Sound and Nat Pops

Chapter 8 briefly touched on the use of natural sound in television stories, but it is perhaps more important in audio pieces. Due to the fact that there is no video to draw the audience into the story, the audio has to serve that purpose. Therefore, sound from the actual event should be placed in the background of stories. This **natural sound** (sometimes referred to as ambient sound, or nat sound) is any sound that is recorded in the field. This natural sound should be recorded at the scene of the event and then played in the background during appropriate times during a recorded story. For example, if a reporter were doing a story on a baseball team and went to batting practice to interview several players, the sound of the crack of the bat might play in the background of the story while the reporter is talking. Such natural sound elements can make the audience feel like they are actually at the event with the reporter.

Another use of natural sound is what is known as a **natural pop** (often shortened to nat pop), which is a brief burst of natural sound at full volume. With a nat pop, that sound would be the only element that is heard during that brief 1-3 seconds. If the reporter at that baseball practice was going to use a nat pop of the coach talking to his players, it might sound something like this:

> Reporter track: AFTER SCORING TWO RUNS IN THE LAST FOUR GAMES, HEAD COACH BLAKE BOWER IS LOOKING FOR IMPROVEMENT AT THE PLATE . . .
>
> Nat pop: "Good swing—that's how to do it."
>
> Coach interview: "We've been struggling to hit lately, and we've been focusing on that a lot in practice this week. Guys are getting dialed in more and I think that it will pay off."

The nat pop of the coach talking to his players once again makes listeners feel like they are there at the practice with the reporter. It also fits in nicely with the flow of the script, which is a key element of any nat pop. The reporter is discussing how they need to get better at hitting, the coach's nat pop references the hitting, and then the coach talks more about the hitting. One of the keys to natural sound and nat pop is not to include them in the story just for the sake of including them. Nat sound and nat pops need to be relevant to the story, or they may end up being distracting to the listener.

Gathering Natural Sound

The process of including natural sound in a story starts when a reporter first gets to the scene of the event. Before starting to gather interviews and information, the reporter should take a few moments to take note of what is happening at the location in terms of sound. What are the noises that will make listeners feel like they are at the scene? Once those elements are determined, the reporter should be sure to get audio-only recordings of the sounds so that they can be included in the completed piece.

It should be noted that there is sound everywhere. Even in quiet locations, there is the hum of an air conditioner or the buzzing of insects in nature. Therefore, while some reporters might get to an area and believe there is no natural sound to be recorded, there is always something out there to capture. In some cases, the silence of the moment can be a part of the story. When sports teams started playing games in empty stadiums after the onset of the COVID-19 pandemic in 2020, the lack of the sound of fans cheering became the sound of the season (Axelrod, 2020). Therefore, if a reporter were doing a story on these games, he or she would likely reference that silence, with a nat pop of players being heard clearly during games due to the lack of fans.

When writing the script, reporters should make note of the nat pops they want to include in the story and include them in the writing. Nat sound and nat pops should not be afterthoughts but should be showcased directly in the script:

> Reporter track: THESE BRAND NEW BASEBALL FIELDS ARE EXACTLY WHAT THESE LITTLE LEAGUE PLAYERS HAVE BEEN LOOKING FOR . . .
>
> Nat pop of player talking to his mom: It's so nice here.
>
> Field Owner: I'M HAPPY TO HEAR THE KIDS SAY THEY FEEL LIKE BIG LEAGUERS BECAUSE THAT'S THE POINT . . .

By writing the nat pop directly into the script, the reporter will know exactly what quote to use and write around it within the script, just as if he or she were writing around a sound bite from an interview.

While nat pops can be a useful tool to help the audience, the reporter should also be careful not to overdo it. Too many nat pops, or ones

Rich Graessle/Icon Sportswire via Getty Images

WFAN's Mike Francesa (left) is considered one of the pioneers of sports talk radio, thanks to his time hosting "Mike and the Mad Dog."

that are too long, can end up being more distracting than helpful. The sound should last just long enough to give the feeling of being there, so usually just a second or two will do the trick. Finally, reporters should be using actual sound from the location. In no circumstances should sound effects found online or sound from another location be used. That would be disingenuous and unethical as a reporter.

Sports Talk Radio

One of the most popular audio options in the world of sports broadcasting is sports talk radio. These shows devote their entire time, and often the entire day, to discussing and debating the latest sports news. While that might seem like a simple concept, sports radio stations have become popular spots for listeners and for broadcasters looking to break into the sports business.

Format of a Sports Talk Radio Show

While there are hundreds of different sports talk radio shows throughout the United States, they are all ultimately very formulaic. The format in a big city like Los Angeles is almost identical to that of a broadcast in a small town in Kansas. However, based on the popularity of these sports talk shows, that formula seems to work.

Each show is traditionally hosted by the same people for a few hours each day. For example, KNBR in San Francisco had the following daily weekday lineup in 2019 (Media Services, 2019):

5am-6am: *The Leadoff Spot with Adam Copeland*

6am-10am: *Murph & Mac*

10am-2pm: *Papa & Lund*

2pm-6pm: *Tolbert, Krueger, & Brooks*

6pm-10pm: *The Mark Willard Show*

10pm-12am: *KNBR Tonight with Drew Hoffar*

As is the case throughout the country on sports talk shows, some of the hosts, such as Greg Papa of *Papa & Lund*, are traditional broadcasters who have worked their way up through smaller radio stations and may also do play-by-play of some teams in that city (Media Services, 2019). Other hosts are former athletes, such as Tom Tolbert of *Tolbert, Krueger, & Brooks*. Tolbert was a basketball player with the Golden State Warriors and made the transition to hosting the show on KNBR when his playing career ended in 1996 (Barney, 2019). Whether former athlete or traditional broadcaster, a host's goals are the same: to discuss the daily sports news in an entertaining and informative way.

The hosts will talk about the day's events, take calls from listeners, and conduct interviews live on the air. The commercial breaks are a key part of the show, as the hosts use those breaks as a way to change the content. For example, the hosts will discuss Topic A for about 12-15 minutes, take a commercial break, and then talk about Topic B or take phone calls about Topic A when the show returns from the break. This allows the show to have a natural flow instead of jumping from topic to topic at random points in the conversation.

Sports Talk Show Hosts

Sports talk show hosts often have one common trait—they are very opinionated about the topics of the day. If a football team decides to change quarterbacks during a losing streak, the talk show host will likely go on the air to say that this is either the greatest decision ever or the dumbest decision ever. Such extreme opinions often play well with the listening audience, because listeners will either have their own views validated or have someone with which to disagree. While that disagreement might seem like something that would cause listeners to change the channel, research has proven otherwise. For example, a study of political talk shows found that 30-40 percent of the audience often disagreed with the hosts but remained loyal listeners to the show (Emmons, 1995).

If there are multiple hosts on a show, they are often on opposite sides of an issue. This can lead to a shouting match between the two as they argue about which of them is correct. Perhaps the most famous sports talk show duo of all time, Mike Francesa and Chris "Mad

Dog" Russo of WFAN in New York City, made an entire career out of arguing with each other about sports teams and athletes in New York and beyond (Paumgarten, 2004). Audiences were drawn to the arguments between the two, such as the time a debate about building a new Yankee Stadium resulted in an almost 10-minute long disagreement about how long it took to use the bathrooms at the team's stadium at the time (Mike & The Mad Dog, 2019).

Despite the yelling and arguing that often makes these shows seem chaotic, being a sports talk show host involves a great deal of research and preparation. For example, on the KNBR lineup discussed earlier, Mark Willard is the sole host for *The Mark Williard Show* from 6 p.m. to 10 p.m. That means Willard has to be able to discuss a variety of topics for four hours by himself. If he simply shows up to work without doing any research, he will not be able to discuss the teams intelligently, have prepared questions for guests, or respond quickly to the callers on his show. Therefore, he needs to read numerous news articles, watch games, and follow along with what fans are discussing on social media.

This preparation is also key to determining what the hosts will discuss on that day's show. For example, New York City sports talk radio hosts have two NFL teams, two NBA teams, two MLB teams, three NHL teams, a WNBA team, and a variety of other local sports and athletes about which they can talk every day. Through research, especially now on social media, a host will be able to determine the topics that are of the most interest to the public. If the host spends 15 minutes talking about the NFL's New York Giants but the fans are most interested in hearing about the Jets, then the host might have fans that change the station or tune out entirely. Finding topics that will resonate with the audience is a key part of the preparation for a show.

Shows that are entertaining and well researched can quickly develop a loyal following, which can ultimately give them a strong influence on the city's fan bases. While Russo and Francesa were known for their arguments, they also became some of the most powerful media members in New York City during their time at the top of the ratings chart. Perhaps no situation better showcased influence than when baseball player Mike Piazza in 1998 was about to be traded from the Florida Marlins. Piazza's agent called the *Mike and the Mad Dog* show to see if the hosts could convince the Mets to trade for the slugging catcher. The Mets' general manager said the team was not interested, so the hosts spent the remainder of the show criticizing the Mets for not attempting to make a trade. That led to fans calling in to the show to criticize the team, too. In perhaps the best demonstration of their popularity, listening to Russo and Francesa's show at the time was the Mets' co-owner, who immediately called together the Mets' team officials and demanded they trade for Piazza. The next morning, Piazza was a member of the Mets, and the talk show duo has been widely credited for making the trade a reality (Vasquez, 2017).

Behind the Scenes of a Sports Talk Show

As with any sports broadcasting production, while the on-air people get the majority of the attention from the viewing and listening public, the shows would not be able to be as successful without the behind-the-scenes staff. The three primary off-air jobs with a sports talk show are the producer, the board operator, and the call screener.

The **producer** works closely with the on-air hosts to decide the content of the show. This may involve conducting research, booking guests, and deciding when the hosts will talk about which subjects. Jonathan Kern, formerly an executive producer with NPR, described being a producer as putting together a jigsaw puzzle. There are various elements that have to go together in one show, and it is up to the producer to determine how they all fit with each other (Kern, 2008). The producer must also keep an eye on what is happening in the sports world while the show is going on. The hosts will likely be focused on the show, so the producer will be on the lookout for breaking news or updates to stories the hosts have already discussed. If that happens, the producer will let the hosts know and then reorganize the show quickly so that the new information can be discussed.

The **board operator** (often shortened to board op) ensures that the show is operating successfully technically. This person is primarily tasked with running the audio board that broadcasts what comes out of the microphones to the airwaves. If one host is speaking very loudly, while the cohost has a soft voice, the board operator would use the various sliders on the board to make them sound like they are speaking at similar volumes. The board op would also make sure that callers, both guests and fans, are being broadcast both to the hosts' headsets and to the audience at home.

The **call screener** is in charge of organizing the calls from the listeners at home who want to speak with the hosts on the air. Callers are an important part of most sports talk shows, and it is up to the screener to decide who will make it onto the air and who will not. Often the most desirable trait of a caller is simply to be interesting. A call screener for a political show once said, "A call is like a record—three minutes—and people will either listen to it or turn away" (Emmons, 1995). Therefore, screeners want to make sure that once callers get on the air, they are able to pose an interesting question to the hosts.

It should be noted that at smaller radio stations, the jobs of producer, board operator, and call screener are often done by the hosts themselves. The hosts will make all the show preparations ahead of time, run the audio board during the show, and also bring guests directly on the air during the show. Most radio shows run on a delay, meaning that the conversation happening on the air does not reach the audience until several seconds later. This can help the host if a caller who makes the air says something inappropriate or tries to take the conversation in the wrong direction.

Pro Advice

© Dawn Davenport

Dawn Davenport

Sports radio host, WGFX 104.5, Nashville, Tennessee

Dawn Davenport always figured that her broadcasting future was in television. She started her career as a sportscaster at a television station in Wilmington, North Carolina, and was occasionally called on to be a guest on the local sports talk radio show. However, being a *guest* was as far as she expected it to go: "I never thought, 'Maybe I should do sports talk radio.'" Her career path eventually brought her to Nashville, Tennessee. After more than 10 years at a television station there, with occasional guest radio appearances, a local Nashville station offered her a chance to be a full-time host. That job offer ended up being a historic one, as Davenport became the first woman to host a sports radio show full time in the city. She is currently the cohost of the afternoon sports program on the city's popular 104.5 *The Zone* station.

How much prep work is involved in putting a show together?

The thing that I have found is you have to know about everything. I'm on the air for three hours, and, give or take, I'd say I probably prep for at least five every day. On the weekend, you're watching games, you're watching highlights, and checking stat sheets to make sure that you're on top of everything. So, while you're on the air for just three hours, the prep work people forget about definitely puts you over probably a 40-hour a week job.

Take us through your show routine. What is it like from start to finish?

The top of every hour it's the big headlines that everybody listening cares about. Then it differs within season. When it's more of a slow sports season, like the summer, you come up with different interesting topics to get people involved. You can kind of go outside of the box and it's not necessarily breaking news and what's happening right now. Let's get some kind of discussion and have some fun with that. What's the greatest sporting event you've ever witnessed in person? Things like that you can sort of do in the slower months when there's not as much live action going on. But when we're in football season, I would say 95 percent of our talk is football.

What is it like talking to the callers? Can you prepare for that at all?

Not really. That kind of goes back to your prep work every single day knowing at least a little about every single story or every single team. If somebody calls and says, "I'm a big Houston Texans fan and I want to talk about their offensive line," you should be prepared to offer something on there. It's not the easiest, but it just all goes back to your prep work.

Sometimes you're off the beaten path with crazy callers who take a show and make it interesting. I think it's important to kind of embrace the kind of unknown with the callers as well because it could turn into something that's really fun and interesting for listeners.

What do you think makes a good radio talk show host?

I think it can be a lot of different things. Like for example, I'm not the kind of radio talk show host that will go in and attack callers and listeners. That's not my style. Now that's maybe very different for some of the other local shows here in Nashville. I think the bottom line, being successful on the radio, and, let's be honest, in journalism in general, is prep work—what you put in.

Make sure you're knowledgeable about what you're talking about. Make sure you're read up on the national stories. That's tons of reading, and that's something I didn't do early in my career. Read the local papers, read the national papers, get on Twitter, read the blogs—do all of that. Find out what people are interested in and what sparks interest. Then utilize those topics to pull people in.

Is being a sports radio talk show host a fun job?

It's a blast! In my career, I've done a little bit of everything. [Sideline reporters] have 30 seconds to get your story across. In local [television] sports, you have a minute and a half on a Tuesday night to hit local sports. Well, guess what? In sports talk radio, you have three hours. You can really dive deep into stories. You can get to know people who listen to your show, you can utilize all of your knowledge and your research to start an interesting conversation and you never know what you're going to get. Every day is different. You might know your topics and I think good radio hosts have a rundown of "This is what we're focusing on today," but the thrill of the unknown, when you have no idea what direction your show might go in, makes it really fun.

Types of Sports Talk Radio

While the format of sports talk radio shows is normally the same for all broadcasts, the content within those shows can vary greatly based on where the show is based. The differences between national and local radio sports talk shows can be seen in the audience and in what the hosts are discussing on a daily basis.

National Sports Radio

Shows that are from national radio networks, such as ESPN Radio, are played throughout the country on local affiliates. Programming from national entities will focus on the big sports stories of the day throughout the world. This leads to a focus on the most popular sports and athletes who have a large national following, since fans from all over the country are all listening to the same shows. For example, ESPN Radio's nationally broadcast shows will be heard in all 50 states at the same time, so the hosts need to have topics that will interest all of them. Therefore, regionally popular leagues, such as NASCAR, might not get much attention on these national shows because fans in certain areas are not very interested.

Local Sports Radio

While national and syndicated radio shows have a large audience, most sports talk radio shows focus on local sports and are heard in a specific area. For example, sports radio station KILT is based in Houston, Texas, and is primarily focused on Houston sports. This station is not heard throughout the country over the traditional radio airwaves (although most stations can now be heard anywhere through the internet). This localization allows for a much more focused content selection by the hosts because they know exactly what fans in that city are most interested in hearing. A host in Lexington, Kentucky, could spend an entire three-hour show talking about the University of Kentucky basketball team because that is unquestionably the most popular topic in that city. However, if a national show attempted that same format, it would likely not garner much interest outside of Kentucky.

National or Local?

While there are these two very different methods of hosting a sports talk radio show, one has not been proven to be better or more successful than the other. In fact, what makes them different is ultimately part of the appeal. In Boston, the local sports talk radio stations dominate the ratings, while the national broadcasts from ESPN Radio barely register any listeners (Finn, 2020). In a city like Boston, where the Red Sox, Patriots, Celtics, and Bruins are immensely popular, this focus on local sports has proven to be a smart decision.

However, not all cities in the United States have the demand for a local sports station, so national broadcasts provide sports talk content for many Americans. For example, Coos Bay, Oregon, is not home to any major sports teams, but it does have a sports talk radio station. Instead of filling the day's lineup with local hosts with little local sports to discuss, the majority of the programming on that network is syndicated from national media outlets. For cities like Coos Bay, national programming allows sports fans to still be able to listen to sports talk radio.

Podcasting

Hosting a sports talk show on a commercial radio station can involve years of hard work to even have the opportunity be on the air. However, new technologies have made it easy to produce and distribute sports talk shows globally with just a few clicks of a mouse on a computer. The creation of **podcasts** has allowed many people to create their own program with little financial commitment and have the potential for it to be available throughout the world. A podcast is an audio recording that listeners can download to a mobile device and play at their convenience.

History of Podcasting

The creation of the genre of podcasting is ultimately connected to the invention of the iPod, hence the name *pod*cast—a combination of iPod and broadcast (Hammersley, 2004). While MP3 players existed previously, it was the iPod that revolutionized the market. It had a simple interface and was small for easy portability, making it very popular almost instantly. Users added music to the device's library through their CDs or online sources (Costello, 2020). While perhaps primarily created as a music device, these spoken word audio files became increasingly popular as more people began using MP3 players. Many point to 2005 as the year podcasts hit the mainstream, when the *New Oxford American Dictionary* selected "podcast" as their Word of the Year (Bottomley, 2015a).

As technology evolved, the opportunity for users to access podcasts became easier. In June 2005, Apple added a podcasting section to their iTunes music store (Neumayr & Kerris, 2005). These podcasts could now be downloaded directly to a user's device, increasing availability throughout the world. Additionally, iPods evolved into iPhones, allowing the audience to have one device that could do a number of different things. By 2020, podcasts could be downloaded onto nearly any mobile device—not just Apple products—through a variety of different online locations.

Popularity of Podcasting for Listeners

The opportunity for anyone to download podcasts has helped make them one of the fastest

Robert Laberge/Getty Images

In this podcast, the hosts are interviewing a NASCAR driver for a show that will be recorded and distributed later over the internet.

growing media options available. Since 2005, more than 700,000 podcasts have been created, and millions are downloaded by users (Miller, 2019). This popularity can be attributed to several different factors, including multitasking, portability, and the option of a show for nearly anyone.

Multitasking

Many leisure activities, while designed to entertain or distract, also require nearly full attention from the audience. For example, a movie can be background noise while someone is working on a different project, but if the viewer is not watching the screen the entire time, he or she may miss important details. With the audio-only aspect of podcasts, listeners' visual attention can be elsewhere while the show plays. More than half of those surveyed in 2019 said they listened to podcasts while doing housework, driving, or cooking (Edison Research, 2019).

Portability

The ability to multitask while listening to a podcast is also connected to the idea of the portability of the medium. If someone wants to watch a television program, they either have to be sitting in front of the television or have a streaming device to watch. Thanks to small audio devices that can fit in a user's pocket, podcasts can essentially go wherever the listener is going. Users regularly cite portability as the key reason they start listening to podcasts (Perks & Turner, 2019).

Something for Everyone

The increase in podcasts has led to an abundance of shows about almost anything that might be of interest to the audience. There are shows about everything from knitting to plumbing (Lamirand, 2020; Winsper, 2020). Podcasts about sports remain one of the more popular genres available, with shows focusing on teams, leagues, fantasy sports, and individual athletes. This wide range of topics means that there should be at least one podcast created that would be of interest to nearly everyone.

Popularity of Podcasting for Creators

The fact that there is a podcast for everyone demonstrates the popularity of these audio shows for content creators as well. With millions of Americans saying that they listen to podcasts regularly, there are many opportunities to create a show that has the potential to have an audience. Three of the primary reasons that podcasts have become increasingly popular for creators is that they can be inexpensive to produce, allow for more material to be shared, and give the hosts an opportunity to give their opinions.

Inexpensive to Produce

As will be discussed in greater detail later in this chapter, one of the most appealing parts of podcasts for content creators is the fact that they can be incredibly inexpensive to produce. While someone could certainly invest in an expensive microphone, editing software, and a home recording studio, the most basic podcast can be done for almost no cost at all using materials the host likely already owns. The show can be recorded on a mobile phone, edited with free audio editing software (such as Audacity), and then uploaded to a free audio streaming website (such as SoundCloud).

Empty the Notebook

For print or on-air journalists, the amount of material gathered during a story can be overwhelming. However, not all of that information can make it into the final piece. Therefore, podcasts can be used to "empty the notebook" and report all the details that were cut from the story. For example, if a reporter conducted a 30-minute interview with a source, only a few seconds of that interview will make it into a broadcast piece or a web story. In a podcast, the reporter can run the entire interview and give the audience a chance to hear more about the topic.

Show Some Personality and Give Opinions

Reporters traditionally have to be impartial when on the news, so they are unable to show much of their personality or give their own opinions. A podcast allows reporters to show another side of themselves. Reporters can give more analysis on the day's news and not be strictly impartial. It is important to make sure that giving opinions on a podcast is acceptable at the company for which that reporter works. Many news outlets would not want their reporters showing any signs of bias on a podcast.

Before Starting a Podcast

The opportunity to start a podcast can be an exciting one, but rushing into recording the first episode can be a mistake. Many different aspects of the show must be determined before getting started. Hosts should know what their show is about, who the audience is, and what the format will be.

What Is the Show About?

This seems like an easy enough question to answer, but in many cases it is best to be as specific as possible when deciding what the show is going to be about. For example, perhaps a podcaster wants to create a show about basketball. That seems like a good topic, but the term "basketball" is a very broad. College? Professional? Women's? Men's? A specific team? Tips on how to play better? Simply saying that a show is about basketball could open up the podcaster to disappointment from listeners if the episodes do not talk about the aspect of basketball for which they were hoping. Therefore, it's best to be as specific as possible when coming up with the concept for the show—a host should be able to describe his or her show in two sentences or less. This description should be in the podcast notes when putting it online, and the hosts can relay this information at the beginning of the episode. Here is an example: "Welcome to *Party with the Pelicans*—your podcast home for the latest news from the NBA's New Orleans Pelicans. I'm your host Kylie Anderson."

Who Is This Show For?

When planning the concept for the show, the hosts should take time to recognize who the audience for this show is. For *Party with the Pelicans*, the host would almost certainly aim the content toward Pelicans fans. However, not all fans are the same. Is this show for diehard fans who know every statistic, player fact, and game result? Or is the show designed for casual fans who want more information on the team but do not want to get bogged down in the specific details of the club? Those are two entirely different shows, so the podcast host should decide early in the show's creation in which direction he or she would like to go.

- **Hardcore fans**: "This week on the show we're going to analyze the shot chart and advanced analytics of college star Sam Kerr and how he might fit in with the Pelicans should they be able to take him with the 15th pick in the upcoming draft."
- **Casual fans**: "This week on the show we're going to discuss the last three games for the Pelicans and interview beat writer James Berry about the upcoming road trip."

What Is the Format?

Once the creator has determined what the show is about and who the intended audience is, it is time to settle on a format for the episodes. Three of the more popular formats for sports podcasts are an interview show, a recap show, and a news show. An interview show is one where the host would have a different guest each week and then interview that person for the entirety of the episode. A recap show would feature more commentary and analysis of events that have happened. Finally, a news show would be similar to an evening newscast in which an anchor discusses various news items and occasionally has reporters out in the field filing stories. In some cases episodes can be a combination of these elements, with a brief recap of events followed by an interview with an expert.

Perhaps the biggest decision when starting up a podcast is deciding who will be the host. In all likelihood, the person who created the idea will serve as the host, but it is worth examining if having a cohost can improve the quality of the show. For example, if episodes of *Party with the Pelicans* are going to be an hour of analyzing individual plays from previous games, that can prove to be difficult for one person to talk about for the entire time. In that case, having a second person to talk to, argue with, and come to conclusions with could help the pacing of the show and help fill the time allotted to the show. Having a second host can also be a help when planning the episodes because the two hosts can bounce ideas off of each other and split up some of the off-air tasks required to create a successful show.

Equipment Needed for a Podcast

As stated previously, a podcast can be created almost for free using equipment that a podcaster probably already owns or can download inexpensively. However, if someone is hoping to turn podcasting into a career, it is worth investing in some more professional equipment that will make the show sound better and easier to produce.

Microphones

Perhaps one of the most important purchases is a microphone that can connect directly into a computer (using a USB port) or a recording device. A microphone will be needed for everyone who is on the podcast, so if there are two hosts (or a host and a guest) there will need to be two different microphones. In addition to the microphone, a **pop filter** should be purchased to cut down on the popping noises that can occur when someone is talking into a microphone. If interviewing outside, a **windscreen** should be used to cut down on the impact of the wind on the recording. The windscreen slides directly over the microphone, while the pop filter is placed directly in front of it.

Headphones

Headphones allow the podcast host to keep track of how the audio sounds during the recording. This can help the host know if he or she needs to be closer to or farther away from the microphone. Headphones can also help identify any interference or unwanted noise that might create a distraction during the podcast. Headphones should also be worn while editing the audio of the podcast.

Editing Equipment

It is possible to record and save a podcast without any editing, but it is not recommended. There are plenty of free or very inexpensive options available such as Audacity. More experienced podcasters may wish to ultimately invest in audio editing programs that have more features, such as Avid's Pro Tools or Adobe Audition. Using editing equipment allows the host to include music, edit out mistakes, and insert commercials or other promotional materials into the middle of the podcast after the recording has been completed.

Location, Location, Location

While not technically equipment, where the podcast is recorded is a very important part of the production process. To put it as simply as possible, the episodes should be recorded in a quiet room. Microphones are wonderful at picking up the voices being spoken into them, but they are also great at picking up *every* noise in the room. Is the air conditioner making a loud noise? That will certainly be on the recording. Loud traffic noises outside? Be prepared for those to be part of the recorded show. Therefore, it is important to find a location that has little to no noise when the room is empty.

Additionally, rooms can often have an echo in them. Podcasters may wish to hang acoustic panels on the wall (a comforter or blanket will do the trick, too). However, if a podcaster has the financial means, it is worth examining the possibility of renting a studio for the recording of the show. These rooms are designed with the sole purpose of getting quality audio during a session, so if there are not any quiet options

MAJOR MOMENTS

Sports Podcasting Goes Political . . . Until It Doesn't

In 2008, Bill Simmons was one of the most prominent employees at ESPN. He had his own column at ESPN.com, was executive producer of the popular *30 for 30* documentary series, was the author of a *The New York Times* best-selling book, and hosted his own podcast called *The B.S. Report* (Masisak, 2009). In April of that year, Simmons, who normally interviewed athletes, sports journalists, and his closest friends, landed an interview with U.S. presidential candidate Barack Obama. The fact that Obama had agreed to appear on a podcast showcased the power of this emerging media platform.

However, the interview was not to be. Just before the two were set to record, ESPN pulled the plug and canceled the scheduled interview. A network spokesman said at the time, "Fans don't expect political coverage on our outlets" (Stelter, 2008, para. 2). Simmons was upset, later saying, "I really had a hard time dealing with that" (Miller & Shales, 2011, p. 650), and eventually left ESPN in 2015 following several disputes with management (Sandomir, 2015).

The story showcases the early struggles that many major media outlets had with podcasts. While they encouraged their reporters to have shows, they did not entirely know what to do with them or how popular they would become. An interview with the future president of the United States would have been a major coup for the network, but they seemed unsure about having that talk on a podcast. Perhaps not surprisingly, the network did eventually reschedule an interview with Obama, although it was conducted by Stuart Scott on ESPN's popular television program *SportsCenter* about four months later (Powell, 2008). Simmons did eventually get his own interview on the *B.S. Report* with Obama in 2012, giving him the honor of hosting the first-ever podcast with a sitting U.S. president (Simmons, 2012).

available, then booking studio time may be a good investment. If all else fails, a solo podcast can always be recorded in the closet. The clothes act as an audio diffuser and the rooms are usually fairly quiet. The host can just bring his or her computer and microphone into the closet and record the show in there.

Recording

There are many steps that should be followed before recording the actual podcast episodes. Even after the format has been decided, the equipment purchased, and the location selected, several more boxes must be checked. Hosts should take time to plan each episode before recording, come up with a consistent format, and then assure that all the equipment is working properly before starting the show.

Planning Each Episode

Before recording each show, the host should know exactly what is going to be discussed. While the majority of the conversation in a podcast is spontaneous, an outline with general topics and points to be addressed can be helpful during the taping of the show. Often podcast hosts will have a point they want to make during the show but they forget once the show is moving along during the taping. Having a list of bullet points that the host can refer to during the show can ensure that all the topics that are planned to be discussed actually make the final taping.

Have a Similar Rundown

While each show will have differing content, the basic order and rundown of the show should be similar for each episode. Listeners should be able to download an episode and know exactly what they are going to get. Creating a format that can be relied on for each show can also make preparations much easier for the hosts because they will know what content they need to include.

Party with the Pelicans ***Weekly Rundown***

Segment one: Theme song

Segment two: Brief introduction of the hosts and what is on this week's episode

Segment three: News and notes

Segment four: Recap of this week's games

Segment five: Interview with expert

Segment six: Player of the Week announcement

Segment seven: Preview of upcoming week's games

Segment eight: Goodbye from the hosts

Segment nine: Theme song

Double- and Triple-Check Everything

Once a script has been created, a format has been decided upon, and the hosts have been determined, it is time to record the show. When everyone has sat down in front of the microphones and the record button has been hit, the host should double- and triple-check that everything is working properly. Is the show recording? Are all the microphones plugged in and recording at the proper volume level? There is nothing worse than finishing a show and then realizing that one button was not pushed properly, causing the hosts to rerecord the entire episode from the beginning.

Distribution

Once the podcast is recorded, it is on to the next step. This might be one of the most important parts of all—making sure that people can actually listen to it. Hosts must figure out where to put the podcast online, how to let people know about it, and when to start thinking about future episodes.

Getting It Out There

After recording the show and exporting it as an MP3 file, the podcast now needs a distribution home. Uploading the shows to an audio-specific hosting network such as SoundCloud or Libsyn can be an easy way to have the show available online. Hosts would only need to send the link to those who might be interested in listening. Additionally, setting up a feed will allow for new episodes to be added to the list and will alert followers that the latest show is now available for listening.

The next step is to ensure that people can listen to the podcast on as many different devices as possible. Therefore, users want to get their feed picked up by Apple Podcasts, Spotify, Stitcher, Google Podcasts, and other popular destinations where people listen to podcasts. Most of these programs make it very easy to connect and offer detailed directions on the steps that need to be followed.

Promotion

Just because a podcaster is making an entertaining and informative show does not mean that people will automatically start listening. Television and radio hosts have a built-in audience network that has been created over decades of simply existing. People in one city may have grown up watching Channel 6 at home because that is what their parents and grandparents watched. A podcast that is started this month will not have that same legacy on which to fall back. Instead, the hosts of the show need to rely on promotion in an attempt to earn listeners.

As will be discussed in chapter 11, social media has become an important part of both journalism and the world of sports. Fans are using social networks to follow athletes and get the latest updates on their favorite teams and sports. Podcast hosts should take advantage of this and not only have their own personal social media accounts but also create one specifically for the show. That account should be updated regularly with content updates, bonuses, and a behind-the-scenes view of the show.

Additionally, having guests on the show can also turn into a promotional tool. The followers of the guests can possibly become followers of the podcast with the right updates. When the episode comes out, hosts should send the link directly to the guest and see if they would be willing to share the episode with their own audience. Fans of that guest will hopefully download the show, and if they enjoy the episode they might download another.

Promoting the show can be as much work as actually creating the episodes themselves. Hosts need to figure out ways to get the show in front of as many people as possible, and that can prove to be very time-consuming. However, the rewards can be worth it as a large audience can only improve the reach of the show.

Create a Consistent Schedule

A podcast should follow a consistent distribution schedule. Fans should be able to know that, for example, every Monday a new episode of *Party with the Pelicans* is going to be available. Keeping to that schedule will not keep the listeners guessing as to when they can expect a new episode. It is similar to radio and television programs for which fans know that a specific show is going to be on the air at the same time on the same channel each week. Viewership of popular sitcoms would likely plummet if viewers did not know when it was going to be on.

While it is a good idea to be consistent, new podcast hosts should also be careful to pace themselves in the beginning weeks of a program. If a show is airing every day in the first month it comes out, fans are going to expect that show to be in their feeds every day for as long as the podcast airs. Instead, hosts should make less frequent shows in the beginning and instead focus on quality over quantity. If the show proves to be successful, then more weekly episodes can be added later on.

CHAPTER WRAP-UP

HK*PROPEL* ACTIVITIES

HK*Propel* includes examples of audio stories with excellent use of natural sound and natural pops.

SUMMARY

While television broadcasting might get the majority of attention in most media circles, there has been a renaissance in the world of audio broadcasting. Sports talk radio stations throughout the United States are devoted to discussing the latest sports news every minute of the day. Hosts give their opinions, talk about the latest news, and interview athletes and coaches from the biggest events in sports.

Sports audio can also be "on the go" with the development of a podcast. These shows can be created with very little initial start-up cost, but they still involve a great deal of work. The preparation can be time-consuming, but the payoff can be rewarding. Podcast episodes can be distributed on networks that have a user base of millions, possibly creating the opportunity for a big audience.

Phil Cole/Getty Images

CHAPTER 10

Live Sports Production

CHAPTER OBJECTIVES

Broadcasting a live game on either radio or television is a very different skill set from anchoring or doing recorded stories. In addition, live sports involves an entire team of behind-the-scenes crew members that help make the games look and sound pleasing. Therefore, this chapter focuses on live sports broadcasting, including the following:

- Understanding how a live sports broadcast works
- Knowing the steps involved in preparation to do play-by-play of a live sports broadcast
- Recognizing the different styles required when broadcasting various sports
- Identifying the various jobs involved with a live sports broadcast beyond just the play-by-play announcer

As stated in chapter 2 of this book, there is perhaps no bigger business in the world of the sports media than live sports. Television and radio networks spend billions of dollars to have the opportunity to be the exclusive broadcast home of various sporting events. With that sort of investment, it is no surprise that these networks invest money beyond just the rights fees in order to put on the best broadcast possible. In many cases, that means hiring top announcers, producers, and behind-the-scenes talent in order to make the production run smoothly.

Live sports broadcasts are games that are broadcast in their entirety live on a television or radio network. For the purposes of this chapter, live studio productions such as *SportsCenter* on ESPN or a local evening newscast will not be

MAJOR MOMENTS

Do You Believe in Miracles? YES!

In 1980, there were very few teams more successful than the men's hockey team for the Soviet Union. The U.S.S.R. team had won four Olympic gold medals in a row and were the heavy favorites to win again during the 1980 games in Lake Placid, New York. Standing in their way to reach another gold medal matchup was a United States team that was the heavy underdog. As most sports fans know, the game became one of the biggest upsets in sports history, as the U.S. team won 4–3 (Brock, 1980). While the game has been called "the top sports moment in the 20th century" (Goldberg, 1999, para. 7), the story behind the broadcast and the broadcaster is just as remarkable.

With the clock winding down, ABC broadcaster Al Michaels uttered perhaps the most famous words in the history of sports broadcasting: "Do you believe in miracles? Yes!" It has been labeled the best sports call ever (Vaccaro, 2015). After that game, Michaels became one of the most prominent announcers in sports history, calling the World Series, Super Bowl, and a variety of other top events (Michaels, 2014). However, his path to the "Miracle on Ice" game was actually quite fortuitous. In 1980 he was chosen to broadcast all Olympic hockey games simply because, of all the ABC broadcasting staff, he was the only one who had ever done play-by-play for a hockey game. Michaels himself would later admit his luck, saying in a 2020 article, "You talk about getting fortunate. As I tell people to this day, there were not a lot of miracles on the biathlon course" (Reedy, 2020b, para. 17).

In retrospect, one of the most amazing aspects of the "Miracle on Ice" game is that it probably should not be part of this chapter about live sports production—the game was not shown *live* on television in the United States. Instead, one of the most famous moments in Olympics history was televised on tape delay. The puck dropped at 5:00 p.m. local time in New York, and management determined that too few people would be home to watch (especially on the West Coast). Instead, ABC elected to record the game and then show it later during prime time at 8:00 p.m. (Allen, 2015). The game was not even shown in its entirety, as ABC edited out several portions of the game to save time. A producer with ABC later said they did not expect the United States to keep the game close, let alone win, so they had plans to show other sports during the action when the Soviet lead became too great (Sandomir, 2000). ABC did admit before the broadcast started that the game was already over, but they did not give the result. However, because of the fact that cable television was still in its beginning stages and there was no internet to reveal up-to-the-second scores, many people watching the game did not know how it was going to end (Reedy, 2020b).

---

discussed. Instead, the focus will be on games that are broadcast live.

Every regular season NFL game is broadcast live on television and radio. While the action on the field might start at kickoff, putting together these broadcasts is much more complex than showing the few hours during which the game is happening. Instead, these productions are a complex concert of a whole team of people getting the game on the air. While the on-air broadcasters might get the majority of the attention, there are numerous behind-the-scenes producers, directors, and technicians that keep everything running smoothly. This goes for team sports, individual sports, and large sporting events such as the Olympics.

Play-by-Play

During a live sports broadcast, the most prominent on-air person is the **play-by-play announcer**. This is the person who describes the action as it happens to the audience watching or listening. They will update the situation before the play, describe what is happening during the game, and then announce what the result of that play means. For example, in a softball game, a play-by-play announcer might describe a home run as follows:

> Olivia Churchill is at the plate for the Scorpions now. She singled in her first time up. The pitch from Manning, and Churchill with a big blast. It's deep to right field—and it is gone! Home run, Olivia Churchill. That is her ninth home run of the season, and the Scorpions take a 2–0 lead over the Bobcats here in the fourth inning.

The announcer told the audience who was up and what she did last time she was at the plate. The announcer then described the action as it was happening before recapping what the home run means by giving a statistic about the batter's season and, most importantly, updating the score. While it often sounds smooth during a broadcast, being a play-by-play announcer is much more than simply describing the action.

Before the Game Starts

A play-by-play announcer might be best known for his or her work during the actual broadcast of the game, but the process of broadcasting an event starts well in advance of the first pitch or opening whistle. In fact, the preparation beforehand is essential to the announcer's success during the game. This research is used to help the announcer learn the players, understand storylines, and develop a confidence that he or she can talk about the game beyond describing what is happening on the field.

Reading Game Notes

In many cases, the teams themselves provide information directly to the media in the form of **game notes**. These are usually several pages of information that contain a variety of different facts and statistics that may be of interest to the announcing team. These statistics might include recent trends ("winners of their last four series"), what happened previously when these two teams played ("snapped a four-game losing streak last night"), or which players are playing particularly well at the moment ("Martinez had four home runs in his last six games"). These statistics could even be a little obscure, such as what the team's record is when tied after eight innings or the record when they score less than three runs.

The game notes will also focus on several sport-specific facts that an announcer may want to discuss during the game. For example, a baseball game's game notes may focus on the starting pitcher for that night, giving statistics on how he plays in that stadium, his record against that night's opponent, and how he fares during a day or night game. It would then provide a recap of that pitcher's recent outings. A similar section would then focus on the various batters in the starting lineup, with brief statistics about how they are playing for the season and in a more recent period. Additionally, no matter what the sport, the game notes will likely contain each player's jersey number, position, height, and hometown. Notes for college sports will also include the player's year in school. Table 10.1 provides an example of what a basketball roster in the game notes for a women's college basketball team would look like.

One of the most helpful sections for a play-by-play announcer is the **pronunciation guide**. Some names can be difficult to say or are not pronounced how they appear. This guide can help announcers be sure they are saying the names correctly. For example, based on the most common pronunciation, most people would likely pronounce basketball star Stephen Curry's name as "Steven," but he pronounces it "Steffen." Therefore, the guide would indicate the correct way to say his name. For names that might be difficult to figure out how to say, the pronunciation guide would use phonetic spellings. Al-Farouq Aminu, another basketball player, would have al-fah-ruke ah-ME-new for his phonetic spelling. However, even with the phonetic spelling in the media guide, announcers should still check every pronunciation verbally with a team official (such as a sports information director for a college team). Western Kentucky University play-by-play announcer Brett Williams said, "I've learned not to trust pronunciation guides without double-checking. Time and

TABLE 10.1 Basketball Roster for Wildcats Basketball

##	Name	Pos.	Ht.	Yr.	Hometown (High School)
0	Vanessa Dickens	G	5-8	Sr.	Albany, NY (Albany H.S.)
1	Samantha Quinn	G/F	5-7	Fr.	Leland, NC (Smith H.S)
3	Sarah Paige	G	6-1	So.	Boston, MA (Freedom H.S.)
4	Rachel Reid	G/F	5-10	So.	Lincoln, NY (Friends H.S.)
11	Carolyn Gibson	G/F	6-2	So.	Ventura, CA (Ventura H.S.)
14	Fiona Murray	G	5-11	Fr.	Edina, MN (Edina H.S.)
20	Wendy McDonald	F	6-3	Jr.	Toledo, OH (Riverbank H.S.)
21	Zoe Abraham	G	5-7	Sr.	Portland, OR (Redwood H.S.)
24	Lisa Campbell	G	5-10	Jr.	St. Louis, MO (Central Academy)
25	Sarah Rees	F	6-3	Jr.	Miami, FL (Oak Grove H.S.)
30	Ava Poole	F	6-4	Sr.	Miami, FL (Coast H.S.)
44	Nia Poole	F	6-1	Fr.	Cleveland, OH (Springfield H.S.)

again I've seen phonetic spelling and thought to myself 'there's no way that's actually pronounced like that,' and upon asking them, it isn't."

The amount of material in a set of game notes can vary from team to team and school to school. For example, the game notes for a professional football team are often incredibly detailed because they have a large staff that can take the time to work primarily on these notes. Smaller teams or college programs may have just one person devoted to that team, and he or she may also be working with several other teams at the same time. Therefore, those notes may not be as in-depth as bigger schools.

While game notes are normally updated before every game, the **media guide** is a much more detailed information book that is completed before the season begins. This contains biographies of team leadership, players, historical information, statistics, and an entire staff directory. These can be helpful at the beginning of the season but can become obsolete as the year moves along, because the preseason rosters and statistics become dated and the updated game notes become timelier. Additionally, the amount of information in these media guides can sometimes be overwhelming. For example, the NFL's Carolina Panthers put out a media guide in 2019 that was over 500 pages long (Carolina Panthers, 2019).

Reading Local Newspaper Articles

If the play-by-play announcer is not covering a team with which he or she is overly familiar, a visit to the website of the local newspaper can be an excellent source of information. Local writers are often embedded with a team and know them better than almost anyone other than the players and coaches themselves. Therefore, reading articles written by those local **beat writers** can provide some behind-the-scenes stories and information that the announcer can relate while broadcasting the game (so long as he or she cites those sources on the air).

Talking With Coaches

Before broadcasting the game, play-by-play announcers should meet with the coaches from both teams in order to get a better sense of each team and what they think about their opponent. In a formal setting, announcers will have these initial meetings through a conference call a few days before the game or a press conference. These events are usually attended by numerous media members, so the information gathered there will likely be very guarded by the coach. However, in a one-on-one interview closer to game day, a coach might be more willing to reveal some information that can be exclusive to that announcer. In a less formal setting such as a high school game, announcers may want to reach out to the coach by telephone or ask if they can come to practice to talk with the coach there. For coaches who may not be familiar with the process, it is worth letting them know that any information they share with the announcer is just for the broadcast and will not be shared with the opposing coach.

These meetings can be some of the most valuable preparation an announcer can make before the game. An announcer can find out who is playing well, who might be struggling, the mood of the team, and whatever special preparations or game plans the team might have for the upcoming game. In some cases, a play-by-play announcer may record these meetings with the coaches so that the conversation can be played during the pregame show. In those cases, the announcer should make it very clear to the coach that the conversation is being recorded and that it will be played for the entire audience to hear.

In any case, the announcer must be able to discern what information he or she can say on air and what needs to be kept confidential. For example, while general game plans and philosophies are fair game, detailed strategies should not be shared with the public. A coach might also privately share the full extent of a player's injury, but it is likely that the team staff will release a vague official description for media use. Understanding these differences is key to maintaining coaches' trust and the announcer's credibility. Even information that cannot be used during the broadcast can be helpful, as it often makes the announcer better prepared for what he or she may see and lowers his or her chance of being caught off guard.

Watching Previous Games

Head coaches watch games involving their opponents before they face off; likewise, play-by-play announcers should attempt to watch previous games of the two teams they are about to broadcast. This is an opportunity to see the teams in action beforehand so the announcer has an idea of what to expect during the game. It can be especially helpful in sports such as basketball, because the announcer can see what plays the team runs in certain situations, the playing style of the team, and what adjustments the coaches might be looking to make. Ultimately, watching these games should help the announcer anticipate what might happen next.

Creating a Spotting Chart

After completing all of the research, it is time for one of the most important steps for a play-by-play announcer: creating his or her **spotting chart**. These charts, sometimes called spotting boards, allow announcers to quickly reference player information and statistics without needing to memorize everything. The chart will lie in front of announcers on the table, loaded with information on each player. For example, for football, a chart will likely have each player's name, number, height, weight, and some statistics. There may also be some room to write down additional information about each player, such as accolades ("reigning Conference Player of the Week"), recent trends ("Has scored a touchdown in ten straight games"), or personal tidbits ("Mother has completed a marathon on every continent").

These charts are often quite large, bigger than a traditional piece of paper, because a lot of information needs to be squeezed onto them. When he broadcast *Monday Night Football*, ESPN's Sean McDonough used two 11-by-17" pieces of card stock that he would stick together (Steinberg, 2017). Football announcers will often have at least four sheets—one for the home team's offense, one for the home team's defense, one for the visiting team's offense, and one for the visiting team's defense—with perhaps an additional sheet for special teams. When he does football, play-by-play announcer Adam Amin tapes those four primary sheets to a manila folder, with a team's offense on one side and their defense on the other (Turori, 2013).

However, there is no one specific way to make a spotting chart. Each individual play-by-play announcer should create something he or she can easily understand. Some charts are handwritten, while others are typed up on the

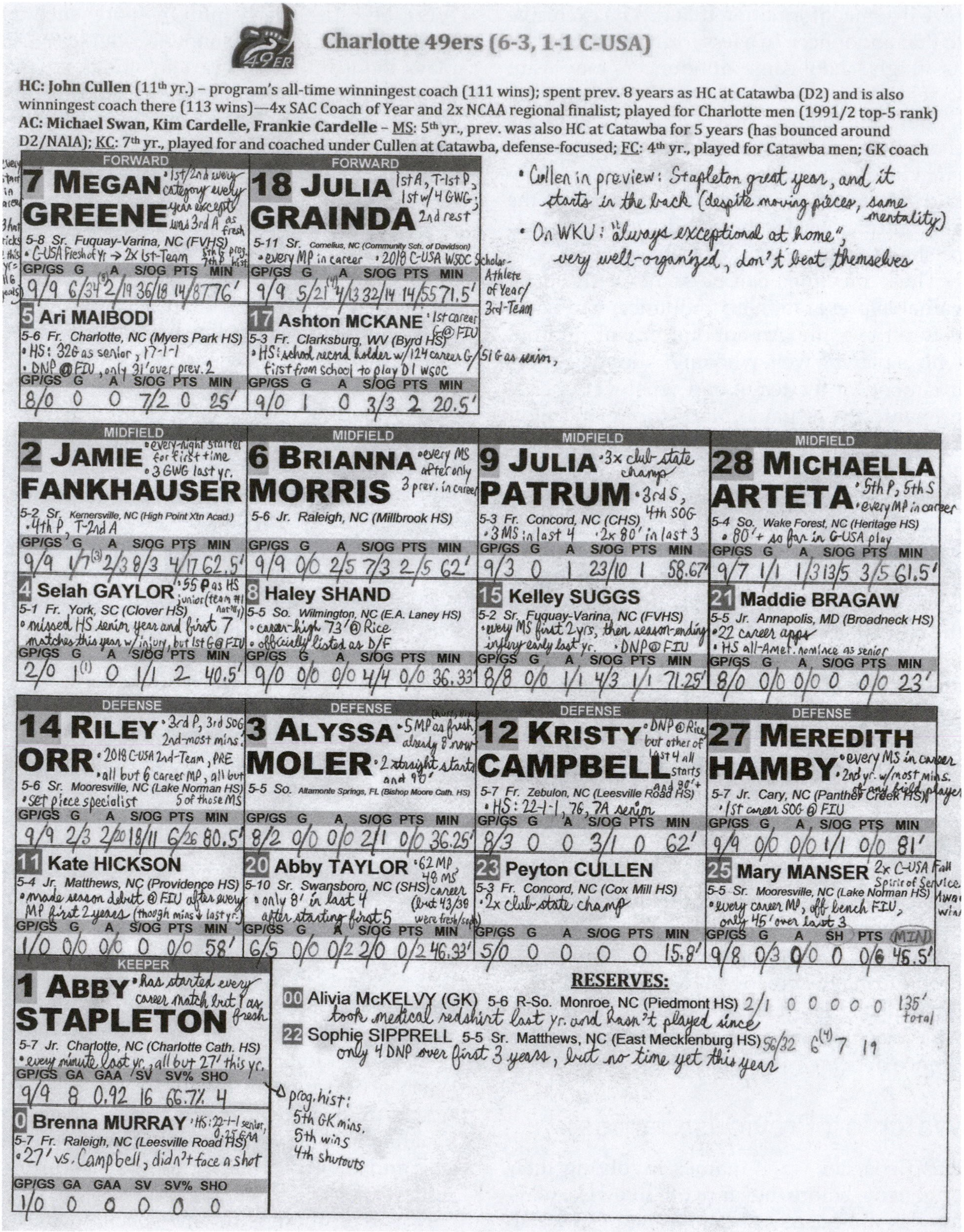

Charlotte 49ers (6-3, 1-1 C-USA)

HC: John Cullen (11th yr.) – program's all-time winningest coach (111 wins); spent prev. 8 years as HC at Catawba (D2) and is also winningest coach there (113 wins)—4x SAC Coach of Year and 2x NCAA regional finalist; played for Charlotte men (1991/2 top-5 rank)
AC: Michael Swan, Kim Cardelle, Frankie Cardelle – MS: 5th yr., prev. was also HC at Catawba for 5 years (has bounced around D2/NAIA); KC: 7th yr., played for and coached under Cullen at Catawba, defense-focused; FC: 4th yr., played for Catawba men; GK coach

• Cullen in preview: Stapleton great year, and it starts in the back (despite moving pieces, same mentality)
• On WKU: "always exceptional at home", very well-organized, don't beat themselves

FORWARD

7 MEGAN GREENE • 1st/2nd every category every year except was 3rd A as fresh
5-8 Sr. Fuquay-Varina, NC (FVHS)
• C-USA Fresh of Yr → 2x 1st-Team

GP/GS	G	A	S/OG	PTS	MIN
9/9	6/34	2/19	36/18	14/87	76′

18 JULIA GRAINDA 1st A, T-1st P, 1st w/ 4 GWG; 2nd rest
5-11 Sr. Cornelius, NC (Community Sch. of Davidson)
• every MP in career • 2018 C-USA WSOC Scholar-Athlete of Year/3rd-Team

GP/GS	G	A	S/OG	PTS	MIN
9/9	5/21	4/13	32/14	14/55	71.5′

5 Ari MAIBODI
5-6 Fr. Charlotte, NC (Myers Park HS)
• HS: 32G as senior, 17-1-1
• DNP @ FIU, only 31′ over prev. 2

GP/GS	G	A	S/OG	PTS	MIN
8/0	0	0	7/2	0	25′

17 Ashton MCKANE • 1st career G @ FIU
5-3 Fr. Clarksburg, WV (Byrd HS)
• HS: school record holder w/ 124 career G/51 G as senior, first from school to play D1 WSOC

GP/GS	G	A	S/OG	PTS	MIN
9/0	1	0	3/3	2	20.5′

MIDFIELD

2 JAMIE FANKHAUSER • every-night starter for first time • 3 GWG last yr.
5-2 Sr. Kernersville, NC (High Point Xtn Acad.)
• 4th P, T-2nd A

GP/GS	G	A	S/OG	PTS	MIN
9/9	1/7	2/3	8/3	4/17	62.5′

6 BRIANNA MORRIS • every MS after only 3 prev. in career
5-6 Jr. Raleigh, NC (Millbrook HS)

GP/GS	G	A	S/OG	PTS	MIN
9/9	0/0	2/5	7/3	2/5	62′

9 JULIA PATRUM • 3x club state champ • 3rd S, 4th SOG
5-3 Fr. Concord, NC (CHS)
• 3 MS in last 4 • 2x 80′ in last 3

GP/GS	G	A	S/OG	PTS	MIN
9/3	0	1	23/10	1	58.67′

28 MICHAELLA ARTETA • 5th P, 5th S • every MP in career
5-4 So. Wake Forest, NC (Heritage HS)
• 80′+ so far in C-USA play

GP/GS	G	A	S/OG	PTS	MIN
9/7	1/1	1/3	13/5	3/5	61.5′

4 Selah GAYLOR • 55 P as HS junior (team #1 Nat'lly)
5-1 Fr. York, SC (Clover HS)
• missed HS senior year and first 7 matches this year w/ injury, but 1st G @ FIU

GP/GS	G	A	S/OG	PTS	MIN
2/0	1	0	1/1	2	40.5′

8 Haley SHAND
5-5 So. Wilmington, NC (E.A. Laney HS)
• career-high 73′ @ Rice • officially listed as D/F

GP/GS	G	A	S/OG	PTS	MIN
9/0	0/0	0/0	4/4	0/0	36.33′

15 Kelley SUGGS
5-2 Sr. Fuquay-Varina, NC (FVHS)
• every MS first 2 yrs, then season-ending injury early last yr. • DNP @ FIU

GP/GS	G	A	S/OG	PTS	MIN
8/8	0/0	1/1	4/3	1/1	71.25′

21 Maddie BRAGAW
5-5 Jr. Annapolis, MD (Broadneck HS)
• 22 career apps • HS all-Amer. nominee as senior

GP/GS	G	A	S/OG	PTS	MIN
8/0	0/0	0/0	0	0/0	23′

DEFENSE

14 RILEY ORR • 3rd P, 3rd SOG, 2nd-most mins • 2018 C-USA 2nd-Team, PRE • all but 6 career MP, all but 5 of those MS
5-6 Sr. Mooresville, NC (Lake Norman HS)
• set piece specialist

GP/GS	G	A	S/OG	PTS	MIN
9/9	2/3	2/20	18/11	6/26	80.5′

3 ALYSSA MOLER • 5 MP as fresh, already 8 now • 2 straight starts and 90′
5-5 So. Altamonte Springs, FL (Bishop Moore Cath. HS)

GP/GS	G	A	S/OG	PTS	MIN
8/2	0/0	0/0	2/1	0/0	36.25′

12 KRISTY CAMPBELL • DNP @ Rice but other of last 4 all starts and 90′+
5-7 Fr. Zebulon, NC (Leesville Road HS)
• HS: 22-1-1, 7G, 7A senior

GP/GS	G	A	S/OG	PTS	MIN
8/3	0	0	3/1	0	62′

27 MEREDITH HAMBY • every MS in career • 2nd yr. w/ most mins. of any field player
5-7 Jr. Cary, NC (Panther Creek HS)
• 1st career SOG @ FIU

GP/GS	G	A	S/OG	PTS	MIN
9/9	0/0	0/0	1/1	0/0	81′

11 Kate HICKSON
5-4 Jr. Matthews, NC (Providence HS)
• made season debut @ FIU after every MP first 2 years (though mins ↓ last yr.)

GP/GS	G	A	S/OG	PTS	MIN
1/0	0/0	0/0	0	0/0	58′

20 Abby TAYLOR • 62 MP, 48 MS career
5-10 Sr. Swansboro, NC (SHS)
• only 8′ in last 4 after starting first 5 (but 43/39 were fresh/soph)

GP/GS	G	A	S/OG	PTS	MIN
6/5	0/0	0/2	2/0	0/2	46.33′

23 Peyton CULLEN
5-3 Fr. Concord, NC (Cox Mill HS)
• 2x club state champ

GP/GS	G	A	S/OG	PTS	MIN
5/0	0	0	0	0	15.8′

25 Mary MANSER 2x C-USA Fall Spirit of Service Award winner
5-5 Sr. Mooresville, NC (Lake Norman HS)
• every career MP, off bench FIU, only 45′ over last 3

GP/GS	G	A	SH	PTS	MIN
9/8	0/3	0/0	0	0/6	45.5′

KEEPER

1 ABBY STAPLETON • has started every career match but 1 as fresh
5-7 Jr. Charlotte, NC (Charlotte Cath. HS)
• every minute last yr., all but 27′ this yr.

GP/GS	GA	GAA	SV	SV%	SHO
9/9	8	0.92	16	66.7%	4

prog. hist.: 5th GK mins, 5th wins, 4th shutouts

0 Brenna MURRAY • HS: 22-1-1 senior, 0.25 GAA
5-7 Fr. Raleigh, NC (Leesville Road HS)
• 27′ vs. Campbell, didn't face a shot

GP/GS	GA	GAA	SV	SV%	SHO
1/0	0	0	0	0	0

RESERVES:

00 Alivia McKELVY (GK) 5-6 R-So. Monroe, NC (Piedmont HS) 2/1 0 0 0 0 0 135′ total
took medical redshirt last yr. and hasn't played since

22 Sophie SIPPRELL 5-5 Sr. Matthews, NC (East Mecklenburg HS) 56/32 6 7 19
only 4 DNP over first 3 years, but no time yet this year

Broadcaster Brett Williams' spotting chart before a Charlotte 49ers soccer game.

computer. Whatever system is used, play-by-play announcers should be sure to use the same format for each game and keep them neatly organized so that they know exactly where to find the details they are looking for.

During the Game

Play-by-play announcers should do as much preparation as possible before the game starts because once it begins, it can be a whirlwind of activity. He or she has to call what is happening in the game while also getting instructions from a producer, working around commercial breaks, and weaving in commentary and information from the other members of the broadcast team. Having that preparation done ahead of time gives announcers one less thing to worry about, because they do not have to focus on looking up statistics on the internet or finding storylines midgame.

The goal of a game broadcast is to make the audience feel like they are at the game themselves. This means describing the action, giving updates on the score and individual statistics, and relaying what it is like inside the stadium or arena. The audience should be able to watch the game and know who is active in the game and what they are doing. A fan watching should never say "who was that?" or "what just happened?" If so, the play-by-play announcer has not done his or her job.

Depending on the game, giving updates on statistics can be done with the help of the team's media staff or by the announcer's own scorekeeping. At larger events, there will be a tablet or computer near the play-by-play announcer's table that gives constant updates on the score and statistics. Additionally, a member of the team's staff may distribute printed-out statistics at various breaks in the action. High school games often do not have official statistics that can be readily relayed to broadcasters, so announcers for those games will have to count on their own scorekeeping for those stats. No matter what level of sport being broadcast, many announcers keep their own scorebooks so they can easily update statistics throughout without needing to rely on someone else to provide them the information.

It is important to remember that not all of the audience will be tuning in from the beginning of the game until the end. Some will get in the car and turn on the radio in the middle of the first half, while others might tune in just in time for the dramatic conclusion. Those not following from the start have missed out on what has already happened and, most importantly, the score. Keeping those fans in mind, announcers should give the time and score every minute or so while recapping some of the big storylines perhaps every 10 to 15 minutes.

Often at sporting events, the action off the playing field can be just as memorable as the actual game itself. Therefore, announcers should not shy away from describing those moments, too. They can talk about how the coach is screaming on the sidelines or how a player is limping off after an injury, and, if the crowd suddenly gets very loud, the play-by-play announcer should reference that excitement of the fans.

Sport-Specific Play-by-Play Tips

As mentioned in chapter 7 about shooting sports, there is no one way to do play-by-play of a sporting event. Often it depends on the sport being talked about, as the pacing of the event often plays a key role in how it is discussed. For example, the play-by-play of a quiet and slow-moving golf broadcast is very different from the play-by-play of a nonstop, high-energy basketball game. The following sections include play-by-play tips for some of the more popular sports broadcast on television and radio.

Football

For football play-by-play announcers, perhaps the most important statistics they should remind fans of are the down and the distance remaining for a first down (such as "2nd down and 5 yards to go"). For radio announcers, including the yard line that the ball is on is also essential. It may feel like overkill at first, but announcers should be giving this information before every play, even though those numbers are already on the screen for people watching on television. With radio, it is crucially important to give that information in between when a play ends and before the ball is snapped for the next play.

Once the teams are lined up, the announcer can identify the formation and perhaps spotlight where a few key players are on the field. For example, a radio announcer might say, "Second down and seven yards to go for the Pirates. They line up with three receivers out wide, with Blake Grant alone on the left side." That lets the fans watching on television know who is where and allows those listening on radio to get a mental picture of the action.

Football is a complex sport to broadcast, because there are 22 people on the field at all times, and they are all going in different directions with various goals. Therefore, the best advice for a football play-by-play announcer is simply to follow the ball. The wide receivers might be all running different routes, so it would be impossible to say what they are all doing. Instead, he or she can describe what the quarterback is doing and what happens to the person who has the ball.

Finally, football announcers should remember to give the time and score on a regular basis. Since there is not frequent scoring as there is with basketball, announcers can sometimes go a long time in between having to update the score. Therefore, play-by-play announcers, especially those on radio, should develop a mechanism that helps remind them to give the time and score at regular intervals. This is true for any sport that doesn't have frequent scoring. Examples of such a mechanism could be every first down in football, or after the first pitch of every at bat in baseball. No matter what, it is still essential on radio to give the time and score every 60 to 90 seconds.

Basketball

Basketball can often be nonstop action, with players running up and down the court, the score constantly changing, and players subbing in and out of the game on a regular basis. Therefore, basketball announcers have a great deal to keep up with very few breaks in between. While the sports are very different, many of the same play-by-play rules for football are also appropriate for basketball.

Due to the fact that a basketball score changes on almost every possession, announcers should be saying the score frequently. On radio, the score should be provided after every basket, while television play-by-play announcers can perhaps wait until a few baskets have been scored to update. Another way to possibly decide when to give a score update is following something remarkable happening score-wise, such as if a team goes on a long run in which the other team does score (such as, "Gators on an 8–0 run to push their lead to 12 . . .").

Also similar to football, the best way to follow the action for a basketball play-by-play announcer is simply to follow the ball. He or she can say who has the ball, who they pass it to, who is guarding the player, who grabbed the rebound after a miss, and where players are located on the court. A basketball announcer might describe a play as follows:

> Wallace dribbling past half-court and gives a quick pass to Bell. He holds the ball at the top of the key where he's guarded by Sean Lewis. And it's knocked away by Lewis—the pass up ahead to Owen Miller for the easy layup. Bruins now lead by seven with about five minutes left here in the second quarter. . . .

Someone watching or listening at home would be able to understand who has the ball, what happened during the play, and what the resulting basket means for the game. One of the keys is properly identifying who has the ball once the ball crosses half-court. Since there are only 10 players on the court (unlike the 22 for football), this should be an easier task. However, because the game moves so quickly, the research done beforehand becomes even more important for basketball. Announcers will not have time to see who has the ball, see that the player is wearing number 22, look down at their chart to see who is number 22, say that player's name, and then look back up to get back to the action. In that time, the ball might have moved to a different player or the entire play may be over. Therefore, memorizing player names and uniform numbers is a key part of basketball play-by-play preparations because the action moves so quickly that the announcer must do much of the identification immediately. It is also wise for a basketball announcer to study the headshots on the teams' rosters, if available, and to watch closely during warm-ups. Since basketball announcers almost always call the game from court level and since the players do not wear helmets or pads, it can be easy to memorize and identify players by their physical appearance. Early in the shot clock is a good time for an announcer to give a quick fact or story, say the time and score, and restate the stakes of the game.

Baseball and Softball

Baseball and softball are very similar, as the basic rules and gameplay for the two sports are alike. When it comes to delivering play-by-play, both are indeed similar in that filling time when the ball is not in play is often the majority of the announcer's job. From the simplest play to the most important hit, the actual action of a game happens in brief bursts. For example, a pitch that results in a swinging strike takes less than 2 seconds to occur, while a home run—from the pitcher's windup to the ball going over the fence—will take less than 10 seconds. Then, depending on the pitcher, there could be least 30 seconds before the next pitch is thrown. Therefore, between pitches there is an abundance of time that needs to be filled. As stated previously, that means the research required before a baseball game is immense. The announcer can talk about past performances before the pitch ("Williams is oh for seven lifetime against this pitcher"), describe what the play that just happened means ("That's home run number 12 on season for Williams"), or relate a personal or professional story ("Williams is on his third team in the last five seasons"). The announcer should also be using that downtime to remind fans of the balls and strikes count, how many people are on base, and the number of outs when a new batter is up and give regular reminders about the score. It is important to remember, however, that baseball and softball games are usually several hours long, so announcers should pace themselves with these facts and statistics and not run through them all in the first two innings.

When the ball is in play, the announcer should describe the flight of the ball off the bat, mentioning all the players it comes in contact with ("Williams with the ground ball to short. Lee scoops it up and throws over to Skinner at first for the out"). Ultimately, the goal of a play-by-play announcer in baseball is to paint a picture of what is happening during a game so the people at home can understand what is going on.

However, sometimes with baseball, especially on television, it is best for the announcer to simply be quiet and let the crowd noise tell the story. When Cal Ripken Jr. broke Lou Gehrig's consecutive-games-played record, announcer Chris Berman said, "Let it be said that Number 8, Cal Ripken Jr., has reached the unreachable star." He then remained silent for 19 straight minutes as the stadium cheered wildly for Ripken as he made his way around the stadium (Nelson, 1995, para. 8). Another silent baseball announcer moment happened in 2019 when Jose Altuve hit a walk-off home run in Game 6 of the American League Championship Series to send the Houston Astros to the World Series. Immediately after the ball cracked off Altuve's bat, Fox Sports announcer Joe Buck enthusiastically yelled, "Altuve has just sent the Astros to the World Series!" (Clapp, 2019, para. 4) and then did not say another word for the next minute and a half. One reporter said that it was "a pro move" by Buck who "lets the moment do the talking" (Clapp, 2019, para. 6).

Hockey

Hockey is one of the most challenging sports to be a play-by-play announcer for because of the fast-moving action and the small puck that can be sometimes hard to spot from the higher levels of the arena (which is where the announcers are usually placed). Additionally, at least in the higher levels of play, many of the players are international, which can lead to some unfamiliar names and pronunciations for announcers.

Many announcers will narrate every pass, shot, deflection, and line change that happens during a game. However, due to the speed of the action, that is not always possible. Play-by-play announcers can often get tongue-tied trying to relay everything that is happening. Therefore, play-by-play broadcasters might take a breath when one team is regrouping in its defensive zone and then try to be as accurate as possible as they move forward and try to create a scoring opportunity. Regroups are also a prime opportunity for the announcer to give the time and score and reset the stakes.

Additionally, the action is often repetitive, so announcers in hockey can find themselves saying the same things over and over again: "Johnson passes to Smith. Smith passes to Spencer, who passes it back to Smith. . . ." That means that announcers will sometimes have to get creative: Mike "Doc" Emrick is credited as once using 153 different terms to describe a puck moving during a game (NPR, 2018).

As with basketball, it is imperative for a hockey announcer to memorize the names and numbers of every player to be able to keep up with the speed of the game. Depending on the level, announcers may have access to line sheets, team-produced documents that show which players will usually be on the ice at the same time. These are helpful but cannot fully replace an announcer's ability to identify any skater by his or her number at any moment.

Golf

While many sporting events consist of nonstop action or brief bursts of intense play, golf is a sport in which a slower pace is something an announcer will have to remember while broadcasting. One of the most difficult aspects of broadcasting golf is that it is happening over an entire course, and not all directly in front of the announcers. Therefore, the lead play-by-play announcer is often more of a conductor, not necessarily giving the updates himself or herself but instead introducing other announcers on various parts of the course. For example, the lead play-by-play announcer may say, "Let's go to our reporter Warren Scott on the 8th hole for an update on our leader." After Scott's report, the announcer may then send viewers to the announcer on the 16th hole where that person can describe a golfer putting for an eagle.

When describing a shot, the play-by-play announcer will want to recap what hole the golfer is on, his or her score, how far away he or she is from the hole, and what club is about to be used: "15th hole, this is Diana Kerr. She is 3 shots back of the leaders. Kerr is about 150 yards away from the hole and has a 7-iron in her hands." Keeping with the quiet tone around a golf course, these words are often delivered in a hushed tone with only the most amazing shots getting any type of excitement from the announcers.

Tennis

Tennis on television is perhaps one of the easiest sports to do play-by-play for because the announcers do not actually do play-by-play. Instead, they will simply update the score in between points and perhaps add a relevant statistic. Once the play starts, instead of describing every forehand and backhand in a tennis rally, the announcer will simply be quiet and let the action play out with only the natural sound of the match being heard. After the play is over, an announcer may recap what happened while showing an instant replay, give an updated score, and then be quiet again before the next point begins.

Soccer

Soccer is a unique sport in that the clock is always running so there are very few stoppages in the action. However, despite that "always-on" format, often not many goals are scored. Therefore, announcers are instead describing passes, penalties, and various free kicks. With the constant action, play-by-play announcers in soccer should not feel the need to describe every single second of the game. Instead, they can pause in parts for a few seconds to let the crowd noise come through on the broadcast. They can also take time to convey storylines surrounding the game and anecdotes about the players. However, when a play is developing or a goal is scored, announcers should be sure to convey the excitement of the moment.

Radio Versus Television Play-by-Play

While the goal of a play-by-play announcer is to describe the action as it happens during a live sporting event, there are some differences with the job if the broadcaster is doing a game on television versus doing a game on the radio. Perhaps the most obvious difference is that the fans can actually see what is happening if they are watching on television. Therefore, television broadcasters can often let the video tell the story instead of needing to describe every detail. Additionally, most television broadcasts have the score displayed the entire time on the screen. This does not mean that television play-by-play announcers do not need to say the score, however, as they should still be giving regular updates on who is in the lead and how much time is remaining.

Radio play-by-play announcers are essentially the eyes of the listener, so they have to make sure that the audience can not only follow along with the action but can also picture it as if they were at the game. Therefore, radio announcers must be much more descriptive with their call of the game. They can describe the jersey colors, the players' appearance, the weather, and other visual elements that the fans at home are missing out on by not watching themselves. A radio announcer may also wish to give descriptions of locations to help with the visualizations, such as "the Devils are moving from left to right." Therefore, while television and radio play-by-play announcers are watching the same game, how they broadcast it is often very different.

Pro Advice

© Kevin Fitzgerald

Kevin Fitzgerald

Play-by-play announcer

Kevin Fitzgerald knew early on that he wanted a career as a play-by-play announcer. "My passion was always play-by-play. I always thought that was so much fun—the way that you prepare for a game, being on site, the live 'we don't know what is going to happen' element to covering live sports." The Syracuse University alum was the winner of the Jim Nantz Award during his senior year, awarded to the top college sports broadcaster in the United States.

Fitzgerald jumped right in after graduation, serving as an announcer for a few universities before landing the lead play-by-play announcer job for the Fireflies, a New York Mets minor league baseball affiliate in Columbia, South Carolina. Kevin also started announcing college sports for ESPN, where he has been a play-by-play announcer for basketball, softball, and baseball. "I really like [doing a variety]. For me, it kinda provides a freshness. I always love jumping from one sport to the next."

Walk us through the process of doing a game. What happens before you even get there?

Whenever you finish the prior game, you're already pivoting to your next game. You could go two weeks without seeing the same team, or you could get the same team three times in the same week, so you have to keep tabs from afar on the league you are on and the teams you are going to see.

I'm already looking ahead to . . . okay, what did Georgia and LSU do last night? What did they do during the week? Who is their best player? What type of team are they? I put it all into a chart. I've got it categorized by the starters, reserves, there is information for the coaches, team stats, player stats, bio info, talking points, and general points about the team. You're just compiling all that stuff onto your chart so you have it in front of you when you are calling a game.

Then you head to the game?

We'll always fly in or drive in the day before. I like to get in early enough so that I can attend practice the day before. You can fly in and fly out the day of the game, but are you really getting

(continued)

Kevin Fitzgerald *(continued)*

to know coaches and players? That day before at practice is a great place to pick up some details, pick up some nuggets for the broadcast.

Day of—you go to shootaround. You gather any last-minute information. Make sure you study your notes. We get to a game an hour and a half before tip and we're sitting there antsy. We just want to go. We've done all our work and we're ready. We love it. That's the best part once you get close. Once that producer counts down, 3-2-1, in your ear, and you're on the air and have some fun.

Can broadcasters mute a game on TV and do their own play-by-play for practice? Is that silly or is that actually worth doing?

When I was a kid, I was playing video games and I was doing that. So, if it's silly, then I'm right there with them. For many of my colleagues, our stories start right there: "I was watching a game or playing a video game and we were commentating the action by ourselves in front of our gaming system."

To be good at something you need repetitions. The more often you do something, the better you can develop your routine. Athletes talk about it all the time. The rookie doesn't have the routine that Tom Brady has. Once you gather more and more opportunities, you simply learn what's the best way to success at something.

The beauty of this is that you can go do homework at any given moment. There's no excuses. There is a sporting event on any time, everywhere, anywhere. You can watch who you like, you can be a sponge listening to some of your favorite play-by-play broadcasters, and you can do it at any point, every night you can flip on a game. You're not there to steal, but more so model what you do. I'll leave a notebook on my coffee table next to my TV because I'll write things down that I like when I hear them.

Role of the Color Commentator

Many beginning play-by-play announcers, or those working for smaller teams, will likely be doing a broadcast solo, so it is up to just him or her to fill all of the airtime. However, as the broadcasts get bigger, the on-air staff grows as well, and the second addition to the team is often what is known as the **color commentator** (or color analyst). This job is often filled by a former player or coach who gives an expert opinion about what is happening during the action.

The job of the color commentator is to provide more information beyond just the general description of the action that the play-by-play announcer is giving. For example, in a football game, the play-by-play announcer might describe how the quarterback is sacked by a defensive lineman: "Johnson back to pass. Here comes the pressure and he is sacked by Colin Russell for a six-yard loss." It is then up to the color commentator to explain how and why the sack happened. On television, the color commentator may use a video **instant replay** to help illustrate his or her point, while a radio announcer will simply retell what happened: "Johnson had no chance on that one. Someone on the offensive line missed an assignment and Russell was able to run untouched up the middle. Looked like someone didn't do their job on that play."

An analyst should be using their personal experiences to help tell the story of what happened during a specific play or sequence. This is why these jobs are often awarded to former players and coaches, although there are some journalists who have been successful in this role. For example, longtime *Sports Illustrated* baseball writer Tom Verducci was an analyst for Fox Sports during the World Series in 2015

(Sherman, 2015). Additionally, perhaps one of the most famous sports broadcasters of all time, Howard Cosell, was a reporter who acted as a color commentator for numerous sports despite never having played professionally himself (Ribowsky, 2011).

Just like the play-by-play announcer, the color commentator must do plenty of work before the broadcast even begins. However, instead of memorizing names and statistics, the analyst will instead research what a team has been doing recently. Ultimately, he or she is watching previous games as if they were a player, trying to figure out what the opponent is doing on specific plays. By studying these tendencies, the color commentator is able to inform the audience about what to look for before a play even begins. For example, if a football team lines up in a specific formation, the color commentator should mention what the team has done from this setup previously and which players to watch closely. Starting in 2019, NFL commentator Tony Romo (a recently retired quarterback) earned a reputation for being able to identify what was going to happen in a game before it did. His predictions ("this has to be a run") were right nearly 70 percent of the time (Cohen & Beaton, 2019). An article in *The New Yorker* summarized one of these sequences:

> *"Gronk is out wide!" he said at one point, referring to the Patriots' tight end Rob Gronkowski. "Watch this safety! If he comes down, it's a good chance he's throwing out there!" The safety came down, and the throw, from the Patriots' quarterback, Tom Brady, to Gronkowski, was complete (Helfand, 2019, para. 2).*

Romo's research before the games allowed him to recognize what might happen during the plays, and his predictions made him one of the most popular color commentators for football. It also made him a rich man: CBS signed him to a 10-year, $180 million dollar contract in 2020 (Marchand, 2020).

Ultimately, it is the goal of the color commentator to educate the audience. While many viewers and listeners may have a great deal of knowledge about a sport, a former player or coach can provide information that the average viewer may not know. By telling the audience what might happen before a play, and then why and how something happened after a play, the color commentator is able to let fans know what it is like to be coaching or playing in the game.

Role of the Sideline Reporter

Many game broadcasts used to consist of only a play-by-play announcer and a color commentator, but the on-air team now often contains a third member: the **sideline reporter**. This person does exactly what the title implies in that they are normally next to the field of play, reporting what is happening up close. While the play-by-play announcer and color commentator are usually sequestered in a booth high above the game so they can see the entire field of play more clearly, the sideline reporter is up close to the action and able to move around freely in the areas in which the media is allowed to stand. This sideline location allows them to see what is happening on the bench, hear what the players and coaches might be saying, and get injury updates direct from the trainer. For example, if a player is suddenly not in the game, the sideline reporter would be able to ask the trainer or team official why the player is out, and then would give that update on the broadcast direct from field level. Additionally, sideline reporters are also often counted on to conduct pregame, in-game (during halftime, for example), and postgame interviews with players and coaches on the field.

While the title of the job is primarily known as *sideline reporter*, it should be noted that this is not a job only for sports that have sidelines. There are courtside reporters in basketball, rinkside reporters in hockey, pit reporters in auto racing, and reporters who stand near the dugouts during baseball games. No matter what the sport, the job of the sideline reporter is to give fans a better sense of what is happening on the field during the game.

Wesley Hitt/Getty Images

The sideline reporter is often tasked with interviewing coaches or players after a big game.

Before the Game

Prior to games, the sideline reporter will be part of the team that meets with the coaches and players. During this time, the sideline reporter will be looking for tidbits of information that he or she can give during their segments when the game is going on. Additionally, sideline reporters will watch previous games involving the teams, read local newspapers for stories, and research the releases sent out by the team (Clapp, 2015). Fox Sports' Laura Okmin is the third-longest tenured sideline reporter in NFL history, and her preparation is one of the reasons she is still going strong: "I do just as much work as my analyst and as my play-by-play guy. We watch the same football, we read the same amount of articles, we do the same amount of meetings, we have the same conversations, and yet, if you boil down what my Sunday is, it probably means I spoke for about three minutes." For beginning sideline reporters, the fact that it is just three minutes on television can be one of the most difficult parts to accept.

Don't Count Hits

While sideline reporters do a great deal of research before the game, their segments on the air are often very brief. Therefore, one sideline reporter estimated that "90% of your preparation doesn't get used" (Reedy, 2020a, para. 10). During the game, the sideline reporter will be constantly giving updates to the behind-the-scenes producers of the broadcast, even though those reports are not always seen on television. For example, in an NFL playoff game, sideline reporter Erin Andrews saw a player getting out of the medical tent and returning to the game. She gave that information to the play-by-play announcer during the commercial break and he said it when the game was back on (Reedy, 2020a). While the sideline reporter got the information, she was not the one who gave the report on the air. Okmin said, "Just as important as me being on camera to deliver a story is me talking to my announcers during a commercial break and telling them 'Hey guys, I'm watching this, just so you know. If you want to use this, I'm watching the quarterback, I'm not going to do a report on it, but his left thumb is bothering him.' Or telling my director, 'make sure you get the camera on this player because he's walking into the tunnel.'"

Even though she's part of the team, Okmin said it can be hard at first to accept what exactly the job entails: "It's hard to walk out of a game where you have prepared so hard all week. Every Saturday night I send a list of my favorite things to my producer and there is a list of 18-20 stories, and there is a chance I'm going to get two of them on. So, there's all these great things that just get left on paper. And that does a number on you for a long period of time."

However, it is the work behind the scenes that ultimately might be the most important part of the job for the sideline reporter. While he or she may only be on camera a few times, the contribution is much larger than that. Okmin said, "When I was a young sideline reporter, I would count my hits and that would determine what my day was. If I had three hits, it was a bad day. If I had seven hits, it was a tremendous day. It's bigger than just trying to get yourself on camera. So now it's not 'how many hits did I have,' it's 'how did I help us get better today?' Did everyone in the truck and everyone in the booth, did they feel that I was their eyes and ears and that they could they count on down on the field?"

Mashed Potatoes Analogy

While many sports broadcasters may dream of being a sideline reporter, Okmin says that should not be the only goal. While she is one of the most accomplished sideline reporters in broadcasting history, that's not how she identifies herself: "The last thing I describe myself as is a sideline reporter. I'm an executive producer. I created a production company. I created a show built on my relationships that I got from the sidelines. And so, look at all these things I've done that I'm really proud of and oh, by the way, I'm also the third-longest tenured sideline reporter."

While it might seem like a strange analogy, Okmin describes sideline reporting as mashed potatoes. "It's a great side of mashed potatoes. I love mashed potatoes, but I'm not going to order my entrée of just mashed potatoes. It won't fill me up. It won't sustain me. It's going to make my filet mignon better, but I need to work on my filet mignon." Ultimately, she believes that broadcasters should be working on a primary career and have sideline reporting be something that they can do in addition to that main job. "You can look at a woman on the sidelines and think, 'I love that, that's great'—and it is. It's a great gig, but I want them look at women who have been doing it for a long time, and I want them to think not, 'how do I land a sweet gig?' but 'how do I have a sustainable career?' "

Homer or Impartial?

Play-by-play announcers and color commentators who work for a national network covering a variety of different teams often sound very different from the broadcast partners who only cover one team. The difference ultimately comes down to the concept of impartiality. A national network announcer will be listened to by fans of both teams and also those who are fans of neither team who are simply watching the game for entertainment. Therefore, these national announcers do not want to show any favoritism toward either team, because it could alienate some of the audience.

However, broadcasters who report on one team throughout the year are not usually impartial, sometimes openly rooting for their team to win during the broadcast. These broadcasters, often called "homers" because they are biased toward the hometown team, have the potential to become very popular with fans because they are viewed as fans themselves.

There may be no more famous homer than former Chicago White Sox play-by-play announcer Ken "Hawk" Harrelson. The former major leaguer, who surprisingly never played for the White Sox during his career, was known for saying "Yes!" after White Sox home runs, criticizing umpires after calls with which he did not agree, and calling the White Sox "the good guys" during the game (Diamond, 2012; Hyman, 2015). Harrelson said, "Let's just say that if we're losing, you're going to know it. I won't sound happy" (Diamond, 2012, para. 3). In 2012, *The Wall Street Journal* analyzed all the home team announcers in baseball and determined that Harrelson and his color commentator Steve Stone were the most biased of any team. In fact, the newspaper counted up all the biased comments the two made during a game and found that they were more biased than all 29 other MLB broadcast teams *combined* (Diamond, 2012). When told by the reporter that he was at the top of the "most biased" list, Harrelson replied, "You just made my day. That's the biggest compliment you could give me" (Diamond, 2012, para. 11). While Harrelson's broadcasts were not universally loved (the website HeaveTheHawk.com was created as an effort to get him removed from the broadcasts), he was widely respected by many in the industry. In 2020, shortly after his retirement, he was named that year's winner of the Frick Award, given to the broadcaster for their contributions to the game by the Baseball Hall of Fame (Francis, 2020).

Team announcers should frame their stories and narration from the perspective of the team. There should be a noticeable difference in the energy they provide when their team does something good as opposed to when the opponent does. However, while Harrelson made a long career out of it for the White Sox, these team announcers should not openly root for their team or provide an unfair depiction or analysis of the game due to their bias. Only on rare occasions should announcers be overtly biased.

Starting in 2014, Turner Broadcasting showed games from the men's college basketball Final Four on three different stations at the same time and gave the national audience a chance to choose what type of broadcasters they wanted to listen to. On TBS, fans would hear the traditional broadcast team of impartial announcers doing the championship contest (Associated Press, 2014). However, on the channels TNT and TruTV, each team had school-specific announcers broadcasting the game. These included former players from each school and broadcasters who had reported on the team throughout the season (NCAA.com, 2014). For example, when Kentucky played Wisconsin in one of the semifinal games that season, the Kentucky announcers were on TNT, while the Wisconsin announcers were on TruTV. During that first year of this experiment, many unsuspecting fans tuning into the games on one of these team-centric broadcasts were confused and outraged at how biased the announcers were. During the Kentucky–Wisconsin game, fans who did not realize they were watching the Kentucky-centric broadcast on TNT went to Twitter to complain. Tweets included "This one announcer on TNT is so biased for Kentucky and it's really getting annoying" and "Am I watching TNT or the Kentucky Wildcats network?" (Cooper, 2014, para. 6;7).

Of course, even though national announcers are supposed to be impartial (and the vast majority truly are), that does not stop some fans from believing that every announcer hates their team. Joe Buck is a longtime announcer for Fox Sports and has been the lead play-by-play announcer for numerous Super Bowl games and World Series matchups. In his job at Fox, Buck is expected to remain neutral while calling a game. However, that has not stopped many fans from accusing him of favoring one team over another, with some going as far as petitioning Fox Sports to have him removed due to his supposed biases (Agrest, 2020). Buck himself chalks up the misunderstanding to the fact that he gets excited on the air when anything important happens and that fans of the team on the wrong end of that play take offense: "Not only did you lose, but I'm screaming and yelling because another team just beat you" (Kelly, 2020, para. 3).

Behind-the-Scenes Jobs of a Live Sports Production

While it is often the play-by-play announcers, sideline reporters, and videographers who get much of the attention, an entire staff of people is backing up the people seen during a broadcast. For a live sports production, all these people must work in harmony for the show to go off without a hitch. Following is a partial list of behind-the-scenes staff who work on a live sports production (Owens, 2016; Schultz, 2005; Zumoff & Negin, 2015):

- **Producer**—Oversees the production of the event and is responsible for the show content. Usually the producer is the person "in charge" of a broadcast.
- **Director**—Instructs camera operators on what to shoot, decides which camera shots should be shown on the broadcast, and communicates with the replay and graphics technicians.
- **Technical director**—Pushes the buttons on the switcher that selects the cameras and effects that have been requested by the director.
- **Associate director**—Is primarily focused on some of the action that is not game-specific, such as the timing of commercial breaks.
- **Audio supervisor**—Mixes the sounds coming from the various microphones during the broadcast. This includes the sound from the crowd, the on-field action, the announcers, and the broadcast's music and sound effects.
- **Replay operator**—Monitors cameras that are not live on the broadcast and determines which one has the best angle or vantage point for a replay after play has concluded.
- **Graphics operator**—Creates graphics and uses the machine that puts text and graphics on the screen.
- **Spotter**—Assists the crew and the announcers in looking for events during the game that those with other jobs may miss. For high-level football broadcasts, one or more spotters will help the announcers identify players involved in a given play by pointing to them on the announcers' spotting charts.
- **Grip**—Helps during setup and breakdown of the event by carrying equipment, placing cable, and assisting with whatever else is needed to get ready for the broadcast. This person may also work with camera operators during the game to hold cables while the videographer is shooting.

Chapter 7 discussed how to shoot video of a game for a live sports production. Obviously for television, videographers are a big part

Christof Koepsel/Bongarts/Getty Images

Inside the television truck of a live broadcast, where the production team monitors the various camera shots from around the stadium to decide which angles to show during the game at key moments.

of making sure the home audience sees the action as it happens. There is no set number of videographers working a game; instead that number depends on the importance of the event. For example, a typical regular-season NFL game will have between 12 and 20 cameras covering the action (Impact of Television, n.d.). That setup will likely include three cameras positioned high on one side of the field, with one at the 50-yard line and the other two between the 20- and 25-yard lines on each side of the field. There are also numerous cameras located on the field to get a lower angle. However, for big events, the number of cameras more than doubles. For example, for the Super Bowl in 2020, Fox Sports used more than 100 cameras to capture the action. While not all of them were manned, they were all monitored by someone in the production truck (Kerschbaumer, 2020).

CHAPTER WRAP-UP

HK*PROPEL* ACTIVITIES

HK*Propel* includes a behind-the-scenes video from a play-by-play announcer as he prepares to broadcast a minor league baseball game.

SUMMARY

Becoming a play-by-play announcer is the dream job for many looking to enter the field of sports broadcasting. The chance to be able to describe some of the biggest sporting events in the world to millions of people watching on television or listening on the radio is an incredible opportunity. However, the path to becoming a great play-by-play announcer involves a great deal of preparation and practice. The amount of work required to prepare for a broadcast before the game even begins can be overwhelming. However, that prep work will make for a much smoother call of the game because the announcer will be ready for almost any scenario that arises. Announcers should also be well versed in the various sports they are being asked to broadcast and understand the different tips and tricks required for each one. Finally, just like the athletes they are covering, announcers will most likely only improve by practicing. That means doing as many games as possible and perhaps even turning down the volume on the television and doing their own play-by-play of a game they are watching.

Phil Cole/Getty Images

CHAPTER 11

Social Media

CHAPTER OBJECTIVES

Whether it is statistics from a game or updates on team news, sports fans want the latest information immediately. To get that fix, many are turning to social media to get that up-to-the-second update. For sports broadcasters, this has given them a new way to both communicate with the audience and deliver news. This chapter focuses on the role of social media in the daily routine of broadcast sports media, including the following:

- Recognizing the impact of social media on the jobs of sports broadcasters
- Understanding the differences among the types of social media
- Creating an effective social media presence
- Utilizing best practices when using social media as a sports broadcaster

Chapter 6 discussed how the internet added new work responsibilities to the daily routine of sports broadcasters. They previously only had to focus on their sportscasts, but the increased importance of websites meant that they had to turn their audio and video stories into written pieces that could appear online. While websites increased the workload, perhaps no online development has altered the jobs of sports broadcasters more than social media.

Blogs (The Old Social Media)

Before discussing the impact of social media, it is worth examining the precursor to the various platforms: blogging. **Blogs** are websites that provide constant updates on a topic or event through posts that are usually displayed with the newest content at the top of the page. Blogs became increasingly popular in the early 2000s due to the availability of free, easy-to-use websites (Blood, 2000). As more people gravitated to blogs, staff members at television stations joined the trend and created their own (de Zúñiga et al., 2011). While newsrooms used blogs for a variety of purposes, sports departments often seemed uninterested. When sports broadcasters started a blog, that decision was more often at the directive of management and not of their own accord (Schultz & Sheffer, 2009). In fact, one local sports broadcaster labeled blogging "a waste of time" (Schultz & Sheffer, 2008, p. 188).

However, while blogs may not have been a big hit for sports broadcasters at the time, many elements of what has made social media popular had their roots in blogging. At the time, "live blogging" of sporting events was a popular way to use this new initiative. Instead of simply talking about the story afterward, reporters would use blogs to provide live updates of the action throughout the event. During the 2007 Masters golf tournament, ESPN's Jason Sobel would update his blog every three to five minutes with the latest news from the course, trivia questions, and jokes (Gisondi, 2018). At the time, these updates enabled fans to follow along with the action if they could not be there physically or watch on television. Now Twitter has become the home for these sorts of updates, as journalists send tweets that provide the latest information on an important game.

Perhaps the more lasting impact of blogs was revealing the importance of interaction with the audience. Through comment sections on blogs, readers could directly contact the author of the blog or interact with other users. This was a dramatic change from when media outlets would simply deliver the news in a one-way relationship—the media would deliver the news and the audience would consume it. Blogs allowed the audience to be a part of the news process. The use of blogs was one of the first attempts to get direct viewer input into the stories of the day, an initiative that would soon become more commonplace. Eventually, online initiatives began moving away from blogs and focusing more on services such as Facebook that had even greater interactivity features (Yu, 2012).

At one time, blogs were considered the top new technology trend in newsrooms (de Zúñiga et al., 2011), but now hardly any television or radio station has a blog on its website. Instead, much of what made blogs unique and appealing has been replaced with social media.

Types of Social Media

The world of social media is littered with services that either dropped dramatically in popularity (such as Myspace) or went away completely (such as Vine) (Chokshi, 2019; Newton, 2016). However, as of the writing of this chapter, four social media networks where journalists can reach their audience in a way that is different from traditional broadcast methods remain popular: Facebook, Instagram, Snapchat, and Twitter.

Facebook

Facebook is a social network on which users can post updates and personal information to be seen by other users of the site. By the end of 2019, it was the most widely used social media network, with 2.45 billion people worldwide logging into the platform each month, 1.62 billion of those people being considered "active" members (Sehl, 2019). The hub of the site is each individual user's news feed. In this location, information and stories from people or businesses with which the user has connected will show up for the user to read. These posts could be text, photos, or videos. Users have the option of liking the post, commenting on the post, or sharing the post with their own followers (Walker, 2019). In 2016, Facebook launched **Facebook Live**, which allowed users to stream live video straight from their mobile device to their news feed (Simo, 2016).

Facebook provides media outlets with the opportunity to create a page for the entire organization as a whole or individual journalists to create their own page. Users can follow those journalists, and then all the updates from the organization or the journalist will show up in that user's feed. For journalists, this has created a scenario in which their stories can be consumed by a much larger audience than was previously possible. The creation of Facebook Live has allowed sports journalists to provide live video updates from games and interact with the audience immediately without needing expensive live equipment or satellite technology.

Instagram

Instagram is a photo and video-sharing application in which users post media to their page. The posts can have captions accompanying the image or video. Much like Facebook (which owns the service), users decide which accounts they want to follow after which posts from those selected accounts will show up in the news feed. Posts can then be "liked" or commented on (Moreau, 2020). In early 2019, 37 percent of adults in the United States used Instagram, with 67 percent of 18- to 29-year-olds reporting that they had an account (Perrin & Anderson, 2019).

Sports journalists often use Instagram to post photos from events. The social network is less of a news delivery service and more of a way to provide a behind-the-scenes element for fans. Therefore, while it is a popular app among a younger generation of sports fans, it has not captured the attention of the sports media as much as the other options listed in this section.

Snapchat

The social network **Snapchat** had 360 million users in January 2020 and was, at the time, one of the fastest growing social networks in the world. The private messaging service allows users to post photos and videos (known as "snaps") that disappear from the site after a set number of seconds (O'Connell, 2020). Additionally, users can put their "snaps" in a sequence that viewers can watch as a "story" (a feature also popular on Instagram). The service is popular with people ages 25 and younger (Clement, 2019).

The sports media began harnessing the popularity of Snapchat in 2016 when NBC agreed to a partnership with the social network, allowing clips of events to be shown over the service (Frier, 2016). This was a landmark deal, as it was the first time that NBC had allowed footage of the Olympics to be shared on a platform not owned and operated by the network (Martin, 2016). That decision turned out to be a wise one for NBC, as the footage on Snapchat was viewed 2.2 billion times for a total of 230 million minutes during the two weeks of the Olympics (Patel, 2016).

Other networks quickly followed suit, perhaps none more aggressively than ESPN. In late 2017, ESPN launched a version of its popular highlights show *SportsCenter* that would air exclusively on Snapchat (Petski, 2017). The Snapchat version of the show was just a few minutes long, but less than two months later it was getting millions of views a day. Reflective of the user base, ESPN stated that 75 percent of the audience was teenagers or young adults (Brady, 2018). The success of *SportsCenter* on Snapchat resulted in the network creating a deeper investment in the social platform, with additional shows added to the online roster (Flynn, 2019).

Twitter

Perhaps no social media network has had a bigger impact on sports journalism than **Twitter**. The site debuted in 2006, and by 2009 the sports world was "obsessed" with it (Gregory, 2009, para. 2). Twitter allows users to send messages, or **tweets**, from a computer or mobile device. The brevity of the messages was a key component to the service: tweets were originally capped at just 140 characters each, but that was increased in 2017 to 280 (Larson, 2017). Tweets are displayed immediately after being posted in a user's **timeline** and provide news, commentary, embedded photos or videos, links to articles or video, or whatever else the author of the message decides to write about. Users are able to follow accounts that have content that interests them and get the latest information from those accounts delivered directly to their Twitter timeline. Users can also search for topics or keywords in tweets (Mansfield, 2010). In addition, Twitter users utilize hashtags in order to have conversations around a specific topic (Johnson, 2009).

When it comes to sports, the owners of the Twitter platform have invested heavily in the ability to show live games. The social network reached deals with the NFL, MLB, and NHL to show regular season games on Twitter (Bucholtz, 2019). While these deals with leagues have brought an increased sports presence, Twitter was already popular with sports journalists and fans. Journalists acknowledged that, while not always required by management, having a professional Twitter account that is used for job purposes is "industry standard" (Adornato, 2014, p. 18).

Social Media Lingo

From hashtags to handles, the world of social media has its own language that users should know before diving deep into the various applications. Following is a list of various terms and symbols that are often used online:

- @—The @ sign is used to contact another user on most social media networks.
- #—The # is the symbol that should be placed before a hashtag.
- **Avatar**—The profile photo of the user of the account. This can be a photo of anything and not necessarily the person.
- **Direct message (DM)**—A private message sent from one user to another through the social network's messaging service. These messages cannot be read by the public.
- **Favorite**—A feature on Twitter that allows users to signify that they enjoy the tweet.
- **Handle/Username**—How a person or organization is identified on social media. For example, ESPN's Twitter handle is @ESPN, while ESPN baseball writer Jeff Passan's handle is @JeffPassan.
- **Hashtag**—Used to identify a key word or topic that can then be searched for by other users. Hashtags are often used to group together posts related to a topic or event. For example, all posts about the World Series may use #WorldSeries.
- **Link**—A web address that takes users to the selected website.
- **Retweet**—A feature on Twitter that allows users to take an existing tweet and put it into their own timeline. The user can either retweet the original message exactly or quote the original message and then add their own comment above it.
- **Tagging**—Linking a picture or video to another user. If a baseball writer composed a post with a photo of four players in it, he or she may wish to "tag" those players in the photo so they will know there is a post with them in it.

Impact of Social Media on Sports Broadcasting

While social media has had a tremendous impact on the jobs of many different types of journalists, perhaps no job in the media has been impacted as greatly as that of the sports broadcaster (Sanderson, 2011). Programs such as ESPN's *SportsCenter* used to be where people would tune in to get the latest scores and highlights from that day's games. However, now highlights are on social media almost instantly, and so the need to wait until late at night to see what happened is not necessary (Wong, 2019). Instead of competing with the benefits of Twitter, sports broadcasters have instead embraced what Twitter can offer to the audience. Journalists now use Twitter to send out news directly and immediately to their followers at any time of the day, not just during the 6:00 p.m. and 11:00 p.m. broadcasts. While this has addressed the need that the audience has for immediacy, it also means that being a sports broadcaster has essentially become a 24-hour-a-day, 7-day-a-week job. One local sports broadcaster said about Twitter, "It's taxing and sometimes annoying, but it's a part of the job" (Hull, 2016e, p. 526). However, another was even less positive about the constant work, saying that they "don't like being plugged in 24/7" (Hull, 2016e, p. 526).

However, for many broadcasters, the option to not use social media during their off-hours is not a possibility. Even though the majority of the local sports broadcasters surveyed in 2016 said that management does not require

Pro Advice

© Reva Labbe

Reva Labbe

Senior social media specialist at ESPN

Reva Labbe is the senior social media specialist at ESPN. In this role, she focuses on working with ESPN's on-air talent on their personal social media pages. Reva was initially hired to work on the college football social media handles before focusing on the accounts for the popular *College GameDay* broadcast. In addition to college football, Reva has been able to cover NBA games, NFL games, and UFC events. In her current role she works with individual on-air personalities at ESPN to help them get more comfortable with their personal social media accounts.

I think a lot of people would love to have a job like yours, so how did you get started working in social media?

It must have been my freshman or sophomore year and I was home for winter break. I was watching all the bowl games and I was on Twitter at the same time. I had this epiphany moment where I realized "Hey, I guess I could do this for a job." I remember my mom being like—"No you can't." And I was like, "No mom, this is a real job now!"

While I was in school at the University of Florida, I was an unpaid intern with Rivals for about three years, working on their social media. That opportunity parlayed into my first paid opportunity, which was a seasonal position with the Chick-fil-A Peach Bowl. After working with them for a year, I made the jump to ESPN.

What is the goal of social media at a place like ESPN? Is it all about promoting the broadcast?

We think that if people want to watch the show, they're going to watch it regardless. I think we can influence it to some regard, but you won't necessarily see overt "tune-in" messaging. It's more organic or subtle.

We view what we're doing as our own entity, and we've created our own niche. But we also try to stay true to the feeling and the overall nature of what broadcast is doing. We're not completely different from the broadcast, but we also know there are tons of people who follow us on social who may not be watching the broadcast.

Obviously, ESPN is one of the top places to work as a sports broadcaster, but what advice do you give the ESPN reporters that sports broadcasters at every level can use?

I tell them to be authentic to themselves in who they are. And everyone is different. A lot of them are concerned about specific things—they don't want to show their families or show their personal lives—and I tell them that this is your platform, and you can show as little or as much as you want. As long as you're authentic to yourself, that's all your fans want.

I also try to tell them to remember that this isn't TV, because sometimes when they get on TV they think that they need to be super buttoned up. But I tell them that on social, you can be more casual, you can be more relaxed, you don't have to be in the suit. You can be more casual on social media and more laid-back. I think they're enjoying that social media atmosphere more now.

What has been one of your favorite parts of the job at ESPN?

I like to push [the broadcasters] a little bit, and it has been cool to see them embrace so much more. If you go to Kirk Herbstreit's Instagram account, he does so much more video content now, and it's really cool because he's opened up so much and now, he loves doing these all-access, behind-the-scenes videos to where he never did that before. If you love college football, there is nothing cooler than watching a 15-minute video with Kirk Herbstreit in the middle of a college football Saturday and he'll answer your questions. The fact that they're willing to try new trends is really cool to see. But I just tell them—just be authentic.

them to tweet when they are not on the clock, they still do so. One said, "So many stories and story updates first come to light on Twitter, we can't afford to ignore it" (Hull, 2016e, p. 527). An ESPN executive stated that Twitter has created a "second-by-second news cycle" (Fry, 2012, para. 14).

Despite the added work responsibilities and constantly being "on the clock," Twitter remains a popular work tool for sports broadcasters. A survey of 113 local sports broadcasters throughout the United States found that 90 percent either "liked" or "loved" Twitter, with one simply stating, "I LOVE Twitter" (Hull, 2016e, p. 527). Social media outlets have made gathering information for the evening sportscast much easier. Breaking news is often first reported on Twitter, so broadcasters are able to get the latest information for their show directly from their social media news feeds. One said, "If you follow the right people, you can get information on stories before the official press release" (Hull, 2016e, p. 528).

Traditionally, one of the challenges for a broadcaster was getting a final score from a high school game. Television broadcasters will often shoot a few minutes' worth of highlights at a game before moving on to the next one and are rarely there for the conclusion to get the score themselves. Therefore, they would have to rely on a coach or parent to call the television station with a final score before the evening sportscast. Now, many high school teams have their own social media accounts that are updated throughout the game. These accounts give scores, statistics, and even updates on rain delays (Hull, 2016e). On a night when there are multiple games happening in an area (such as a Friday night during high school football season), Twitter has become the place to turn to for the broadcaster. One estimated that 90 percent of their high school football scores are gathered from Twitter and that "some coaches don't even call or text anymore. They will tweet me and include a link with results, or a photo of kids with a trophy. It's great" (Hull, 2016e, p. 528).

The impact of social media on sports broadcasters has been tremendous. While it has added more work to an already full plate, many do not seem to mind this. They say that networks such as Twitter have made them more prepared when going on the air, given them an easier way to gather information, and allowed them to connect with viewers in an entirely new way. Ultimately, it has, as one sports broadcaster put it, "made life easier" (Hull, 2016e, p. 529).

Setting Up a Social Media Account

While the various social media platforms have different methods of delivering information, they all have similar steps to setting up an account. Users will traditionally register with an email address and then answer several personal questions in order to finalize the process. When it comes to the public-facing elements of the account, the most important steps may be when users must create a username (or handle) and upload a profile picture. While these might seem like fairly straightforward decisions, they are anything but.

While broadcasters have the option of making their username whatever they want (as long as it has not been already taken by someone else), almost all sports broadcaster usernames fall into one of three categories: (1) name only, such as @SusanJones; (2) name with station call letters, such as @SusanJonesWABC; or (3) name with additional word, such as @SusanJonesSports or SusanJonesTV. In a 2016 study of 200 Twitter accounts of local sports broadcasters, the most popular option of these three was the use of the station call letters in the account (45.5 percent). However, this may not have been their decision. About half of the users from that study said that station management had instructed them to put the call letters in the username (Hull, 2016a).

While having the station's call letters in the username may make sense during the sportscaster's employment there, the fact is that most broadcasters live nomadic lives when it comes to their careers. Broadcasters will often move from city to city as they work their way up the career ladder. That means that having station call letters in a username can result in making multiple changes to that name or having to start over with a new account in each new city. For example, local sports broadcaster Jordan Conigliaro has worked for a variety of television stations and has had to change his Twitter handle along with those moves. In 2015, Conigliaro worked for WCYB in Bristol, Virginia, and his Twitter account was @WCYB_Jordan. By 2020, he had moved to Pittsburgh for WPGH, created a new Twitter account, and used @JordanC_PGH as his handle there.

Therefore, it is recommended that, when first setting up an account, broadcasters create social media usernames that are either just their names or their names with an added word (such as TV). This way the account can move with the broadcasters without needing to change the username. In a 2015 study, one sports broadcaster said that he used his Twitter account for more than just work-related tweets, so he did not believe that his station call letters needed to be in there:

> *I feel my Twitter is more a reflection of myself than it is my employer. I do represent my employer when I am on Twitter, but in the same way I represent them when I go out to buy groceries. Just because I am employed by a TV station doesn't mean I need to add call letters to my driver's license or credit cards. (Hull, 2015, p. 137)*

The profile photo is often the first thing that the audience sees when visiting a social media account. Therefore, broadcasters should decide how they would like the public to see them. A profile photo could be something work-related (such as the official headshot on the website or a shot of the broadcaster working) or something more casual (such as a picture with family). Ultimately, it comes down to the personal preference of the broadcaster. In that 2016 study, the majority of the 200 broadcasters (77.5 percent) used a photo of them working as their profile picture (Hull, 2016a).

When setting up a social media profile, broadcasters and their employers may wish to make explicitly clear what will happen to that account should the two sides part ways in the future. For many of the work-related tools, this ownership is clear. For example, when a broadcaster uses a camera or microphone, those items are clearly the property of the station. However, what about a social media account? If a journalist uses his or her Twitter account to give updates on the latest sports news, does the station own that account or is it the property of the individual journalist?

When sports reporter Andy Bitter left the *Roanoke Times* in 2018, he planned to take his @AndyBitterVT Twitter account, and its 27,000 followers, with him to his new job. However, the newspaper claimed that the account, which was previously run by another reporter before Bitter took it over, was owned by them and therefore Bitter could not continue to use it (Phillips, 2018a). Bitter then countersued the newspaper for more than $150,000, alleging defamation (Phillips, 2018b). Ultimately, before the case could go to trial, the two settled, with Bitter getting to keep the account while sending a tweet announcing the Twitter account of the new Virginia Tech beat writer for the *Roanoke Times* (Phillips, 2018c). While the settlement did end the legal battle, it did not answer the question of "Who owns a social media account?" As one reporter following the case wrote, "It looks like that murky grey legal area between social media, reporters, and their media companies will remain just that for the foreseeable future" (Keeley, 2018, para. 7).

Proper Use of Social Media

Despite the importance of social media to the daily routine of sports broadcasters, many reporters having never been properly trained on how to use it. A 2016 study found that more than half of local sports broadcasters surveyed had not received formal training (Hull, 2016b). This was especially true for broadcasters in their thirties who had not gotten training in college, from their employer, or on their own. For that age group not to get lessons in college is not surprising because social media was not available then. Therefore, it would have to fall on the employer to provide an education on how to use the various networks. However, that is not always successful, as one broadcaster who received social media lessons from his employer said they were "a waste of time"

MAJOR MOMENTS

Being First vs Being Correct

On January 26, 2020, former NBA player Kobe Bryant was killed in a helicopter crash in Calabasas, California, along with eight other people who were on board (Branch, Bogel-Burroughs, Mervosh, & Jordan, 2020). Less than an hour after the helicopter crashed, law enforcement was alerted to the fact that the former Los Angeles Lakers star was one of the casualties. However, before the authorities were able to personally deliver this news to Bryant's wife, celebrity and entertainment news outlet TMZ reported on Twitter that Bryant had died in the crash. The Los Angeles Sheriff's Department strongly criticized the coverage, with Sheriff Alex Villanueva saying at a press conference the next day, "It would be extremely disrespectful to understand that your loved one . . . perished and you learn about it from TMZ. That is just wholly inappropriate" (Darcy, 2020, para. 5). Another member of the Los Angeles Sheriff's Department tweeted, "I understand getting the scoop but please allow us time to make personal notifications to their loved ones. It's very cold to hear of the loss via media. Breaks my heart" (Murakami, 2020). While TMZ's founder Harvey Levin later stated that he was assured that Bryant's family knew the news before his website tweeted it, he did acknowledge that the families of the other people on board may not have known (D'Zurilla, 2020). When it comes to being first, TMZ will ultimately get credit for being the original news outlet to report the information. However, at what cost? The website was strongly criticized by both celebrities (D'Zurilla, 2020) and the police (Darcy, 2020) for the speed with which they reported the information, and the concerns about the news going public before families could be notified is valid. However, ultimately TMZ did get the story correct. Not everyone who reported information on social media could say the same.

ABC News reporter Matt Gutman stated that four of Bryant's daughters had died in the crash (Cachero, 2020). This information was spread on social media but was ultimately incorrect (only one of Bryant's daughters was on board). Gutman had to apologize on Twitter for his error (Gutman, 2020) and was suspended by the network (Cachero, 2020). Additionally, before all the victims were identified, reports circulated on Twitter that Bryant's former teammate Rick Fox had also died in the crash (Tracy, 2020). Fox, who was not on the helicopter, was at home when he said his phone kept buzzing with people making sure he was alive (Alexander, 2020).

The death of Kobe Bryant revealed two major concerns regarding social media: the rush to be first and the importance of getting the news right. Information spreads quickly on social media, so, despite the pressures to be first, journalists must be sure that their information is correct before hitting send.

(Hull, 2016b, p. 36). Therefore, the next few sections will focus on the various ways in which to use social media when sending out messages to followers: delivering news, promotional messages, interacting with the audience, and creating a public/private balance (Hull, 2016c).

Delivering News

Perhaps the most obvious use of social media is to deliver news updates. While most broadcast stations have social media accounts that cover the entire newsroom operations (news, weather, and sports), sports news is often an afterthought. A study found that less than 9 percent of messages on television station Twitter accounts were related to sports (Armstrong & Gao, 2010), so it will ultimately be up to the sportscasters to send out their own sports updates.

The first method of delivering news updates would be via straightforward sports news. This could include hirings, firings, injury updates, player updates, and team information. For example, if a local player wins an award, the broadcaster can send out a quick update on Twitter.

Joe Reporter @JoeReporter2020
Penguins shortstop Peter Thomson is the BBL Player of the Week. He hit .438 with 3 HR and 10 RBI in 5 games.

This tweet does not have a great deal of information in it, but it contains the important parts of the story. The audience now knows that Thomson won the award and what his statistics were for the week. The broadcaster may wish to include a photo of the player or, if it has already been written, a link to the story that has been posted to the station website.

Another way to deliver news is to provide updates on games as they are happening. This can be especially effective for games that are not on television or the radio. For example, very few high school games are broadcast to a mass audience. Therefore, social media allows for journalists at the games to send frequent updates about what is happening. At a minor league baseball game, a journalist may send a tweet about a big hit that scores a few runs.

Joe Reporter @JoeReporter2020
B3: Thomson with a 2-run double. Penguins now lead 4–1.

This tweet is simple and concise, but it also provides the all the key details. It is the bottom of the third inning (B3) and Peter Thomson just hit a double that scored two runs, giving the Penguins a 4–1 lead. Tweets like these can be very helpful to fans who are not able to watch or attend a game.

In addition to straightforward updates, tweets from games can also provide the follower a feeling of what it is like to be there. This can happen by the describing some of the scenes that will not be apparent through just reading the statistics. At that same baseball game, Thomson is up again in the inning following his base hit and this time the result is much different. However, it is the action beyond the play that followers may find most interesting.

Joe Reporter @JoeReporter2020
B4: Thomson hit by a pitch. Penguins players yelling at the Eagles' pitcher from the dugout. Fans aren't happy either. Starting to get a little rowdy here.

A fan reading the box score can easily deduce that Thomson was hit by a pitch in the fourth inning. However, the reporter's tweet gives more information beyond that one pitch. Now the audience knows the Penguins players are angry and the fans are, too. These can be good ways to showcase the action beyond the traditional scoring plays and give the audience a sense of what it is like to be at the game.

Sending these updates during games can be an effective way to keep the audience informed of what is happening; however, the broadcaster should be aware of how many messages he or she is sending. It is highly possible that sending updates too frequently will end up making the audience less interested in the content. There is no need to send a tweet after every single play and clog up the timelines of followers. Instead, broadcasters should stick to key moments such as scoring plays, important statistics, and descriptions that make the followers feel like they are at the game, too.

Promotional Messages

One of the aspects of social media that is appealing for broadcasters is the ability to draw more attention to their work. Twitter and Facebook both allow for direct links to be placed within the messages being sent, so followers can easily go directly to the website for the complete story. For example, in a story about a player injury, the tweet contains the key facts, with a link to the station website for fans who want more information within the entire story.

Joe Reporter @JoeReporter2020
Penguins SS Thomson to miss three games after being hit by pitch on Saturday. Full story: www.wyyy.com/Thomson

The idea of using social media as a promotional tool is important for two reasons: financial and personal. The financial implications revolve around advertising for the station as a whole. While social media can be an effective tool for distributing content and interacting with the audience, it ultimately is not a money-making endeavor for broadcast stations or individuals. A tweet can get five million likes or just five likes and the station will get the same amount of money from it: $0. However, the station can get revenue from advertising on its website. Therefore, driving the audience to the website can possibly increase the number of visitors, which can ultimately allow the station to charge more for advertising. Therefore, broadcasters should include links to the website when posting messages on both Twitter and Facebook. In addition to promoting content on the website, broadcasters can also promote content that will be coming up on the broadcasts later that day. More viewers there can also translate to higher advertising dollars for the station.

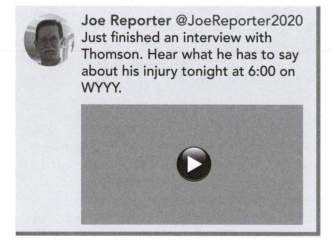

Joe Reporter @JoeReporter2020
Just finished an interview with Thomson. Hear what he has to say about his injury tonight at 6:00 on WYYY.

Using social media as a promotional tool can also benefit journalists personally. One of the main objectives when doing a story is to get it viewed, read, or listened to by as many people as possible. More readers can possibly lead to more followers on social media, and journalists with more followers, rightly or wrongly, are often considered more popular and established than those with fewer followers. Therefore, if a journalist can get his or her stories to a wider audience, that can lead to some personal benefits, such as a better reputation, job possibilities, and perhaps more money from an employer. Stations ultimately will want to keep (or hire away) journalists with high follower counts because that could translate to a bigger audience for the station.

While it would seem that promotional messages would be an important part of a daily social media routine, one examination found that broadcasters were rarely using Twitter for that purpose. A 2016 study found that while the majority of local sports broadcasters were sending promotional tweets, only about 8 percent of their entire tweet content was of a promotional nature (Hull, 2016d). Perhaps broadcasters do not see one tweet or one Facebook post as a way to increase their audience. However, that would be a mistake, as the strength of weak ties demonstrates that one tweet can make a big difference. The **strength of weak ties** states that people who someone knows closely are strong ties, while casual acquaintances are weak ties. In the spreading of information, the weak ties are often more effective in getting the message out to a new and wider audience (Granovetter, 1973).

For example, a broadcaster sends a tweet that contains a link to a story about a famous soccer player making an appearance in the city in which the broadcaster works.

Joe Reporter @JoeReporter2020
Soccer superstar Diego Gonzalez showed up at a high school soccer game in Springfield today. See what happened next: www.wyyy.com/SoccerStar

This tweet could then be retweeted by a local viewer. That retweet now shows up in the feed of that viewer's family, who lives in a different state, causing them to click on the link to see the story, causing it to go national. That fan then retweets it again, causing it to be seen by an entirely new audience, including a diehard fan of Gonzalez's professional team. She then retweets it again, causing it to be seen by other fans of that team who are located throughout the world. That broadcaster's tweet, through just a few retweets, has gone global. Ultimately, it was the weak ties of people who never would have seen the tweets in the first place that helped it reach worldwide viewership. This might seem like an unlikely scenario, but the strength of weak ties has been shown to be effective in the world of sports. In 2013, the UNC–Wilmington swimming and diving teams were able to get celebrities with large followings to retweet their messages, allowing them to get over 14,000 signatures on a petition to save their team from elimination, despite none of the athletes having more than 300 followers (Hull, 2014b). Therefore, while it may seem like a promotional tweet will only impact a broadcaster's followers, the strength of weak ties demonstrates that a few fortunate retweets or repostings can make a message go global.

Interaction With the Audience

For decades, news delivery was a one-way interaction between the journalist and the audience. In television, the broadcaster would talk about the latest sports news during the evening sportscast and the audience could only listen. That made the audience very passive, because they could not directly participate in the news delivery and could not interact with the journalists. Social media has changed that dramatically as now broadcasters and writers are more accessible than ever. Interaction with followers can happen in a variety of ways, such as answering questions, asking the audience for its opinion, or simply injecting themselves into viewer conversations. If broadcasters can develop positive interactions on social media, that could lead to a larger and most supportive audience online, which could lead to stories being spread more readily and a larger following.

Joe Reporter @JoeReporter2020
30 minutes until first pitch for the Penguins. I've got time for quick Q&A. What's on your mind Penguins fans?

One of the more popular ways to get audience engagement on social media is to ask for it directly. Many journalists will do question-and-answer sessions on social media. This gives direct feedback to followers and also gives the broadcaster a sense of what is on the minds of his or her audience. For example, if in the previous example several people all ask a similar question, that will let the reporter know that there is an interest in that specific topic. With that knowledge, the broadcaster may do a story on that topic in the future since he or she knows that is something about which many people are already curious. Therefore, social media can be used as a form of crowdsourcing to see which topics are worth pursuing for the broadcaster.

Joe Reporter @JoeReporter2020
Penguins to start Joseph Dywer on the mound tonight. It's his first start since coming off the injured list.

Go Pens! @PenguinsFan
@JoeReporter2020 Will he be on a pitch count?

Joe Reporter @JoeReporter2020
@PenguinsFan Manager says no restrictions on pitch count, but I'm guessing the first few innings will be key.

Another opportunity for interaction with followers would be if they respond to something that the broadcaster has tweeted. In the above message, the reporter gives information about a pitcher coming back from injury. The tweet contained just the basic information, but a diehard fan wants to know even more before the game starts. By responding directly to this fan's question, the broadcaster is able to demonstrate his or her knowledge of the team and also provide the information that this fan is requesting. In the future, this fan may first turn to this specific reporter for the latest information on the team.

While social media has changed much for broadcasters as far as their daily routine, the ability to interact with viewers and listeners is perhaps the most dramatic change. Broadcasters should embrace this opportunity by connecting with the audience in order to possibly develop a greater connection. If the audience feels that the broadcaster will personally respond to questions, they might be more willing to follow them on the broadcast and become a loyal audience member.

Maintaining a Public–Private Balance

While social media has given broadcasters the opportunity to interact with the audience, it has also provided them a chance to reveal more about their personal lives. Traditionally, the audience only gets to know the broadcaster during the few minutes that he or she is on the air during the day. That leaves little time for the broadcaster to reveal any personal details, so any non–work life information is usually a quick tidbit. However, due to social media being an "always-on" service and broadcasters being expected to use it nearly 24/7, many are using social networks to reveal more personal details about their lives. This is known as the public–private balance on social media, as broadcasters decide how much of their private lives to reveal while also discussing their public, job-related activities (Hull, 2017).

Research has demonstrated that people may be more likely to follow people who are like themselves and may even develop a bond with celebrities they believe they are "friends" with because of that similarity (Horton & Wohl, 1956). Social media posts that reveal more information about their personal lives allow the audience to find things they have in common with broadcasters.

Joe Reporter @JoeReporter2020
For my money, Joe's Pizza on Main Street is the best pizza in Springfield.

For example, this tweet has nothing to do with sports or the latest news, but it could ultimately be a post that gets a great deal of reaction from followers. Those who also love Joe's Pizza will feel a connection with the reporter, while others may respond with their own suggestions. This simple tweet shows more of a personal side of the broadcaster (he loves pizza and loves a local establishment) and has the potential to endear himself to the audience even further.

Joe Reporter @JoeReporter2020
Great Saturday with the family! Daughter's soccer game in the morning, family hike in the afternoon, and ice cream for dinner. This is the life!

This tweet reveals that the broadcaster has a family, something many of his followers may appreciate learning; they will likely be able to relate to his story about his great day. Even those without young kids may simply enjoy the fact that his dinner consisted of ice cream. Social media posts like this one will not make his audience any more informed about the latest sports news, but they will help make the reporter more than just a face on the evening news by introducing part of his personal life to the public.

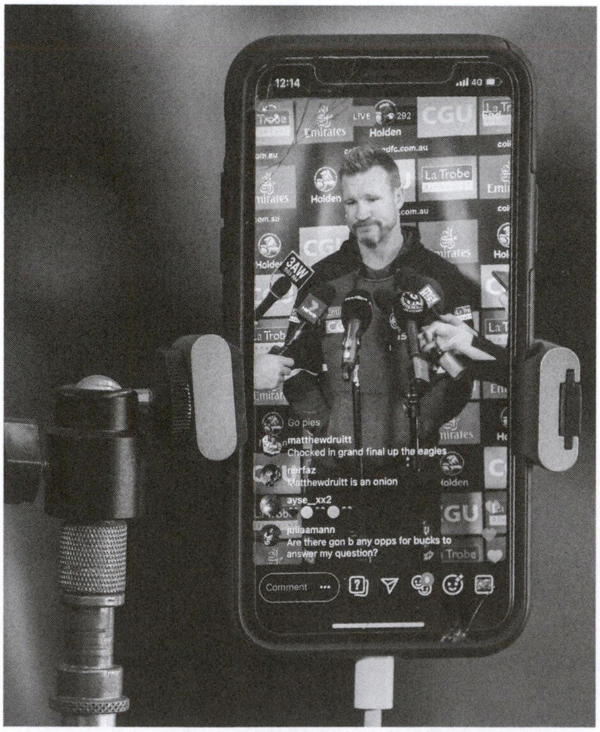

Michael Dodge/Getty Images

Sports broadcasters are able to use social media to live stream press conferences and get immediate feedback from their followers.

A 2017 study of local sports broadcasters found that in a national sample of almost 20,000 tweets, about 22 percent of the posts were about the broadcasters' personal lives. These messages related humorous things that happened at work ("Had to stand on a chair to interview a player today #shortgirlstruggles"), revealed personal sports opinions ("I love our defense"), and gave details about their home life (including posting pictures of their kids in Halloween costumes) (Hull, 2017). While revealing information about their personal life can be an aspect of their social media use, broadcasters should also remember why people are following them in the first place. So, while an occasional tweet about movie preferences, favorite foods, or frustrations at the DMV might be a welcome addition to the timeline, the primary focus should always be delivering the latest sports news and scores to followers.

Social Media Policies

While there are a variety of different uses for social media, many companies explicitly spell out how their employees should be using these services. Many media outlets have their own social media guidelines, which are often provided to new hires and are updated when necessary. For example, ESPN created their social media guidelines in 2011, made small changes in 2012, and revisited them entirely in 2017 after some employees created negative headlines for the company after controversial tweets (Brady, 2017; Skipper, 2017). Those tweets focused on the political opinions of ESPN personalities, so the updated policy explicitly stated the following:

> *Our engagement on social platforms such as Facebook, Twitter and Instagram should be civil, responsible, and without overt political or other biases that would threaten our or your credibility with the public. Do nothing that would undercut your colleagues' work or embroil the company in unwanted controversy. (Social media, 2017, p. 1)*

Avoiding political topics is something that other media outlets have also spelled out in social media policies. *The New York Times* updated its social media policy approximately one month before ESPN did. While the newspaper has reporters working on politics, health, international news, and a variety of other topics, the policy makes it clear that everyone, no matter what they are reporting on, has the same guidelines. Much like ESPN, *The New York Times* policy states: "In social media posts, our journalists must not express partisan opinions, promote political views, endorse candidates, make offensive comments or do anything else that undercuts The Times's journalistic reputation" (The New York Times, 2017, para. 20). Those policies apply to everyone at the newspaper, including the sports department, as stated in the follow-up bullet point: "These guidelines apply to everyone in every department of the newsroom, including those not involved in coverage of government and politics" (The New York Times, 2017, para. 22).

The New York Times policy also touches on the subject of how, while the accounts of individuals are associated with those journalists, they are representing the newspaper at the same time. Therefore, any negative tweet that comes from that individual's account will ultimately be associated with the newspaper as a whole. Reporter Nick Confessore said the following:

> *The reality is that my Twitter account is a Times account. The Times does not control it, but the Times is held accountable for what appears on my feed. Indeed, the casual reader interprets my social accounts as an extension of our digital platforms, for good and ill. I think all of us at the Times need to embrace this as the price of our employment by a major media institution. (New York Times, 2017, para. 25)*

While ESPN and *The New York Times* are large, national organizations, many local television stations have their own social media policies. However, these policies are often created on the national, corporate level and are consistent throughout the country. For example, as of 2021, Gray Television owns and operates stations in 94 of the 210 television markets in the United States (Gray Television, n.d.). The 2014 Gray Television employee handbook is a 49-page document, broken up into 27 different sections. Of those, no section is larger than the 7 pages devoted to the company's social media policy. The document is divided into prohibited conduct, general guidelines, and discipline if those guidelines are violated (Gray Television, 2014).

While media ownership groups throughout the world all have their own policies, the best advice for journalists is simply to use common sense when using social media. The Gray Media policy stated that broadcast standards apply to work accounts, so if something is not appropriate for the television audience, then it is not appropriate for social media either (Gray Television, 2014). No matter who the employer, that policy is a good one to follow for broadcasters using social media. Ultimately, ESPN reporter Don Van Natta may have put it best when he said, "When in doubt, don't tweet it out" (Brady, 2017, para. 31).

Social Media in Action

One of the advantages of social media is that it allows reporters to provide constant updates of a situation while covering a story. Instead of waiting until the next newscast or simply updating one story on the station's website, social media gives reporters the opportunity to deliver breaking news and updates immediately. In some cases the story is not urgent, but the reporter can still use social media to provide updates and encourage people to stay tuned to traditional broadcast formats for more information later in the day.

To demonstrate how social media can help a sports broadcaster keep his or her followers updated during a fluid situation, an example of a reporter finding out about a big story will be used. In this scenario, a sports broadcaster (Joe Reporter) is heading to the practice of a minor league baseball team (the Penguins) to gather elements for a preview story about an important series against their rival (the Eagles) happening in the upcoming weekend. This should be a fairly straightforward story that broadcasters will likely do dozens of times in a year. Typically, the broadcaster goes to practice, interviews the key players and coaches, gets some video and photos of the practice, and then heads back to the television or radio station to edit it together for the next sportscast and to write the website story.

Before heading to the stadium, Joe first sends a tweet to let his followers know the story on which he is working. This lets Joe's followers know that he is going to be there and that they can expect updates about the upcoming series against the Eagles. For fans of the Penguins, this might make them want to keep an eye on Joe's feed so that they can get the latest news. It can also let them know that there will be more information about the team during the evening news, which may motivate more people to watch or listen to that broadcast.

Joe Reporter @JoeReporter2020
I'm heading to Penguins practice shortly to get some updates before the big series vs the Eagles. Stay tuned for updates.

After going into the stadium and seeing the team starting to warm up, Joe immediately notices there is an important development happening that no one in the media had yet reported. The Penguins' star shortstop, Peter Thomson, appears to be injured. This is the type of breaking news that can be delivered on social media through a one-sentence update. After confirming that it is in fact Thomson on crutches, the broadcaster quickly composes a tweet and sends it to his followers.

Joe Reporter @JoeReporter2020
Update from Penguins' practice: Shortstop Peter Thomson is on crutches with his left foot in a walking boot. I'm attempting to get more information.

For fans of the Penguins, this tweet is likely to generate a great deal of interest. This quick update could garner several comments, likes, and retweets from concerned fans. Through the strength of weak ties, this interaction from Joe's followers could result in the message being seen by a much larger audience than normal.

By ending the tweet with the update that he is attempting to get more information, that may motivate fans to keep checking back with Joe's account for more details. It is important to remember that if a broadcaster promises that he or she is going to get more information, he or she should follow through on that promise.

In order to get that update, Joe approaches the Penguins' manager, who agrees to do a quick interview before practice. The broadcaster records it on his usual video camera for the evening news, but when asking about Thomson he also records the manager using the video features of his phone at the same time. By having it on his phone, he is able to quickly send the video from the interview out to his followers on social media without needing to take the time to get to a computer, upload the video from his video camera, and send that file. Joe quickly finds the portion of the interview on his phone that he wants to send to his followers, edits out the unnecessary part, and posts the sound bite to both his Twitter and Facebook accounts.

Joe Reporter @JoeReporter2020
It's a broken foot for Thomson. Manager says he'll miss 4-6 weeks.

As practice is starting up, the broadcaster responds to some Twitter and Facebook posts from his followers who want more information about the team and Thomson's injury. This interaction is a key component to social media, allowing Joe to make a personal connection with his followers. Instead of simply delivering the news through a one-way conversation, Joe is able to answer questions and create a two-way flow of information. Research has demonstrated that followers are more likely to feel a connection with journalists and celebrities who respond to social media posts. Using the information that he gathered from his interview with the manager, Joe can directly answer questions that fans might have.

Go Pens! @PenguinsFan
Oh no! We are lost without Thomson. @JoeReporter2020 who will play shortstop now?

Joe Reporter @JoeReporter2020
@PenguinsFan Manager says it is Austin Sanderson's job to lose, but he'll look at all possibilities.

Additionally, Joe may wish to do a quick Facebook Live session from the field so that he can provide a more broadcast-style update. This would also allow for interaction with his followers in that he could answer questions being posed at the bottom of the screen.

Once practice starts, broadcasters can continue to give updates and behind-the-scenes photos on social media of what is going on with the team. However, this will likely prove to be a balancing act for Joe. As stated previously, social media has added to the workflow of broadcasters and now gives them more to worry about when doing their job. In addition to getting video and interviews for his story that will air later that night, Joe should continue to post updates on social media. While he is hopeful that many will watch the late news, he does have an attentive audience now that knows he is at practice and is following his breaking news story. Therefore, it would be a good idea to continue to engage that audience. Therefore, Joe can take a quick break from shooting video to use his phone to take a picture of the possible replacements at shortstop who are vying for the job.

Joe Reporter @JoeReporter2020
Looks like Penguins' manager Chip Godwin wasn't kidding when he said everyone will get a shot to replace Thomson. Lots of players lined up at short.

By using social media to cover this story, Joe was able to let his followers know that he was going to the Penguins' practice, provide a breaking news update as soon as he was alerted to Thomson's injury, send out video interview clips with the manager on multiple social media accounts, respond to his followers' questions through both text and video, and then provide constant updates of the situation.

A Week of @CollegeGameDay

While the previous scenario was fictional and involved just one reporter in one day, the real thing at a place such as ESPN is an enormous undertaking. One of the most popular shows on ESPN is *College GameDay*. Each week, this college football pregame show airs live on Saturday morning from the location of one of the major games of the week. These broadcasts traditionally happen on campus, with hundreds of fans lining up behind the hosts with their own homemade signs, hoping to make the broadcast. The show is wildly popular with fans and critics, bringing in high television ratings and numerous Emmy Awards.

However, while the broadcast portion of the show is widely celebrated, the online components are also key to the show's success. Reva Labbe was a part of the social media team for *College GameDay*, and while the broadcast airs on television on Saturday, she said the social media accounts were a week-long project.

Sunday and Monday

Immediately after the Saturday night games end, the *College GameDay* team is already thinking about the next show and the content that can be on the social media accounts throughout the week. One of the biggest aspects is announcing where the live show will take place, which is often decided late Saturday night or Sunday morning. Labbe said making the announcement is an important part of the social media accounts and that she often does not know the destination until about 30 seconds before she clicks post on the tweet: "We are watching just like everyone else to see who is winning and who is losing before we decide where we are going next week."

"Once it's official, you're immediately hitting the ground running," Labbe said. "I need to immediately draft the email to the school's SID to see who is the best player that I can get on campus for a behind-the-scenes, all-access interview with Maria Taylor. You're trying to get all your ducks in a row." Many of the staff members work from home on Sunday and Monday.

Tuesday

With everyone back in the office on Tuesday, the face-to-face planning for the upcoming show and social media aspects begins. Two different plans are starting to come together: one for items that need to get done at ESPN headquarters in Bristol, Connecticut, and another for what they want to do when they get on-site.

Much of the on-location social media items cannot be gathered until they are actually there, so this time is spent coming up with a plan for what they will do once they are on campus. However, the items from the Bristol office can start coming together at this time. "We need to make sure that we have graphics, all these different animations, highlight videos and all this other sort of stuff that needs to be created before we go to the site of the game," Labbe said.

Wednesday

Wednesday is a workday in Bristol as the social media team puts the final touches on the material that is created there.

Thursday

Thursday is a travel day for those who are on-site during the *College GameDay* broadcast. That makes for a great deal of remote working for those who are part of the traveling crew: "We are usually in the office only one or two days a week during the fall."

Friday

Friday is the start of crunch time for the entire *College GameDay* team. This is when they will interview players for social media content but not necessarily ask about the game. Labbe said, "We like to do fun things that don't really have anything to do with the game, but we really like to show these players' personalities outside of just Xs and Os." In addition, they are editing video, making graphics, and creating content so that it will be ready to go on Saturday.

Saturday

Everything that they've done all week leads up to a full day of games on Saturday, so it's no surprise when Labbe stated that "Saturday is a 20-hour day." The social media team is showcasing homemade signs that fans brought to the *College GameDay* set, monitoring games, and looking for the historic and the interesting about which to send messages. Those fan signs in the background of the show are a key part of the social media effort: "If you're watching on TV you'll see a bunch of signs. You can see some of them, but it's hard to see all of them. So some people follow on social media just to see the funniest sign of the day. That's definitely a niche that we've carved out for us, and we know that's our bread and butter."

At the same time, they are also weaving in the content that was created earlier in the week back in Bristol, finding the perfect time to post that tweet or Instagram post. During the showcase game of the week, the team is sending updates from the game with pictures, video clips, and interviews.

By the end of Saturday night, they are all exhausted, but it's also time to start the weekly process all over again. "It's a lot of work. I think a lot of people think that it's just so much fun. And it is a lot of fun, but it's also a lot of work. It's a grind. It's 17 weeks of nonstop, and it feels like a roller coaster. You get spun out at the end and think, 'how did we get here?' "

Athletes and Social Media

While broadcasters are using social media to provide the latest updates to their followers, these social networks have also created some new competition when it comes to providing news about athletes: the athletes themselves. Professional and amateur athletes have some of the most followers on Twitter (Gaines, 2012) and are using sites like Twitter to create positive exposure for themselves, engage fans, and increase their own visibility (Pegoraro, 2010).

Athlete use of social media is perhaps most disruptive to journalists because it allows sports stars to make a direct connection with fans. Traditionally, when there was news about an athlete, the only way for that information to get out to the public was through the media. Teams would make their players available for interviews, and the journalist would get sound bites from the players and then play them on the broadcast. Athletes, beyond interactions at staged events like autograph signings, had little way of making direct contact with fans. This put the media in the role of the **gatekeeper**. The concept behind gatekeeping is that the media ultimately decides what information is released to the public. Before social media, if an athlete talked to a reporter about several different topics, it was up to the journalist to decide which stories were covered and which ones were ignored (Shoemaker & Vos, 2009). In that relationship, the journalist held almost all of the power when it comes to athletes communicating with fans. Social media has turned that balance upside down.

During the 2013 Masters golf tournament, many of the participants spent their time away from the course sending out tweets to their followers about everything from what they bought in the gift shop to on-course strategy (Hull, 2014a). One of the most visible uses of Twitter during the week involved the world's most famous golfer, Tiger Woods. He used the service to avoid the media and deliver a message directly to his followers. Instead of participating in a press conference before the third round, Woods turned to Twitter to explain his opinion on the two-stroke penalty he had been assessed after an illegal drop the day before. After hitting the ball into the water on the 15th hole, Woods dropped a replacement ball a few feet behind where he had hit his previous shot. This was a violation of PGA Tour Rule 26, which states that the player should play his ball "as nearly as possible" to the spot of the first ball (Crouse, 2013). To address what happened, Woods sent out five consecutive tweets in which he explained the drop from his perspective, what happened the next morning, how the penalty was assessed, and how he accepted the penalty (Harig, 2013). Fans of Woods were able to get this information directly from Woods and not have to wait for the media to report it.

In 2018, LeBron James was one of the most coveted free agents in the NBA. Reporters spent months attempting to guess what team James would sign with (Reisinger, 2018; Stein, 2018), and it had the potential to be one of the biggest "scoops" of the year for the reporter who was the first to reveal it. However, no reporter got the scoop. Instead, James' agent made the announcement through Twitter by tweeting a picture of a press release stating that James was signing with the Los Angeles Lakers (Joseph, 2018b). This allowed James to control the message himself, as he and his team could decide when the announcement would be made public.

Athletes can also use social media to speak out against and possibly correct journalists. Previously, athletes had few opportunities to respond if a broadcaster reported something with which the athlete disagreed. However, social media has now given them that platform. In 2018, reporter Ed Bouchette sent a tweet that stated Steelers' receiver Antonio Brown was injured during practice. Shortly afterward, Brown went to his Twitter account, retweeted Bouchette's original post, and wrote, "You making [expletive] up." Bouchette later sent another tweet stating that Brown was not hurt (Joseph, 2018a).

All of these examples demonstrate how social media has the ability to disrupt sports broadcasting (Hull & Lewis, 2014). With athletes using social media to connect directly with fans and show a side of their private lives, it could be media members left in the dark. Athletes previously needed journalists to deliver the latest news and show a behind-the-scenes look at their lives. Now, sports stars can do it themselves by sending a tweet, posting a photo to Instagram, or creating a brief Snapchat video. Therefore, broadcasters must embrace social media themselves to get information directly to followers while also keeping track of what athletes are sending out on the various platforms.

CHAPTER WRAP-UP

SUMMARY

Social media has had a tremendous impact on the daily routine of sports broadcasters. Fans now expect the latest sports news to be delivered as it is happening, so journalists need to be both following social media and posting to it almost immediately after a story breaks. That has turned the profession into a job in which broadcasters are seemingly always working. Despite that extra work, the majority of local sports broadcasters report having a positive impression of Twitter. Social media platforms such as Facebook, Instagram, and Snapchat also provide opportunities for sports broadcasters to deliver the latest news, interact with the audience, and reveal portions of their personal life that they may not have been able to discuss while on the air. Although social media has created competition from athletes as they report their own news, the opportunity to reach the audience in a different format is one that broadcasters should continue to embrace.

Phil Cole/Getty Images

CHAPTER 12

Careers in Sports Broadcasting

CHAPTER OBJECTIVES

For many jobs, getting hired involves simply sending a one-page resume and taking part in an interview with a potential boss. However, getting hired in sports broadcasting, especially for those hoping to be on air, is a much more involved process. The paper resume is just the start, as candidates need to have relevant broadcast experience, a multimedia reel, and a way to publicly showcase their work. In order to get candidates ready to enter the field, this chapter focuses on the job search, including the following:

- Identifying what might be a realistic first job in the industry and how to find it
- Examining avenues for potential experience
- Formatting a written resume and video/audio resume reel
- Recognizing the importance of self-marketing

Every broadcaster, no matter what level, has needed that first job to get into the industry. Television broadcasters do not start at *SportsCenter*, and the first-ever game for a radio play-by-play announcer is not the Super Bowl. Ultimately, the path to that dream job can be a long one, but broadcasters can start the process years earlier through careful planning and making sure that they are doing everything possible to make themselves more marketable for the first job and the ones after that.

Be Realistic

Before starting the job search, it is important to be realistic with what a first job might be. While anchoring ESPN's *SportsCenter* might be a dream job, that will not be a starting point after graduating from college. The career paths of national anchors demonstrate that it could be years before that ESPN appearance becomes a reality. In 1995, Sage Steele started her career at WSBT in South Bend, Indiana, before moving to WISH in Indianapolis, Indiana, until 1998. That year she took a job at WFTS in Tampa, Florida, for two years and then left that job for Fox Sports Net in Tampa. In 2001, she started a six-year run at Comcast SportsNet in Washington, D.C. before finally landing at ESPN in 2007 (ESPN Press Room, n.d.). Her 12-year career path to *SportsCenter* is certainly not unique, as national sports broadcasters have resumes filled with local television and radio experience, while major league play-by-play announcers often have decades of minor league experience.

Therefore, it is important to be realistic when thinking about what might be a good first job in the world of sports broadcasting. For those looking to get an on-air television job, a smaller city in a local market can be an excellent way to break into the business. From there, one can hopefully move to bigger and bigger cities until a possible call comes from ESPN. For sports talk radio, a similar start in smaller cities hosting an off-hours show can potentially lead to more opportunities in bigger sports-crazed areas. For those looking to do play-by-play or behind-the-scenes of live games, openings at smaller colleges or minor league teams can be an excellent way to break into the business. These first jobs might not be exactly what a broadcaster wants to do for decades, but they are often an excellent way to get a career started.

Getting Relevant Experience

Even though the opportunities in smaller cities and with smaller teams might be easier to get for a first job, that does not mean that someone can simply walk in off the street and start broadcasting. Those trying to enter the field should be looking to gain relevant experience before starting their official job search. While broadcasting-based college classes will provide important lessons and class projects in

Jeff Gross/Getty Images

Reporting from the All-Star Game is a dream assignment, but it likely won't be a sports broadcaster's first job. Climbing the career ladder is an important part of the industry.

which students create content, there is more that should be done. In fact, a survey of broadcasters revealed that prior experience was the most important factor for getting that first job (White, 2018). Finding an external opportunity to go above and beyond what is learned in the classroom can be valuable for honing work skills and for networking.

Student Media

For college students, perhaps the best place to start gaining experience is through student media. Many higher education programs have student television, radio, or newspaper organizations that either are directly affiliated with the school or operate independently. While run by amateur college students, these media outlets often act as professional media organizations. At many places, these student media members are given spots on press row and in the interview room directly next to those who work in the field. For college students looking to break into sports broadcasting, these opportunities can allow students to cover sports while learning the ropes along the way.

At Boston University, the student radio station WTBU has a sports department in which students can host their own sports talk shows, create podcasts, and do live play-by-play of various Division 1 sporting events on campus. At the University of Florida, the student newspaper *The Alligator* gives students the opportunity to cover all of the Gators' sporting events and publish stories in print and on the newspaper's website. Students involved with SGTV at the University of South Carolina followed the men's basketball team all the way across the country to Arizona for the Final Four in 2017. Additionally, students at SGTV host weekly sports recap shows, report on the field or court after games, and do live play-by-play of the club hockey team. Those are some specific examples of student media opportunities at colleges, but there are hundreds at schools of all sizes throughout the United States that offer similar opportunities. Even though a position might be with a student organization, it should be treated like a professional job. The experience and stories gained through student media can be helpful when applying for internships and jobs. Anyone seeking to get involved with student media should check in with the student activities office or, if their school has one, the department that offers journalism or communication classes.

Internships

In addition to the college media options offered at schools, students should explore the possibilities of getting an internship at a professional station. These internships will not only provide the student with work experience, they also can sometimes be used for course credit. Previous research has demonstrated that internships are often just as valuable as the journalism classes that a student takes on campus (Mandella, 2018; McDonough, Rodriguez, & Prior-Miller, 2009).

Not only are internships important for getting work experience, many employers now see them as almost a necessity to being hired as a broadcaster. In the eyes of some newsroom management, an internship can take the place of a first job. One news director said, "I do count an internship as previous professional experience" (Wegner & Owens, 2013, p. 32). This might be because, in many newsrooms, interns are given a tremendous amount of responsibility. A news director said that staff reductions are a big reason for this: "Many newsrooms have reduced the number of staff in their building, so interns may be gaining more hands-on, practical experience at the television station" (Wegner & Owens, 2013, pp. 32-33).

In a survey of local television sports broadcasters who had been on the job for less than five years, the vast majority (94 percent) said they had an internship while in school. They cited the hands-on experience as the most valuable part of that experience. One of the broadcasters in the survey wrote that during his internship, his supervisors "allowed me to take charge of my own experience and get out of it what I put in. Seemingly nothing was off limits" (Hull & Romney, 2021, p. 145).

Freelancing

Some newsrooms have freelance opportunities for those looking to gain additional experience. One of the best ways to help out a professional newsroom's sports department is to offer help with high school sports. Many newsrooms—broadcast, newspaper, or online—have only a few journalists to cover all the various high school sporting events going on in that area. For example, on a high school football Friday night, many television stations devote an entire 30 minutes to its coverage of the games. However, getting to all those games can be challenging if the staff is just a handful of people. That is where **freelance journalists** can help out. These journalists are not employed by the news organization but instead report on games or events on a case-by-case basis.

In the world of broadcasting, a freelance journalist might be able to shoot and edit video of a high school football game and then transfer the file over the internet to the television station. This gives the freelance journalist valuable experience and also helps him or her develop a connection with a local television station. While a broadcaster may only be interested in working for a television or radio station, offering to freelance for a newspaper during high school games can also be a rewarding experience. As stated in chapter 6, writing for websites has become an important part of the broadcaster's daily routine, so sharpening that style of writing can be a valuable exercise. Additionally, any experience working with a professional newsroom will look good on a resume, even if it is a broadcaster working with a newspaper.

During live sporting events, major networks will occasionally hire freelancers to work on the crew for games. These freelancers will help set up equipment; carry cables before, during, and after games; and assist in any other ways that are requested. Such opportunities are an excellent way to get in the door for those looking to work behind the scenes in broadcasting; however, it is up to the individual to make that opportunity happen. Newspapers and television stations are likely not going to put out open calls looking for people to help. Instead, those looking to freelance should be proactive and contact sports departments to see how they might assist in that capacity.

Networking

As in many industries, being in a position to get a job in sports broadcasting can often be a question of "who do you know?" Creating a network of people that can be trusted to provide feedback, give career advice, and help prepare one for a job opening can be helpful in breaking into the industry. Internships are an excellent place to start that network, as one's supervisor can turn out to be a long-term mentor to be counted on throughout an entire career.

Also, many sports media–related organizations provide opportunities for networking with other beginners and those who are seasoned professionals. The National Sports Media Association (NSMA) has student memberships that give those who sign up access to their annual hall of fame banquet and special member-only seminars throughout the year. Other organizations worth exploring include the Association for Women in Sport Media (AWSM) and Sportscasters Talent Agency of America (STAA). Minority students should strongly consider joining the National Association of Black Journalists (NABJ), National Association of Hispanic Journalists (NAHJ), and Asian American Journalists Association (AAJA). Those organizations pride themselves on being a strong network for minorities in the industry.

It is also suggested to try to connect with those who already have a job in the field. If someone wants to be a radio host, they should email those who are currently hosts to see if they have any career advice. The worst that can happen is that the person simply does not respond. However, if that connection is made, it could result in some excellent career advice and a possible reference in the future.

The Written Resume

As with almost any job, applicants will need a written resume when applying. These resumes are a way to demonstrate a candidate's work experience and skills. For sports broadcasters looking for a job, most resumes follow the same generic format. One of the first accepted rules of a resume is that it should not be longer than one page. Hiring managers will, in some cases, get over 100 applicants for a job, so they are not looking to read pages and pages of information. Some applicants will format their resumes two columns, while others will list everything from top to bottom in a single column. Both formats are acceptable.

For those doing a resume in which everything is placed in one list, the applicant's name and contact information should be at the very top. This should include an address, phone number, email address, and, as will be discussed later in this chapter, an online portfolio website link. The goal is to make it easy for the hiring manager to contact a candidate in whom he or she is interested.

Directly below the contact information should be the candidate's relevant work experience. While those in other industries might suggest that education should be in that spot, management in the broadcasting field wants to see what journalism experience the applicant has. As stated previously, student media, internship, and freelance experience have become almost a "must" when it comes to getting that first job. Therefore, this experience should be listed directly below the contact information so that it can be referenced immediately. The various jobs should be listed in reverse chronological order, so the most recent should be at the top. Each listing should include the job title, employer, location, and dates. These experiences should focus primarily on journalism-related jobs. That includes internships, student media, and any sort of volunteer or freelance work. While a job at the coffee shop might have helped pay the bills throughout school, that is not something in which news directors will be overly interested. They want to know that a candidate has been in a newsroom before and has some journalism experience. Below each listing, approximately three bullet points can describe exactly what the candidate did at that position. Not all internships are the same, so hiring managers will want to know exactly what an applicant did at his or her internship. These descriptors should be very specific and should be about one sentence each.

A listing of appropriate skills that the applicant has should follow the work experience. These skills should focus more on journalistic and technical elements and not vague personal descriptions. Relevant skills can include proficiency in computer software programs, social media expertise, and knowledge of various video and audio equipment. A vague skill such as "works well with people" should not be included because a hiring manager cannot discern what exactly that means.

Finally, at the bottom of the resume should be the candidate's education. This section should not be much more than a line or two, with the institution, year of graduation, and major included. Any relevant journalism awards or scholarships can be added, but it is not necessary to list a grade point average.

For a resume with an alternative look, the following is an example of a two-column resume from Claudia Chakamian. She is a television sports broadcaster who landed a job in Minnesota shortly after graduating from the University of South Carolina. She has her contact information directly below her name in the left column, with her education and skills below that. Her phone number and email have been blocked out for the purposes of this textbook but appear in the actual resume. Chakamian had a wealth of journalism experience while in college, so she devoted the entire right column to that list, with a brief description of each.

References do not have to fit on the one-page resume and can instead be included on a separate second page. These references should be people who can speak about the applicant's potential to succeed within a professional newsroom. They can include internship supervisors, student media advisors, and journalism professors. The candidate should ask permission from a potential reference before listing him or her. It is important to know that the reference will say good things about the candidate and also helpful to the reference to know that a phone call or email from an employer might be coming.

While many job applicants will create one version of their resume and simply send that

Claudia Chakamian

SPORTS JOURNALIST

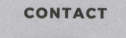

CONTACT

[redacted]@gmail.com

(803) [redacted]

www.cchakamian@wixsite.com/claudiachakamian

linkedin.com/in/claudia-chakamian

@C_Chakamian

ClaudiaChakamianReports

EDUCATION

UNIVERSITY OF SOUTH CAROLINA

May 2018

Bachelor of Arts, *Broadcast Journalism*

Minor, *Sport and Entertainment Management*

SKILLS

- Premiere
- Sony NX cameras
- Canon DSLR
- Social Media Analytics
- SAS Audio Console
- InDesign
- ENPS
- Public Speaking
- Microsoft Office
- Tricaster
- OpXStudio Client

PROFESSIONAL EXPERIENCE

WEEKEND SPORTS ANCHOR/SPORTS REPORTER

KQDS FOX 21 | July 2018 - Present | Duluth, MN

- Produced and anchored sports blocks for weekend shows and produced and co-anchored 30 minute sports show every Friday
- Shot and wrote highlights from local games
- Conducted interviews and shot video for weekly athlete feature segment, as well as for other stories

PRODUCTION INTERN

Ryan Seacrest Studios | Jan 2018 - May 2018 | Charlotte, NC

- Broadcast weekly radio/television show for 200+ patients at Levine Children's Hospital
- Produce videos and flyers showcasing events going on with the studio

SPORTS EDITOR

The Daily Gamecock | Sept 2014 - May 2018 | Columbia, SC

- Run weekly production meetings and edited articles from a 20-person staff
- Work with photo, social media and design to enhance sports content
- Write recaps, previews and features about USC athletics

SPORTS ANCHOR, REPORTER, PRODUCER

Carolina News | Aug 2017 - Dec 2017 | Columbia, SC

- Rotated through each position in the newsroom to help put on the live, daily news show
- Pitched stories, conducted interviews and edited packages to meet 3:30 p.m. deadlines

SIDELINE REPORTER

Wareham Gatemen | May 2017 - Aug 2017 | Wareham, MA

- Conducted live interviews with athletes and coaches as well as find stories for in-game hits
- Worked with broadcast team to live stream all 45 games

EXECUTIVE PRODUCER

Capital City Sports | Sept 2014 - May 2017 | Columbia, SC

- Trained and managed a 30 person staff
- Finalized staffer's highlights and put together weekly episode

Example of a two-column resume from an early-career broadcaster.

same one to every job opening, it is worth creating different versions for different job listings. If a job posting specifies a skill a candidate should have, a candidate who has that skill should list it somewhere in the resume. If knowledge of certain computer software is preferred, such as Adobe Premiere, then someone proficient should be sure to include that fact.

The Resume Reel

In addition to a written resume, those looking to be hired at a professional radio or television station should include a sample of their professional work. Before the digital era, for television broadcasters, that meant compiling their best work and putting it onto VHS tapes, while radio broadcasters made cassette tapes full of stories. These VHS and cassette tapes were then mailed all over the country every time there was an opening. When sportscaster Dawn Davenport was looking for her first job, those VHS tapes were a key part of the job search. "I remember going to Walmart and buying a big box of blank VHS's, putting my reels on them, and sending them out everywhere. I would then drive to local TV stations and pass them my resume tape in person," recalled Davenport (Privott, 2020, para. 6). While getting video and audio resumes in the hands of those doing the hiring has not changed, the process has. Thanks to technology, resume tapes have become resume reels and are now posted on online websites such as YouTube for video or SoundCloud for audio. Searching YouTube for "broadcasting reel" will result in hundreds of results for people looking for their next job. There is no one answer to the question "what should a resume reel look like?" However, most news directors and reporters would likely agree on the basics.

Television Resume Reel

For a television resume reel, the video should start with a graphic that lists the reporter's name and contact information. Some may be nervous to put their phone number on a public website, so listing just an email address on that graphic is acceptable. The contact information graphic should be on the screen for about five seconds.

Following the opening graphic, a reporter **standup** montage should take place. A standup occurs when a reporter can be seen in the story reporting from an event as opposed to being in the studio. For sports reporters these standups can be at games, at practices, outside stadiums, or at any other relevant location. While there may be some debate about what a reel should look like, there is one element on which everyone can agree: reporters should put their best standups first. As harsh as it may seem, because television is a visual business many news directors will make up their minds regarding a candidate within the first 15 seconds of viewing a resume reel. They are watching for how a reporter looks and sounds. If that news director is not impressed right away, that reel will be stopped pretty quickly. Those reporters who save the best standups for later on in the reel might end up with hiring managers never even seeing it. Therefore, the best standups should go first. Approximately 6 standups can go at the beginning, with each one about 10 seconds long. These standups can be shot during internships, at student media, during class projects, or just by working with a friend and going out to shoot various standups of each other all over town. If the job involves anchoring, some anchoring clips on the set can be included in this montage.

After the reporter montage, it is time to include some packages. However, it is important to not solely include packages that are too sports-focused. While a story breaking down a defense or analyzing a big play might be excellent, sports reporters should also include stories that go beyond the traditional Xs and Os. News directors are looking for sports reporters who can reach the entire audience, not just die-hard sports fans. Therefore, a feature story about an athlete that is not heavy on sports terminology should also be included. Three solid packages should be included in this portion of the reel, but those looking for an anchor position can have two packages and one anchoring segment. However, if the job listing is for a reporter position, then a reel full of anchoring will likely not get much traction.

At the end, include the same identifying graphic that was at the beginning of the reel. If the hiring manager has made it all the way to the end, this is a good way to have a name and contact information directly in front of them. Ultimately, a completed resume reel should be less than 10 minutes long.

Andy Guerra is an executive producer at a television station in Texas and is heavily involved in the hiring process. He sees many resume reels and says that how a reporter looks and sounds in those standups at the beginning are what he's looking for right away: "I want to see that you have compelling, interactive, creative, useful standups, live shots, that kind of thing that you can function in the outside world, not just in a studio where the lights are perfect, the mic is perfect, and you've got a prompter in front of you." However, he's also looking for variety. Even if a reporter is at one location, Guerra wants to see the reporter take advantage of the environment. "If you're standing in front of a stadium three times, I don't need to see that more than once. So, show me when you're standing in front of a stadium, show me when the game was just wrapping up and you were there when they rushed the field. Show me when you were talking to the player all by himself after the game, heartbroken that they lost. Show me a cool standup in the middle of their practice. But we don't need three or four of the same things." For more from Guerra, including his tips for breaking into the television sports broadcasting business, check out his Pro Advice later in this chapter.

Radio Resume Reel

Those looking to enter radio journalism will be asked to submit an **air check** of a show in which they participated. An air check is a recording of a radio or television program. Someone hoping to host a sports talk show will be asked to send in a portion of a sports show air check that they have appeared on previously. These segments should showcase all the various skills needed to be successful in the field, including an interview with a coach or player, interactions with callers, and a solo piece that showcases how the host keeps an audience's attention.

Radio reporters would create a reel similar to that of a television reporter, although they would instead focus on the stories. An audio reel with three or four stories back to back can be submitted to demonstrate the reporter's voice, reporting style, and writing. It is recommended that those stories be different in order to showcase the versatility of the person applying for the job. For example, submitting three stories all previewing the same college football team's games might make the hiring manager wonder if that is all that reporter can do.

Play-by-Play Resume Reel

Similar to radio announcers, play-by-play announcers should send air checks when applying for jobs. These air checks should not be of just the game-winning touchdown or the buzzer-beating three-pointer, however. Instead, the reel should include an entire unedited segment from a game. This demonstrates that the announcer can describe the game even during the less exciting parts and broadcast an entire game without making mistakes. For example, a baseball or softball announcer might include an unedited inning, and a hockey, football, or soccer announcer might include an entire unedited 15-minute block of action. While the goal is to showcase that the broadcaster can broadcast an entire game, that does not mean that any random segment should be chosen. Instead, broadcasters should look for a baseball inning in which a home run is hit or a soccer segment in which a goal is scored.

In addition to the actual game, many play-by-play announcers will also have to conduct a pregame and postgame interview with a coach or player that will either be live or recorded to be broadcast later. Therefore, play-by-play announcers should have an additional reel in which they can showcase the unedited recordings of these interviews. Hiring managers will want to see that the broadcaster can have a compelling conversation with a coach in which good questions are asked, the interactions are comfortable, and the audience learns something. These interviews are often sponsored ("The Bill's Tire Shop Post Game Show"), so station managers want to make sure these

Pro Advice

© Andy Guerra

Andy Guerra

Executive producer, KFOX/KDBC, El Paso, Texas

When a job opens up at a local television station, applicants from all over the country start putting together resume reels. At KFOX and KDBC in El Paso, Texas, executive producer Andy Guerra is typically one of the first to screen those applying for jobs. When there is an opening in the sports department, he's even busier than usual. While a news reporter job opportunity might get around 50 applicants, he says, "I think the sports jobs probably would have 90, if not 100-plus, people apply." With his years of experience as an executive producer and a producer in major markets such as Denver and Phoenix, Guerra has seen it all and has a good idea of what makes a promising candidate.

When you're hiring sports broadcasters, what are you looking for?

When we look for a reporter, if somebody doesn't have the best on-air presence, we tell ourselves, "You know, I like the way this person seems to write. We can coach them. We can teach them how to be on TV." I think that when you're looking for a sports person, there's a little bit less room for that. You want somebody who brings a lot of energy and who does well at carrying a broadcast. You want someone who has the energy, who jumps off the screen, but not as part of a skit. Stand out because you have good energy, and you have good pacing, and because you're fun to watch, not because you have some cheap gimmick.

What are some of the pitfalls you see from sports candidates?

I see a lot of guys who are trying too hard to be funny, a lot of guys who are trying to stand out for the wrong reasons because they wear unusual pants or coats or have an unusual hair style. Maybe that gets somebody's attention in market 160, but by the time you are getting into the top 100, not even the top 100, top 120 or 130 even, we don't have time for that. You can have fun all you want. You can have a really nice feature story with the star of the local college team or some really popular coach, but we don't need you to be compromising who you are just to turn a few heads.

What advice would you give someone looking to try to break into the field of sports broadcasting?

You have to be willing to go all in. Kill everything you do. Maybe you didn't want to do that particular story on that day. Kill it. Want to beat the competition for your sake. Everyone says this is a thankless job at first. I wish that we could pay more. I wish that there were enough people so you didn't have to work holidays and all that when you're starting, but it's part of paying your dues. So, it's understanding what you're up against from the start, and being willing to go all in so that you get your reps. In the long run that's going to benefit you, especially if you're trying to break into the sports world. Guess what? Big-time college games are on Saturdays and the NFL is on Sundays, because sport is entertainment. Even if it's local minor league, chances are there's going to be a weekend series, too.

Know what you're getting into and do it because you want to. I don't need you to take the coach's phone call on your off-hours for my sake. Sure, that's a win for the station, but at the end of the day if you have those instincts, that commitment to your job that you don't care if you're off the clock, you're going to take five minutes to set up an interview. Yeah, it benefits me on Saturday when we have a great story nobody else had, but when you have five, six, a dozen great stories you can show a recruiter down the line that you got because you put in five extra minutes, because you were willing to take a call on your day off, because you didn't shy away from staying an extra hour—that's to your benefit.

interview segments go well in order to keep the advertisers happy. Broadcasters should be able to demonstrate that an interview will be compelling, no matter the result of the game.

The Online Portfolio

Journalists are now going beyond just sending out a simple one-page resume and a couple of YouTube links when applying for jobs. Instead, they are creating websites that can house all their best work and making it even easier for hiring managers to learn more about potential employees. If a job becomes open, a reporter can send the website link that will contain a reel, additional stories, a pdf of the resume, and contact information. Perhaps most importantly for newsroom management, this allows for all the important details about the reporter to be in one location, so an executive producer does not have to search a variety of different documents or links to find the appropriate materials.

Those looking to create an online portfolio can get the process started at any number of the free website-building options. Many of those sites make it very easy to create a portfolio with just a little bit of time and effort. In addition, many offer opportunities to buy a domain name to make the website even easier for anyone to remember. For example, if Jane Sportscaster signs up for a website through Wordpress, her domain name might be JaneSportscaster.wordpress.com. If she pays an additional fee, the domain JaneSportscaster.com could be her home page.

As for what should go in an online portfolio, it is simply a collection of the reporter's best work organized into different sections for ease of navigation and reading. The home page should have a professional photo of the sports broadcaster and also include his or her name, job position, and current affiliation. If Jane Sportscaster is a student at the University of Texas, she should indicate this—with her estimated graduation date—on the home page. The resume reel should also be embedded on the home page. News directors should not have to click to other pages to find this important clip, so it should be placed prominently on the home page. By embedding it on the page, the news director also will not have to go to another page to view it, as it should start playing with just one click.

In addition to the home page, the online portfolio should have subpages that provide other information, including "stories," "resume," and "contact." The *stories* page can have YouTube clips of individual packages all listed on the page. This gives news directors a chance to see stories beyond what is in the resume reel. The *resume* page should be a written-out version of the reporter's resume, with an option to download a pdf version as well. Finally, a *contact* page should include the reporter's email address, not a "contact box" that has to be completely filled out. A news director wants to be able to contact candidates directly, and contact boxes can be cumbersome. The contact page should also include relevant links to social media accounts used for news purposes. For example, if an Instagram page is private and only used for personal photos, there is no sense in adding it to the contact page. These three subpages should be easy to locate from anywhere on the website, which most free website builders can assist with through creation of a navigation system using headers at the top of the page.

Once the online portfolio has been created, it is important to remember to keep updating it. Many journalists will create an online portfolio and then never touch it again until it is necessary to start a new job search. Instead, every time a reporter completes a story of which he or she is proud, it should immediately be added to the website. Additionally, resume reels should be updated every six months or so. One never knows when a news director might be looking for a sports reporter and specifically request a link to his or her latest work. Instead of having to update two years' worth of work overnight, searching through hours of archives to find that *one* story that should be there, a consistently refreshed portfolio will take much of the stress out of the application process. Also, news directors might stumble upon an online portfolio on their own, and if that page has not been updated, the reporter would not be putting his or her best material out there.

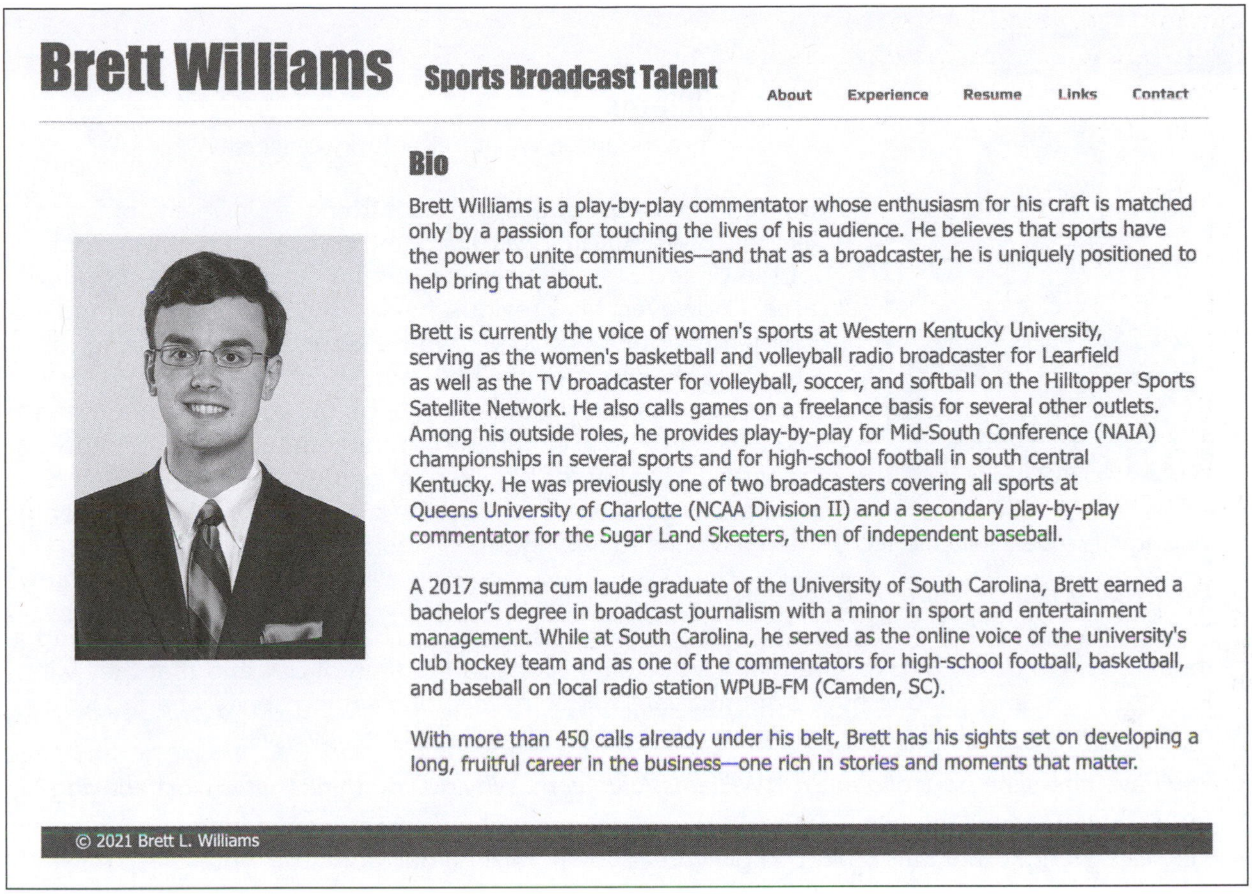
Brett Williams Sports Broadcast Talent
About Experience Resume Links Contact
Bio
Brett Williams is a play-by-play commentator whose enthusiasm for his craft is matched only by a passion for touching the lives of his audience. He believes that sports have the power to unite communities—and that as a broadcaster, he is uniquely positioned to help bring that about.
Brett is currently the voice of women's sports at Western Kentucky University, serving as the women's basketball and volleyball radio broadcaster for Learfield as well as the TV broadcaster for volleyball, soccer, and softball on the Hilltopper Sports Satellite Network. He also calls games on a freelance basis for several other outlets. Among his outside roles, he provides play-by-play for Mid-South Conference (NAIA) championships in several sports and for high-school football in south central Kentucky. He was previously one of two broadcasters covering all sports at Queens University of Charlotte (NCAA Division II) and a secondary play-by-play commentator for the Sugar Land Skeeters, then of independent baseball.
A 2017 summa cum laude graduate of the University of South Carolina, Brett earned a bachelor's degree in broadcast journalism with a minor in sport and entertainment management. While at South Carolina, he served as the online voice of the university's club hockey team and as one of the commentators for high-school football, basketball, and baseball on local radio station WPUB-FM (Camden, SC).
With more than 450 calls already under his belt, Brett has his sights set on developing a long, fruitful career in the business—one rich in stories and moments that matter.
© 2021 Brett L. Williams

Courtesy of Brett Williams.

An example of an online portfolio of a play-by-play announcer.

Social Media

When applying for broadcasting jobs, candidates will often have to submit a resume, resume reel, and online portfolio. However, even if it is not listed as a portion of the job application, a candidate can be assured that hiring managers will be looking at that person's social media accounts. As discussed in chapter 11, social media has become an important part of the job for sports broadcasters, so management will want to make sure that these accounts are professional.

Knowing that these accounts are a key part of the job, those looking to start a career in sports broadcasting should treat their social media as if they already have the job. That means going back through *every single post* on all of the social media platforms and deleting any posts that are inappropriate for the workplace. That old photo from a wild Friday night at the bar might have been a fun memory that someone wanted to remember forever online, but a news director might look at it differently. Pictures and posts that you would not want any boss to see should be eliminated. Meredith Dean is the CEO and founder of *The Dean's List*, a digital branding company that empowers people to land their dream job. Dean has a simple policy when it comes to the social media accounts of her clients: "WWMD—What Would Marty do? Marty is my 90-year-old grandmother. If she shouldn't see it, then you probably shouldn't be posting it. Trust your gut."

Setting a social media account to "private" does not mean that it is safe from news directors. While there are hundreds of journalism outlets throughout the country, it is ultimately a very small field because there is so much movement from city to city. Through their years on the job, news directors probably know someone who knows the applicant. When hiring her own

Pro Advice

© Brett Williams

Brett Williams

Play-by-play announcer, Western Kentucky University

As he was getting ready to graduate from the University of South Carolina, Brett Williams was one of the many candidates throughout the United States looking to get their start in a play-by-play career. However, his previous freelancing and student media experience got him noticed, and he landed an announcing job with Queens University of Charlotte. About a year later, he was off to Western Kentucky University to be the voice of the women's basketball team. Since then, he's added other Western Kentucky sports and a variety of high school games to his resume. After landing two great jobs within just about a year of his graduation, Williams is a true success story when it comes to finding that first job in sports broadcasting.

How would you describe the job search?

Not for the faint of heart. Obviously for so many of these jobs, you have tons of people wanting them. So, how do you make sure that they actually give you the time of day and that they will listen to your tape? I had to have a strong reel, I had to have strong writing ability. I had to learn how to put all those skills together to learn how to catch the eye of employers.

You have an online portfolio at BrettWilliamsVoice.com. Why do you think that is worth having?

I think it's about your brand. Rather than sending people to a personality-free YouTube page, they can go right there and get to know you as you're telling your story from your perspective. It is a good foundation for me to build that brand online. The color scheme is the same as the one on my resume, some of the verbiage is the same, and I want to make sure that everything on there is mirrored on my Twitter and Instagram. The website gives you the biggest space to build that out so that really is the home base for it.

How important is networking?

It is absolutely essential. Being able to build positive relationships with people and stay in touch with them will help you get a potential inroad to a job. Somebody might say to you, "Hey, this is about to come open, I think you'd be a good fit for this," or "Reach out to this person, they might be able to help you." And that's true even outside of looking for a job. It's having resources to critique your tapes and give you advice overall.

What is your advice for those looking to get that first job in play-by-play?

The first thing is you have to get the reps. And if you don't have opportunities available, you've got to find ways. You've got to network, you've got to get your name out to local high school radio outlets, you've got to create opportunities for yourself. It takes a lot of ingenuity; it takes being scrappy—you have to want this.

Second, try to get reps in as many sports as you can. It's pretty common in this industry to start at a Division 2 or Division 3 school, and those jobs will involve a lot of different sports. I called 11 different sports at Queens [University] and because of those volleyball and soccer tapes, I was able to sell myself here. I only came [to Western Kentucky] to do women's basketball, but at the end of my first year here, they decided to create their own outlet and they needed someone to call these other games. I just went to them and said, "Here are my tapes." Having that in your back pocket will be helpful to you. How do you work your way up the ladder? By being as diverse as possible and versatile as possible, you give yourself the best chance.

interns at *The Dean's List*, Meredith Dean said, "If an applicant is private on Instagram, I find someone who is a mutual connection of ours that follows them. I ask that connection to then screenshot or record the applicant's feed just to make sure this person is being appropriate on social media since they will ultimately be a representation of my company online."

In addition to going back to delete old posts, prospective broadcasters should start treating their accounts like professionals even before they get the job. They should link to news articles, provide appropriate commentary on events, and post stories on which they have worked. This gives an employer an idea of how that broadcaster might use social media when he or she is officially on the job.

The Job Search

Once a candidate's written resume, resume reel, and online portfolio are ready to send out, it is time to find jobs for which to apply. While many schools provide networking opportunities, it is often up to the individual to find a job on his or her own. A survey of over one hundred students and broadcast employers found that job postings were the most common way to land a job (White, 2018). A good starting point for those looking to break into the field is JournalismJobs.com. Candidates on this website can search by medium, location, and job title. There are also sports journalism–specific job websites, such as SportsJournalists.com. Organizations will often have job listings also, with the Sportscasters Talent Agency of America (STAA) listing openings for their members while also helping prepare members to apply for those jobs.

Local television and radio stations are often owned by a major national corporation. For example, as of 2021, Gray Television owned stations in 94 of the 210 television markets in the United States. These large organizations can be an excellent way to work up the career ladder because they often try to promote from within. If a sports broadcaster works in one of the many starter markets in which Gray has a station, they might have a better chance at getting a job at a larger Gray station when a job there becomes open. Many of these large ownership groups have a "careers" tab on their website that lists current openings at every station within the company. Based on previous openings at local television stations, a potential job ad might look like this:

The NBC affiliate in (City, State) is looking for a full-time Sports Reporter/Anchor to join our news team. You will be required to cover and report on sports news daily on a variety of platforms including the internet and social media. Responsibilities include:

- Shoot and edit daily sports content for multiple newscasts and digital properties
- Develop and grow sources within local high school and college teams
- Anchor sports on weekend evenings
- Perform other duties as assigned by management

Requirements:

- BS/BA in journalism or communications
- Working knowledge of camera and editing gear
- A valid driver's license, good driving record, and proof of insurance
- One year of experience as a sports reporter

Send reel and resume to (News director's email address).

A key for these job listings is to read them very closely. If a listing is looking for a reporter, then a resume reel full of anchoring clips will likely quickly be eliminated. Candidates should know exactly what the job listing states the company is looking for and then format the written resume and resume reel to make them appear to be a perfect applicant for the opening.

CHAPTER WRAP-UP

SUMMARY

The job search in any field can be a challenge, but that may be especially true in sports broadcasting. In other industries, if two great candidates apply for a job, that company might end up hiring both of them. In broadcasting, there is only one weekend sports anchor at each television station, and that means only one person will be hired, even if there are a number of well-qualified candidates. Therefore even if a candidate has a "can't-miss" resume and experience, the job search might still take some time.

The key is to make sure that a candidate is best positioned to make that search go as smoothly as possible. That starts by getting experience through student media or internships. Creating a clearly written resume will showcase that previous experience, while a resume reel will demonstrate that the candidate has the ability to perform the job. An online portfolio gives applicants a place to put all their materials, so a hiring manager can go to just one website to get all the necessary information. Unfortunately, there is no secret to finding that first job. It comes through preparation that starts years earlier putting one self in the right position to be the best candidate for an opening.

Phil Cole/Getty Images

CHAPTER 13

Issues and Ethics in Sports Broadcasting

CHAPTER OBJECTIVES

Sports broadcasting is about much more than just who won the game and who was the leading scorer. In the modern era, special attention has to be paid to who is receiving the coverage and how those people are discussed. It must also be acknowledged that sports broadcasting has traditionally not been a welcoming environment for all those looking to enter. If someone is fortunate enough to enter the field, many ethical situations will likely arise while on the job. Therefore, this chapter focuses on issues and ethics in sports broadcasting, including the following:

- Recognizing the importance of telling the stories of athletes from diverse backgrounds
- Understanding the difficulties women, people of color, and people who identify as LGBTQ+ face entering and succeeding in the field of sports broadcasting
- Identifying ethical situations and how to respond when they present themselves

When she was first starting out in sports broadcasting, current Fox Sports broadcaster Laura Okmin thought she had finally made it. The then-22-year-old had her first job at a television station in Alabama and was getting ready to interview a high school football coach. "Right before he came up, I was having a moment. I was really proud of myself. 'You've done it. You've made it.' " As she was feeling that pride, the head coach was walking toward her holding a football in one hand and a basketball in the other. Even as she retells the story over

20 years later, Okmin recalls what happened next as if it happened yesterday, reenacting the coach's words from memory: "Little girl, I just wanted to make sure you knew the difference between a football and a basketball. A basketball is round, and a football is oblong." Her moment of pride was over.

While Okmin's story is certainly upsetting, it is far from unique when describing the obstacles many face when breaking into sports media. In fact, it is not even unique for Okmin herself: "That's just one example. I could literally give 100." The media, especially the sports media, is dominated by white men. White men have the majority of on-air positions, and they are in many positions of leadership in media organizations, too. This can make it difficult for minorities to break into the business.

However, it is not just the demographics of the people doing the stories that cause many of the issues in sports broadcasting. Coverage of sports is no longer just who won the game and who scored the most points. Instead, societal issues have become a key part of the sports landscape. What is happening in the real world can no longer be ignored by broadcasters, as stories involving Black athletes, women, people who identify as LGBTQ+, and people of color are now nearly daily reports. As these issues move to the forefront, many sports broadcasters are having a hard time "sticking to sports."

Coverage of Race, Gender, and Sexuality

For decades, sports journalists focused only on the games themselves. The majority of those in the field were white men who paid little attention to the athletes' stories off the field or the issues that those athletes might be facing in society. However, those days are over. Athletes are choosing to speak out regarding issues of race, gender, and sexuality, and the sports media has little choice but to cover those topics. In order to understand this change, it is important to recognize how this evolution happened and what sports broadcasters can do to make sure they cover these topics properly and respectfully.

It is first important to understand the role that the media plays in stories broadcast to the audience. Chapter 11 discussed the role of gatekeeper and how journalists are the ones who ultimately decide what information reaches the viewers and listeners. If a head coach has a press conference and discusses five different topics, journalists have the power to determine which of those stories they will report in their broadcast. For example, figure 13.1 shows the five stories from that press conference on the left side of the image. All of the stories are then known by the reporter who was at that press conference (represented by the shaded

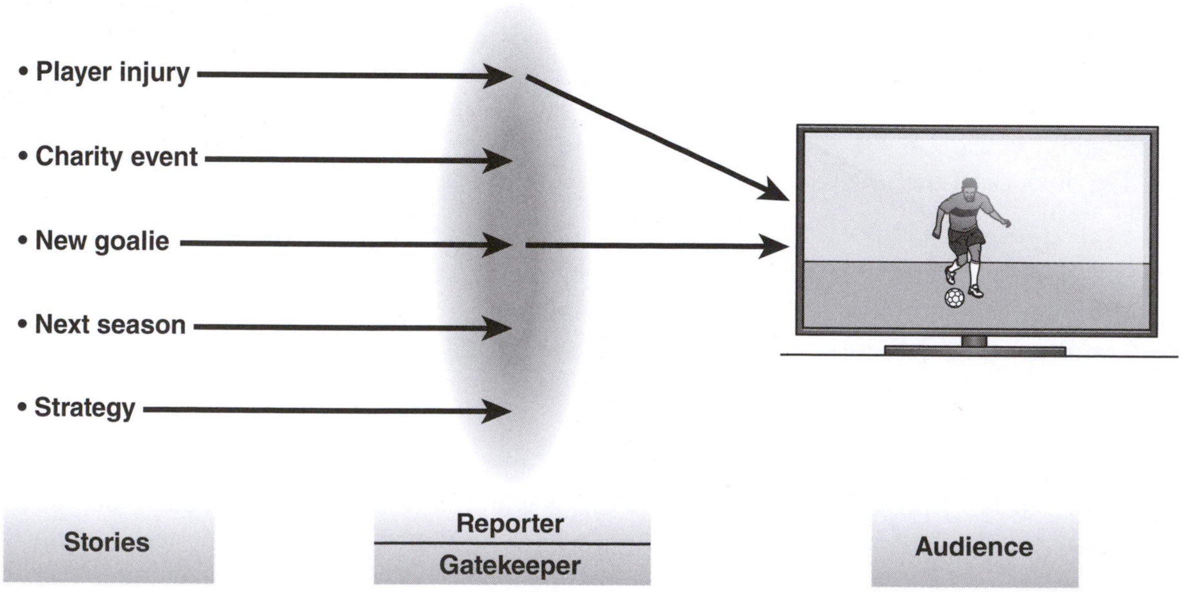

FIGURE 13.1 Gatekeeping theory.

area in the middle of the image). That reporter then acts as the gatekeeper to decide which of the stories he or she will inform the audience about. In this example, only the stories about the player injury and the new goalie make it to the audience. This means the viewers will not learn about the charity event, the next season, or team strategy from that broadcaster.

While the concept of gatekeeping has been relevant for decades in the media environment, it has taken on new importance as more attention has been paid to stories regarding race, gender, and sexuality. Ultimately, the gatekeepers themselves have become the focus of how these stories are reported. Due to the fact that the sports media is primarily an industry populated by straight, white men, stories involving minority races and ethnicities, women's sports, and LGBTQ+ issues have often been either ignored or reported improperly.

Coverage of Race and Ethnicity in Sports

Muhammad Ali was one of the first athletes to force sports media members to closely examine how they covered race. Born Cassius Clay, the boxer changed his name to Muhammad Ali in 1964 for religious reasons. However, many media members refused to acknowledge this change. As discussed in chapter 1, broadcaster Howard Cosell was one of the few sports broadcasters who did call Ali by his new name, and others were soon to follow. Ali's dominance in the boxing ring made it difficult for media members to ignore the boxer's wishes.

In 1968, following the 200-meter finals in the Olympics, Americans Tommie Smith and John Carlos raised their fists on the medal podium to signify Black unity. It remains one of the most overtly political statements in the history of the Olympics, and media members were mixed in their reactions. *Sports Illustrated* chose not to run the historic photo, while the *Pittsburgh Courier* newspaper put them on the front page (Maraniss, 2018). For years, the media has wrestled with the proper way to cover racial issues.

However, it is not just coverage of Black athletes with which the sports media has traditionally struggled. In Major League Baseball, many of the players have Hispanic backgrounds, and their first language may not be English. If those

Bettman/Contributor

ABC Sports' Howard Cosell is credited as being one of the first broadcasters to call Cassius Clay by his new name, Muhammad Ali.

players are quoted directly, it may appear that they are not intelligent because those players are not as proficient in the English language as a native speaker. In 2016, Houston Astros' star Carlos Gomez was upset with the *Houston Chronicle* after the paper used a quote of his. Gomez said that the author "did it intentionally to ridicule me" (ESPN News Services, 2016, para. 3).

Native Americans have long protested names that they have considered racist, including the former name of the Washington NFL team. In this case, sports media members were put in a difficult spot. It is difficult to report on a team without saying the name of the team, but Native American advocacy groups pushed for sports broadcasters to avoid using the slur. It was not until 2020 that Washington elected to officially drop the name, saving media members from this difficult scenario.

As will be discussed later in this chapter, one element of the sports media that makes these issues challenging to cover is the lack of diversity in sports broadcasting. Those who do not have the same background as the athletes or coaches they are covering should make an effort to better understand them. This might involve a meeting away from the cameras or a chance to have that subject tell their story on their own terms. It is important to recognize possible sensitive issues that could arise in the coverage of that team or player.

Coverage of Women's Sports

Perhaps the watershed moment in women's sports occurred in 1972 with the passing of the federal civil rights law Title IX in the United States. This new law essentially stated that women have the same rights as men when it comes to playing sports at the high school or college level (Women's Sports Foundation, 1998). Women's sports participation skyrocketed: fewer than 300,000 girls played high school sports in 1971, but 2.8 million were playing 30 years later (Lee, 2016). While

Bettmann/Getty Images

During the 1968 Olympics, Tommie Smith (center) and John Carlos (right) bow their heads and raise black gloved fists in a protest against the ongoing injustices facing Black Americans in the civil rights struggle.

women were not only playing more, they were also excelling. Women's tennis star Billie Jean King beat former men's Wimbledon champion Bobby Riggs in the "Battle of the Sexes" in 1973 (Rothman, 2017), while golfer Nancy Lopez, basketball player Nancy Lieberman, and Olympians Peggy Fleming and Mary Lou Retton were becoming stars in their respective sports. In the Olympics, it was the women who were becoming the stars of the United States team—they won more gold medals and more overall medals than men did in the 2016 Summer Games (Myre, 2016). While one might reasonably consider this the golden era of women's sports, that was not the case when it comes to media coverage. In 2013, a group of academics published "Women play sport, but not on TV" (Cooky, Messner, & Hextrum, 2013). While the title might seem extreme, the research backs up the claim. The trio discovered that coverage of women's sports might actually have gotten worse over the years, and that media attention focuses primarily on men's sports (Cooky et al., 2013).

When women do get media coverage, it is often not up to the same standards. When Corey Cogdell won a bronze medal in the women's trap shooting event in the 2016 Olympics, the *Chicago Tribune* identified her not by name on social media but instead as follows: "Wife of a Bears' lineman wins a bronze medal" (Chicago Tribune, 2016). In other sports, women are often given media coverage not for their athletic accomplishments but for their looks. A simple web search of "female golfers" returns results that include "Top 10 Hottest Female Golfers" and "20 Hottest Women of Golf" among the first suggestions.

Women's sports are, in many cases, in a "chicken-or-the-egg" scenario when it comes to media coverage: they do not get covered because they are not as popular, but they cannot get more popular without coverage. *The Boston Globe*'s Dan Shaughnessy once said that his job was to focus on what he believed his audience wanted to read about, and he did not believe that included women's sports (Ottaway, 2016). However, without introducing women's sports to the audience, how will readers and viewers know about these teams?

Joe Scarnici/Getty Images

Corey Cogdell won a bronze medal in the 2016 Olympics but was identified as "wife of a Bears lineman" and not by her name in the *Chicago Tribune*.

Sports broadcasters should make an effort to include both men's and women's sports when covering local teams. On the high school level, girls' basketball games often take place immediately before the boys' games, so a broadcaster can get there early enough to get highlights of the end of the girls' game and then the beginning of the boys' game. Most high schools also have the softball and baseball fields in close proximity to each other, so on nights they are both home, it is possible to get video of a few innings from each field. In many cities throughout the United States, there is nothing bigger than high school or college football. While those games should still be the top story in many rundowns, that does not mean that women's sports should be ignored. While football might dominate the NCAA fall schedule, sports broadcasters should also attempt to cover women's soccer, field hockey, or volleyball when the opportunities arise. Covering women's sports can start to even the playing field when it comes to equitable coverage and can also lead to some great stories. While most people probably know the story of the star running back, covering the women's soccer team might open the broadcasters up to a remarkable athlete that few know about. Traditionally, these teams are also more willing to work with the media because they are happy to get the coverage that may have been lacking previously. While most people are itching to talk to the biggest male athletes, it is often the women who have the best stories to tell.

Coverage of LGBTQ+ in Sports

For decades, an athlete's sexual orientation was something that rarely made it into sports coverage. However, as more sports personalities have come out as gay, their personal stories have, in some cases, become a major part of their identity. While Jason Collins carved out a solid 13-year career in the NBA, he will most likely be remembered more as the first openly gay active player in the NBA, NFL, NHL, or MLB (Beck & Branch, 2013). In 2014, Michael Sam became the biggest story in the lead-up to the NFL draft when he announced that he was gay. ESPN was broadcasting the draft and, despite Sam being picked in the last round, had cameras stationed in his house to get his reaction (Associated Press, 2014).

While stories such as Collins' and Sam's have become more frequent, the sports media has not always covered LGBTQ+ athletes with the proper respect. During training camp, ESPN's Josina Anderson reported on Sam's showering habits with his teammates, which caused a great deal of criticism and forced the network to issue a statement that they regretted the story (Chase, 2014). In 2016, Brazilian beach volleyball player Larissa Franca won a match in the Olympics and hugged her wife on the sidelines following the victory. On the NBC broadcast, the announcer described Franca's wife as her "husband," which once again resulted in an apology from a regretful network (Perez, 2016).

GLAAD, an organization developed to promote positive and equal media coverage of the LGBTQ+ community, lists several suggestions for those looking to report on openly gay athletes. In a media reference guide, the organization writes that while LGBTQ+ athletes playing professionally is still relatively new, "it is also important to acknowledge that any athlete's first and more important role is simply to play and excel at their sport" (GLAAD, n.d., para. 5). The organization also suggests highlighting players from every level of sport, talking to a wide variety of athletes, and treating anti-LGBTQ+ comments with the same level of attention that other public figures would receive (GLAAD, n.d.). Sports broadcasters should also be sure to use proper pronouns, terms, and language when describing individuals. GLAAD suggests asking individuals which pronouns they prefer if one is unsure of what descriptors to use. It is traditionally more important to ask for clarification than to assume someone's gender identity or sexual orientation.

Women in Sports Broadcasting

While covering the various backgrounds of the athletes playing in the games can be a challenge, it is sometimes the backgrounds of the broadcasters themselves that can be a difficult hurdle to overcome. When Phyllis George was named cohost of *The NFL Today* on CBS in 1975, she became the first woman to have a prominent role in sports broadcasting (Sandomir, 2020). The former Miss America's role on the pregame show meant that millions of young women could now see themselves in a similar position. However, just because that job was now attainable, that did not mean the road to get there was smooth. If a woman did happen to get a prominent sports broadcasting job, they were often faced with many obstacles once there.

Getting Access

When women started reporting on professional sports in the late 1960s and 1970s, they could cover the games but had issues with access after the contest was over. All professional sports leagues had rules that banned women from the locker room, even if they had a media pass (Vogt, 2013). While this might seem like a minor issue, it essentially meant that the women had fewer opportunities to write a full recap of the game. Without locker room access, they would only be able to interview players who were willing to come out and talk to them. Many athletes chose not to do this, so the women reporters were left with incomplete stories in which they did not have quotes from some of the best players in the game. It ultimately took a lawsuit for this to change. It was not until *Sports Illustrated* writer Melissa Ludtke sued Major League Baseball following the 1977 World Series that women were granted the same access to the locker room. One sportswriter compared Ludtke's quest to open the locker room to Jackie Robinson becoming the first Black player in Major League Baseball: "Those were steps taken by very brave people, steps that advanced society, and I'll always believe that" (Baranauckas, 2013, para. 14).

"Don't Know What the Hell They're Talking About"

While women have earned some high-profile positions at sports broadcasting outlets throughout the world, they have not always been welcomed warmly by other media members, athletes, or fans. Sports broadcasters, male or female, will often face criticism due to the fact that the job is a very public one. However, a search through the history of women in sports broadcasting reveals that women have had a more challenging time than men.

Women in the sports media are often questioned about their sports knowledge. Andy Rooney, a former commentator on the popular news program *60 Minutes*, once remarked: "The only thing that really bugs me about television's coverage is those damn women they have down on the sidelines who don't know what the hell they're talking about" (ESPN News Services, 2002, para. 2). Rooney was one of many who equate a person's sex with their knowledge of sports. Perhaps in Rooney's mind since women did not play professional football, they weren't qualified to discuss the sport on television. This, of course, completely ignores any preparation and research that the vast majority of female sports broadcasters do each day to stay up to date on their job. Implying that a woman cannot report on football simply because she is a woman is an incorrect way of thinking.

Judged on Appearance

Television sports broadcasting is a visual medium, so those entering the field are often judged on their appearance. However, that judging appears to be harsher and more frequent for women. ESPN's Tony Kornheiser was live on his radio show in 2010 at the same time that Hannah Storm was hosting *SportsCenter*. Kornheiser began criticizing his colleague's outfit: "She's got on her typically very, very tight shirt. She looks like she has sausage casing wrapping around her upper body. . . . I know she's very good, and I'm not supposed to be critical of ESPN people, so I won't. But Hannah Storm, come on now! Stop! What are you doing?" Kornheiser was suspended for two weeks for his comments (Lisi, 2010, para. 4), but that hardly stopped others from making similar remarks.

This focus on looks can often put women in a no-win situation. ESPN's Sarah Spain said, "Either you're too beautiful and you don't know what you're talking about, or you're too ugly and I don't want to watch you" (Markham, 2013, para. 20). The importance, and sometimes criticism, of a sports broadcaster's looks does appear to be a females-only issue. Erin Andrews, a reporter for Fox Sports, pointed out the double standard that comes along with appearance-related observations: "I always bring up the fact that people are so worried about what I'm doing or that I care about the way I look . . . [but] we have some of the best-looking guys at Fox. They are wearing gorgeous suits. They have a hair and makeup team there powdering them. They work out all the time. [They're] beautiful men wearing beautiful clothes, and no one says anything about that. That's the only time I kind of get salty about it, because I'm like, how am I any different from these guys?" (Buxton, 2016, para. 4).

Social Media Negativity

For all the advantages of social media described in chapter 11, there can also be negative experiences. Women in the industry often face vulgar and offensive comments from fans hiding behind an anonymous social media account. A simple web search or a look through the replies to a tweet from a female sports broadcaster will quickly showcase some of the awful comments with which these women must deal. Journalist Julie DiCaro has been one of the most outspoken about the impact of these tweets. In a first-person story for SI.com, DiCaro summarized her feelings:

> *Make no mistake, these tweets are not meant to express disagreement. They are calculated to destroy, demean, and denigrate the women they target in a public forum. It's not enough for such fragile men to simply tell a woman she's wrong, or even that she's stupid. These comments attempt to cut much deeper, striking women at what misogynists see as their most valuable characteristics: appearance, sexual purity, sweetness and submissiveness. (DiCaro, 2015, para. 22)*

The following year, DiCaro and fellow Chicago sports journalist Sarah Spain joined forces to create the "More Than Mean" video. In the 4 minute and 15 second video, unsuspecting men read some of the mean tweets that have been sent to the two women over the years. As the video progresses, the journalists and the men involved become increasingly uncomfortable as the two sides sit just feet apart while the tweets are being read (Just Not Sports, 2016). Response to the video was overwhelmingly positive, with other sports journalists relaying how much they could relate to the tweets DiCaro and Spain had received (Mettler, 2016).

Sports Radio

While more women have entered the field of sports broadcasting as a whole, the job of sports radio host is still a very male-dominated position. In 2020, women made up less than 5 percent of the on-air hosts of sports radio stations in Canada (Beckstead, 2020). The numbers are similar in the United States, where there are very few women sports radio hosts in large cities and on nationally syndicated shows. When NBC Sports announced a weekday, 12-hour, syndicated sports talk channel, one online commenter pointed out that not a single host on the new venture was a woman (Walker, 2020).

Pro Advice

© Laura Okmin

Laura Okmin

Sports broadcaster and founder of GALvanize

While Laura Okmin might best be known as one of the longest tenured sideline reporters in broadcast television history, she has also served as an executive producer, started her own production company, and had a nationally syndicated television show. Despite all her successes, it has not been smooth sailing to get to the point where she is now. She has frequently had to overcome negative perceptions of her work simply because she is a woman: "I realized that I was going to have to prove myself and that getting a job didn't mean I was ready for this world."

Okmin has more than proven herself, as the Emmy Award winner has covered multiple Super Bowls, World Series, Olympics, and NBA and NHL championships. Now she is paying it forward. Okmin started GALvanize, a company designed to help the next generation of female sports broadcasters. She hosts seminars around the country in which young women learn about the industry and work on their broadcasting skills, all while empowering each other and developing a strong network of female role models and supporters.

We've talked throughout this chapter about some of the difficulties facing women in the field of sports broadcasting—including your own story about the football coach insultingly making sure you knew the difference between a football and a basketball. What impact do comments like those have on the women trying to make it in sports broadcasting?

I went from how excited and how proud I was to how embarrassed I was. I really was introduced to a world that I suddenly realized didn't want me there. That stuck with me for an incredibly long time. That voice in my head was always with me. Every person that I met, I basically pictured that coach. And maybe they weren't as obnoxious about it, but I felt that. And what happened was that those voices became my voice. For a really long time, I felt like I wasn't invited to it. I got to the party, but I wasn't warmly invited. For a really long time, it made me feel like every single day I had to prove myself over and over and over again. That was exhausting.

Is it safe to say that social media has made these criticisms worse?

For so many of us who have been doing this for 30 years, it was perceived voices in our heads. Now these women are legitimately getting on their phone and hearing these voices in real time. They're reading people telling them about their hair, and their face, and their body. And that absolutely kills me that these young women have to deal with that. But if they work on it when they are younger, it will only make them better in every way. Not only as a broadcaster, but more importantly as a woman, as a human being.

So, is it any better than it used to be for women in this field?

Everyone always thinks the answer is going to be "it is so much better." And in some ways it is, such as in numbers. At big events like the Super Bowl and the World Series, I would count the women, and I would do it on my hands. In the beginning you'd need one hand, and then it got to two hands and then you'd think "I can't count anymore." And that's awesome.

But where I can still count on one hand is where it counts. It's the women who are in power. It's the women who are decision makers. The women who are hiring. That's where we have not come any further. The same people are in those offices, and I don't think this business is going to truly change for women until there are women who have a voice. Not just that they have a seat at the table, but they are running that table. And I'm saying women, but I could also be saying women of color and men of color. Representation matters so much, not just on TV, but who is hiring the people we're seeing on TV and what content we're covering.

One of the things you've done to help young women trying to enter the field of sports broadcasting is creating GALvanize. How does that fit into all this?

Everyone thinks that we work on getting better on camera and working on interviews—and we do. But 95 percent of GALvanize camps are about confidence. That's always what we do. If you can make yourself feel good about who you are, and not question if you belong, then you're not going to let someone else get into your head. I think the biggest thing is working on confidence as hard as they're working on their reel. Working on feeling good about themselves as much as they're working on prepping on an interview.

For more information on GALvanize, visit https://lauraokmin.com/galvanize/

Dawn Davenport is one of the few woman sports talk show hosts in the country, serving as cohost of a program in Nashville, Tennessee. She said that the lack of female sports radio hosts now has a major impact on how many there might be in the future: "I didn't grow up listening to women do sports talk radio. It was just very rare. For the most part, it's a newer thing to actually hear women in sports talk radio, so we need more to be able to further that." Davenport said her time as a sideline reporter at ESPN helps her gain additional respect from her audience and cohosts, which has helped her transition into the male-dominated field. She views her role on the radio as a privilege, saying, "I hope other women out there can hear it and understand that sports talk radio is an option for you, and a really fun one, and a really great one."

Small Steps to Advancement

While it continues to be an uphill climb for women in sports broadcasting, there have been small victories along the way. On ESPN, Linda Cohn became the longest tenured anchor on *SportsCenter*, and she has hosted over 5,000 of the episodes in the network's history (Hall, 2018). In 2014, CBS Sports debuted a sports talk show that featured all-female talent (Fleming, 2014). When Amazon started broadcasting NFL games, they tapped Hannah Storm and Andrea Kremer as the announcers, making them the first all-female broadcast team to call an NFL game (Feldman, 2018). *USA Today* columnist Nancy Armour said that how players interact with female media members is one of the most positive changes that has occurred: "This generation of athletes in their 20s and 30s have grown up being covered by women. Seeing women in the sports media is not foreign or shocking to them" (Strauss & Bellware, 2020, para. 22).

Racial Minorities in Sports Broadcasting

When it comes to minorities in sports broadcasting, one of the biggest concerns is a lack of representation—something that is not a new trend. Dating back to the early days of sports journalism, the field was dominated by white men. If an outlet did have a Black journalist, he or she was forced to primarily cover Black athletes. As the years have progressed not much has changed as far as the number of minorities in these roles.

An examination of ESPN announcers during high school football's national signing day found that 98 percent were white (Lewis, Bell, Billings, & Brown, 2020). Play-by-play broadcasting is dominated almost entirely by white men (Curtis, 2020), and research has suggested that this lack of minorities in these roles contributes to the racialized language in coverage of sports on television (Eastman & Billings, 2001). When swimmer Simone Manuel became the first African American ever to win an individual swimming medal at the Olympics in 2016, reporter Jesse Washington tweeted that he was the only Black journalist at Manuel's press conference afterward (Washington, 2016). Richard Lapchick, who runs The Institute for Diversity and Ethics in Sport, calls diversity in media sports departments "imperative" to offering a different perspective (Lapchick, 2018). A 2020 survey of Black local sports broadcasters across the United States found that the majority believed there should be more journalists of color in newsrooms (Hull, Walker, Romney, & Pellizzaro, 2020).

Stick to Sports

As athletes and teams become more vocal about social issues, it has become increasingly difficult for sports broadcasters to focus only on the games. When professional athletes protested racial injustices in 2020, refusing to play in that night's matchups, the sports media had no choice but to report on this development. Instead of focusing on the action, journalists had to examine the issues involved with these protests. However, many fans use sports as an escape from the real world, so when media members talk on social media about topics other than sports, the response from followers is often "stick to sports."

While there are certainly many positives to social media for sports broadcasters, it can also create a situation in which media members discuss topics that are not what their bosses would like them to discuss. Most newsrooms have a hierarchy system in which content must be approved by an editor or producer. However, a personal social media account does not traditionally have those levels of approval. A sports broadcaster can type out a tweet, hit send, and then it is out there for the world to see. When Donald Trump was elected president in 2016, many sports media members expressed their opinions on social media, essentially interrupting their traditional sports content to provide their own personal political opinions. Perhaps no example of this garnered more attention than when in 2017, ESPN's Jemele Hill tweeted that the president was a "white supremacist." Reactions came from all over, including from President Trump himself (Best, 2017). While ESPN elected not to suspend Hill for the incident (she was suspended a month later for another social media violation), it did force the network to reassess its own social media policy.

Later that year, ESPN publicly released its new social media policy. Highlights included a reminder that "ESPN's focus is sports" (ESPN, 2017, para. 5) and that "ESPN is a journalistic organization (not a political or advocacy organization)" (ESPN, 2017, para. 4). The policy further states that news reports "should not include statements of support, opposition, or partisanship related to any social issue, political position, candidate or office holder" and that individuals should not take any political positions themselves on social media (ESPN, 2017, para. 14). This policy is similar to that of *The New York Times*. That organization's social media guidelines state that its journalists must not express partisan opinions, promote political views, endorse candidates, or make offensive comments. That newspaper's policy is also very explicit that these rules are not just for news writers, as it is written that "these guidelines apply to everyone in every department of the newsroom, including those not involved in coverage of government and politics" (The New York Times, 2017, para. 22).

Sports broadcasters should be acutely aware of the social media policies at their place of employment before tweeting anything that is outside the realm of their job duties. A violation of a policy could result in suspension or even termination. If someone is not sure of that policy, it would be advisable to stay away from posting politically focused messages until it is clear what is and what is not allowed by the company.

Ethics in Sports Broadcasting

Broadcasters often face a variety of ethical issues when it comes to covering sports. These issues may not seem like a big deal, but they can often have consequences later on. The primary goal of having a good ethical base for a sports reporter is to appear impartial when covering a team or an athlete. If a broadcaster cheers, accepts gifts, or treats people poorly, the team, athletes, or fans might question that broadcaster's ability to report fairly.

No Cheering in the Press Box

For decades, sports media members have been told there is no cheering in the press box. This means that sports media members are supposed to be impartial and should not act like fans. If a media member gives the impression that he or she is rooting for (or against) a particular team, that could give the impression of biased coverage. For example, if a Dallas Cowboys fan is covering the team as a sports broadcaster and openly rooting for the team, then one might rightly wonder if that sports broadcaster is going to report negative stories about the team or only focus on positive storylines.

This can be especially difficult when covering college sports, as media members might be graduates of that institution or, in the case of student media, still be enrolled there. Journalists must put those allegiances to the side and report on teams as an independent media member. This can be hard for student media, as players on the team are often contemporaries and perhaps even classmates. Student journalists should strive to separate themselves from their "student" identity and instead focus on the "journalist" aspect. An attempt to be independent should also be reflected in the clothes worn to these events. While college bookstores are often filled with very nice (and very expensive) team polo shirts, media members should not wear any team-branded clothing to games or events. That goes both for the team and a rival, so one should not wear an Ohio State sweatshirt to report on a University of Michigan sporting event.

No Free Stuff (Except Food)

Big sporting events often provide free gifts to media members covering the game. These can be physical items such as backpacks or tickets to the game that the journalist can give to others. On free giveaway nights, the T-shirt, hat, or bobblehead might also be available in the press box. While it may be difficult, journalists should decline these gifts because accepting them might give the impression of favoritism. The Associated Press Sports Editors (APSE) ethical guidelines state that members should accept "no deals, discounts or gifts except those of insignificant value or those available to the public" (APSE, n.d., para. 6). If a gift cannot be returned, the APSE suggests donating that gift to charity (APSE, n.d.).

MAJOR MOMENTS

Newsworthiness vs Privacy

In 2015, the New York Giants' Jason Pierre-Paul was considered one of the best defensive players in the NFL. However, it was something that happened during the off-season that made bigger headlines than anything he had done on the field. On July 5, multiple media members reported that Pierre-Paul was injured lighting fireworks at his home the previous night. Early reports were vague, noting that what happened was not believed to be career-threatening, but that he had suffered injuries to some of his fingers and thumb (Bieler, 2015a). One reporter stated that Pierre had "dodged a bullet" and had suffered only skin injuries (Bonesteel, 2015, para. 2). However, days later, an ethically questionable report proved those earlier stories false.

On July 8, ESPN's Adam Schefter tweeted out an image of Pierre-Paul's medical chart that showed that the player's injuries were, in fact, more serious than many had reported. The chart showed that Pierre-Paul had to have one of his fingers amputated earlier that afternoon (Schefter, 2015). While the photo was proof that his story was correct, many questioned both how Schefter had gotten that picture and if he should have published it on Twitter. Additionally, if someone at the hospital had given that information out without Pierre-Paul's permission, it would be a violation of his privacy through the Health Insurance Portability and Accountability Act (HIPAA) Privacy Rule (Bieler, 2015b). By February 2016, it became clear that the Giants' star was not happy with his medical records being posted, as he filed a lawsuit against ESPN and Schefter. The lawsuit stated that ESPN showed "blatant disregard for the private and confidential nature of plaintiff's media records" (Marsh, 2016, para. 5).

While Schefter himself was not in violation of HIPAA laws because it was technically the hospital that released Pierre-Paul's records without his permission, the reporter's tweet raised many ethical questions. Schefter himself would later admit, "In hindsight I could have and should have done even more here due to the sensitivity of the situation. There should have been even more discussion than there was due to the sensitivity of the story; that's on me" (Deitsch, 2015, para. 30).

This case is an excellent example of some of the ethical quandaries in which sports reporters can find themselves. Technically, Schefter himself did not break any laws with his tweet, but that does not mean it was ethically the right decision. The ESPN reporter published private information about a career-altering injury that was wrongfully and illegally leaked to him by a hospital worker. While the lawsuit between ESPN and Pierre-Paul was eventually settled out of court (Payne, 2017), Schefter said the case was one that will stick with him for the rest of his career: "You think about it, you learn from it, and it becomes a part of your experience and thought process for if and when a similar difficult situation and decision should happen to arise again" (Deitsch, 2015, para. 34).

The one exception to the "no-free-stuff" rule is food in the press area. Often sports broadcasters have to leave the anchor desk and go directly to a game, with no time to stop for dinner. Because of this, some teams will offer a modest buffet (think sandwiches, hamburgers, or pizza) for the media covering the event. It is generally accepted that this free food will not sway a reporter's coverage because it might be the only chance he or she has to eat that night. Therefore, eating the press box food is considered an acceptable "free" item to receive, but reporters should check with station management first.

The Golden Rule

The Golden Rule is the idea that one should "treat people as you would want to be treated." That is a good philosophy in many aspects of life but can be especially true for sports broadcasters. When covering a team or athlete, having compassion, especially during a difficult time, can be a good way to develop a positive relationship with those people. Broadcasters can think to themselves "how would I want someone to approach me in this situation?" and use that as a guide for challenging scenarios. Additionally, following The Golden Rule can also be a good way to help avoid some of those ethical situations that might cause problems in the future.

CHAPTER WRAP-UP

HK*PROPEL* ACTIVITIES

Examples of ethical situations that sports have encountered are provided in HK*Propel*. Using those situations as a guide, reflect on how a sports broadcaster should handle these events and what should be done to avoid unnecessary conflicts.

SUMMARY

Being a sports broadcaster has become more than just talking about sports. As the identities of the athletes evolve and those playing the games become more vocal about societal issues, the sports media must be aware of how to properly report on these developments. The media should be able to cover these topics respectfully while also considering how their personal political opinions might influence their own reporting.

Additionally, the media must strive to provide equitable coverage to everyone participating in sporting events, regardless of race, sex, gender, sexual orientation, or ethnicity. While doing this, sports broadcasters must also avoid some of the ethical issues that can arise during coverage. These two topics go hand in hand: broadcasters should treat others how they would like to be treated and not put themselves in situations that could cause a problem in the future.

GLOSSARY

180-degree rule—The rule that the camera should stay on one side of an imaginary axis drawn on a field or court. For example, if the imaginary line is drawn from one goalpost to another in football, the camera should stay on just one side of the field for the entire game.

@—The sign used to contact another user on most social media networks.

#—The symbol placed before a hashtag.

A-roll—The process in a video edit in which the reporter's track and the interviews are edited together.

Active voice—The subject performs the action stated by the verb.

Actuality—A radio sound bite from a prerecorded interview.

Air check—A recording of a radio or television program.

Assembly edit—The process of putting down video clips in the order in which they will ultimately be seen on the broadcast. Should be done first when editing.

Associate director—During a live broadcast of a sporting event, the associate director is primarily focused on action that is not game-specific, such as the timing of commercial breaks.

Associated Press—A news-gathering organization that provides breaking news updates, written stories, videos, and photos to news outlets throughout the world.

Attribution—Identifying who provided information or who said a specific quote.

Audio level—Displays how loud something is.

Audio supervisor—During a live broadcast of a sporting event, the audio supervisor mixes the sounds coming from the various microphones during the broadcast. This includes sounds from the crowd, the on-field action, the announcers, and the broadcast's music and sound effects.

Avatar—The profile photo of the account user. This can be a photo of anything and not necessarily the person.

B-roll—The process in a video edit in which the reporter track is covered with video shot out in the field. It is supplemental video that helps tell the story visually to support what the reporter and interview subjects are talking about.

Backlit—When the dominant light is behind the subject. In these situations, the subject will appear very dark.

Beat writers—Sports reporters focused on one specific team, league, or sport. These writers are often considered experts in the topic about which they write.

Blogs—Websites that provide constant updates on a topic or event through posts usually displayed with the newest content at the top of the page.

Board operator—Runs the audio board that broadcasts what comes out of the microphones. Commonly shortened to board op.

Call screener—In charge of organizing the calls from sports talk radio listeners at home who want to speak with the hosts on the air.

Closed-ended questions—Designed to get a specific response.

Color commentator—The broadcaster during a live sports broadcast who gives an expert opinion about what is happening during a game. Sometimes referred to as a color analyst. This job is often filled by a former player or coach.

Cutaway—A shot of something that is not part of the main action, for example, a shot of the crowd during a football game.

Debate shows—Television broadcasts in which multiple media members debate topics surrounding the latest sports news.

Diamond structure—A broadcast writing format for putting together a package. The story starts with a narrow focus, then widens out to include more information, before ending with a narrow focus.

Direct message (DM)—A private message sent from one user to another through a social network's messaging service. These messages cannot be read by the public.

Direct quotes—When the author uses the exact words from an interview subject and includes them in the story.

Director—During a live broadcast of a sporting event, the director instructs camera operators what to shoot, decides which camera shots should be shown on the broadcast, and communicates with the replay and graphics technicians.

Establishing shot—The first shot in a video highlight. It demonstrates where the action is taking place or introduces a key element in the story.

Facebook—A social network on which users can post messages, photos, or videos that will appear on the news feed of those who follow that user.

Facebook Live—A streaming video service through Facebook that allows users to stream live video directly from their mobile device.

Favorite—A feature on Twitter that allows users to indicate that they enjoy a tweet.

Focus—A camera feature that allows the subject to be seen clearly.

Freelance journalist—Journalist not employed by a news organization but instead reporting on games or events for that organization on a case-by-case basis.

Gain—A camera feature that can be used to increase the brightness of the video. Should be used in situations in which there is not adequate light, for example at night in an area that is not well lit.

Game notes—Several pages of information containing a variety of different facts and statistics about the teams involved in a game. These are produced by media officials that work with the teams.

Gatekeeper—Media that decides what stories reach the public and which ones are not reported on.

Graphics operator—During a live broadcast of a sporting event, the graphics operator creates graphics and uses the machine that puts text and graphics on the screen.

Grip—During a live broadcast of a sporting event, the grip helps during setup and breakdown of the event by carrying equipment, placing cable, and assisting with whatever else is needed to get ready for the broadcast. This person may also work with camera operators during the game to hold cables while the videographer is shooting.

Handheld microphone—A microphone that picks up audio from what is directly in front of it.

Handle/username—How a person or organization is identified on social media. For example, ESPN's Twitter handle is @ESPN, while ESPN baseball writer Jeff Passan's handle is @JeffPassan.

Hashtag—Used to identify a key word or topic that can then be searched for by other users. Hashtags are often used to group together posts related to a topic or event. For example, all posts about the World Series may use #WorldSeries.

Highlight—A video recap of a sporting event in which important plays are shown.

In point—Sets where the edit will begin.

Indirect quotes—When the author of a story does not use the exact words from an interview subject and instead summarizes the general idea stated by the subject. This is also known as paraphrasing.

Insert—A button on a video-editing program that will insert the selected video clip in between the two selected clips on the timeline.

Instagram—A photo and video-sharing social media network in which users post media to their page and it shows up in the timeline of those who follow that user.

Instant replay—After a live play that viewers have just watched during a game broadcast, the play is shown again to allow the audience to see it for a second time. The instant replay is often from a different angle and at a slower speed than the live version.

Interview—A conversation in which one person asks questions while another person provides answers.

Inverted pyramid—A journalistic style of writing that is popular in newspapers and on websites. It dictates that the most important information should go at the beginning of a story, followed by the important details in the middle and the supporting and background information at the end.

Iris—A ring on the camera lens that determines how much light is being shown. The iris can be used to adjust video that is either too dark or too light.

Kicker—The upbeat and happy story that traditionally ends most newscasts.

Lavalier microphone—A small microphone that clips onto a person's shirt.

Lead—The beginning of a news story. It should contain the most important information in the piece.

Linear video editing—Video editing from tape to tape. Plays are chosen from one tape and then copied onto a second tape in sequential order.

Links—Website visitors click on these to visit a specific location on the internet defined by the author. These are more formally referred to as hyperlinks.

Live sports broadcast—Games that are broadcast in their entirety live on a television or radio network.

Logging—Writing down everything that someone has said during a recorded interview. Also known as transcribing.

Lower third—A graphic that appears at the bottom of the screen that identifies what is on the screen. It can be a person, a location, or, in sports, a final score.

Markets—The United States is divided into 210 markets where people in that area all receive the same television or radio station. New York City is the largest market, so it is Market #1. Glendive, Montana, is the smallest market, so it is Market #210.

Media guide—A book published by the media officials working with a team that contains information about the players, coaches, and team officials. There are also sections on team history and statistical records.

Metadata—Additional information about the selected video clip.

Mult box—An audio device that splits one audio signal into several signals. Allows for media members to get sound from one microphone.

Natural pop—A brief burst of natural sound at full audio level.

Natural sound—Any sound occurring naturally recorded in the field. This sound should be playing in the background of video packages or audio wraps. Sometimes referred to as ambient sound.

ND filter—A camera feature that can be used to increase the darkness of the video. Should be used in situations where there is too much light present. An example would be during the day when the sun is at its brightest.

Nonlinear video editing—Video editing on a computer. Video is recorded on a computer from tapes or camera cards and then edited using specialized software before the finished product is exported for viewing.

Off the record—None of the information can be used in the broadcast.

On-camera lead—The anchor provides a sentence or two of information about a game before the video of highlights begins to play.

One Frame Back—A button on a video-editing program that will move the video back one frame. This is good for making precise edits.

One Frame Forward—A button on a video-editing program that will move the video forward one frame. This is good for making precise edits.

On background—The broadcaster can use the information but can only give a vague description of where it came from.

On deep background—The broadcaster can use the information, but the source cannot be identified.

On the record—Everything within the interview can be used, including the information, the source, and direct quotes.

Open-ended questions—Allow interview subjects flexibility in their answers.

Out point—Sets where the edit will end.

Overmodulated—When the volume of an audio clip is so loud it becomes distorted and difficult to hear.

Overwrite—A button on a video-editing program that will overwrite whatever is on the timeline when selected.

Package (PKG)—A self-contained television story that includes recorded multiple reporter tracks, sound bites, and relevant video that matches what the reporter is talking about.

Pan—A camera movement in which the camera moves from side to side on a flat, horizontal plane.

Partial quotes—When a writer uses just a small portion of what someone says in a story, essentially combining a direct quote with an indirect quote.

Passive voice—The subject is acted upon by the verb.

Play-by-play announcer—The person who describes the action to the audience watching or listening as it happens.

Play—A button on a video-editing program that will play the video clip.

Podcasts—Digital audio files that can be downloaded and played at the listener's convenience. Podcasts usually consist of a host talking about a topic through his or her commentary, an interview, or storytelling.

Pop filter—A screen placed in front of a microphone used to eliminate popping sounds occasionally generated during audio recordings.

Press conference—An interview to which members of the press are invited to hear from someone in a formal setting.

Press release—An official statement delivered by an impacted party to the media for the purpose of informing journalists about the latest developments.

Producer (television)—During a live broadcast of a sporting event, the producer oversees the production of the event and is responsible for the show content. Usually the producer is the person in charge of a live sports broadcast.

Producer (radio)—Works closely with the on-air hosts at a sports talk radio show to decide the content of the show. This may involve conducting research, booking guests, and deciding what the hosts will talk about and when.

Program window—The window in the upper right of most video-editing programs where the finished video will be displayed. Sometimes referred to as the program monitor.

Project window—The window in the lower left of most video programs where the imported clips will be displayed. Sometimes referred to as the bin window.

Pronunciation guide—A section of a media guide or game notes that provides the proper phonetic pronunciation for names of athletes and coaches.

Rating—The approximate number of people who are watching a given television or radio program.

Razor tool—Used in Adobe Premiere to cut a clip into two separate clips. Looks like a razor blade.

Reader—In television, an anchor is reading a script while being shown on television. In radio, the anchor is reading a script with no other audio elements included in the story.

Re-creations—When a radio play-by-play announcer would take information sent from a telegraph and re-create the action for the audience. The practice was discontinued in the 1990s.

Replay operator—During a live broadcast of a sporting event, the replay operator monitors additional cameras that are not live on the broadcast and determines which one has the best angle or vantage point for a replay after the play has concluded.

Retweet—A feature on Twitter that allows users to import an existing tweet into their own timeline. The user can either retweet the original message exactly or quote the original message and then add their own comment above it.

Rundown—The order in which stories will appear in the newscast.

Scoop—An exclusive story.

Search engine optimization—Increasing the amount of people who visit a particular website by increasing the visibility of that website on a web search engine.

Selection tool—Used in Adobe Premiere to select a clip that should be modified. Looks like an arrow.

Shared services agreement—An arrangement in which two local television stations in the same television market agree to share news operations while still legally acting as two different entities.

Shot sheet—A document used by sports broadcasters when doing highlights on television. It takes the place of a script and instead has a basic description of the highlight, along with perhaps an important fact.

Sideline reporter—The broadcaster during a live sports broadcast who stands on the sidelines and is able to relay information from field level. This person often provides updates on injuries and interviews the coaches at halftime and after the game.

Snapchat—A social media network that allows users to post photos and videos that disappear from the site after a set number of seconds.

Solo interview—An interview in which one media member speaks to one individual.

Sound on tape (SOT)—An edited piece of an interview showing interview subject talking on camera.

Sound edit—The process of making sure that the volume of various clips in a video-editing timeline are all at appropriate and equal levels. This should be done after the assembly edit is completed.

Source window—The window in the upper left of most video-editing programs where individual clips are previewed before being edited. Also, where in and out points are selected. Sometimes referred to as the source monitor.

Sports information director (SID)—A person who works for a college sports team to deliver statistics, team notes, and player notes to media members. Sports information directors are often tasked with arranging interviews between the media and players or coaches.

Spotter—During a live broadcast of a sporting event, the spotter assists the crew and the announcers with looking for events during the game that others might have missed.

Spotting chart—A reference sheet created by a play-by-play announcer in which the players' uniform numbers, statistics, positions, and personal stories are arranged for easy access during a game. These are sometimes referred to as spotting boards.

Standup—When a reporter can be seen reporting from an event as opposed to being in the studio.

Stream—Playing a video or audio file so that people can watch it as it is happening. Is an alternative to downloading.

Strength of weak ties—People who someone knows closely are strong ties, whereas casual acquaintances are weak ties. In the spreading of social media information, it is the weak ties that are often more effective in getting the message out to a new and wider audience.

Studio shows—Television broadcasts in which anchors or commentators report on or discuss the latest sports news.

Syndicated—National shows that are leased to local stations in order to play that programming.

Tagging—Linking a picture or video to another user. If a baseball writer composes a post with a photo of four players in it, he or she may wish to "tag" those players in the photo so they will know there is a post with them in it.

Take Still Photo—A button on a video-editing program that will take a photo of whatever is in the player window.

Technical director—During a live broadcast of a sporting event, the technical director pushes the buttons on the switcher that selects the cameras and effects requested by the director.

Teleprompter—Displays the scripts on a piece of glass directly in front of the camera for the anchor to read during the sportscast.

Television market—The United States is divided into 210 television markets, ranging from the biggest (New York City is Market #1 because it is the most populated) to the smallest (Glendive, Montana, is Market #210 because it has the least number of viewers). The newscasts in each market are limited to the people living in that specific viewing area.

Tilt—A camera movement in which the camera moves up and down on a flat, vertical plane.

Timeline (video editing)—The main section of a video-editing program where the majority of the editing will take place. Clips are dragged from the player window to the timeline when editing, displaying the video and audio.

Timeline (social media)—A sometimes chronological display of the posts from people followed by the user.

Tripod—A three-legged stand that stabilizes what is sitting on it. Used in video recording to hold up a camera and keep it stable.

Tweet—A 280-character message sent on Twitter. Tweets can contain links, photos, videos, and other multimedia elements.

Twitter—A social media network that allows users to send short messages to followers that will show up on others' timelines.

Viewfinder—Part of the camera that shows what is being shot through the lens. It is used by the videographer to get the desired shot.

Voice-over (VO)—A reporter or anchor reads a television script while video is playing on the screen.

Voice-over to sound on tape (VO/SOT)—A reporter or anchor reads a television script while video is playing on the screen followed immediately by an edited interview.

VU (volume unit) meter—Displays a visual representation of the volume being recorded on audio or video equipment.

White balance—A camera setting that informs the device what color is white. With this information, the camera is able to determine all the other colors for recording.

Windscreen—A foam cover placed over a microphone. When used outside it helps reduce the chance of wind affecting the recording. It also helps protect the microphone from dirt and debris.

Wipe—The process in which the video from one story ends and the video from the next story begins immediately.

Wrap—A radio piece in which a reporter records his or her voice track and includes sound bites edited into the piece.

Zone focus—A videographer uses this to prefocus on the field of play with the knowledge that everything that comes into that area will be in focus. Used primarily in live television sports productions.

Zoom—Using camera lens technology to make subjects appear closer (zoom in) or farther away (zoom out). The camera itself does not move.

REFERENCES

Chapter 1

1939 NFL League Standings. (n.d.) *NFL.com*. www.nfl.com/standings/league/1939/reg

Anderson, D. (1975, October 2). Title retained after ugly end to the "Thrilla in Manila." *The New York Times*. www.nytimes.com/2016/06/11/sports/title-retained-after-ugly-end-to-the-thrilla-in-manila.html

Associated Press. (2002, January 10). CNN to scrap struggling sports network, replace it with new cable network. www.newson6.com/story/5e3680942f69d76f62094a3e/cnn-to-scrap-struggling-sports-network-replace-it-with-new-cable-network

Badenhausen, K. (2013, July 24). NBC nabs NASCAR tv rights for $4.4 billion. *Forbes*. www.forbes.com/sites/kurtbadenhausen/2013/07/24/nbc-nabs-nascar-tv-rights-for-4-4-billion

Barnhouse, W. (1988, November 19). Heidi Game. *Reading Eagle*, 10.

Baysinger, T. (2013, March 7). Fox isn't shy about challenging ESPN. *Broadcasting+Cable*. www.nexttv.com/blog/fox-isnt-shy-about-challenging-espn-119233

Best, N. (2011, June 16). First time, long time for Bill Mazer. *Newsday*. www.newsday.com/sports/columnists/neil-best/first-time-long-time-for-bill-mazer-1.2962262

Best, N. (2016, August 12). The Rio Olympics, NBC ratings and "total audience delivery." *Newsday*. www.newsday.com/sports/olympics/the-rio-olympics-nbc-ratings-and-total-audience-delivery-1.12168143

Billings, A., Angelini, J.R., & MacArthur, P.J. (2018). *Olympic television: Broadcasting the biggest show on earth*. Routledge.

Brady, J. (2018, January 18). ESPN's evolution: Snapchat, esports and attribution guidelines. *ESPN.com*. www.espn.com/blog/ombudsman/post/_/id/912/espns-evolution-snapchat-esports-and-attribution-guidelines

Breech, J. (2020, February 5). 2020 Super Bowl rating revealed: Chiefs-49ers ranks as the 11th most-watched show in TV history. *CBS Sports*. www.cbssports.com/nfl/news/2020-super-bowl-ratings-revealed-chiefs-49ers-ranks-as-the-11th-most-watched-show-in-tv-history

Britannica. (n.d.) Radio. www.britannica.com/topic/radio/Juvenile-action-and-adventure-series#ref1123774

Brooks, T., & Marsh, E. (2007). *The complete directory to primetime network and cable TV shows 1946–present* (9th ed.). Ballantine Books.

Caldwell, D. (2014, September 30). When Fordham introduced football to television. *The Wall Street Journal*. www.wsj.com/articles/when-fordham-introduced-football-to-television-1412123075

Catsis, J.R. (1996). *Sports broadcasting*. Nelson-Hall Publishers.

CCTA. (n.d.) History of cable. https://calcable.org/learn/history-of-cable

Chad, N. (1987, October 18). To TV sports fans, ESPN grows from novelty to necessity. *The Washington Post*. www.washingtonpost.com/archive/sports/1987/10/18/to-tv-sports-fans-espn-grows-from-novelty-to-necessity/497e6ee0-dc18-42f0-b868-e72e3567d739

Chansky, A. (2005). *Blue blood. Duke-Carolina: Inside the most storied rivalry in college hoops*. Thomas Dunne Books.

Chase, C. (2015, December 8). The real story of Howard Cosell, John Lennon and the shocking "MNF" announcement. *For the Win*. https://ftw.usatoday.com/2015/12/howard-cosell-john-lennon-monday-night-football-video

Coelho, A.L. (2015, May 12). Scott Van Pelt signs extension with ESPN; Will take over midnight (ET) SportsCenter as solo anchor. *ESPN Press Room*. https://espnpressroom.com/us/press-releases/2015/05/scott-van-pelt-signs-extension-espn-will-take-midnight-et-sportscenter-solo-anchor

Columbia Athletics. (2009, May 17). Columbia vs. Princeton: First televised sporting event marks 70th anniversary. https://gocolumbialions.com/news/2009/5/17/3738874

Cotey, J.C. (2005, August 24). ESPNU to add to college saturation. *Tampa Bay Times*. www.tampabay.com/archive/2005/02/25/espnu-to-add-to-college-saturation

Covil, E.C. (n.d.). Radio and its impact on the sports world. *American Sportscasters Online*. www.americansportscastersonline.com/radiohistory.html

Cramer, M. (2016, September 12). As tv and football celebrate 65 years of marriage, the relationship grows deeper. *The Dallas Morning News*. www.dallasnews.com/opinion/commentary/2016/09/12/as-tv-and-football-celebrate-65-years-of-marriage-the-relationship-grows-deeper

Draper, K. (2018, April 12). ESPN tries to get with a mobile, app-driven world. *The New York Times*. www.nytimes.com/2018/04/12/sports/espn-app.html

Emmys. (n.d.) ABC's Wide World of Sports. www.emmys.com/shows/abcs-wide-world-sports

ESPN Front Row. (2018, December 18). *First SportsCenter 1979*. [Video]. *Vimeo*. https://vimeo.com/307153790

ESPN Press Room. (2011, April 21). 50th anniversary of Wide World of Sports celebrated. https://espnpressroom.com/us/press-releases/2011/04/50th-anniversary-of-wide-world-of-sports-celebrated

Esposito, G. (2018, October 10). Inside ESPN's Snapchat SportsCenter strategy. *Front Office Sports*. https://frontofficesports.com/espns-snapchat-sportscenter-strategy

Fabrikant, G. (1987, June 9). It's first and goal for ESPN. *The New York Times*. www.nytimes.com/1987/06/09/business/it-s-first-and-goal-for-espn.html

Fang, K. (2015, December 28). In its first five years, Longhorn Network isn't the success than ESPN had hoped for. *Awful Announcing*. https://awfulannouncing.com/2015/in-its-first-five-years-longhorn-network-isnt-the-success-that-espn-had-hoped-for.html

Fitzpatrick, F. (2016, February 4). First televised NFL game: An Eagles defeat. *The Philadelphia Inquirer*. www.inquirer.com/philly/sports/eagles/20160205_Eagles_lost_first_televised_NFL_game.html

Fleming, J. (2020, May 22). ESPN's "This is SportsCenter" campaign turns 25: Adweek picks our favorite spots. *AdWeek*. www.adweek.com/brand-marketing/espns-this-is-sportcenter-campaign-turns-25-adweek-picks-our-favorite-spots

Flint, J. (2020, October 14). Amazon expands NFL coverage with playoff game. *The Wall Street Journal*. www.wsj.com/articles/amazon-expands-nfl-coverage-with-playoff-game-11602702168

Florio, M. (2015, December 2). 30 years ago tonight, Monday Night Football had its highest rating ever. *Pro Football Talk*. https://profootballtalk.nbcsports.com/2015/12/02/30-years-ago-tonight-monday-night-football-had-its-highest-rating-ever

Frager, R. (1993, October 1). Whether you get it or not, ESPN2 has no tied to the tried and true. *The Baltimore Sun*. www.baltimoresun.com/news/bs-xpm-1993-10-01-1993274121-story.html

Fry, M.C. (1973, March). Radio's first voice . . . Canadian! *IEEE Canada*. www.ieee.ca/millennium/radio/radio_birth.html

Given, K. (2016, February 20). Nazis pioneered broadcasting . . . and made Jesse Owens a star. *WBUR*. www.wbur.org/onlyagame/2016/02/20/jesse-owens-olympics-germans-nazi-radio

Halberstam, D.J. (2019, September 29). Born 80 years ago, college football on TV was limited by the NCAA's grip until stopped by the Supreme Court. *Sports Broadcast Journal*. www.sportsbroadcastjournal.com/born-80-years-ago-college-football-on-tv-was-limited-by-the-ncaas-grip-until-the-supreme-court-said-let-go

Hale, D.M. (2018, November 30). ACC Network set to launch August 2019. *ESPN.com*. www.espn.com/college-sports/story/_/id/25419387/acc-network-set-launch-august-2019

Haring, B. (2018, November 17). NFL's "Heidi" game remembered, changed pro football tv rules. *Deadline*. https://deadline.com/2018/11/nfls-heidi-game-remembered-changed-pro-football-tv-rules-1202504298

Heistand, M. (2008, June 8). Jim McKay's wide world spanned eras. *USA Today*. https://usatoday30.usatoday.com/sports/columnist/hiestand-tv/2008-06-08-mckay_N.htm

History.com Editors (2020, August 25). First televised Major League Baseball game. *History*. www.history.com/this-day-in-history/first-televised-major-league-baseball-game

Hofmeister, S. (1997, September 4). ESPN agrees to buy cable tv's Classic Sports Network. *Los Angeles Times*. www.latimes.com/archives/la-xpm-1997-sep-04-fi-28622-story.html

Hu, J. (2001, October 30). Baseball officials plan live video streaming. *CNET*. https://archive.is/20120711061344/http://news.com.com/2100-1023-275123.html

KDKA. (2010, April 1). KDKA firsts. https://pittsburgh.cbslocal.com/2010/04/01/kdka-firsts

Kissel, K.P. (1992, November 10). HBO started 20 years ago in Wilkes-Barre. https://apnews.com/article/7234e60624a3ac1b2c33c4fb690dc235

Kohler, J. (2013, March 19). Michael Roarty dies at 84; marketer helped build Anheuser-Busch brand. *Los Angeles Times*. www.latimes.com/local/obituaries/la-xpm-2013-mar-19-la-me-michael-roarty-20130319-story.html

Koplovitz, K. (2015, September 30). How Muhammad Ali, Joe Frazier and satellites changed tv history. *Media Village*. www.mediavillage.com/article/how-muhammed-ali-joe-frazier-and-satellites-changed-the-course-of-television-history

Koppett, L. (1999, Spring). Baker Field: Birthplace of sports television. *Columbia College*. www.college.columbia.edu/cct_archive/spr99/34a.html

Leddy, C. (2015, September 28). The fight that helped cable take flight. *Multichannel News*. www.nexttv.com/news/fight-helped-cable-take-flight-394103

Leitch, W. (2007, February 1). The last days of ESPN2. *Deadspin*. https://deadspin.com/the-last-days-of-espn2-233272

Leverette, M., Ott, B.L., & Buckley, C.L. (2008). *It's not TV. Watching HBO in the post-television era*. Routledge.

Martin, D. (2020, September 11). Bellator MMA announces move from Paramount Network to CBS Sports Network.

www.mmafighting.com/2020/9/11/21432619/bellator-mma-announces-move-from-paramount-network-to-cbs-sports-network

McAtee, R. (2018, April 2). What ESPN's new streaming service doesn't have and what it needs. *The Ringer*. www.theringer.com/sports/2018/4/2/17190026/espn-plus-streaming-service-april-12

McGowen, R. (1939, August 26). First day for the small screen. *The New York Times*. https://archive.nytimes.com/www.nytimes.com/packages/html/sports/year_in_sports/08.26.html

McKay, J. (2002, December 13). The end of innocence. *ESPN.com*. www.espn.com/abcsports/columns/mckay_jim/2002/0904/1427112.html#

Melvin, P. (2018, September 20). ESPN+ hits one million paid subscribers in just over five months. *ESPN Press Room*. https://espnpressroom.com/us/press-releases/2018/09/espn-hits-one-million-paid-subscribers-in-just-over-five-months

Miller, J.A., & Shales, T. (2011). *Those guys have all the fun*. Little, Brown and Company.

Morton, J. (2019, August 18). Five years on, student-athletes made SEC Network a success. *Tuscaloosa News*. www.tuscaloosanews.com/news/20190818/five-years-on-student-athletes-made-sec-network-success

Mullin, B. (2019, March 18). ESPN, UFC reach exclusive pay-per-view deal. *The Wall Street Journal*. www.wsj.com/articles/espn-ufc-reach-exclusive-pay-per-view-deal-11552939288

Nagle, D. (1988, January 2). ESPN, Inc.: 1987 in review. *ESPN Press Room*. https://espnpressroom.com/us/press-releases/1988/01/1987-marks-espns-biggest-year-yet

National Baseball Hall of Fame. (n.d.). 2016 Ford C. Frick award winner Graham McNamee. https://baseballhall.org/discover-more/awards/frick/graham-mcnamee

NCAA. (2020). College football history: Notable firsts and milestones. www.ncaa.com/news/ncaa/article/2020-01-31/college-football-history-notable-firsts-and-milestones

NFL Ops. (n.d). Impact of television. https://operations.nfl.com/the-game/impact-of-television

Nielsen. (2008, September 5). Beijing Olympics drew largest ever global tv audience. www.nielsen.com/us/en/insights/article/2008/beijing-olympics-draw-largest-ever-global-tv-audience

Nufer, D. (1991, August 26). Present at the re-creation. *Sports Illustrated*. https://vault.si.com/vault/1991/08/26/present-at-the-re-creation-bob-robertson-broadcasts-baseball-games-the-old-fashioned-way-making-it-up-as-he-goes-along

Olympic.org. (n.d.). Squaw Valley 1960. www.olympic.org/squaw-valley-1960

Ota, K. (2017, November 13). ESPN launches *SportsCenter* on Snapchat. ESPN Press Room. https://espnpressroom.com/us/press-releases/2017/11/espn-launches-sportscenter-snapchat

Pallotta, F. (2015, February 2). Super Bowl XLIX posts the largest audience in TV history. *CNN.com*. https://money.cnn.com/2015/02/02/media/super-bowl-ratings

Pallotta, F. (2021, January 22). NBC Sports Network to shut down by the end of the year. *CNN.com*. https://www.cnn.com/2021/01/22/media/nbc-sports-network-shut-down/index.html

Pierson, D. (1987, March 16). NFL finally opens the door to cable. *Chicago Tribune*. www.chicagotribune.com/news/ct-xpm-1987-03-16-8701210017-story.html

Pro Football Hall of Fame. (n.d.). Ebbets Field hosts football history. www.profootballhof.com/football-history/the-1930s-and-the-first-televised-game

Reedy, J. (2019, May 1). Fox Sports 1 showing patience, growth with studio lineup. https://apnews.com/article/5ce025b37a1543b0ab26dfc28294af38

Reynolds, M. (2014, January 23). YES adds simulcast of "The Michael Kay Show" to its weekday lineup. *Multichannel News*. www.nexttv.com/news/yes-adds-simulcast-michael-kay-show-its-weekday-lineup-356401

Romano, F.V. (2017). *The golden age of boxing on radio and television: A blow-by-blow history from 1921 to 1964*. Carrel Books.

Rosenthal, P. (2019, September 8). How ESPN—now 40 years old—changed the sports world from your growing cable bill and round-the-clock programming to the glut of bowl games. *Chicago Tribune*. www.chicagotribune.com/sports/breaking/ct-cb-espn-40th-anniversary-changed-sports-20190906-ogxokpxedjgwdekdlmgudb6myq-story.html

Sandomir, R. (1996, November 1). Plays of the day, all day, every day. *The New York Times*. www.nytimes.com/1996/11/01/sports/plays-of-the-day-all-day-every-day.html

Sandomir, R. (2001, September 11). Sports business; YankeeNets getting own cable network. *The New York Times*. www.nytimes.com/2001/09/11/sports/sports-business-yankeenets-getting-own-cable-network.html

Sandomir, R. (2005, November 23). One night in 1970, the revolution was televised. *The New York Times*. www.nytimes.com/2005/11/23/sports/football/one-night-in-1970-the-revolution-was-televised.html

Sandomir, R. (2006, August 11). ABC Sports is dead at 45; Stand by for ESPN. *The New York Times*. www.nytimes.com/2006/08/11/sports/othersports/11sandomir.html

Sandomir, R. (2008, December 31). Fans who can't get enough are getting more. *The New York Times*. www.nytimes.com/2009/01/01/sports/baseball/01sandomir.html

Sandomir, R. (2013, May 2). SEC will start TV network in 2014. *The New York Times*. www.nytimes.com/2013/05/03/sports/ncaafootball/sec-will-have-own-tv-network-starting-in-2014.html

Sandomir, R. (2015, August 10). NBC retains rights to Premier League in six-year deal. *The New York Times*. www.nytimes.com/2015/08/11/sports/soccer/nbc-retains-rights-to-premier-league-in-six-year-deal.html

Sandomir, R. (2016, June 4). Muhammad Ali and Howard Cosell: Foils and friends bound by mutual respect. *The New York Times*. www.nytimes.com/2016/06/05/sports/muhammad-ali-and-howard-cosell-foils-and-friends-bound-by-mutual-respect.html

Schneider, J. (2019, March 4). Graham McNamee: Radio's first superstar announcer. *Radio World*. www.radioworld.com/columns-and-views/roots-of-radio/graham-mcnamee-radios-first-superstar-announcer

Schneider, M. (2019, December 27). Top rated shows of 2019: Super Bowl LIII, "The Big Bang Theory," "Game of Thrones" dominate. *Variety*. https://variety.com/2019/tv/news/top-rated-shows-2019-game-of-thrones-big-bang-theory-oscars-super-bowl-1203451363

Selyukh, A. (2016, April 5). Twitter wins NFL deal to stream 2016 Thursday night football. *NPR*. www.npr.org/sections/thetwo-way/2016/04/05/473099436/twitter-wins-nfl-deal-to-stream-2016-thursday-night-football

Sengwe, S. (2020, August 4). ESPN Plus reaches 8.5 million subscribers in Disney's Q3 2020 earnings report. *The Streamable*. https://thestreamable.com/news/espn-plus-reaches-8-5-million-subscribers-in-disney-s-q3-2020-earnings-report

Shales, T., & Miller, J.A. (2011). *Those guys have all the fun: Inside the world of ESPN*. Little, Brown and Company.

Shapiro, L. (1995, April 24). Howard Cosell dies at 77. *The Washington Post*. www.washingtonpost.com/wp-srv/sports/longterm/memories/1995/95pass12.htm

Sidelinger, B. (2020, September 21). High schools to live-stream games for fall sports. *WABI*. www.wabi.tv/2020/09/21/high-schools-to-live-stream-games-for-fall-sports

Slater, J. (2018, January 22). 45 years ago today: "Down goes Frazier! Down goes Frazier!" *Boxing News 24/7*. www.boxing247.com/boxing-news/45-years-ago-to-day-down-goes-frazier-down-goes-frazier/88647

Smith, R.A. (2001). *Play-by-play: Radio, television, and big-time college sport*. Johns Hopkins University Press.

Sunset, B. (2008, October 27). This is SportsCenter campaign. *Marketing Campaign Case Studies*. http://marketing-case-studies.blogspot.com/2008/10/this-is-sportscenter-campaign.html

The Raiders Film Vault. (2019, September 26). *Raider History: The Heidi Game* [Video]. YouTube. www.youtube.com/watch?v=vsrxpLly_Vw

Thomas, R.M. (1995, April 25). The man in the yellow blazer. *The New York Times*. http://archive.nytimes.com/www.nytimes.com/packages/html/sports/year_in_sports/04.25.html

TLPFAS. (2010, December 3). *John Lennon shot 12-8-80 Howard Cosell tells the world twice that John Lennon was dead* [Video]. YouTube. www.youtube.com/watch?v=n73GFvAyIjs

Umstead, R.T. (2002, June 6). From classic sports to college sports. *Multichannel News*. www.nexttv.com/news/classic-sports-college-sports-136683

Valinsky, J. (2018, March 9). Facebook to exclusively stream 25 MLB games. *CNN*. https://money.cnn.com/2018/03/09/technology/facebook-mlb-deal/index.html

Voepel, M. (2020, August 10). WNBA partners with Twitter to stream 10 games on social media platform. *ESPN.com*. www.espn.com/wnba/story/_/id/29633085/wnba-partners-twitter-stream-10-games-social-media-platform

Vogan, T. (2015). *ESPN: The making of a sports media empire*. University of Illinois Press.

Washburn, P.S., & Lamb, C. (2020). *Sports Journalism: A history of glory, fame, and technology*. University of Nebraska Press.

We R Tacoma. (2020, September 7). Bob Robertson: Remembering R beloved broadcaster. www.wertacoma.com/bobrobertson

Wingfield, N. (2017, April 4). Amazon will stream N.F.L.'s Thursday night games. *The New York Times*. www.nytimes.com/2017/04/04/business/media/amazon-stream-nfl-thursday-night-football.html

Chapter 2

Abrahamson, A. (2003, June 7). NBC wins rights to 2010, 2012 Olympics. *Los Angeles Times*. www.latimes.com/archives/la-xpm-2003-jun-07-fi-oly7-story.html

Adams, V. (1964, January 25). C.B.S.-TV to pay $28.2 million for 2-year pro football rights. *The New York Times*. www.nytimes.com/1964/01/25/archives/cbstv-to-pay-282-million-for-2year-pro-football-rights.html

Andreeva, N., & Johnson, T. (2019, December 27). Cable ratings 2019: Fox News tops total viewers, ESPN wins 18-49 demo as entertainment networks slide. *Deadline*. https://deadline.com/2019/12/cable-ratings-2019-list-fox-news-total-viewers-espn-18-49-demo-1202817561

Associated Press. (2016, August 4). How to watch The Olympics without a TV. *NBC News*. www.nbcnews.com/storyline/2016-rio-summer-olympics/how-watch-olympics-without-tv-n623111

Bachman, R. (2012, November 21). ESPN strikes deal for college football playoff. *The Wall Street Journal*. www.wsj.com/articles/SB10001424127887324851704578133223970790516

Bassam, T. (2019, November 11). Reports: CBS secures shock Champions League US rights deal. *SportsPro*. www.sportspromedia.com/news/champions-league-tv-rights-cbs-univision

Bennetts, L. (2016, November 3). Joan Rivers's remarkable rise to (and devastating fall from) comedy's highest ranks. *Vanity Fair*. www.vanityfair.com/hollywood/2016/11/joan-rivers-last-girl-before-freeway-excerpt

Breech, J. (2017, April 4). Amazon wins NFL bidding war to stream Thursday Night Football games in 2017. *CBS Sports*. www.cbssports.com/nfl/news/amazon-wins-huge-bidding-war-to-stream-thursday-night-football-games-in-2017

Breech, J. (2020, February 5). 2020 Super Bowl ratings revealed: Chiefs-49ers ranks as the 11th most-watched show in TV history. *CBS Sports*. www.cbssports.com/nfl/news/2020-super-bowl-ratings-revealed-chiefs-49ers-ranks-as-the-11th-most-watched-show-in-tv-history

Carter, B. (2008, August 24). On TV, timing is everything at the Olympics. *The New York Times*. www.nytimes.com/2008/08/25/sports/olympics/25nbc.html

Chad, N. (1987, March 13). NFL's new TV deal is set: ESPN to get 8 Sunday night games. *Los Angeles Times*. www.latimes.com/archives/la-xpm-1987-03-13-sp-5390-story.html

Cozart, L. (2014, April 17). #TBT: As NBA Playoffs on ESPN and ABC loom, a look at early days of league coverage. *ESPN Front Row*. www.espnfrontrow.com/2014/04/tbt

Crouse, L. (2008, August 15). In pool or out, Olympic star stands apart. *The New York Times*. www.nytimes.com/2008/08/16/sports/olympics/16phelps.html

Crupi, A. (2020, November 5). ESPN eliminates 500 positions as Disney budgets for a multi-billion-dollar rights spree. *Yahoo! Finance*. https://finance.yahoo.com/news/espn-eliminates-500-positions-disney-140346813.html

Curtis, B. (2018, December 13). The great NFL heist: How Fox paid for and changed football forever. *The Ringer*. www.theringer.com/nfl/2018/12/13/18137938/nfl-fox-deal-rupert-murdoch-1993-john-madden-terry-bradshaw-howie-long-jimmy-johnson-cbs-nbc

de Moraes, L. (2019, May 21). 'Big Bang Theory' series so-long crowd grows to 23.4M in live+3. *Deadline*. https://deadline.com/2019/05/big-bang-theory-series-live-plus-three-day-viewing-23-44-million-viewers-tv-ratings-1202619990

Dempsey, J. (1996, December 3). CBS, TNT team for games. *Variety*. https://variety.com/1996/scene/vpage/cbs-tnt-team-for-games-1117466417

Draper, K. (2020, October 22). TV ratings for many sports are down. Don't read too much into it. *The New York Times*. www.nytimes.com/2020/10/22/sports/tv-ratings-sports.html

Fainaru-Wada, M., & Fainaru, S. (2013, October). *ESPN.com*. www.espn.com/sportsnation/chat/_/id/49069/league-of-denial-authors

Fang, K. (2015, January 25). The NFL on TV has changed dramatically over the last 50 years. *Awful Announcing*. https://awfulannouncing.com/2015/nfl-tv-changed-dramatically-over-the-last-50-years.html

Flood, B. (2020, January 31). The first Super Bowl was broadcast on two networks, but you're not allowed to watch it today. *Fox News*. www.foxnews.com/media/first-super-bowl-tv-broadcast

Gagnon, B. (2013, November 6). The 8 biggest moments in the 10 year history of NFL Network. *Awful Announcing*. https://awfulannouncing.com/2013/the-8-biggest-moments-in-the-10-year-history-of-nfl-network.html

Gaines, C. (2015, December 7). ESPN has lost more than $2 billion because of cord cutting. *Business Insider*. www.businessinsider.com/espn-cord-cutting-losses-2015-12

Gaines, C. (2017, March 7). Cable and satellite TV customers pay more than $9.00 per month for ESPN networks whether they watch them or not. *Business Insider*. www.businessinsider.com/cable-satellite-tv-sub-fees-espn-networks-2017-3

Garcia, A. (2018, January 31). NFL and Fox Sports sign 5-year deal for 'Thursday Night Football.' *CNN*. https://money.cnn.com/2018/01/31/media/nfl-thursday-night-football/index.html

Gaughan, J. (2015, August 11). Premier League just keeps getting richer: Another whopping payday as NBC agrees to $1billion deal to retain US rights. *Mail Online*. https://www.dailymail.co.uk/sport/sportsnews/article-3193629/Premier-League-set-1billion-windfall-new-NBC-live-TV-rights-deal.html

Gerard, J. (1989, January 6). ESPN will pay $400 million for baseball-game rights. *The New York Times*. www.nytimes.com/1989/01/06/business/espn-will-pay-400-million-for-baseball-game-rights.html

Gorman, S. (2008, August 17). Phelps' Olympic feat lifts NBC to 18-year record. *Reuters*. www.reuters.com/article/us-olympics-nbc/phelps-olympic-feat-lifts-nbc-to-18-year-record-idUSN1732689420080818

Hibberd, J, & Landreth, J. (2008, August 24). Beijing Olympics end with massive viewership. *Reuters*. www.reuters.com/article/us-olympics-television/beijing-olympics-end-with-massive-viewership-idUSN2547356720080825

Hiestand, M. (2005, April 18). Football shuffle: MNF to ESPN; NBC gets Sundays. *USA Today*. https://usatoday30.usatoday.com/sports/2005-04-18-nbc-abc_x.htm

Isidore, C. (2014, May 7). NBC nails Olympics right through 2032. *CNN*. https://money.cnn.com/2014/05/07/news/companies/nbc-olympics/index.html?iid=EL

James, M. (2004, August 23). Will ABC sack 'Monday Night Football'? *Baltimore Sun*. www.baltimoresun.com/business/bal-abc0823-story.html

King, A. (2017, August 2). How TV ratings work. *Jalopnik*. https://jalopnik.com/how-tv-ratings-work-1795820157

Koo, B. (2019, October 17). ABC's best shot at a NFL TV package is gaining some momentum. *Awful Announcing*. https://awfulannouncing.com/nfl/abcs-best-shot-at-a-nfl-tv-package-is-gaining-some-momentum.html

Lewis, J. (2008, November). BCS to ESPN? *Sports Media Watch*. www.sportsmediawatch.com/2008/11/bcs-to-espn

Lippman, J. (1990, September 7). Fox network gets cable affiliates deal with TCI. *Los Angeles Times*. www.latimes.com/archives/la-xpm-1990-09-07-fi-566-story.html

Lucia, J. (2019, September 30). ESPN officially announces Bundesliga ESPN+ deal, reportedly paying $30 million per year. *Awful Announcing*. https://awfulannouncing.com/espn/espn-officially-announces-bundesliga-espn-deal-reportedly-paying-30-million-per-year.html

McClintock, P. (2020, January 28). Super Bowl LIV: Most movie ads sitting out the big game as prices soar. *The Hollywood Reporter*. www.hollywoodreporter.com/news/super-bowl-liv-movie-ads-sitting-big-game-as-prices-soar-1273888

Mulligan, T.S. (1992, July 25). Barcelona '92 Olympics: TripleCast sales remain woefully short of projections. *Los Angeles Times*. www.latimes.com/archives/la-xpm-1992-07-25-sp-3983-story.html

Nagle, D. (1986, January 2). ESPN, Inc.: 1985 in review. *ESPN Press Room*. https://espnpressroom.com/us/press-releases/1986/01/1985-banner-year-for-espn

NBC Sports Group. (2019, December 30). NBC's "Sunday Night Football" concludes season on pace to be TV's #1 primetime show for unprecedented 9th consecutive year; 2019 season averages 20.5 million viewers, best in four years. *Press Box*. https://nbcsportsgrouppressbox.com/2019/12/30/nbcs-sunday-night-football-concludes-season-on-pace-to-be-tvs-1-primetime-show-for-unprecedented-9th-consecutive-year-2019-season-averages-20-5-million-viewers-b

Newberry, P. (2008, August 17). 2008 Beijing Olympics—Phelps wins 8 golds. *AP News*. https://apnews.com/article/virus-outbreak-beijing-tokyo-2020-tokyo-olympics-jason-lezak-ab5fce1bc5ad1dc462772a9d931e00c7

Nielsen. (n.d.) TV ratings. www.nielsen.com/us/en/solutions/measurement/television

Noriega, E. (2018, October 29). From slow-motion to live TV. '68 Olympics impacted how we watch today. *Global Sports Matters*. https://globalsportmatters.com/mexico/2018/10/29/from-slow-motion-to-live-tv-68-olympics-impacted-how-we-watch-today

Ourand, J. (2020, November 17). Bassmaster leaving ESPN for Fox Sports after two-decade run. *Sports Business Journal*. www.sportsbusinessdaily.com/Daily/Morning-Buzz/2020/11/17/Bassmaster.aspx

Parker, R. (2015, February 13). 2026 World Cup TV rights awarded without bids; ESPN 'surprised.' *Los Angeles Times*. www.latimes.com/entertainment/envelope/cotown/la-et-ct-2026-world-cup-tv-rights-20150213-story.html

Petski, D. (2017, October 27). 'The Simpsons' showrunner gets back at George H. W. Bush. *Deadline*. https://deadline.com/2017/10/the-simpsons-showrunner-al-jean-george-h-w-bush-1202196474

Porter, R. (2021, February 9). TV Ratings: Super Bowl hits 14-year low. *Hollywood Reporter*. www.hollywoodreporter.com/live-feed/tv-ratings-sunday-feb-7-2021-super-bowl

Reedy, J. (2019, August 24). A look at the seminal broadcasting moves that define the NFL. *AP News*. https://apnews.com/article/e3b17485ab1e4044a379b45f78bcabf1

Riley, C. (2011, June 7). NBC snags Olympics through 2020. *CNN*. https://money.cnn.com/2011/06/07/news/companies/nbc_olympics/index.htm?iid=EL

Sandomir, R. (1992, June 29). Olympics; Triplecast: An Olympian blunder or innovation? *The New York Times*. www.nytimes.com/1992/06/29/sports/olympics-triplecast-an-olympian-blunder-or-innovation.html

Sandomir, R. (1993, December 18). Fox network outbids CBS for rights to pro football. *The New York Times*. www.nytimes.com/1993/12/18/us/fox-network-outbids-cbs-for-rights-to-pro-football.html

Sandomir, R. (1995a, August 8). Olympics; For $1.27 billion, NBC accomplishes an Olympic sweep. *The New York Times*. www.nytimes.com/1995/08/08/us/olympics-for-1.27-billion-nbc-accomplishes-an-olympic-sweep.html

Sandomir, R. (1995b, December 13). Olympics; $2.3 billion deal to give NBC rights to future Olympics. *The New York Times*. www.nytimes.com/1995/12/13/sports/olympics-2.3-billion-deal-to-give-nbc-rights-to-future-olympics.html

Sandomir, R. (1998, January 13). Pro Football: CBS guarantees billions to get N.F.L. back. *The New York Times*. www.nytimes.com/1998/01/13/sports/pro-football-cbs-guarantees-billions-to-get-nfl-back.html

Sandomir, R. (2005, November 23). One night in 1970, the revolution was televised. *The New York Times*. www.nytimes.com/2005/11/23/sports/football/one-night-in-1970-the-revolution-was-televised.html

Sandomir, R. (2011, September 8). ESPN extends deal with N.F.L. for $15 billion. *The New York Times*. www.nytimes.com/2011/09/09/sports/football/espn-extends-deal-with-nfl-for-15-billion.html

Sandomir, R. (2016, April 3). TBS acquires N.C.A.A. Final and fewer eyeballs. *The New York Times*. www.nytimes.com/2016/04/04/sports/ncaabasketball/tbs-acquires-ncaa-final-and-fewer-eyeballs.html

Shapiro, L., & Farhi, P. (1998, January 14). ABC keeps Mondays in record NFL deals. *The Washington Post*. www.washingtonpost.com/archive/politics/1998/01/14/abc-keeps-mondays-in-record-nfl-deals/13e3aff9-ef15-4967-86e4-a61c9aa3c673

Shapiro, L., & Maske, M. (2005, April 19). 'Monday Night Football' changes the channel. *The Washington Post*. www.washingtonpost.com/archive/politics/2005/04/19/monday-night-football-changes-the-channel/e1b638b6-52dd-4442-a996-5ae25f8bc21f

Sharbutt, J. (1998, December 2). NBC gets rights to 1992 Olympics for $401 million. *Los Angeles Times*. www.latimes.com/archives/la-xpm-1988-12-02-sp-1175-story.html

Spence, J. (1988, November 20). Views of sport; Are Olympic TV rights worth the price? *The New York Times*. www.nytimes.com/1988/11/20/sports/views-of-sport-are-olympic-tv-rights-worth-the-price.html

Stanhope, K. (2017, June 15). NBC Universal sets Olympic Channel launch date. *The Hollywood Reporter*. www.hollywoodreporter.com/news/nbcuniversal-sets-olympic-channel-launch-date-1013975

Stewart, L. (1992, August 10). No medals for NBC, gold for Triplecast. *Los Angeles Times*. www.latimes.com/archives/la-xpm-1992-08-10-sp-4894-story.html

Stewart, L. (2002, January 23). NBA finalizes $4.6-billion TV contract. *Los Angeles Times*. www.latimes.com/archives/la-xpm-2002-jan-23-sp-nbatv23-story.html

Stewart, L. (2004, November 23). Fox lands BCS deal for $330 million. *Los Angeles Times*. www.latimes.com/archives/la-xpm-2004-nov-23-sp-bcstv23-story.html

Strauss, B. (2020, November 5). ESPN announces hundreds of layoffs as pandemic, cord-cutting upend sports television. *The Washington Post*. www.washingtonpost.com/sports/2020/11/05/espn-layoffs-coronavirus

Tayler, J. (2014, April 9). Houston Astros get 0.0 television rating for game against Los Angeles Angels. *SI*. www.si.com/mlb/2014/04/09/houston-astros-get-0-0-television-rating

UPI. (1993, July 28). NBC to pay $456 million for 1996 Olympics. www.upi.com/Archives/1993/07/28/NBC-to-pay-456-million-for-1996-Olympics/7747743832000

Weinstein, S. (1989, March 8). "Married" . . . with controversy: Stars defend sitcom that's getting ratings. *Los Angeles Times*. www.latimes.com/archives/la-xpm-1989-03-08-ca-321-story.html

Wulf, S. (1993, December 27). Out Foxed. *Sports Illustrated*. https://vault.si.com/vault/1993/12/27/out-foxed-rupert-murdochs-upstart-network-snatched-the-nfl-from-cbs-in-a-coup-that-will-change-the-face-of-televised-sports

Zinser, L. (2008, November 18). ESPN outbids Fox Sports and wins B.C.S. rights. *The New York Times*. www.nytimes.com/2008/11/19/sports/ncaafootball/19bcs.html

Chapter 3

Affleck, J. (2016). New ball game: Covering sports, with teams as competitors. In G. Sweeney (Ed.), *Global corruption report: Sport* (pp. 352-357). Routledge.

Breech, J. (2020, February 5). 2020 Super Bowl ratings revealed: Chiefs-49ers ranks as the 11th most-watched show in TV history. *CBS Sports*. www.cbssports.com/nfl/news/2020-super-bowl-ratings-revealed-chiefs-49ers-ranks-as-the-11th-most-watched-show-in-tv-history

Busbee, J. (2015, May 3). Periscope proves a new method for pirating Mayweather-Pacquiao. *Yahoo*. https://sports.yahoo.com/blogs/boxing/periscope-proves-an-easy--free-method-for-pirating-mayweather-pacquiao-051526318.html

Costolo, D. [@dickc]. (2015, May 3). *And the winner is . . . @periscopeco* [Tweet]. Twitter. https://twitter.com/dickc/status/594725651854139392

FloridaGators.com. (n.d.) Chris Harry. https://floridagators.com/staff-directory/chris-harry/66

Edison Research. (2020, March 19). *The infinite dial 2020*. www.edisonresearch.com/the-infinite-dial-2020

ESPN. (2020, May 20). *Stephen A. thinks Jayson Tatum, not Luka Doncic, will become NBA's best player* [Video]. YouTube. www.youtube.com/watch?v=9w-jnhRWNbQ

ESPN Press Room. (n.d). ESPN, Inc. fact sheet. https://espnpressroom.com/us/espn-inc-fact-sheet

Finlay, J.P. (2011, March 18). WSFX to lose general manager Thom Postema. *WilmingtonBiz*. www.wilmingtonbiz.com/marketingmedia/2011/03/18/wsfx_to_lose_general_manager_thom_postema/2338

French, A., & Kahn, H. (2012, July 11). The sound and the fury. *Grantland*. https://grantland.com/features/don-imus-mike-mad-dog-fall-rise-first-all-sports-talk-station-wfan

Gagnon, E. (n.d.) Posts [LinkedIn page]. www.linkedin.com/in/emily-gagnon-21800295

Gaines, C. (2013, March 8). Criticism of latest 'First Take' controversy is exactly what ESPN wants. *Business Insider*. www.businessinsider.com/criticism-of-latest-first-take-controversy-is-exactly-what-espn-wants-2013-3

Hall, A. (2019, October 22). Outside the Lines evolving as 30th anniversary year approaches. *ESPN Press Room*. https://espnpressroom.com/us/press-releases/2019/10/outside-the-lines-evolving-as-30th-anniversary-year-approaches

Harry, C. (n.d.) Posts [LinkedIn page]. www.linkedin.com/in/chris-harry-5002921a

Hofheimer, B. (2016, October 19). ESPN signs Tony Kornheiser and Michael Wilbon to new multi-year extensions as *Pardon the Interruption* marks 15th anniversary. *ESPN Press Room*. https://espnpressroom.com/us/press-releases/2016/10/espn-signs-tony-kornheiser-michael-wilbon-new-multi-year-extensions-pardon-interruption-marks-15th-anniversary

Hull, K., & Romney, M. (2020). Welcome to the big leagues: Exploring rookie sports broadcasters' adjustment to new careers. *Journalism & Mass Communication Educator*. Advance online publication.

Jenkins, C. (2000, August 9). League's web site links teams to internet to be just like TV: Profit making. *USA Today*.

Keller, T. (2018, February 7). ESPN's podcast business benefits from history. *ESPN*. www.espnfrontrow.com/2018/02/espns-podcast-business-benefits-from-history

Lewis, D.J. (2020, April 18). Apple podcasts surpasses 1 million podcasts. MyPodcastReviews. https://mypodcastreviews.com/apple-podcasts-surpasses-1-million-podcasts

Malone, M. (2012). Raycom-Belo partnership in Arizona starts 'now.' *Broadcasting & Cable, 142*(5), 20.

Mannix, C. (2015, September 10). Periscope, boxing fighting piracy ahead of Mayweather-Berto bout. *SI*. www.

si.com/boxing/2015/09/10/floyd-mayweather-andre-berto-fight-periscope-illegal-streams-showtime

Marchand, A. (2019, November 7). Stephen A. Smith rakes in almost $8M per year on new ESPN megadeal. *New York Post*. https://nypost.com/2019/11/07/stephen-a-smith-rakes-in-almost-8m-per-year-on-new-espn-megadeal

McCarthy, M. (2020, January 20). ESPN being more "strategic" with new podcasts. *Front Office Sports*. https://frntofficesport.com/espn-podcasts-monetize

Miller, J.A., & Shales, T. (2011). *Those guys have all the fun*. Little, Brown and Company.

Mirer, M. (2018). "I did what I do" versus "I cover football." *Journalism Practice, 12*(3), 251-267.

Mullin, B., & Flint, J. (2019, January 29). For Bill Simmons's the Ringer, podcasting is the main event. *The Wall Street Journal*. www.wsj.com/articles/for-bill-simmonss-the-ringer-podcasting-is-the-main-event-11548673244

Pedersen, E. (2015, April 2). Showtime & HBO charging $90 for Mayweather-Pacquiao PPV—update. *Deadline*. https://deadline.com/2015/04/mayweather-pacquiao-hbo-showtime-pay-per-view-1201378147

Pells, E., & Newberry, P. (2009, October 4). For tweets' sake: Sports world adjusts to new media. *Los Angeles Times*. http://articles.latimes.com/2009/oct/04/sports/sp-dog-media4

Pérez-Peña, R. (2009, September 27). As coverage wanes, Los Angeles Kings hire own reporter. *The New York Times*. www.nytimes.com/2009/09/28/business/media/28kings.html

Pfeifer, S. (2015, May 3). Mayweather-Pacquiao fight promoter vows legal action against piracy. *Los Angeles Times*. www.latimes.com/business/la-fi-mayweather-pacquiao-piracy-20150503-htmlstory.html

Ravanos, D. (2020, May 11). The 7 best shows of ESPN's embrace debate era. Barrett Media. https://barrettsportsmedia.com/2020/05/11/the-7-best-shows-of-espns-embrace-debate-era

Sandomir, R. (2015, May 4). Periscope, a streaming Twitter app, steals the show on boxing's big night. *The New York Times*. www.nytimes.com/2015/05/05/sports/periscope-a-streaming-twitter-app-steals-the-show-on-boxings-big-night.html

Shaw, L. (2020, February 11). Spotify pays $250 million for Ringer in podcasting drive. *Bloomberg*. www.bloomberg.com/news/articles/2020-02-11/spotify-said-to-pay-250-million-for-ringer-in-podcasting-drive

Spanberg, E. (2018, May 7). The podcast revolution. *Sports Business Daily*. www.sportsbusinessdaily.com/Journal/Issues/2018/05/07/Media/Podcast.aspx

Stelter, B. (2012, May 28). You can change the channel, but local news is the same. *The New York Times*. www.nytimes.com/2012/05/29/business/media/local-tv-stations-cut-costs-by-sharing-news-operations.html

Strauss, B. (2020, May 14). Amid layoffs and furloughs, sportswriters wonder what will be left of a storied profession. *The Washington Post*. www.washingtonpost.com/sports/2020/05/14/amid-layoffs-furloughs-sportswriters-wonder-what-will-be-left-once-storied-profession

Sullivan, T. (2013). *Imus, Mike and the Mad Dog & Doris from Rego Park: The groundbreaking history of WFAN*. Triumph Books.

Trumpbour, R.C. (2007). *The new cathedrals: Politics and media in the history of stadium construction*. Syracuse University Press.

TV News Desk. (2020, January 3). *RATINGS: ESPN tops cable networks in key demos in 2019*. www.broadwayworld.com/bwwtv/article/RATINGS-ESPN-Tops-Cable-Networks-in-Key-Demos-in-2019-20200103

TVnewscheck. (2013). *FCC's Pai: JSAs, SSAs vital to TV's survival*. www.tvnewscheck.com/article/65356/fccs-pai-jsas-ssas-vital-to-tvs-survival

Warren, C. (2015, May 3). I watched the Pacquiao-Mayweather fight on Periscope and saw the future. *Mashable*. https://mashable.com/2015/05/03/pacquiao-mayweather-periscope

Yanich, D. (2011). *Local TV news & service agreements: A critical look*. Center for Research & Community Service, University of Delaware.

Yanity, M. (2013). Publishing for paydirt: A case study of an athletic department writer. *International Journal of Sport Communication*, 6(4), 478-489.

Chapter 4

Associated Press. (n.d.). Anonymous sources. www.ap.org/about/news-values-and-principles/telling-the-story/anonymous-sources

Boren, C. (2019, February 7). Kevin Durant fires back at media over free agency coverage: 'Grow up.' *The Washington Post*. www.washingtonpost.com/sports/2019/02/07/kevin-durant-is-fed-up-with-media-i-have-nothing-do-with-knicks

Branch, J. (2015, January 27). The Super Bowl's perfect odd couple. *The New York Times*. www.nytimes.com/2015/01/28/sports/football/seahawks-pete-carroll-allows-marshawn-lynch-to-be-himself.html

Cacciola, S., & Stein, M. (2019, June 30). Kevin Durant to join Nets in N.B.A. free agency. *The New York Times*. www.nytimes.com/2019/06/30/sports/kevin-durant-nets.html

Gribble, A. (2012, October 22). The Plaxico effect: Why Alabama freshmen don't speak to reporters. AL.com www.al.com/alabamafootball/2012/10/the_plaxico_effect_why_alabama.html

Huston, C. (2012, November 21). Sumlin touts Johnny Manziel for Heisman, might allow freshman QB to talk to media. CBS Sports www.cbssports.com/college-football/news/sumlin-touts-johnny-manziel-for-heisman-might-allow-freshman-qb-to-talk-to-media

KNBR [KNBR]. (2019, February 6). *Full Interview: Kevin Durant blasts media's treatment of him, tells reporters to "grow up."* [Video file]. YouTube. www.youtube.com/watch?v=v_ZayLMQQ0g

LHSAA. (n.d.). *Post-game press conference interviews.* http://lhsaa.org/affiliations/media-resources/post-game-press-conference-interviews

MacAdam, A. (2015, June 1). "Butt cut what?" A glossary of audio production terms and definitions. NPR Training/Sources https://training.npr.org/2015/06/01/butt-cut-what-a-glossary-of-production-terms/

MLB. (n.d.). *2016 regular season club/media regulation.* http://mlb.mlb.com/documents/2/5/6/174633256/2016MediaGuidelines_dh5n8alt.pdf

NCAA. (n.d.). *Media coordination manual.* NCAA. https://i.turner.ncaa.com/sites/default/files/images/2019/updated_18-19_mc_stats_manual_1.11.19.pdf

NFL. (n.d.). *2018 media access policy.* https://operations.nfl.com/media/3176/2018-nfl-media-access-policy.pdf

Optus Sport. [OptusSport] (2019, July 7). *Alex Morgan helps USA to World Cup glory against Netherlands.* [Video file]. YouTube. www.youtube.com/watch?v=XYGibGLPfCg

Payne, M. (2015, December 30). Marshawn Lynch trademarks "I'm just here so I won't get fined." *The Washington Post.* www.washingtonpost.com/news/early-lead/wp/2015/12/30/marshawn-lynch-trademarks-im-just-here-so-i-wont-get-fined

Pendergast, S. (2012, November 27). Johnny "football" Manziel can speak! Texas A&M QB talks to the media. Houston Press. www.houstonpress.com/news/johnny-football-manziel-can-speak-texas-aandm-qb-talks-to-the-media-6712510

Whittle, J. (2016, August 1). Muschamp explains why freshmen can't speak. The Big Spur https://247sports.com/college/south-carolina/Article/Muschamp-explains-why-freshmen-cant-speak-46538452

Chapter 5

Butera, J. (2015) *Write like you talk.* Author.

Filak, V. F. (2019). *Dynamics of news reporting & writing.* CQ Press.

Halbrooks, G. (2018, December 17). B-roll to VO SOT: Definitions of common TV broadcasting terms. The Balance Careers. www.thebalancecareers.com/common-tv-broadcasting-terms-2315195

Harrower, T. (2013). *Inside reporting. A practical guide to the craft of journalism.* McGraw-Hill.

Kern, J. (2008). *Sound reporting.* University of Chicago Press.

Panthers.com (2019, October 11). *Ron Rivera Friday press conference transcript.* www.panthers.com/news/ron-rivera-friday-press-conference-transcript

Traffis, C. (n.d.) Active vs. passive voice. *Grammarly.* www.grammarly.com/blog/active-vs-passive-voice

Chapter 6

Adler, K. (2019, November 26). No. 1 and best October audience on record for the ESPN app and ESPN Fantasy app. *ESPN Press Room.* https://espnpressroom.com/us/press-releases/2019/11/no-1-and-best-october-audience-on-record-for-the-espn-app-and-espn-fantasy-app

Associated Press. (n.d.a). *About us.* www.ap.org/about

Associated Press. (n.d.b). *AP by the numbers.* www.ap.org/about/annual-report/2018/ap-by-the-numbers

Associated Press. (2019, May 7). Moreland homers, has 3 RBIs to help Red Sox beat Orioles 8-5. *ESPN.* www.espn.com/mlb/recap?gameId=401075268

Baseballhall.org. (n.d.) *J.G. Taylor Spink award.* https://baseballhall.org/discover-more/awards/884

BoardStudios.com, T. (2017, July 24). How to stay ahead of your website visitors' dwindling attention spans. B2BNXT. https://b2bnxt.com/how-to-stay-ahead-of-your-website-visitors-dwindling-attention-spans

Blum, R. (2019, December 11). Yankees sign ace Gerrit Cole on record $324 million, 9-year deal. www.boston.com/sports/mlb/2019/12/11/gerrit-cole-yankees-contract

Brooks, B. S., Pinson, J. L., & Wilson, J. G. (2020). *Working with words.* Bedford/St. Martin's.

Demers, T. (2017, July 20). How to build a strong digital brand in online publishing: Bill Simmons on his career at ESPN. www.digitalexaminer.com/build-strong-digital-brand

ESPN Press Room. (n.d.) *ESPN, Inc. fact sheet.* https://espnpressroom.com/us/espn-inc-fact-sheet

ESPN.com (2009). *Gammons leaving ESPN.* www.espn.com/mlb/news/story?id=4725366

Froke, P., Bratton, A. J., Garcia, O., McMillan, J., & Schwartz, J. (Eds.) (2019). *The Associated Press Stylebook 2019.* The Associated Press.

Gisondi, J. (2018). *Field guide to covering sports.* CQ Press.

Hu, E. (2011, August 17). From broadcast to the web: Writing tips from the digital editors. StateImpact. https://stateimpact.npr.org/toolbox/2011/08/17/from-broadcast-to-the-web-writing-tips-from-the-digital-editors

Knight Foundation. (2019). *Local TV news and the new media landscape.* https://knightfoundation.org/reports/local-tv-news-and-the-new-media-landscape

Miller, J. A., & Shales, T. (2011) *Those guys have all the fun: Inside the world of ESPN.* Little, Brown and Company.

Moran, K. (2020, April 5). How people read online: New and old findings. Nielsen Norman Group. www.nngroup.com/articles/how-people-read-online

Olney, B. (2009, December 11). One of many. ESPN. https://web.archive.org/web/20100211042630/http://insider.espn.go.com/espn/blog/index?entryID=4733669&name=olney_buster&action=login&appRedirect=http://insider.espn.go.com/espn/blog/index?entryID=4733669&name=olney_buster

Pascarelli, P. (2009, December 11). An appreciation of Peter Gammons. ESPN. www.espn.com/mlb/news/story?id=4734632

Pew Research Center. (2019, March 26). For local news, American embrace digital but still want strong community connection. Pew Research Center. www.journalism.org/2019/03/26/for-local-news-americans-embrace-digital-but-still-want-strong-community-connection

Stokes, J. (2005, April 13). 2005 edition of AP Stylebook now available. Associated Press. https://web.archive.org/web/20110119025351/http://ap.org/pages/about/pressreleases/pr_041305a.html

Stovall, J. G. (2012). *Writing for the mass media*. Pearson.

Testa, K. (2009, December 8). Peter Gammons: The reason we can all do what we do. Bleacher Report. https://bleacherreport.com/articles/305200-peter-gammons-the-reason-we-can-all-do-what-we-do

The Missouri Group. (2020). *News reporting and writing*. Bedford/St. Martin's.

WECT.com. (2000, September 28). News Six at 6. WECT https://web.archive.org/web/20001019015018/https://www.wect.com

Wiggins, E., Smith, L, & Sisk, L. (2017). *Writing for mass communications*. Kendall Hunt.

Witz, B. (2013, September 29). Southern California calls Kiffin off the team bus and then fires him. *The New York Times*. www.nytimes.com/2013/09/30/sports/ncaafootball/usc-fires-its-football-coach.html

Chapter 7

Bieler, D. (2016, February 1). Mexican puppets and "Pick Boy" were back for more Super Bowl media day wackiness. *The Washington Post*. www.washingtonpost.com/news/early-lead/wp/2016/02/01/mexican-puppets-and-pick-boy-were-back-for-more-super-bowl-media-day-wackiness

Clapp, B. (2015, June 29). A day in the life: Producing live sports. Work in Sports. www.workinsports.com/blog/live-sports-production-day-in-the-life

Frechette, C. (2012, August 13). How journalists can improve video stories with shot sequences. Poynter. www.poynter.org/newsletters/2012/how-journalists-can-improve-video-stories-with-shot-sequences

Fuller, J. (2019, January 23). Hoggard swimming wins another MEC title. *Star News*. www.starnewsonline.com/sports/20190123/hoggard-swimming-wins-another-mec-title

Lambert, T.A. (2018, February 7). Quay Walker signs with Georgia; fakes out Tennessee fans. *RockyTopTalk*. www.rockytoptalk.com/2018/2/7/16986546/national-signing-day-quay-walker-signs-with-georgia-fakes-out-tennessee-fans

Moore, T. (2020, January 28). Super Bowl Media Day turns into bigger farce with fans paying for entrance, expensive night at venue. *Forbes*. www.forbes.com/sites/terencemoore/2020/01/28/among-other-things-folks-paid-10-for-a-bud-light-to-watch-super-bowl-interviews/#675d9a326867

Owens, J. (2016). *Television sports production* (5th edition). Focal Press.

Rill, J. (2019, December 18). Texas A&M commit Donell Harris fakes out Florida during signing ceremony. *Saturday Down South*. www.saturdaydownsouth.com/florida-football/texas-am-commit-donell-harris-fakes-out-florida-during-signing-ceremony

Schultz, B. (2015). *Sports media: Reporting, producing and planning*. Elsevier.

Wilder, C. (2019, January 29). How the Super Bowl's opening night has evolved into the spectacle it is today. *Sports Illustrated*. www.si.com/nfl/2019/01/29/super-bowl-opening-night-patriots-rams-media-day

Zumoff, M., & Negin, M. (2015). *Total sportscasting: Performance, production, and career development*. Focal Press.

Chapter 8

Curtis, B. (2019, September 4). The Big Show never ends: How Dan and Keith's "SportsCenter" changed TV forever. *The Ringer*. www.theringer.com/2019/9/4/20848656/sportscenter-dan-patrick-keith-olbermann-espn-40-anniversary

Miller, J.A., & Shales, T. (2011). *Those guys have all the fun: Inside the world of ESPN*. Little, Brown and Company.

Scott, D. (2019, September 8). The inside story of SportsCenter's "Big Show" reunion from two of the episode's producers. *ESPN Front Row*. www.espnfrontrow.com/2019/09/the-inside-story-of-sportscenters-big-show-reunion-from-two-of-the-episodes-producers

Chapter 9

Axelrod, J. (2020, July 19). The sounds of silence: Sports try to deal with no fans in the stands. *Pittsburgh Post-Gazette*. https://medina-gazette.com/news/228805/the-sounds-of-silence-sports-try-to-deal-with-no-fans-in-the-stands

Barney, C. (2019, September 17). KNBR, former Warriors player Tom Tolbert agree to multiyear deal. *The Mercury News*. www.mercurynews.com/2019/09/17/knbr-tom-tolbert-agree-to-multiyear-deal

Costello, S. (2020, January 12). History of the iPod: From the first iPod to the iPod classic. *Lifewire*. www.lifewire.com/history-ipod-classic-original-2000732

Edison Research. (2019, April 5). The podcast consumer. *Edison Research*. www.edisonresearch.com/the-podcast-consumer-2019

Emmons, S. (1995, May 10). Just what do talk shows listen for? Radio: Even if your phone call passes the screening, don't forget the genre's first commandments: Thou shalt not be boring. *Los Angeles Times*. www.latimes.com/archives/la-xpm-1995-05-10-ls-64329-story.html

Finn, C. (2020, April 16). WEEI trails far behind The Sports Hub in Boston sports radio winter ratings. *Boston.com.* www.boston.com/sports/media/2020/04/16/boston-sports-radio-ratings-weei

Hammersley, B. (2004, February 11). Audible revolution. *The Guardian.* www.theguardian.com/media/2004/feb/12/broadcasting.digitalmedia

Kern, J. (2008). *Sound reporting. The NPR guide to audio journalism and production.* University of Chicago Press.

Lamirand, D. (2020, March 12). The essential plumbing podcast list for contractors. *Service Titan.* www.servicetitan.com/blog/best-plumbing-podcasts

Masisak, C. (2009, October 26). Simmons is not just a regular "sports guy." *Washington Times.* www.washingtontimes.com/news/2009/oct/26/simmons-not-just-a-regular-sports-guy

Media Services. (2019, June 24). KNBR signs Greg Papa to multi-year deal, new lineup to debut July 16. Cumulus Media. www.knbr.com/2019/06/24/knbr-signs-greg-papa-to-multi-year-deal-new-lineup-to-debut-july-16

Mike & The Mad Dog. (2019, August 1). Best of "Mike and the Mad Dog": An argument over the new Yankee Stadium. *WFAN.* wfan.radio.com/articles/best-mike-and-mad-dog-argument-over-new-yankee-stadium

Miller, J. (2019, July 18). Have we hit peak podcast? *The New York Times.* www.nytimes.com/2019/07/18/style/why-are-there-so-many-podcasts.html

Miller, J.A., & Shales, T. (2011). *Those guys have all the fun: Inside the world of ESPN.* Little, Brown.

Neumary, T., & Kerris, N. (2005, June 28). Apple takes podcasting mainstream. *Apple Newsroom.* www.apple.com/newsroom/2005/06/28Apple-Takes-Podcasting-Mainstream/

Paumgarten, N. (2004, August 23). The boys. *The New Yorker.* www.newyorker.com/magazine/2004/08/30/the-boys-4

Perks, L.G., & Turner, J. S. (2019). Podcasts and productivity: A qualitative uses and gratifications study. *Mass Communication and Society, 22*(1), 96-116.

Powell, B. (2008, August 25). Stu Scott interview with Barack Obama to air on Sports Center tonight. *Awful Announcing.* https://awfulannouncing.com/2008-articles/stu-scott-interview-with-barack-obama-to-air-on-sports-center-tonight.html

Sandomir, R. (2015, May 8). ESPN is splitting with Bill Simmons, who offers an uncharacteristic word count: Zero. *The New York Times.* www.nytimes.com/2015/05/09/sports/bill-simmons-and-espn-are-parting-ways.html

Simmons, B. (2012, March 1). B.S. report: Barack Obama. *Grantland.* http://grantland.com/the-triangle/b-s-report-barack-obama

Stelter, B. (2008, April 16). ESPN drops Obama interview. *The New York Times.* https://thecaucus.blogs.nytimes.com/2008/04/16/espn-drops-obama-interview

Vasquez, F. (2017, July 6). Mike and the Mad Dog brought Mike Piazza to the Mets. *Mets Hot Corner.* www.metshotcorner.com/2017/mike-and-the-mad-dog-brought-mike-piazza-to-the-mets

Winsper, S. (2020, April 1). 15 of the best knitting podcasts. *Gathered.* www.gathered.how/knitting-and-crochet/knitting/10-of-the-best-knitting-podcasts

Chapter 10

Agrest, J. (2020, January 30). Defending Joe Buck is easy; changing detractors' minds is hard. *Chicago Sun Times.* https://chicago.suntimes.com/2020/1/30/21115380/joe-buck-jack-buck-troy-aikman-fox-sports-super-bowl-liv-49ers-chiefs-nfl

Allen, K. (2015, February 20). 6 great myths about the Miracle on Ice. *USA Today.* https://ftw.usatoday.com/2015/02/6-great-myths-about-the-miracle-on-ice

Associated Press. (2014, March 11). Final Four "teamcasts" means biased announcing will be best. www.sportingnews.com/us/ncaa-basketball/news/ncaa-tournament-final-four-teamcasts-means-biased-announcing-will-be-best/c6e4s8i9q43d1xtu7xuetkv72

Brock, H. (1980, February 23). AP was there: An Olympic "miracle on ice" as US shocks USSR. *USA Today.* www.usatoday.com/story/sports/olympics/2020/02/20/ap-was-there-an-olympic-miracle-on-ice-as-us-shocks-ussr/111338174

Carolina Panthers. (2019). 2019 media guide. https://static.clubs.nfl.com/image/upload/v1564188088/panthers/zw6dnlvcpze9zmvo6g0g.pdf

Clapp, B. (2015, March 18). A week in the life of a sideline reporter for the NFL on Fox. Work in Sports. www.workinsports.com/blog/a-week-in-the-life-of-a-sideline-reporter-for-the-nfl-on-fox

Clapp, M. (2019, October 20). Joe Buck lets the moment do the talking after Jose Altuve's pennant-clinching home run. Awful Announcing. https://awfulannouncing.com/fox/joe-buck-lets-the-moment-do-the-talking-after-jose-altuves-pennant-clinching-home-run.html

Cohen, B., & Beaton, A. (2019, January 30). Tony Romo calls plays before they happen. How often is he actually right? *The Wall Street Journal.* www.wsj.com/articles/tony-romo-play-predictions-super-bowl-11548805802

Cooper, S. (2014, April 5). Some people on Twitter are very confused by the biases of the Kentucky Teamcast announcers. Yahoo! Sports. https://sports.yahoo.com/blogs/ncaab-the-dagger/some-people-on-twitter-are-very-confused-by-the-biases-of-the-kentucky-teamcast-announcers-023735276.html

Diamond, J. (2012, September 26). How biased is your announcer? *The Wall Street Journal.* www.wsj.com/articles/SB10000872396390444180004578016652376246198

Francis, B. (2020). Mercy! Ken Harrelson honored by election as 2020 Frick Award winner. National Baseball Hall of Fame. https://baseballhall.org/discover/ken-harrelson-honored-by-election-as-2020-frick-award-winner

Goldberg, J. (1999, December 3). SI awards: Ali the century's greatest. *Hartford Courant*.www.courant.com/news/connecticut/hc-xpm-1999-12-03-9912030176-story.html

Helfand, Z. (2019, January 28). Why Tony Romo is a genius at football commentary. *The New Yorker*. www.newyorker.com/sports/sporting-scene/why-tony-romo-is-a-genius-at-football-commentary

Hyman, D. (2015, April 22). Hawk Harrelson: Baseball's ultimate home still rules on the South Side. *Rolling Stone*. www.rollingstone.com/culture/culture-sports/hawk-harrelson-baseballs-ultimate-homer-still-rules-on-the-south-side-120747/

Impact of Television. (n.d.). Impact of television. National Football League. https://operations.nfl.com/the-game/impact-of-television

Kelly, T. (2020, April 6). Joe Buck reveals why you think he hates your favorite team. Audacy. www.radio.com/sports/joe-buck-reveals-why-you-think-he-hates-your-favorite-team

Marchand, A. (2020, March 2). CBS tried hiring Peyton Manning before giving Tony Romo $180 million. *New York Post*. https://nypost.com/2020/03/02/cbs-tried-hiring-peyton-manning-before-giving-tony-romo-180-million

Michaels, A. (2014). *You can't make this up: Miracles, memories, and the perfect marriage of sports and television*. William Morrow.

NCAA. (2014, April 1). Announcers selected for regionalized Final Four broadcasts. NCAA. www.ncaa.com/news/basketball-men/article/2014-04-01/announcers-selected-regionalized-final-four-broadcasts-tnt

Nelson, J. (1995, September 7). For Cal Ripken Jr., it was 2131 consecutive games. For Chris Berman, it was 19 consecutive minutes of silence. Associated Press. https://apnews.com/a04366413d20fedec70c47654e1d5c48

NPR. (2018, June 5). Mike 'Doc' Emrick is NBC's wizard of hockey play-by-play. NPR. www.npr.org/2018/06/05/617029593/mike-doc-emrick-is-nbcs-wizard-of-hockey-play-by-play

Owens, J. (2016). *Television sports production* (5th ed.). Focal Press.

Reedy, J. (2020a, January 31). Sideline view: Erin Andrews, Chris Myers have key role for Super Bowl. Associated Press. https://apnews.com/ee8ad72c4fb69b1f75beeff319e25e59

Reedy, J. (2020b, February 21). Miracle on Ice shows how much Olympics on TV have changed. Associated Press. https://apnews.com/6167daf10b894dc016008ac3ed488b0b

Ribowsky, M. (2011). *Howard Cosell: The man, the myth, and the transformation of American sports*. W.W. Norton & Company.

Sandomir, R. (2000, February 22). TVSports; "Miracle on Ice" of 1980 looks different today. *The New York Times*. www.nytimes.com/2000/02/22/sports/tv-sports-miracle-on-ice-of-1980-looks-different-today.html

Schultz, B. (2015). *Sports media: Reporting, producing and planning*. Elsevier.

Sherman, E. (2015, October 29). Tom Verducci calls the World Series games then writes about them. Poynter. www.poynter.org/reporting-editing/2015/tom-verducci-calls-the-world-series-games-then-writes-about-them

Steinberg, D. (2017, October 23). What is that giant chart ESPN's Sean McDonough is holding, and where did it come from? *The Washington Post*. www.washingtonpost.com/news/dc-sports-bog/wp/2017/10/23/what-is-that-giant-chart-espns-sean-mcdonough-is-holding-and-where-did-it-come-from

Turori, M. (2013, August 20). Creating a football spotting chart. Sportscasters Talent Agency of America.\ https://staatalent.com/creating-a-football-spotting-chart

Vaccaro, M. (2015, February 21). "Do you believe in miracles?": The 8 best sports calls ever. *New York Post*. https://nypost.com/2015/02/21/do-you-believe-in-miracles-the-8-best-sports-calls-ever

Zumoff, M., & Negin, M. (2015). *Total sportscasting: Performance, production, and career development*. Focal Press.

Chapter 11

Adornato, A.C. (2014). A digital juggling act: New media's impact on the responsibilities of local television reporters. *Electronic News*, *8*(1), 3-29.

Alexander, J.M. (2020, January 29). Former UNC star Rick Fox: inaccurate death report "shook a lot of people in my life." *The News & Observer*. www.newsobserver.com/sports/article239751923.html

Blood, R. (2000, September 7) Weblogs: A history and perspective. Rebecca's Pocket. www.rebeccablood.net/essays/weblog_history.html

Brady, J. (2017, November 2). ESPN's new social guidelines show right instincts. *ESPN*. www.espn.com/blog/ombudsman/post/_/id/896/espns-new-social-guidelines-show-right-instincts

Brady, J. (2018, January 18). ESPN's evolution: Snapchat, esports and attribution guidelines. *ESPN*. www.espn.com/blog/ombudsman/post/_/id/912/espns-evolution-snapchat-esports-and-attribution-guidelines

Branch, J., Bogel-Burroughs, N., Mervosh, S., & Jordan, M. (2020, February 8). "Helicopter went down, flames seen": Kobe Bryant's last flight. *The New York Times*. www.nytimes.com/2020/02/08/us/kobe-bryant-crash-reconstruction.html

Bucholtz, A. (2019, November 2). Twitter and Facebook execs say they now have no plans to bid big on live sports. Awful Announcing. https://awfulannouncing.com/tech/twitter-and-facebook-dont-plan-to-bid-big-on-live-sports-rights.html

Cachero, P. (2020, January 30). An ABC News correspondent was suspended for erroneously reporting on the deaths of Kobe Bryant's children. *Insider.* www.insider.com/abc-news-matt-gutman-suspended-inaccurate-report-kobe-bryants-death-2020-1

Chokshi, N. (2019, March 19). Myspace, once the king of social networks, lost years of data from its heyday. *The New York Times.* www.nytimes.com/2019/03/19/business/myspace-user-data.html

Clement, J. (2019, October 10). Percentage of U.S. internet users who use Snapchat as of 3rd quarter 2019, by age group. Statista. www.statista.com/statistics/814300/snapchat-users-in-the-united-states-by-age

Crouse, K. (2013, April 13). After two-stroke penalty, Woods plays on. *The New York Times.* www.nytimes.com/2013/04/14/sports/golf/woods-faces-disqualification-at-augusta.html

D'Zurilla, C. (2020, January 29). Ellen Pompeo accuses TMZ of abusive behavior after Kobe Bryant death coverage. *Los Angeles Times.* www.latimes.com/entertainment-arts/tv/story/2020-01-29/ellen-pompeo-tmz-kobe-bryant

Darcy, O. (2020, January 26). Police scold TMZ after outlet was first to report death of Kobe Bryant. *CNN.* www.cnn.com/2020/01/26/media/tmz-death-report-kobe-bryant/index.html

de Zúñiga, H.G., Lewis, S.C., Willard, A., Valenzuela, S., Lee, J.K., & Baresch, B. (2011). Blogging as a journalistic practice: A model linking perception, motivation, and behavior. *Journalism, 12*(5), 586-606.

ESPN. (n.d.). *Social media guidelines.* www.espnfrontrow.com/wp-content/uploads/2017/11/NOV-2-RECEIVED-UPDATED-SOCIAL-MEDIA-GUIDELINES-10.221.pdf

Flynn, K. (2019, May 28). "We've just gotten smarter": Why ESPN is rolling out more Snapchat shows. *Digiday.* https://digiday.com/media/espn-snapchat-investment

Frier, S. (2016, April 29). Snapchat scores unique deal with NBC to showcase Olympics. *Bloomberg.* www.bloomberg.com/news/articles/2016-04-29/snapchat-scores-unprecedented-deal-with-nbc-to-showcase-olympics

Fry, J. (2012, July 6). ESPN faces challenges in Twitter era. *ESPN.* www.espn.com/blog/poynterreview/post/_/id/373/espn-faces-challenges-in-twitter-era

Gaines, C. (2012, January 18). The most popular athletes on Twitter. *Business Insider.* www.businessinsider.com/athletes-with-two-million-twitter-followers-2012-1

Gisondi, J. (2018). *Field guide to covering sports.* CQ Press.

Granovetter, M.S. (1973). The strength of weak ties. *American Journal of Sociology, 78,* 1360-1380.

Gray Television. (2014). 2014 Employee Handbook. https://ssa.gray.tv/SHCM/ahess/docs/Employee%20 Handbook.pdf

Gray Television. (n.d.) About—Gray Television. https://gray.tv/about

Gregory, S. (2009, June 5). Twitter craze is rapidly changing the face of sports. *Sports Illustrated.* www.si.com/more-sports/2009/06/05/twitter-sports

Gutman, M. [@mattgutmanABC]. (2020, January 26). Today I inaccurately reported it was believed that four of Kobe Bryant's children were on board that flight. That is incorrect. I apologize to Kobe's family, friends and our viewers. [Tweet]. https://twitter.com/mattgutmanABC/status/1221636913402007552

Harig, B. (2013, April 13). Tiger Woods penalized 2 shots. *ESPN.* http://espn.go.com/golf/masters13/story/_/id/9167230/2013-masters-tiger-penalized-2-strokes-ball-drop-15

Horton, D., & Wohl, R. R. (1956). Mass communication and parasocial interaction: Observations on intimacy at a distance. *Psychiatry, 19*(3), 215-229.

Hull, K. (2014a). A hole in one (hundred forty characters): A case study examining PGA tour golfers' Twitter use during The Masters. *International Journal of Sport Communication, 7*(2), 245-260.

Hull, K. (2014b). #Fight4UNCWSwimandDive: A case study of how college athletes used twitter to help save their teams. *International Journal of Sport Communication, 7*(4), 533-552.

Hull, K. (2015). How local television sports broadcasters are using Twitter: Informing and engaging their followers, promoting their sportscasts, and using self-presentation techniques (Doctoral dissertation, University of Florida). ProQuest.

Hull, K. (2016a, June). *Branding techniques used by local television sports broadcasters in their Twitter profiles* [Paper presentation]. North American Society for Sport Management (NASSM) National Conference, Orlando, FL.

Hull, K. (2016b). A lack of Twitter training for broadcasters. *Journal of Media Education, 7*(2), 32-40.

Hull, K. (2016c). Did I tweet that? Local sports broadcasters are not using Twitter how they think they are. *Journal of Sports Media, 11*(2), 22-44.

Hull, K. (2016d). Examining local sports broadcasters' use of Twitter to cross-promote on-air and online content. *Journal of Media Business Studies, 13*(4), 241-256.

Hull, K. (2016e). "I love Twitter": A case study exploring local sports broadcasters' impressions of Twitter. *International Journal of Sport Communication, 9*(4), 519-533.

Hull, K. (2017). Self-presentation techniques used by local sports broadcasters on Twitter. *The Journal of Social Media in Society, 6*(2), 116-151.

Hull K., & Lewis, N.P. (2014). Why Twitter displaces broadcast sports media: A model. *International Journal of Sports Communication, (7)*1, 16-33.

Johnson, S. (2009, June 5). How Twitter will change the way we live. *Time Magazine.* www.time.com/time/magazine/article/0,9171,1902818,00.html

Joseph, A. (2018a, August 13). Antonio Brown blasts reporter on Twitter over an injury tweet. *USA Today.*

https://ftw.usatoday.com/2018/08/antonio-brown-steelers-reporter-tweet-injury-limping-training-camp-nfl

Joseph, A. (2018b, July 1). LeBron James announced that he would be joining the Lakers in the least dramatic way. *USA Today*. https://ftw.usatoday.com/2018/07/lebron-james-lakers-klutch-announcement-nba-free-agency-los-angeles-rich-paul-reaction

Keeley, S. (2018, November 16). *Roanoke Times* and reporter Andy Bitter settle lawsuits over Twitter account he took with him to The Athletic. Awful Announcing. https://awfulannouncing.com/twitter/andy-bitter-twitter-roanoke-times-lawsuit-settled.html

Larson, S. (2017, November 7). Welcome to a world with 280-character tweets. CNN. https://money.cnn.com/2017/11/07/technology/twitter-280-character-limit/index.html

Mansfield, E. (2010). Celebrity tweeting: Why it does not work for everyone. *O&P Business News, 19*(6), 76-76.

Martin, N. (2016, April 29). NBC strikes deal with Snapchat to share Olympics coverage for first time ever. *The Washington Post*. www.washingtonpost.com/news/early-lead/wp/2016/04/29/nbc-strikes-deal-with-snapchat-to-share-olympics-coverage-for-first-time-ever/

Moreau, E. (2020, May 7). What is Instagram and why should you be using it? www.lifewire.com/what-is-instagram-3486316

Murakami, T. [@LASDMurakami]. (2020, January 26). I am saddened that I was gathering facts as media outlet reported Kobe had passed. I understand getting the scoop but please allow us time to make personal notifications to their loved ones. It's very cold to hear the loss via media. Breaks my heart. [Tweet]. https://twitter.com/lasdmurakami/status/1221578597032329216

Newton, C. (2016, October 28). Why Vine died. www.theverge.com/2016/10/28/13456208/why-vine-died-twitter-shutdown

New York Times. (2017, October 13)..The *Times* issues social media guidelines for the newsroom. *The New York Times*. www.nytimes.com/2017/10/13/reader-center/social-media-guidelines.html

O'Connell, B. (2020, February 28). History of Snapchat: Timeline and facts. The Street. www.thestreet.com/technology/history-of-snapchat

Patel, S. (2016, August 25). 2.2 billion views: How NBCU and BuzzFeed scored on Snapchat during Rio Olympics. *Digiday*. https://digiday.com/media/2-2bn-views-nbcu-scored-snapchat-rio-olympics/

Pegoraro, A. (2010). Look who's talking—athletes on Twitter: A case study. *International Journal of Sport Communication, 3*(4), 501-514.

Perrin, A., & Anderson, M. (2019, April 10). Share of U.S. adults using social media, including Facebook, is mostly unchanged since 2018. Pew Research Center. www.pewresearch.org/fact-tank/2019/04/10/share-of-u-s-adults-using-social-media-including-facebook-is-mostly-unchanged-since-2018/

Petski, D. (2017, November 13). ESPN launches "SportsCenter" on Snapchat. *Deadline*. https://deadline.com/2017/11/espn-launches-sportscenter-snapchat-1202206890/

Phillips, M. (2018a, August 7). *Roanoke Times* owner is suing paper's former Hokies football reporter over Twitter account. *Richmond Times-Dispatch*. www.richmond.com/sports/college/schools/virginia-tech/the-roanoke-times-is-suing-its-former-hokies-football-reporter/article_0b2769fc-a7a4-5474-a34f-bd4d7212a05a.html

Phillips, M. (2018b, August 30). Former *Roanoke Times* reporter countersues for more than $150,000 in Twitter case. *Richmond Times-Dispatch*. www.richmond.com/sports/college/schools/virginia-tech/former-roanoke-times-reporter-countersues-for-more-than-in-twitter/article_0404201e-ea6b-52e3-b8c5-eac46230c69c.html

Phillips, M. (2018c, November 15). Andy Bitter, *Roanoke Times* settle lawsuit over Virginia Tech Twitter account. *Richmond Times-Dispatch*. www.richmond.com/sports/college/schools/virginia-tech/andy-bitter-roanoke-times-settle-lawsuit-over-virginia-tech-twitter-account/article_3ebce8af-ee8f-5a65-82e6-7c3f0c3979bb.html

Reisinger, A. (2018). Destination LeBron. *ESPN*. www.espn.com/espn/feature/story/_/id/22453452/destination-lebron-where-king-james-land-free-agency-summer

Sanderson, J. (2011). *It's a whole new ballgame: How social media is changing sports*. Hampton Press.

Schultz, B., & Sheffer, M.L. (2008). Left behind: Local television and the community of sport. *Western Journal of Communication, 72*(2), 180-195.

Schultz, B., & Sheffer, M.L. (2009). Resisting change: Blogging and local sports media. *Journal of Communication Studies, 2*(4), 372-385.

Sehl, K. (2019, December 20). 27 top Facebook demographics that matter to social media marketers. Hootsuite. https://blog.hootsuite.com/facebook-demographics

Shoemaker, P.J., & Vos, T.P. (2009). *Gatekeeping theory*. Routledge.

Simo, F. (2016, April 6). Introducing new ways to create, share and discover live video on Facebook. Facebook. https://about.fb.com/news/2016/04/introducing-new-ways-to-create-share-and-discover-live-video-on-facebook

Skipper, J. (2017, November 2). ESPN's social media guidelines. *ESPN*. www.espnfrontrow.com/2017/11/espns-social-media-guidelines/

Social media. (2017). https://14iezz3qg8u21xburg-26fglg-wpengine.netdna-ssl.com/wp-content/uploads/2017/11/NOV-2-RECEIVED-UPDATED-SOCIAL-MEDIA-GUIDELINES-10.221.pdf

Stein, M. (2018, June 30). The N.B.A. has the hottest stove. LeBron James is the flame. *The New York Times*. www.nytimes.com/2018/06/30/sports/nba-free-agency-lebron-james.html

Tracy, M. (2020, January 27). In haste to confirm Kobe Bryant news, news media stumbles. *The New York Times.* www.nytimes.com/2020/01/27/business/tmz-kobe.html

Walker, L. (2019, November 12). How to set up Facebook. www.lifewire.com/tutorial-how-facebook-works-2654610

Wong, A. (2019, February 23). Their news isn't new: Sports anchors in the era of social media. *The New York Times.* www.nytimes.com/2019/02/23/sports/sportscenter-anchors-highlights-scott-van-pelt.html

Yu, R. (2012, April 20). More companies quit blogging, go with Facebook instead. *USA Today.* http://usatoday30.usatoday.com/tech/news/story/2012-04-19/corporate-blogging/54419982/1

Chapter 12

ESPN Press Room. (n.d.). Sage Steele. https://espnpressroom.com/us/bios/steele_sage

Hull, K., & Romney, M. (2021). Welcome to the big leagues: Exploring rookie sports broadcasters' adjustment to new careers. *Journalism & Mass Communication Educator, 76*(2), 135-155.

Mandella, A. (2018). *The value of internships in radio broadcasting* [Thesis]. University of Wisconsin–Milwaukee. https://dc.uwm.edu/etd/1869

McDonough, K., Rodriguez, L., & Prior-Miller, M.R. (2009). A comparison of student interns and supervisors regarding internship performance ratings. *Journalism & Mass Communication Educator, 64*(2), 139-155.

Privott, L. (2020, September 9). Nashville women in sports media: Dawn Davenport of 104.5 The Zone. *A to Z Sports Nashville.* https://atozsportsnashville.com/nashville-women-sports-dawn-davenport

Wenger, D., & Owens, L.C. (2013). An examination of job skills required by top US broadcast news companies and potential impact on journalism curricula. *Electronic News, 7*(1), 22-35.

White, L. (2018). Broadcast industry employment report. *Journal of Media Education, 9*(3), 49-83.

Chapter 13

APSE. (n.d.). *Ethics guidelines.* www.apsportseditors.com/apse-ethics-guidelines

Associated Press. (2014, May 12). Networks don't hesitate on Sam. *ESPN.* www.espn.com/nfl/story/_/id/10921644/michael-sam-coverage-networks-was-business-usual

Baranauckas, C. (2013, July 20). 'Let Them Wear Towels,' said early female sportswriters. *The Washington Post.* www.washingtonpost.com/blogs/she-the-people/wp/2013/07/20/let-them-wear-towels-pioneering-female-sportswriters-with-lessons-for-all-of-us

Beck, H., & Branch, J. (2013, April 29). With the words 'I'm gay,' an N.B.A. center breaks a barrier. *The New York Times.* www.nytimes.com/2013/04/30/sports/basketball/nba-center-jason-collins-comes-out-as-gay.html

Beckstead, L. (2020). Pass the mic. https://passthemic.fcad.ryerson.ca

Best, N. (2017, October 10). Donald Trump reacts to ESPN's suspension of Jemele Hill in tweet. *Newsday.* www.newsday.com/donald-trump-reacts-to-espn-s-suspension-of-jemele-hill-in-tweet-1.14422178

Bieler, D. (2015a, July 5). Giants' Jason Pierre-Paul reportedly damages hand in fireworks accident. *The Washington Post.* www.washingtonpost.com/news/early-lead/wp/2015/07/05/giants-jason-pierre-paul-reportedly-damages-hand-in-fireworks-accident

Bieler, B. (2015b, July 8). ESPN's Adam Schefter tweets medical record showing Jason Pierre-Paul had finger amputated. *The Washington Post.* www.washingtonpost.com/news/early-lead/wp/2015/07/08/espns-adam-schefter-tweets-medical-record-showing-jason-pierre-paul-had-finger-amputated

Bonesteel, M. (2015, July 7). Giants' Jason Pierre-Paul could miss 6 games after fireworks incident. *The Washington Post.* www.washingtonpost.com/news/early-lead/wp/2015/07/07/giants-jason-pierre-paul-could-miss-6-games-after-fireworks-incident

Buxton, R. (2016, February 17). Erin Andrews on the problematic double-standard between male and female sportscasters. *Huffpost.* www.huffpost.com/entry/erin-andrews-female-sportscasters_n_56c4cacce4b0b40245c8bd7c

Chase, C. (2014, August 27). ESPN apologizes for report on Michael Sam's showering habits. *USA Today.* https://ftw.usatoday.com/2014/08/espn-apologizes-for-report-on-michael-sams-showering-habits

Chicago Tribune [@ChicagoTribune]. (2016, August 7). Wife of a Bears' lineman wins a bronze medal today in Rio Olympics http://trib.in/2asmvvr [Tweet]. Twitter. https://twitter.com/chicagotribune/status/762401317050605568

Cooky, C., Messner, M.A., & Hextrum, R.H. (2013). Women play sport, but not on TV: A longitudinal study of televised news media. *Communication & Sport, 1*(3), 203-230.

Curtis, B. (2020, July 1). The future of the Black play-by-play announcer. *The Ringer.* www.theringer.com/sports/2020/7/1/21309644/black-play-by-play-announcers-minor-league-baseball

Deitsch, R. (2015, July 12). ESPN's decision to give Caitlyn Jenner an ESPY award, more media circus. *Sports Illustrated.* www.si.com/more-sports/2015/07/12/caitlin-jenner-espnys-espn-adam-schefter-jason-pierre-paul

DiCaro, J. (2015, September 27). Threats. Vitriol. Hate. Ugly truth about women in sports and social media. *Sports Illustrated.* www.si.com/the-cauldron/2015/09/27/twitter-threats-vile-remarks-women-sports-journalists

Eastman, S.T., & Billings, A.C. (2001). Biased voices of sports: Racial and gender stereotyping in college basketball announcing. *Howard Journal of Communications, 12*(4), 183-201.

ESPN. (2017, November 2). *Updated social media guidelines.* www.espnfrontrow.com/wp-content/uploads/2017/11/NOV-2-RECEIVED-UPDATED-SOCIAL-MEDIA-GUIDELINES-10.221.pdf

ESPN News Services. (2002, October 10). *Women sportscasters bristle at commentator's remarks.* www.espn.com/nfl/news/2002/1010/1443917.html

ESPN News Services. (2016, May 13). *Carlos Gomez feels insulted by newspaper's use of quote.* www.espn.com/mlb/story/_/id/15528312/carlos-gomez-houston-astros-discusses-feeling-disrespected-newspaper-column

Feldman, J. (2018, November 25). Hannah Storm and Andrea Kremer set the standard for new style of broadcasts. *Sports Illustrated.* www.si.com/media/2018/11/26/hannah-storm-andrea-kremer-all-female-duo-sportsperson-2018-moments

Fleming, K. (2014, December 26). Meet the women of TV's first all-female sports talk show. *New York Post.* https://nypost.com/2014/12/26/meet-the-women-of-tvs-first-all-female-sports-talk-show

GLAAD. (n.d.). *GLAAD media reference guide—in focus: LGBTQ people in sports.* www.glaad.org/reference/sports

Hall, A. (2018, July 19). Linda Cohn signs new ESPN deal; *SportsCenter* tenure continues, hockey profile increases. *ESPN Press Room.* https://espnpressroom.com/us/press-releases/2018/07/linda-cohn-signs-new-espn-deal-sportscenter-tenure-continues-hockey-profile-increases

Hull, K., Walker, D., Romney, M., & Pellizzaro, K. (2020, August 6-9). *"Through our prism": A survey of Black local sports broadcasters' views and interactions with Black athletes* [Paper presentation]. Association for Education in Journalism and Mass Communication (AEJMC) 2020 National Conference (Minorities and Communication Division), San Francisco, CA.

Just Not Sports. (2016, April 25). *#MoreThanMean—women in sports 'face' harassment* [Video]. YouTube. www.youtube.com/watch?v=9tU-D-m2JY8

Lapchick, R. (2018, May 2). The 2018 Associated Press sports editors racial and gender report card. *ESPN.* www.espn.com/espn/story/_/id/23382605/espn-leads-way-hiring-practices-sports-media

Lee, C. (2016, December 23). Time out: Who carries the ball for women's equality in sports media. *Ms.* https://msmagazine.com/2016/12/23/time-carries-ball-womens-equality-sports-media/

Lewis, M., Bell, T.R., Billings, A.C., & Brown, K.A. (2020). White sportscasters, black athletes: Race and ESPN's coverage of college football's national signing day. *Howard Journal of Communications, 31*(4), 337-350.

Lisi, C. (2010, February 23). Tony Kornheiser suspended by ESPN for 'horrifying' comments about Hannah Storm. *New York Post.* https://nypost.com/2010/02/23/tony-kornheiser-suspended-by-espn-for-horrifying-comments-about-hannah-storm

Maraniss, A. (2018, October 15). The Mexico City Olympics protest and the media. *The Undefeated.* https://theundefeated.com/features/mexico-city-olympics-protest-media-john-carlos-tommie-smith

Markham, I. (2013, May 24). Sports journalism's beauty curse. *The Daily Beast.* https://web.archive.org/web/20130603202641/https://www.thedailybeast.com/witw/articles/2013/05/24/for-women-in-sports-media-beauty-still-the-strongest-currency.html

Marsh, J. (2016, February 24). JPP sues ESPN, Adam Schefter for posting his medical records. *New York Post.* https://nypost.com/2016/02/24/jpp-sues-espn-adam-schefter-for-posting-his-medical-records

Myre, G. (2016, August 21). U.S. women are the biggest winners at the Rio Olympics. *NPR.* www.npr.org/sections/thetorch/2016/08/21/490818961/u-s-women-are-the-biggest-winners-in-rio-olympics

Ottaway, A. (2016, July 20). Why don't people watch women's sports? *The Nation.* www.thenation.com/article/archive/why-dont-people-watch-womens-sports

Perez, A.J. (2016, August 9). NBC's Chris Marlowe calls Olympic athlete's same-sex spouse wrong gender. *USA Today.* www.usatoday.com/story/sports/olympics/rio-2016/2016/08/09/nbc-sports-chris-marlowe-same-sex-spouse-wrong-gender/88491630

Rothman, L. (2017, September 19). How Billie Jean King won the Battle of the Sexes, as told in 1973. *Time.* https://time.com/4938913/battle-of-the-sexes-1973-report

Sandomir, R. (2020, May 16). Phyllis George, trailblazing sportscaster, is dead at 70. *The New York Times.* www.nytimes.com/2020/05/16/arts/television/phyllis-george-dead.html

Schefter, A. [@AdamSchefter]. (2015, July 8). ESPN obtained medical charts that show Giants DE Jason Pierre-Paul had right index finger amputated today. [Image attached] [Tweet]. Twitter. https://twitter.com/AdamSchefter/status/618918579770146816/photo/1

Strauss, B., & Bellware, K. (2020, July 19). For women in sports media, dealing with toxic masculinity is far from new. *The Washington Post.* www.washingtonpost.com/sports/2020/07/19/women-sports-media-dealing-with-toxic-masculinity-is-far-new

The New York Times. (2017, October 13). *The Times issues social media guidelines for the newsroom.* www.nytimes.com/2017/10/13/reader-center/social-media-guidelines.html

Vogt, A. (2013, July 17). ESPN's let them wear towels & the plight of the female sportswriter. *Newsweek.* www.newsweek.com/2013/07/17/espns-let-them-wear-towels-plight-female-sportswriter-237716.html

Walker, D. (2020, December 10). Why aren't more women on sports talk? Because the men in power don't care what they have to say. *Deadspin*. https://deadspin.com/why-aren-t-more-women-on-sports-talk-because-the-men-i-1845852252

Washington, J. [@jessewashington]. (2016, August 11). At Olympic press conference for only black woman to win individual swimming medal, I'm the only black journalist [Video attached] [Tweet]. Twitter. https://twitter.com/jessewashington/status/763943451628965890

Women's Sports Foundation. (1998). *What is Title IX?* www.womenssportsfoundation.org/advocacy/what-is-title-ix

INDEX

Note: The italicized *f* following page numbers refers to figures.

ABOUT THE AUTHOR

Courtesy of Michaela Baker Taylor.

Kevin Hull, PhD, is an associate professor of journalism and the lead instructor of the sports media initiative at the University of South Carolina. Before entering academia, Hull was a television sports broadcaster for an NBC affiliate in North Carolina for about seven years. In this role, he anchored and reported on local sports while also serving as photographer, editor, and producer for his own stories. His work has sent him to the Super Bowl, NCAA Tournaments, and many additional amateur and professional sporting events. Hull won several statewide awards for Best Sports Feature from the Radio and Television News Directors Association of the Carolinas, and his department's sportscasts were the most watched in the market.

As a researcher, Hull focuses primarily on local sports broadcasters throughout the United States. He has studied the challenges new sports broadcasters face, the issues surrounding race and gender in the profession, and how universities are preparing students to enter the field of sportscasting. His published studies have discussed sports media education, how sportscasters are using social media, and sports media internships.